MAKE OURS
MARVEL

WORLD COMICS AND GRAPHIC NONFICTION SERIES

Frederick Luis Aldama and Christopher Gonzalez, Editors

The World Comics and Graphic Nonfiction series includes monographs and edited volumes that focus on the analysis and interpretation of comic books and graphic nonfiction from around the world. The books published in the series use analytical approaches from literature, art history, cultural studies, communication studies, media studies, and film studies, among other fields, to help define the comic book studies field at a time of great vitality and growth.

MAKE OURS MARVEL

MARVEL

MEDIA CONVERGENCE AND A COMICS UNIVERSE

EDITED BY **MATT YOCKEY**

UNIVERSITY OF TEXAS PRESS · AUSTIN

Requests for permission to reproduce material from this work
should be sent to:
    Permissions
    University of Texas Press
    P.O. Box 7819
    Austin, TX 78713-7819
    http://utpress.utexas.edu/index.php/rp-form

♾ The paper used in this book meets the minimum requirements
of ANSI/NISO Z39.48-1992 (R1997) (Permanence of Paper).

LIBRARY OF CONGRESS CATALOGING-IN-PUBLICATION DATA

Names: Yockey, Matt, editor.
Title: Make ours Marvel : media convergence and a comics
    universe / edited by Matt Yockey.
Other titles: World comics and graphic nonfiction series.
Description: First edition. | Austin : University of Texas Press,
    2017. | Series: World comics and graphic nonfiction series |
    Includes bibliographical references and index.
Identifiers: LCCN 2016050503
    ISBN 978-1-4773-1249-0 (cloth : alk. paper)
    ISBN 978-1-4773-1250-6 (pbk. : alk. paper)
    ISBN 978-1-4773-1251-3 (library e-book)
    ISBN 978-1-4773-1252-0 (non-library e-book)
Subjects: LCSH: Marvel Comics Group. | Comic books, strips,
    etc.—United States—History and criticism. | Storytelling in
    mass media. | Motion pictures and comic books. | Comic strip
    characters in motion pictures.
Classification: LCC PN6725 .M34 2017 | DDC 741.5/973—dc23
LC record available at https://lccn.loc.gov/2016050503

doi:10.7560/312490

Contents

ACKNOWLEDGMENTS   vii

Introduction   1
Excelsior! Or, Everything That Rises Must Converge
MATT YOCKEY

CHAPTER 1.   **Reforming the "Justice" System**   39
Marvel's *Avengers* and the Transformation
of the All-Star Team Book
MARK MINETT AND BRADLEY SCHAUER

CHAPTER 2.   **Man Without Fear**   66
David Mack, Daredevil, and the "Bounds
of Difference" in Superhero Comics
HENRY JENKINS

CHAPTER 3.   **"This Female Fights Back!"**   105
A Feminist History of Marvel Comics
ANNA F. PEPPARD

CHAPTER 4.   **"Share Your Universe"**   138
Generation, Gender, and the Future
of Marvel Publishing
DEREK JOHNSON

CHAPTER 5.   **Breaking Brand**   164
From NuMarvel to MarvelNOW! Marvel
Comics in the Age of Media Convergence
DERON OVERPECK

CHAPTER 6.   **Marvel and the Form of Motion Comics**   187
DARREN WERSHLER AND KALERVO A. SINERVO

CHAPTER 7.   **Transmedia Storytelling in the "Marvel Cinematic**   207
Universe" and the Logics of Convergence-Era
Popular Seriality
FELIX BRINKER

CHAPTER 8.   **The Marvel One-Shots and Transmedia Storytelling**   234
MICHAEL GRAVES

CHAPTER 9.   **Spinning Webs**   248
Constructing Authors, Genre, and
Fans in the Spider-Man Film Franchise
JAMES N. GILMORE

CHAPTER 10.   **Playing Peter Parker**   268
Spider-Man and Superhero Film Performance
AARON TAYLOR

CHAPTER 11.   **Spotting Stan**   297
The Fun and Function of Stan Lee's
Cameos in the Marvel Universe(s)
DRU JEFFRIES

CHAPTER 12.   **Schrödinger's Cape**   319
The Quantum Seriality of the Marvel Multiverse
WILLIAM PROCTOR

NOTES ON CONTRIBUTORS   347
INDEX   351

Acknowledgments

No editor could have asked for a better bullpen of writers than the one I worked with on this book. They are one and all to be commended for their diligence, patience, good humor, and dedication in this academic foray into the vastness of the Marvel Universe. And none of this would have been possible, or as pleasurable, without Jim Burr at the University of Texas Press, whose sage stewardship was instrumental in transforming the "What if?" proposition of an anthology about the Marvel Universe into a reality.

MAKE OURS MARVEL

Introduction

EXCELSIOR! OR, EVERYTHING THAT RISES MUST CONVERGE

MATT YOCKEY

I n a letter published in *The Fantastic Four* no. 54 (Sept. 1966), a reader suggests to writer Stan Lee and artist Jack Kirby that the comic book publisher should sign away film rights to their characters to "someone with sufficient cinematic competence. . . . May I suggest Akira Kurosawa as a suitable director? Of course, only your venerable self is worthy of writing the script if such a film is to have any artistic significance." The letters' page editor reassures the fan that upcoming Marvel television productions will feature scripts based on "the actual stories you've seen in the past ishes of our Marvel mags—and the artwork of our new, modern-style TV cartoon features will be photographed directly from the mags themselves. . . . So what you—and a zillion other frantic ones everywhere—will be seeing are actual Marvel stories and art brought to life on your home screen, in glowing color, thru the magic of the most dazzling, off-beat Hollywood trick photography we've seen in years!"

This exchange demonstrates that from very early on in what the company dubbed "The Marvel Age" of comic books, the publisher appealed to a readership that was older and more sophisticated than the children most typically considered the chief consumers of superhero tales. Further, this dialogue between a fan and a major comic book publisher confirms that a desire for the faithful expansion (in terms of both narrative content and innovative style and technique) of Marvel comic books into other media was shared by the company and its readership equally.

While the resultant animated series referenced in the editor's response to the fan's request (*The Marvel Super Heroes*, which originally ran in syndication in the fall of 1966) fell short of the cinematic brilliance the reader was hoping for, it was significant as Marvel's first successful licensing of some of its most popular characters for use in other media. Some fifty years later, the promises offered by Marvel to its fans have been realized likely beyond anyone's expectations in 1966. In August 2009 it was announced that the Walt Disney Company had purchased Marvel Entertainment for a staggering $4 billion, placing Mickey Mouse and Spider-Man (and Donald Duck and Howard the Duck) under the same corporate umbrella. The deal evidenced a remarkable turnaround for Marvel, which had filed for bankruptcy in 1996 (after a major decline in comic book sales), and the company's renewed fortunes speak to the successful proliferation of its comic book characters in other media fields, most especially film and television. Indeed, the corporate and self-contained storyworld known as the Marvel Universe has been well suited to the international and transmedia spread of a readily identifiable Marvel brand. The new era of the superhero blockbuster that effectively began in 2000 with the release of *X-Men* (a 20th Century Fox production) set the stage for Marvel Studios (a subsidiary of Marvel Entertainment) to produce films based on its stable of comic book characters. This era began with *Iron Man* (Jon Favreau, 2008) and has continued with an ever-evolving "Marvel Cinematic Universe" that mirrors the extended continuity of the comic books and that has proven to be tremendously successful globally. Disney's purchase of Marvel is an indicator of the financial viability and cultural power of the Marvel brand, which has effectively retained original Marvel editor in chief and principal writer Stan Lee's spirit of familiarity and audience participation, as well as the spectacular vision of Lee's chief collaborator, legendary Marvel artist and co-plotter Jack Kirby.

The expansion of this ethos and vision in contemporary blockbusters has depended upon that sense of audience participation established in the 1960s, a means of appealing on an individual level by confirming agency within a collective. It is axiomatic that popular culture both creates and satisfies consumer desires, and Marvel has successfully done both in the process of building both a coherent brand and a diegetic universe in the twenty-first century. The generative capacity of popular culture to name and temporarily satisfy consumer desires—a capacity that has only become more germane to the Marvel product with time, owing to the necessity of broadening the brand's appeal beyond the confines of a comic book readership—is produced through a dialectical relationship between production and consumption cultures. This central dialectic is at the heart of what Henry Jenkins terms convergence culture, "where the power of the media producer and the power of the media consumer interact in unpredictable ways" (2).

An example of this process is the reflexive casting of Samuel L. Jackson as Marvel Comics character Nick Fury in the films *Iron Man, Iron Man 2* (Favreau, 2010), and *Captain America: The First Avenger* (Joe Johnston, 2011). Fury began life in the comics in 1963 as the white, cigar-chomping leader of a World War II–era combat unit but was reinvented in 1965 as a member of the Cold War–era spy agency S.H.I.E.L.D. Given that both iterations of Fury were published concurrently, we can see how the polysemic nature of the superhero genre paradoxically facilitates its syncretic capacities, in this case symbolically conflating the national ideological discourse of the Cold War and World War II. The character underwent a third radical transformation when, in 2002, Marvel Comics obtained permission from Jackson to redesign the character in his likeness for the series *The Ultimates* (2002–2004). This unusual maneuver, in which a long-standing character was essentially re-iconicized as a popular movie star, is presented as a remediation of fan desire in an episode in the comic in which a group of superheroes play a game of fantasy movie-casting with Fury. Their debate about whether Brad Pitt would make a good Captain America or Johnny Depp a convincing Iron Man duplicates the same kind of discourse engaged in by fans, embedding reader subjectivity within the diegesis. When posed with the question of who should play him, Fury's response is a condensation of self-evident production power and (implied) fan desire: "Why, Mister Samuel L. Jackson, of course. That's not even open to debate." Fans themselves are role-playing as Hollywood producers when they engage in this kind of activity, but, just as significantly, they assume the roles of comic book producers when they give themselves control over narrative trajectory in a manner that echoes the diegetic propensity for alterations of time and space. As one fan noted in an online discussion about who should play Captain America, "If only we had a time machine. . . . I think [Paul] Newman would be my #1 choice. . . . But why am I talking about that? We have a time machine! I'm gonna go forward in time now and pick some actors who are too *young* to play Cap now. . . . We'll see if that's as much fun" ("All-Time Casting Call").[1] Fantasy casting is one of the most prevalent ways by which fans engage with the meaning-making apparatus of popular culture; their projections of ideal casting frequently go unrealized in reality and are always open to debate when actualized.

In subsequently having Jackson actually play Nick Fury in various

Marvel films, fantasy casting becomes a doubly mediated, self-fulfilling prophecy in which Marvel fan subjectivity is located at the center of a matrix of meanings. The central dialectic between innovation and repetition, what Luca Somigli characterizes in serial comic book narratives as a necessary "sameness with difference," confirms that there is no defining center or "original" text in the iterative, infinitely reproducible universes of the mass commodity and of the superhero (289). Even as we trace back to an "original" text, this text is equalized among all others, each iteration becoming a tributary into a metatextual pool. While a chronologically first appearance by a character can be valued for that originating status, it rarely assumes powers of whole definition. It is typically regarded as a seed that germinates into the multifaceted metatext of any given present moment, affording a more directly affective and active attachment to the character—and Marvel brand—by fans. Thus, we equally allow for Sergeant Nick Fury, leader of the Howling Commandos, and Samuel L. Jackson, star of *Pulp Fiction* (Quentin Tarantino, 1994), as authorizing sources for Nick Fury in *The Ultimates*. Comparably, both fans and the writers and artists of Marvel Comics share authorizing agency. The most appropriate metaphor, then, for mapping these intertextual connections is that of the palimpsest, in which the removal of an "urtext" expands the frames of representation for producers and consumers alike, confirming and actualizing a vaguely defined utopian desire embedded at the heart of the genre and best understood by consumers in affective terms. This principle helps us to understand the vital significance of affect in superhero texts, those spectacular, emotionally charged moments in which an intimate bond with characters becomes a deeply felt, immediate experience. Lee's own signature sign-off line, "Excelsior!," is a wry nod toward the expected affective fun at the heart of Marvel fandom, which is inferred to be an extension of a comparable fun in the making and selling of Marvel products.

Robert Stam's use of the concept of the chronotope (by way of Mikhail Bakhtin) facilitates a richer understanding of the inherently convergent nature of Marvel textual production and consumption in this regard. The identifiable point of convergence, its affectively realizable moment, is that of the chronotope, that "cluster of distinctive temporal and spatial features within a genre that are understood to be relatively stable utterances" and that produce the simulacrum of reality (204). If we consider the Marvel Universe itself as a genre, the relevance of Stam's observation is evident across various media platforms in which we can see seemingly disparate textual iterations reconciled by the power of the company brand. For example, an overview of the various iterations of Nick Fury reveals a series of defining and distinctive chronotopes. The 1963 version of Fury is defined in part by co-creator Jack Kirby's personal and professional connection to World War II (he was a combat veteran and co-created the most iconic, patriotic superhero of that era, Captain America), while the superspy version of 1965, created by Lee and Kirby and further developed by Jim Steranko, depends upon the popularity of James Bond and Steranko's interest in pop-art and op-art effects. What validates each iteration of the character is its strong association with an individual artist who, per company rhetoric, has been allowed to flourish under the aegis of Marvel. Consequently, the more comprehensive glue that holds various chronotopes together within the Marvel Universe is the affect produced in the encounter with each one, guided by the familiar address of the comic books and the inherent continuity of the Marvel Universe. After all, the World War II combat veteran is the same man as the 1960s superspy. In allowing characters to be significantly altered to meet new consumer demands and reflect shifting cultural norms, Marvel marks itself and its fans as particularly sophisticated and aware of the machinations of popular culture.

The chronotope is thus about the context of moments of production, to be sure, but it is also about all the subsequent moments of consumption and re-production. Therefore, we always understand the chronotope in relation to context (time, place, medium); at the same time, we can read historical processes on the surface of a text via an understanding of the chronotope. The convergences between media platforms, the public and private, the textual and the extra-textual, necessarily reassert the symbolic utility of divergences, of disparity and gaps to be constantly overcome between text and reader, producer and consumer. If we look a bit closer at the transmedia history of Captain America, we can see the degree to which Marvel has effectively exploited that fluidity to this day in the building of an audience for the Marvel brand. While a mainstream audience is primarily familiar with Captain America by way of the hugely popular film *Captain America: The First Avenger* and its sequels, the character has actually had a long, though not always illustrious, history on film and television. He was the star of an unexceptional fifteen-chapter Republic Studios serial in 1944, was adapted (very loosely) for a pair of television movies in 1979 that were most charitably described by fans as "cheesy," and was the subject of a feature-length film that went straight to video in 1990. This last adaptation has been particularly useful for many Marvel fans as an illustration of how *not* to adapt a comic book superhero to the big screen. A representative sampling of comments on the film gleaned from the Internet Movie Database (IMDb) includes: "This movie just plain stinks! The costume looks horrible; too many liberties were taken with the characters and the plot lurches forward badly"; and "I'll be brutally honest, I tried to like this movie. Simply because I find the character Captain America interesting. But everything in this movie is done wrong. . . . This is indeed one of the worst films of all time."

These film and television iterations of Captain America have been lost in the shadow cast by the character's reintroduction to the public in *Captain America: The First Avenger*; its sequel *Captain America: The Winter Soldier* (Anthony and Joe Russo, 2014); *The Avengers* (Joss Whedon, 2012); *Avengers: Age of Ultron* (Whedon, 2015); and *Captain America: Civil War* (Anthony and Joe Russo, 2016). Yet they offer valuable insights into the function of "bad texts," those adaptations that are regarded as a violation of the character's essence or viewed as terrible aesthetically (and often both designations are blurred in fans' evaluation of a particular version). These adaptations may not establish a canon, but they typically confirm its boundaries. In order for a boundary to be asserted, it must be violated, and in this way, the "bad" Captain America films are vital to the integrity of the "good" ones. Affect is the determining factor, whether positive or negative. The television movies and the 1990 film are particularly salient examples of the necessary bad text that tacitly validates the latest filmic iteration of the character, at least for many fans.

Fans routinely participate in defining Captain America by disciplining a textual history, asserting the integrity of the character in their evaluation of each iteration. Importantly, this evaluative process also works to assert the integrity of fan subjectivity, which can lead to a more complicated reception of various iterations of a character. It in fact is central to fan discourse, providing the opportunity for fans to assert competing affective responses to texts. Quite frequently, an iteration that happens to be a fan's first encounter with a character can become the subject of deep affective attachment. Consider, for example, this positive review of *Captain America: The First Avenger* posted on IMDb: "I will never forget the 1990 film. That film is how I was first exposed to the character when I was a kid when I had it on VHS and grew up with it. CA: First Avenger is still a great film though." This fan can value both the current cinematic version of Captain America and the version that introduced him to the character in part because his relationship to each version puts him in affective contact with different versions of himself safely regulated by the reliable Marvel brand. Our own origin as a fan is ritualistically returned to in the act of celebrating that first encounter with the fan object. The artistic merits of the original fan object are less important than its place in a personal history.

The preoccupation with beginnings is vividly pronounced in the history of Captain America adaptations, which is essentially determined by a recursive narrative return to points of origin (both the 1990 and 2011 films are largely given over to telling the origin of this character). This dynamic is then reenacted by fan and producers alike in acts of remediation. Thus, the very act of remediation marks the 2011 film as dependent on a vast textual history of the character within the rules of the Marvel Universe. According to director Joe Johnston,

> I was mildly familiar with the comic book, but I wasn't a fan of the comic . . . but once I decided to do it, I read every Captain America comic . . . and . . . researched where he came from and where he started and the various iterations of him over the decades. I wanted the origin of the film to be based on a comic book, but I didn't want to have it be in your face. . . . If there is anything that does not fit into the Marvel Universe, [the Marvel guys] will say, "You are going slightly outside of the lines here." . . . As long as you don't mess with that template, you can pretty much do anything. (Zakarin)

It is a self-validating strategy not only for producers but for consumers as well, and it's a key function of the film's box-office success. In effect, the brand signifier becomes "frozen" in place, erstwhile and perennial. Consider the history of Captain America further. He debuted in his own comic book in 1941, not as a response to World War II, but in anticipation of that war. In fact, the character's Jewish creators, Joe Simon and Jack Kirby, were expressly interested in agitating for US intervention in Europe. Thus the desires of the creators are remediated through their character in the hope that these desires will become the readers' as well. This synthesis of creator/character/reader subjectivity became a trope of many superhero comic books during the war, and it is because of the consensual nature of a wartime culture that such a synthesis became a dominant trait of the superhero genre. As the World War II–era advertisement illustrates (fig. 0.1),

Captain America is the mediating figure in the crystallization of consumer-citizen subjectivity. Becoming a member of the Sentinels of Liberty confirms the reader's ideal citizenship and consumerism. As it says, "wear the badge that proves you are a loyal believer in Americanism." Affect, linked to the dynamic body of the superhero, moves from the superficial patriotism of this ad to the more subjectively experienced affect of internal conflict that defined Captain America in his return to the comics of the 1960s. It also links the "loyal believer in Americanism" to the "True Believer" in the Marvel brand. This is not simply time-travel but a movement from the ideologically secure confines of World War II–era comic books to the more psychologically and narratively complex (but ontologically secure) Marvel Universe.

Similarly, in *Captain America: The First Avenger*, we see the origin of the character represented as a tacit collaboration between Marvel and the audience in a montage sequence that shows Steve Rogers performing as Captain America in a traveling stage show. We then see a key affective moment (Cap striking Hitler) reproduced in a comic book. The iterative performance of ideal super-citizenship is remediated as the iterative consumption of the fantasy narrative, confirming that such consumption itself is a comparable patriotic enterprise. Tellingly, the comic book we see in the film is the cover of the actual first issue of Captain America. Thus the knowing viewer's recognition of this reference to the real world sympathetically aligns him or her with Marvel Studios in an affectively saturated exchange, both between the film and the first issue of Captain America, and between the viewer and multiple points of identification within and attached to the film (the unnamed characters reading the comic book, Captain America, the director).

The production and consumption of the film itself reassert these values of the character in the present and link the viewer to a history of production and consumption and anticipations of future iterations, all organized around the Marvel brand and the Marvel Universe. A central value of text, then, is in being constantly anticipated. These transfigurations are articulated by the specifics of *this* textual iteration (the casting, the direction, the scriptwriting, etc.), which satisfies the desire for change, confirms the authority of defining textual signifiers, and gestures toward the next textual iteration. The blockbuster iteration of the character is placed as the originating textual source for the comic book Captain America. This latest and most successful film version of the character is seen by its producers and many fans as a "corrective" to less well-received versions and as reasserting the

0.1. A call to arms aimed at the consumer-citizen. From *Captain America* no. 5 (Aug. 1941).

integrity of the Captain America metatext even as it confirms the desire for future remediations. This, then, is the secret power of the Marvel Universe: the diegetic and extra-diegetic engagement with tropes of transformation. Like a lava lamp, the Marvel Universe retains a fixed structural dimension that contains a visibly mercurial interior. Always recalling a deeply connected textual history while simultaneously moving toward the future, the Marvel Universe allows fans the pleasures of navigating their own sense of self within its fluid boundaries.

THE SHAPE OF THINGS TO COME

These boundaries were established early on by Stan Lee and his coterie of co-creators. In the 1974 trade paperback collection *Origins of Marvel Comics*, which featured reprints of the first appearances of several canonical Marvel superheroes, Lee composed this introduction to the book's section on the Fantastic Four (FF):

> In the beginning Marvel created the Bullpen and the Style.
> And the Bullpen was without form, and was void; and darkness was
>   upon the face of the Artists. And the Spirit of Marvel moved upon
>   the face of the Writers.
> And Marvel said, Let there be The Fantastic Four. And there was
>   The Fantastic Four.
> And Marvel saw The Fantastic Four. And it was good.

The passage's tongue-in-cheek verbosity and ad-man hyperbole had become Lee's stock-in-trade as a writer and as a general pitchman for Marvel since the debut issue of *The Fantastic Four* in 1961. They certainly obscure the mundane (and inevitably market-driven) reality of the genesis of that comic book title: Marvel's publisher Martin Goodman encouraged Lee to create a super-team comic book after learning of the high sales figures for *The Justice League*, a super-team comic book produced by Marvel's chief competitor, DC Comics. What Goodman certainly could not have predicted was that Lee, burned out after working for the company since 1939, would create, along with artist and co-plotter Jack Kirby, a superhero team unlike any seen before then. While the team's powers were reductively archetypal (the stretchable Mr. Fantastic was water, the Human Torch was fire, the Invisible Girl was air, and the rock-like Thing was earth), their dialogue was

—

written by Lee (a frustrated novelist) in as close to a psychologically realistic manner as superhero comic books had ever been to that point. The heroes bickered among themselves nearly as much as they fought villains such as Dr. Doom, and they eschewed secret identities to live publicly in Manhattan as celebrities. From its characterizations to its actual naming of New York (Lee rejected the fictional stand-ins for New York City that DC routinely used, e.g., Gotham and Metropolis), *The Fantastic Four* aimed for a sense of verisimilitude uncommon for the superhero genre.

Further, Lee encouraged reader participation in the creation of a realistic narrative universe. In the letters page of *The Fantastic Four* no. 4 (May 1962), for example, a reader points out a mistake in a story, and Lee offers $5.00 to any fan who can come up with a credible explanation for the error. This idea evolved later into the No-Prize, a nonexistent prize offered to readers who spotted continuity mistakes or flaws in logic in the stories (thus, paradoxically, fans could assert their own mastery over Marvel producers and compete with one another for a fictional prize in pursuit of making Marvel comic books more realistic). Lee himself wrote some of these early letters using various pseudonyms, showing that modeling and shaping practices of participatory consumption were central strategies by which Marvel branded itself and by which the consumer/producer binary was blurred. As Lee and Kirby found their way with this new approach (over the course of what would be a 102-issue run together that ended in 1970, when Kirby jumped ship for DC), what would become a Marvel style and a Marvel narrative universe emerged, a template for what has become an ever-expanding narrative world that has quite effectively grown beyond the comic book medium and into highly successful television programming and movie franchises.

That Marvel style (and Lee worked hard to convince readers that there was such a thing by throwing around phrases like "The House of Ideas" to describe the company) was heavily predicated on a reinvention of the superhero genre founded on a conflation of two of the primary genres that the company produced in the 1950s: horror and science-fiction monster stories and romances. In the late 1950s, when Marvel was known as Atlas,[2] Kirby created an endless stream of (usually giant) monsters on the rampage in titles such as *Tales to Astonish* and *Amazing Adventures*, but he also illustrated romance titles, many of which were penned by Lee, including *Teen-Age Romance* and *Love Romances*. Many tropes of both the giant monster and the romance genres are readily apparent in the early superhero sagas

—

that the company began producing with *The Fantastic Four* no. 1 (Nov. 1961).[3] In that comic, for example, melodramatic anxiety underscores the team's discovery of their superpowers (which they acquired by being bathed in cosmic rays in outer space). When Sue Storm first uses her power of invisibility, the others express dismay that she may never become visible again. When she reappears, Reed Richards, her fiancé, embraces her, exclaiming, "Thank heavens!! You're all right, my darling!" An upset Ben Grimm (Reed's copilot on their space venture) interjects, "All right, eh? How do you know, wise guy? How do you know she won't turn invisible again? How do you know what'll happen to the rest of us?" Reed angrily replies, "Ben, I'm sick and tired of your insults . . . of your complaining! I didn't purposely cause our flight to fail!" Ben responds, "And I'm sick of you . . . period! In fact, I'm gonna paste you right in that smug face of yours!" Before the two come to blows, however, Ben transforms into a rock-like behemoth, visually a clear descendant of the Kirby monsters of the 1950s and as affectively charged a subject as any Lee created for the romance comics. In fact, when Ben (now dubbed the Thing) attacks Reed with a tree, he also mocks Sue's pleas, saying, "'Reed darling'!! Bah! How can you care for that weakling when I'm here!?" As he swings the tree trunk, Reed quickly pulls his body away like a piece of taffy and then wraps his arms, which have now elongated several feet, around Ben, subduing him. Johnny Storm, Sue's younger brother, overwrought seeing his compatriots so incredibly transformed, bursts into flame. As he says, "When I get excited I can feel my body begin to blaze!"

That their powers can be regarded as embodiments of psychological traits speaks not only to the central conceit of *The Fantastic Four* but also to what would soon become the Marvel Universe more broadly: the physical excesses of the superhero genre are almost always a visual affirmation of the excesses of affect that define character subjectivities. Again, the giant monster and the romance comics of the 1950s figure significantly in this. The Fantastic Four's first adventure is a battle with the Mole Man, a rodent-like man who has taken refuge in the center of the earth to escape the scorn heaped on him by the human race. He takes control of an army of giant creatures he discovers there and proceeds to wreak his vengeance on the surface world. The Mole Man's link between affect and science-fiction monstrousness here serves as a negative counterpoint to the Fantastic Four (the former retreats underground to confirm his emotional ugliness; the latter reach to the stars to secure their potential for greatness), and their differences are most clearly realized by the fact that, unlike the lone Mole

—

Man, the Fantastic Four are defined very strongly as a group. They are either actually family (Sue and Johnny are siblings) or symbolically so, and thus serve in yet another important way as a model for a Marvel Universe of like-minded characters and their readers. Like the Marvel superheroes, readers could be both idiosyncratically themselves and part of a larger group.

In making their characters psychologically realistic (at least by comic book standards), Lee and company managed to make them more iden-tifiable for their readers. While at that time DC generally was producing cookie-cutter stories that were relentlessly one-dimensional in their moral binaries and visual and written characterizations (their superheroes tended to be so bland on both registers that frequently the only thing that dis-tinguished them were their costumes), Marvel began creating a host of variously ill-tempered or misunderstood heroes who were similar only in their estrangement from the normativity of DC. Following up on the success of the Fantastic Four, Marvel brought readers the Incredible Hulk (the monstrous, green-skinned, and always misunderstood alter ego of a mild scientist), the Amazing Spider-Man (a guilt-ridden, neurotic teen), Thor (the Norse god of thunder), and Dr. Strange (a former surgeon who acquired mystical powers in the Far East). In various ways, these characters and others that would rise to popularity over the course of the next several years offered fresh takes on the superhero genre, revitalizing it along with the company's fortunes. Certainly these characters conformed to one of the central tropes of the genre: they were outside of the social norm but always worked to defend it (a conceit key to one of the most popular comic book genres of the 1950s, the western, and its cowboy heroes). Yet, because Marvel's heroes were so extremely unusual visually and psychologically, they more directly called into question the inherent strangeness of the very society (and its members) that they were enlisted to protect. In effect, by foregrounding their characters' sense of alienation, the creators of Marvel superheroes appealed to similar feelings in their readers. DC's depiction of the alien Superman as completely assimilated into American society (to the point that he defines white heteronormativity) offered readers a very different point of identification with an idealized subject.

This point speaks to Cornell Sandvoss's contention that "fantasies of resemblance allow for [a] simultaneously projective and introjective relationship between fan and object" (81). This sort of affective relation-ship between characters and audience is key to the success of Marvel, and the company has routinely exploited it, foregrounding psychological

---

insecurities as a means of bridging the gap between fantasy and real life. The technique makes the act of consumption much more intimate than it could be otherwise and requires that the personal address of the text (in the characters' psychological realism and in Lee's editorial voice) is redirected back to Marvel as a corporate textual sign. According to Sandvoss, in such an interaction "the object of fandom forms part of the self" (100). Accordingly, Marvel comics are no longer simply external objects, but become an externalization of the self. Lee's common address to the Marvel fans as "True Believers" can thus be understood to indicate a belief in the power of personal transformation through acts of consumption. The Marvel faithful ultimately are confirming a faith in self, echoing the iterative psychological dramas of Marvel stories themselves that are neatly reinforced by the cyclical consumption of these narratives.

Fantasies of resemblance were also encouraged between fans and creators by a number of editorial decisions made at Marvel that were not common in the comic book industry at the time, thus personalizing the company itself for readers. For example, Lee's decision to alter the standard address of the fan missives published in the letters pages from "Dear Sir" or "Dear Editor" to "Dear Stan and Jack," and even to make use of nicknames (calling himself Stan "The Man" Lee, for example), did much to encourage fantasies of resemblance. Marvel did the same at times by renaming the characters themselves (for example, "Shell Head" for Iron Man, or "Goldilocks" for Thor), a technique that provided a comparable sense of familiarity for readers with creators and their characters. Lee created a sense of affective authenticity and intimacy with his readers that became a key ingredient in the development of a Marvel brand. Moreover, his direct address to readers in his columns and the letter pages often extended to the covers and stories of the comic books themselves in a manner that is simultaneously self-aggrandizing and self-effacing. For example, on the opening splash page of *The Amazing Spider-Man* no. 66 (Nov. 1968), the credits read: "Brought to you in all its brain-blasting brilliance by: Stan (The Man) Lee, Johnny (Ring-a-Ding) Romita [and] amazingly abetted by: Dazzlin' Don Heck & Slick Mick Demeo." The image of the villain Mysterio looming above the model of an amusement park is adorned at the bottom with a caption shaped like an arrow, helpfully encouraging the reader to turn the page. The text in the arrow reads: "And now, let's prove that the mighty men of Marvel haven't lost the masters' touch—!"

Central to this "masters' touch" was the creative license that Lee allowed his artists, or, perhaps more accurately, Lee's ability to recognize the enormous talents of creators like Kirby and his general willingness to step out of their way. Dubbed "the King" by Lee himself, Kirby was more vital to the shaping of the Marvel Universe than any other artist/co-plotter. His wildly cosmic vision was the perfect counterpoint to Lee's psychological angst, neatly exemplified by the introduction of the Inhumans in *The Fantastic Four* no. 45 (Dec. 1965). A group of super-evolved beings from the island nation Attilan, the Inhumans include Black Bolt, who, because his power is the ability to emit shockwaves vocally, never speaks; Medusa, whose mountainous red hairdo (which looks like a bouffant rinsed in cosmic rays) can be animated by her into tendril-like appendages; and Lockjaw, a teleporting creature who looks like a giant boxer with antennae. As Sean Howe notes, "With the introduction of the Inhumans, it was suddenly apparent that the Marvel Universe was infinite. . . . [A]s each issue tumbled into the next, picking up momentum, expanding the cast, the grand space opera absorbed forgotten characters and established the relationships between them all" (72). Typical of the collaboration between Lee and Kirby, the Inhumans are introduced into the Marvel Universe when Johnny Storm falls in love with Crystal, the sister of Medusa. Affect, then, is the key to accessing a world beyond oneself, a diegetic conceit that is also central to the consumption of these cosmic comic book tales. The creation of a Marvel Universe was strongly informed by a sense of intimate rapport between the company and its readers, with both the characters and the writers and artists equally serving as intermediaries between the corporate entity "Marvel Publishing" and readers. The seemingly infinite nature of the diegetic Marvel Universe was reflected extra-diegetically, per Lee's hyperbolic editorial voice, by the apparently boundless creativity and innovation of the company's stable of talent (collectively dubbed the "Marvel Bullpen") and the requisite good taste and intelligence of its readership.

The resurgence of the superhero in Marvel's hands was due in large part to the publisher's unorthodox approach to creating content. The Marvel style was informed by the collaboration encouraged at the company between writers and artists, which resulted in a looser and freer creative process than the more assembly-line-like system in place at DC. At DC, a writer (under the often heavy-handed stewardship of an editor) would produce a completed script that would then be passed along to an artist to illustrate. Thus the two primary creative forces behind a comic never met, exchanged notes, or collaborated in any organic way. The Marvel method

0.2. *Fantastic Four* no. 51 (June 1966).

was much less rigid and required a more synergistic relationship between writer and artist. As the principal writer in those early years, Lee would typically provide the artist with a brief outline, usually a single typewritten page (though sometimes Lee would simply discuss his story outline face-to-face with the artist). After the artwork was completed, Lee would write the text for the captions, word balloons, and thought bubbles. In fact, as the company's unique approach to the superhero genre became progressively more popular throughout the 1960s, and Lee became preoccupied with shilling the company's ever-expanding line of comics on college campuses and in the media, this approach became increasingly necessary.[4]

Aside from the more creatively relaxed production style, there were a number of other elements that set the Marvel product apart from that of its chief rival in the 1960s: centrally, Stan Lee's editorial vision and soap opera writing style, and the striking artistry of many of Marvel's coterie of artists (which, in addition to Kirby, included Steve Ditko, Gene Colan, John Romita, Jim Steranko, and John Buscema, among others, as well as talented inkers such as Chic Stone and Joe Sinnott, and colorist Stan Goldberg). The company's emphasis on the unique talents of its stable of creators was key to its success with college-age readers. Marvel balanced the rigorously conservative demands of the mass market with a clear appeal to individualism; thus, the notion of a "Bullpen" signifies a collective working toward a shared goal in a playful manner, and a House of Ideas suggests both domestic security and creative innovation. *The Fantastic Four* no. 51 (June 1966) is one of the most celebrated Marvel comic books of this period and arguably best represents the company's innovative approach to superhero comic books. This issue depicts Ben Grimm in a soul-searching funk about his monstrous appearance. Kirby offers what has become one of his most iconic images with the opening splash page of a morose Thing standing in a rainstorm on a New York street (fig. 0.2).

The dramatically static nature of the image (so in contrast with Kirby's usual depictions of dynamic bodies in impossible motion) heavily underscores the emotional turmoil below the Thing's orange, rocky surface, which was played out in Lee's purple prose (reflexively summed up by the Thing's self-admonishment about "sounding like a soap opera"). Quite simply, it is a superhero comic book about what it means to be a hero, while acknowledging an intense ambivalence about being super. A parallel plotline, in which fellow FF member Reed Richards is tasked with mastering "the space-time principle," and is temporarily trapped in "a four dimensional universe" called the Negative Zone (which Kirby represented in part through the spectacular and innovative use of photo collage), echoes Ben Grimm's existential self-reflection. As Charles Hatfield has noted, Marvel comics of this period "partook of a childlike sense of wonder: the young reader's sense of being overawed by a huge, looming world" (*Hand*, 153). This childlike sense of wonder is essential to unpacking the value of Marvel comic books at this time because, while Hatfield suggests that Marvel's audience was predominantly children, the fact is that adults made up a growing segment of their readership. For example, a letter published in *The Fantastic Four* no. 21 (Dec. 1963) is from a reader who identifies herself as a fifty-three-year-old grandmother. Thus, the relatively sophisticated artwork and concepts induced a childlike sense of wonder for a reader in her fifties, for example, as much as it might for one under ten (as Lee writes in response to this letter, "Congratulations to all of you young-in-heart fans!").

Arguably what most strongly facilitated the maturation of Marvel narratives alongside the evolving sensibilities of their readership was Kirby's visionary artwork, which reimagined the visual and conceptual possibilities of the genre literally on a cosmic scale. As Hatfield observes, "The most visionary and invigorating element of Marvel was Kirby's graphic mythopoesis, that is, his talent for ideation and world-building *through drawing.* . . . He drew worlds into being"(*Hand*, 153). While Kirby drew stunning, even cosmic worldscapes (an approach that Lee, serving as unofficial art director, encouraged other Marvel artists to emulate), Lee poured psychologically realistic characters into them. It was this synthesis of the external and the internal that most strongly defined the developing Marvel Universe throughout the 1960s, and that was more fully explored in the 1970s by writers such as Roy Thomas, Doug Moench, and Steve Gerber and writer-artist Jim Starlin.

As space explorers who are perpetually weighed down by the gravity of their emotions, the Fantastic Four are arguably the quintessential superheroes of the 1960s. This was an era in which American society was compelled to examine defining national values by way of the increasingly volatile discourse surrounding the civil rights movement and the Vietnam War, while at the same time it was inspired to support the race to the moon as a symbolic victory for universal liberty and peace. The inner turmoil of Marvel superheroes (from the perennially insecure Spider-Man to the tormented Hulk) offered catharsis for a nation that was itself contending with the tension between its best and worst selves. In fact, the social anxieties

—

of the decade were perhaps most profoundly informed by the assassination of President John F. Kennedy in 1963, a blow to the national psyche that arguably required that subsequent depictions of American heroes reflect ambivalence regarding the youthful optimism of the Kennedy era. Thus the typical Marvel superhero is defined in equal parts by optimism and self-doubt. Such characterizations proved quite meaningful to the college-age audience that Marvel attracted. Their angst-ridden superheroes, always simultaneously questioning and shouldering the burdens of their roles as heroes, echoed a corresponding uncertainty about identity typical of young adulthood and exacerbated by the social tensions of the period. Consequently, Marvel characters became popular icons on college campuses, a phenomenon reinforced and mirrored by the enthusiastic welcome Lee received on the college lecture circuit. In a 1965 poll by *Esquire* magazine, college students ranked Spider-Man and the Hulk as two of their favorite counterculture symbols (alongside the likes of Bob Dylan and Che Guevara).

BRING ON THE BRAND GUYS

Marvel branded itself in explicit contrast to DC, which Lee would constantly refer to in the pages of Marvel comic books as their Distinguished Competition, a label that acknowledged DC's dominance in the field while also subtly undermining its comic books with the hint of staidness and staleness. DC was for squares, Marvel was for True Believers. As Lee put it, "I tried to make the readers feel they're more than just casual readers but we're all part of a family, we're all part of an inner-group. We're having fun and the outside world isn't aware of it. And I tried doing that with the Soapbox column I wrote, with the Bullpen page" (Zakarin). Marvel's promotion of highly stylized artists worked in symbiotic rapport with Lee's editorial voice, so that it was not only that Lee came across to readers as a chummy uncle, but that he came across as one with a lot of very cool friends. In this way, Marvel touched on the affective appeal of the emergent underground comix scene of the era, while steering well clear of its politically and culturally challenging content. As Charles Hatfield observes, "The countercultural comix movement—scurrilous, wild and liberating, innovative, radical, and yet in some ways narrowly circumscribed—gave rise to the idea of comics as an acutely personal means of artistic exploration and self-expression" (*Alternative*, ix). Marvel appropriated the signifiers of difference and hip otherness with both its characters and its creators as a means of engaging its readers in a triangular dialogue that challenged hegemonic ideas of the superhero as a reductive symbol of good, of comic books as disposable entertainment, and of the reader as a child (or childish).

Take, for example, Steranko's work on *Captain America* no. 111 (March 1969), in which the illustrator employs a highly surrealistic style to depict a hallucination suffered by Captain America's sidekick, Rick Jones (figs. 0.3 and 0.4). The emotional crux of this story, like that of all of Lee's Captain America tales in this period, is Captain America's lingering guilt over the death of his sidekick Bucky in World War II. This inner conflict is further complicated by his efforts to train Rick Jones as a replacement. Steranko radically revises Lee's predictable trope of regret and self-doubt by representing Captain America's guilt as a transference-induced death trip experienced by Rick. The regulated flow of narrative action via sequential panels is utterly disrupted here by the bold use of sequential images occupying single splash pages. Like Rick himself, the reader is pitched into an LSD-inspired vortex in which the principle threat is not that of physical death, but of the annihilation of identity. The sequence poses that most fundamental of questions to the reader—"Who am I?"—and implicitly provides the answer in the act of consumption itself ("I am a Marvel fan, because Marvel comics are so amazing, so incredible, so uncanny.").

The Marvel superhero's essential appeal and the contrast between the Marvel and DC superheroes are both apparent in how the companies' characters were appropriated by a 1960s youth culture. Lee's strategy to create a sense of belonging to an inner group was confirmed by fans in their affective responses. For example, the band Country Joe and the Fish, best known for its anti–Vietnam War song "I-Feel-Like-I'm-Fixin'-to-Die Rag," recorded "Superbird" in 1967, a musical swipe at Lyndon Johnson that links the president and Superman as simplistic emblems of national identity to be rejected ("He's flying high way up in the sky just like Superman, / But I've got a little piece of kryptonite, / Yes, I'll bring him back to land"). The song's narrator then promises to recruit the help of Marvel superheroes to rid the world of the threat of Superbird ("I got the Fantastic Four / and Doctor Strange to help him on his way"). This clear articulation of the deep cultural divide between the ideologically conservative Superman and the stable of Marvel heroes was later reflexively echoed in *Nick Fury, Agent of S.H.I.E.L.D.* no. 15 (Nov. 1969), in which Country Joe and the Fish briefly appear at a concert performing "Superbird." This knowing wink to readers effectively confirmed Marvel's hipness in stark distinction to the ever-square DC. This

0.3. Steranko takes readers on the ultimate guilt trip. From *Captain America* no. 111 (March 1969).

0.4. The altered states of Captain America. From *Captain America* no. 111 (March 1969).

difference in company cultures is further exemplified by Lee's August 1969 "Soapbox" entry, in which he notes that Country Joe and the Fish are visiting the Marvel office as he is writing, thereby effectively making creative producers (both the Marvel bullpen and the rock group) and their audiences collaborators in the production of a vaguely antiestablishment ethos.

Such vagueness was, of course, quite intentional, and it is worth noting that Marvel's characterizations were not more politically explicit than those of DC's characters. Certainly many of the Marvel superheroes had at least two dimensions to Superman and Batman's one, but Marvel (like any prudent corporate entity) generally steered clear of overt political statements. The fact that characters such as the Hulk and Spider-Man were embraced by college students indicates the degree to which Marvel successfully touched on general affective tropes of resistance to appeal to a countercultural sensibility without being "counter" to anything specifically. When the company did evoke social unrest, it was rarely about the war in Vietnam or civil rights. For example, the cover of *The Amazing Spider-Man* no. 68 (Jan. 1969) features Spider-Man swinging above a group of angry students holding protest signs, and is emblazoned with the provocative title of that issue's story, "Crisis on the Campus!" The crisis that the students are protesting is the proposal by the administration at Empire State University to turn a dorm for low-income students into private housing for visiting alumni. Lee's script does employ countercultural buzzwords of the era. In a curious move, the leader of the protest, Josh, is African American, and the support for low-income housing is racialized by the use of terms such as "whitey" (directed at Peter Parker), "soul brother," and "Uncle Tom." Peter himself sympathizes with the students' cause, but he refrains from joining them because of his personal dislike of Josh. The protesters are thus aligned with the superhero in their fight against injustice (the administration is dismissed by the students as "the establishment"), but the superhero himself is not incorporated into their political actions. Meanwhile, the narrative is mostly taken up with Spider-Man's habitual self-doubt and self-pity and a subplot in which the villainous Kingpin steals a rare tablet from the very dormitory the students are protesting about. Consequently, Spider-Man's battle with the Kingpin also requires that he save the protesters; he remains sympathetic, but he is also superior to them in his role as superhero. The protesters may be at odds with "the establishment," but they need Spider-Man (and because Spidey is misunderstood and threatened by the police, he reflects and actualizes the protesters' perceptions of unjust persecution).

Reader identification with Spider-Man thus coalesces around Peter's self-doubt, his outsider status as Spider-Man, and his affective alignment with the counterculture. The very ideological opaqueness of Marvel superheroes then encourages readers to fill in the gaps, making them complicit in the production of meaning.

Marvel's success, then, was partially developed around affective tropes aimed at a postpubescent audience and sustained by an increasingly complex storyworld identified as the Marvel Universe. By 1972 Marvel was the most successful comic book publisher in the field, distinguishing itself from DC in part by creating a richly complex narrative world that connected nearly all of the comic books it published. While this strategy was certainly a shrewd marketing ploy to sell more comics, Marvel also recognized, starting in the early 1960s (well before the editors at DC did the same), that comic book audience members were not only interested in following narratives across titles and over an extended period of time, but also in building individual libraries of comics and continuing to buy new ones long after conventional wisdom dictated they would lose interest. If Marvel was the House of Ideas, then, in contrast, DC was a Factory of Ideals, a company stuck in the past, generally producing aesthetically and moralistically uncomplicated fairy tales with little or no recognition that the audience for comics could be older or might continue reading beyond their childhood and early teen years, and be interested in complex, multi-issue, multi-title storylines. Marvel readers actively participated in the construction of the meaning of Marvel because, by extension, it reflected their own meaning, their own identity; they had grown up with superhero comic books, and now the Marvel superheroes were growing up along with them.

Marvel's ability to appeal to readers' desires to both be part of a group and strongly individualistic was a canny strategy and was perhaps one of the most instrumental ways by which the company engaged them. Key to this strategy was Lee's willingness (some would say eagerness) to become the face and voice of Marvel. He created a familiar and familial rapport with readers that, like the content of the comics themselves, fostered an empathetic connection with readers by projecting an affective authenticity. As Marvel narratives became increasingly complex, running across consecutive issues of a title and even from title to title, captions would frequently remind readers about previous plot points and in what other comics they appeared. Lee also developed a bank of catchphrases and slogans, such as "'nuff said!" and "Excelsior!" Lee and Kirby even sometimes appear as

—

themselves within the diegesis of the comics (starting a practice that would be continued in later years by other Marvel creators), such as in *The Fantastic Four* no. 10 (Jan. 1963), in which we see the two in the Marvel offices struggling to come up with a new villain for the Fantastic Four. Suddenly Dr. Doom enters the room and forces Lee to invite Reed Richards to discuss future comic book plots, so that the villain can kidnap him when he arrives. Such self-reflexivity foregrounds the presence of comic book producers and puts them in more intimate rapport with the readers by allowing them to serve as intermediaries between fan and object, per Sandvoss's dynamic of projection and introjection. Lee and Kirby's appearance in the diegesis creates and actualizes reader desire to enter the storyworld, blurring the boundary between production and consumption cultures in the process.

These various strategies legitimate fan subjectivity, a key trope of Marvel comic books. Lee was careful to always make his readers feel as though they shared in the creation of the Marvel line. In the letters page of *The Fantastic Four* no. 24 (March 1964), Lee makes this appeal to his audience: "It is our intention, here at Marvel, to produce comics which are so well-written and well-drawn, that they'll elevate the entire field in the minds of the public! After all, comic magazines are an art form, as creative and enjoyable as any other! It is up to *us*, the producers, and *you*, the fans, to make comics something to be proud of." The Marvel Style required writers and artists to work synergistically together, and Lee's rhetoric implicated readers in this process as well. Such rhetoric validates the purchase of Marvel comics by readers by branding the product as art, in the process validating the readers themselves as sophisticated connoisseurs who share in the responsibility (and benefits) of the creation of the Marvel Universe, which is both a narrative one and an extra-diegetic one of fans and producers in sympathetic alliance.

This alliance also benefited from coincidental shifts occurring in comic book fandom at the time. Comic book fandom first became a nationally organized entity in the early 1960s, a fact underscored by two key historical developments. First, in October 1964, fan Jerry Bails published the first issue of *CAPA-Alpha* in response to the explosive growth of fanzines in 1963 and 1964. *CAPA-Alpha* solicited work from fans, and Bails published what he considered to be the best of that work in each issue (future Marvel writer and editor in chief Roy Thomas was an early contributor). Second, this period also saw the creation of the earliest comic book conventions, beginning with a modest event in Detroit in May 1964, but then advancing to a more fully realized effort in July in New York that featured comic book-industry guests (including Ditko and Marvel secretary Flo Steinberg). Fans were increasingly becoming more aware of and connected to one another, validating their fandom as they continued to read comics long after many of their peers had given them up as a childish pursuit.

Again, both the increasing sophistication of Marvel comics and the company's ability to appeal to readers as tacit collaborators in the shaping of the Marvel Universe dovetailed neatly with these separate developments in fandom itself. Marvel also seems to have recognized these trends, as evidenced by its creation of an in-house fan club, The Merry Marvel Marching Society, in late 1964. One of the items that members received when they signed up was a 45 rpm record that featured brief sound bites from various members of the "Marvel Bullpen." Again, Marvel saw the value of maintaining a familiar rapport with readers and aptly exploited this avenue to sell comic books and ancillary products. This strategy on the part of the company speaks to what Paul du Gay regards as a "'cultural economy'. . . [that] draws attention to the ways in which forms of economic life are cultural phenomena; they depend on 'meaning' for their effects and have particular discursive conditions of existence" (6–7). The early 1960s then saw comic book readers coming together to recognize themselves and each other as such, and Marvel responded in kind by facilitating self-identification as a Marvel fan, at least partially dissolving the barrier between producers and consumers. It is significant, for example, that in *Origins of Marvel Comics*, Lee invokes his own childhood love of the pulp character The Spider as a primary motivation for creating Spider-Man. He thus articulates a narrative of transformation from fan to professional that makes his own textual self-production in the comic books more personal and identifiable for readers. As Lee states, "We tried to talk to the readers"; equally telling, he observes, "I always wanted to be in the advertising business" (Zakarin).

Lee's interest in advertising is not particularly surprising, given that consumer culture grew stronger after the Depression in the United States, neatly coinciding with the birth and growth of comic books and the superhero genre that came to dominate it. The success of Marvel in the 1960s can, in fact, be traced back to the key period in which the medium and the superhero genre took shape, World War II, and the conflation of citizenship and consumerism. At this time, according to Lizabeth Cohen, "to ensure the speedy arrival of this postwar utopia of abundance, patriotic citizens were urged to save today (preferably through war bonds) so that they might become purchaser consumers tomorrow" (70). The low-cost purchase of superhero comic books, which frequently featured anti-Axis propaganda, allowed consumers to buy into fantasies of American exceptionalism and triumphalism over both the Axis and the Depression. The superhero also served as an indication of the utopian affect implied to follow victory over these elements. The purchase and later recycling of comic books (for paper drives) facilitated the realization of this utopian vision. It is of further interest, then, to consider how this period has come to be romanticized by fans as the "Golden Age" of the superhero comic book, and why these discarded comic books, sacrificed as part of the utopian consumerist vision of the time, have become such rare collectors' items from the "Silver Age" on. The era is "golden" both in terms of the infancy of the superhero genre and in terms of the collectability of the comic books in which they appeared.

These labels (which originated as marketing tools by comic book back-issue dealers in the early 1960s, when such a market was first becoming organized and more widespread) are certainly echoed in the appellation "The Marvel Age," which became a routine slogan that the company employed to brand its products as both of the moment and also rich with historical potential. Interestingly, one of the earliest instances of the phrase is on the cover of *Strange Tales* no. 114 (Nov. 1963), which features Captain America and the Human Torch battling each other, and a caption that exclaims, "From out of the Golden Age of Comics into the Marvel Age, Captain America Returns to Challenge the Human Torch!" What is so compelling about this terminology is that Captain America had effectively disappeared from newsstands in 1949 (a revival of the character in 1953 was short-lived). While the Human Torch is a member of the Fantastic Four, the character is visually based on a World War II–era hero of the same name and with approximately the same powers (though an android). While the story reveals that this is not the real Captain America after all (it is a villain posing as Cap), it is still quite telling that the cover depends upon reader knowledge of company history and familiarity with the relatively new term "Golden Age." Clearly, Lee felt that readers were familiar enough with it that the notion of a "Marvel Age" could have traction with them. In fact, the issue (and especially the cover) was something of a test to gauge reader interest in the possible return of Captain America. Conforming to a by now familiar self-reflexive tone, the story concludes with a scene in which Johnny Storm consults "his prized collection of old comic mags." Of Captain America, he recalls enthusiastically, "Boy! I sure dug this guy the most!" (fig. 0.5). In the

—

0.5. *Strange Tales* no. 114 (Nov. 1963).

final panel Johnny wonders what became of Cap, musing, "Is he still alive? Will he ever return? I'd sure like to know!" A thought balloon conjures up the real Captain America (that is, the authentic Cap is constituted by the conflated desires of Johnny and the readers), and a direct-address caption states, "You guessed it! This story was really a test! To see if you would like Captain America to return! As usual, your letters will give us the answer!"

Having been duped by an imposter, just as the reader is when looking at the cover, Johnny is inspired to recover his love of the original character by returning to his comic book collection. Thus the Silver Age character's affective attachment to the Golden Age character informs and validates a comparable response in readers, as measured by their written responses to the challenge posed at the end of the story. Presumably the reaction was favorable, for the "real" Captain America was reintroduced in *Avengers* no. 4 (March 1964), a "physical" embodiment for Johnny and a textual one for readers of personal desires recovered by the affirmation of memory produced by contact with comic books of the past. This new "Marvel Age" was thus ostensibly the product of a dialogue between the company and its readers. Lee recalls: "I think I really treated the whole line as a gigantic advertising campaign. I don't mean that we tried to put anything over on anyone, but I felt we had good stories, and we were all very excited about what we were doing. I wanted the readers to feel the same way, to feel that we were all part of an 'in' thing that the outside world wasn't even aware of. We were all sharing a big joke together and having a lot of fun with this crazy Marvel Universe" (Daniels 105).

One of the key aspects of Marvel's approach in this period was this embrace of a perceived outsider status to affectively cohere a brand identity. Certainly this strategy was augmented by the increasing importance of market segmentation in postwar America, which appealed more directly to ideas of individualism than earlier marketing approaches, and was, to a large extent, a response by advertisers to the influence exerted by consumers. As Cohen observes, "it was no accident that the rise of market segmentation corresponded to the historical era of the 1960s and 1970s, when social and cultural groups such as African Americans, women, youth, and senior citizens began to assert themselves in a way that came to be called 'identity politics,' where people's affiliation with a particular community defined their cultural consciousness and motivated their collective political action" (308). Marvel's rise in sales over the course of the 1960s (culminating in it supplanting DC as the top comic book publisher) was also fueled to a large degree by the company's ability to recognize and appeal to an older demographic while still bringing in new young readers. The company's emphasis on a sophisticated meta-continuity, its investment in artistic creativity, its appeal to an outsider status, and its canny knack for making affective bonds with readers were all important aspects of its success.

Marvel's success in the 1960s was strongly dependent on its constant self-promotion as an iconoclastic publishing house, its stable of outsider heroes, and its address to readers as collaborators in the company's ostensibly irreverent enterprise. According to Cohen, postwar America saw "a new commercial culture that reified—at times even exaggerated—social difference in the pursuit of profits, often reincorporating disaffected groups into the commercial marketplace" (309). Clearly this was a strategy that Marvel successfully pursued, but it's also one that the company enhanced by facilitating long-term brand loyalty with teenagers. Marvel thus appealed to the first age demographic that advertisers had targeted. According to Cohen, "what began as an awareness during and after World War II of a distinctive 'teenage' stage of life, with its own language, customs, and emotional traumas, very quickly developed into a consumer market. . . . Before long, being a teenager became defined as a unique consumer experience" (319). If, per Cohen, the segmentation of children as consumers in the 1950s and 1960s "sought to lay the groundwork for a lifetime of consumption," Marvel improved upon this idea by promoting a lifetime of Marvel brand loyalty, making the consumption of Marvel products a unique experience (320). And when Lee exhorted readers to follow the dictum "Make Mine Marvel!"

he was not only inspiring a lifetime commitment that was consistent with a postwar consumer ethos, but also cementing a company philosophy that positioned it for maximum advantage in the current era of globalization and multiplatform storytelling.

ACADEMICS ASSEMBLE!

The goal of this present anthology is to chart some key points of the fluid borders of the Marvel Universe in order to contribute to a deeper understanding of how and why the Marvel brand has been so dependable and changeable for both producers and consumers for over half a century. The essays that follow explore some of the most fascinating and complex developments of that universe, which began as an inspired attempt to catch up with DC in the world of comic book publishing, and which has become one of the most successful transmedia enterprises of the twenty-first century. These essays are categorized according to their focus on either Marvel comics or films, although such a division is not meant to assert a clear distinction between these categories (as evidenced by the transmedia references in many of the chapters). Such a separation does indicate the historically significant position of comic books as foundational texts for the ever-expanding textual universe that recursively draws on its past as it continues to evolve.

In the opening chapter, "Reforming the 'Justice' System: Marvel's *Avengers* and the Transformation of the All-Star Team Book," Mark Minett and Bradley Schauer examine the transmedial life of the Avengers, focusing on narrative formula, characterization, and continuity as key building blocks in the Marvel Universe. They turn to David Bordwell's notion of "historical poetics" as a model for understanding the various permutations in the Avengers metatext over the decades. Minett and Schauer are specifically concerned with the development of the all-star team comic book in its first two years and argue that it was vital to the establishment of a larger storyworld involving all Marvel comic books. In doing so, they offer a productive comparison with industry practices at DC, especially in relation to the all-star team (in their case, the Justice League), that moves us away from a reductive DC/Marvel binary and provides insights into the ways in which the development of a Marvel Universe was inevitably uneven and defined as much by its failures as its success.

Henry Jenkins explores the complicated function of the auteur within the company in chapter 2, "Man Without Fear: David Mack, Daredevil, and the 'Bounds of Difference' in Superhero Comics." Jenkins performs a close analysis of Mack's highly stylized work on Daredevil, focusing on *Daredevil: Echo-Vision Quest*, in order to map out the ways in which the company challenges its own conventions as a means of reasserting its role as a House of Ideas. The essay is rich in visual examples of Mack's highly idiosyncratic approach, exemplified by his use of paints and collage, to illustrate the degree to which Marvel editors allowed Mack to push the accepted limits of the comic book form and the superhero genre. Jenkins borrows a concept from film studies, the "bounds of difference," to articulate how Marvel effectively appropriated a strategy from classical Hollywood cinema by facilitating innovation within the elastic frame of genre conventions. His essay charts how Mack's work enabled a response from readers that, while sometimes contentious (some expressed a strong disapproval of its "artiness"), was valuable to the company as a means of reinvigorating the character of Daredevil and, more significantly, the aura of Marvel as an innovative comic book publisher. Jenkins places Mack's work in a historical framework, comparing it to the comparably innovative work done by Frank Miller and Bill Sienkiewicz on the same character. In doing so, Jenkins's essay suggests that Marvel maintains a long-term commitment to innovation that will likely remain a valuable means by which it will engage with readers well into the future.

The collection then shifts to a nuanced evaluation of Marvel's representation of female characters in chapter 3 with Anna F. Peppard's essay "'This Female Fights Back'! A Feminist History of Marvel Comics." Peppard usefully expands the scholarly discourse regarding representations of women in superhero comic books, which, as she wryly notes, has historically glossed over them as male masturbatory fantasies. In her analysis of such Marvel superheroines as the Cat, Ms. Marvel (later Captain Marvel), and the She-Hulk, Peppard explores the significant ways in which, beginning in the 1970s as a response to feminism, Marvel has sought to address a female readership. In her analysis she observes that the idea of the female reader who might enjoy identifying with a superheroine sans the conventions of melodrama or romance has historically been regarded by comic book producers as being as much of a fantasy as the superheroines themselves. Peppard looks at various marketing strategies aimed at a female readership indicating the degree to which Marvel itself has struggled to understand this readership by consistently approaching female readers as a problem to be solved rather than as simply an audience to be satisfied. In the end, her cogent analysis capably maps Marvel's blind spots and failures in their numerous attempts to incorporate empowered female characters (and, consequently, female readers) into the Marvel Universe. In doing so, she also demonstrates the very real value of correcting Marvel's decades-long myopia regarding female characters and readers.

Derek Johnson addresses a similar issue in chapter 4, "'Share Your Universe': Generation, Gender, and the Future of Marvel Publishing," offering a rigorous analysis of Marvel's recent attempt to reach out to new readers in its "Share Your Universe" campaign. He foregrounds the significance of Marvel's role as a comic book publisher (a role frequently lost in the shadows cast by the movie franchises derived from the comics) and notes the ways in which the radically amplified transmediality of Marvel in recent years has complicated its relationship with longtime (mostly male, mostly older) fans. Johnson's essay identifies a central dialectic in the production and consumption of Marvel products—the old and the new—and the impact that this dialectic has had on Marvel's corporate identity and, consequently, the identity-formation of its fans. He focuses on Marvel's "Share Your Universe" effort, which aimed to draw in a new generation of fans by appealing to veteran fans to serve as institutional gatekeepers. As Johnson argues, this effort was severely handicapped by Marvel's focus on recasting its central fan base (adult males) as fathers; the company thereby handed over to older fans the great responsibility of inspiring a comparable devotion to Marvel comics in a younger generation. As Johnson illustrates, the very gendered and generational ideologies of this approach ultimately proved too problematic, a finding that suggests the very clear limitations that persist regarding fan identity and the superhero genre.

In chapter 5, "Breaking Brand: From NuMarvel to MarvelNOW! Marvel Comics in the Age of Media Convergence," Deron Overpeck brings together a number of thematic concerns in this volume by looking at how Marvel reinvigorated its brand identity in 2000 with the launch of "NuMarvel," in which the company privileged creators over continuity and favored "decompressed" storylines. Both strategies proved quite suitable for the translation of comic book content to the trade paperback form, and this chapter unpacks the degree to which NuMarvel was more of a marketing ploy to grow an audience than it was an attempt to reenergize its existing fan base. Overpeck considers how the company's renewed emphasis on creators (with their Young Guns and Marvel Architects campaigns) privileged the role of creators over the continued development of a dense storyworld, a maneuver that increased sales for flagship titles such as *X-Men* and *Amazing Spider-Man*, coinciding with the successful transition of these characters to movie screens in 2000 and 2002, respectively. Ultimately, Overpeck argues, the reinvention of Marvel beginning in 2000 was an important step in the company's transition from a content-driven company to a licensing-driven one. As such, the company incorporated commercial practices of other media, especially the auteurism of film, as a means of facilitating the transmedia growth of Marvel content. As Overpeck's essay ably demonstrates, these changes actually reconfirmed the central place of comic book production within its ever-changing brand development.

Issues around the transmediality of Marvel content are the chief concern of Darren Wershler and Kalervo A. Sinervo in chapter 6, "Marvel and the Form of Motion Comics." They evaluate how Marvel's various forays into the world of motion comics have compelled the company to privilege circulation over continuity and a historical record, both chief characteristics of the production and consumption of Marvel comics in print form. If readers have long valued the print comic book as an archive of the Marvel Universe, Wershler and Sinervo ask, in what ways is the integrity of that universe, and the relationship between the company and its fans, altered by the abandonment of a material archive? In addressing this issue, they make a compelling case for the value of digital comics as a means of proliferating the Marvel brand while maintaining its reputation as an innovator in the comic book industry. Yet, as the authors observe, the fact that actual innovation is minimized in the production of motion comics contradicts such rhetoric. In pursuing its interest in mining a new market, Marvel has focused on only one aspect of the digital form (motion comics) that inherently hinders creativity. Ultimately, they contend, Marvel's turn toward the digital comic book market seems driven by a desire to reconfigure comic books as ancillary products of the films based on Marvel characters and storylines. Their essay compels us to consider the future of comic books as more than simply an abstraction of the past, the vaguely recalled source material for the films.

The anthology shifts its focus to Marvel films beginning with chapter 7, "Transmedia Storytelling in the 'Marvel Cinematic Universe' and the Logics of Convergence-Era Popular Seriality," by Felix Brinker. This chapter offers a detailed study of the Marvel Cinematic Universe (MCU) as developed in film and television by Marvel Studios. Brinker considers how the template

—

for a rich storyworld that Minett and Schauer mapped out in chapter 1 now utilizes a number of media platforms. He looks at how the inevitable promotion of transmediality, resulting from the proliferation of digital media in recent years, is key to the serialization of Marvel texts across media platforms. Further, he considers the role of this digital environment in the development of the self-reflexivity that has been so strongly characteristic of the Marvel product for decades. Finally, Brinker makes a compelling argument that the MCU now stands as a game-changing model for a new kind of seriality. In this way he productively moves the conversation about the Marvel Universe into a larger consideration of a rapidly changing mediascape and the pivotal and leading role that Marvel is playing in reshaping it.

In chapter 8, "The Marvel One-Shots and Transmedia Storytelling," Michael Graves considers a particular strategy by which the Marvel Universe and the comic book audience's relationship with it have expanded. Graves examines the short films that are only included in the Blu-ray and digital releases of the Marvel theatrical films, which provide further backstory for characters and deepen the links between the films. Graves looks at how these Marvel One-Shots conform to and deviate from Henry Jenkins's seven principles of transmedia storytelling, modifying Jenkins's concepts of extractability and immersion. Although for Jenkins, these concepts are generally opposed to each other, Graves emphasizes the unidirectional flow of the Marvel Universe, showing that extractability and immersion can in fact be utterly consistent with one another. From this position Graves illustrates the degree to which the construction of the Marvel Universe is as dependent upon its audience as it is upon its producers. His analysis of the One-Shots reveals the more pronounced value in them of characters who are relegated to supporting roles in the films. The development of these characters deepens the textual heft of the films by providing fuller backstories and strengthening narrative connectivity. In typical Marvel fashion, this strategy is not simply canny marketing; it also reinforces the Marvel ethos of pluralism and difference as a subjective asset rather than an ideological disruption to be contained and managed.

In chapter 9, "Spinning Webs: Constructing Authors, Genre, and Fans in the Spider-Man Film Franchise," James N. Gilmore explores the ways in which paratexts have become valuable tools of negotiation between audiences, producers, and texts, using the Spider-Man franchise as Exhibit A. He specifically evaluates the ways in which special edition DVD/Blu-ray releases of the films use features such as filmmakers' commentaries to appeal to fandom by exploiting the cache of insider knowledge, consumer participation, and brand value. Gilmore traces the roots of this strategy back to Stan Lee's editorial presence in the Marvel comics of the 1960s, and to how Lee replicated discursive practices but also complicated them in considerations of authorship, adaptation, and genre. In considering how the Spider-Man films are positioned as a "fan's franchise," Gilmore challenges the conventional take that DVD/Blu-ray special features are secondary to the filmic text. He articulates the significant ways in which they allow that text to be not only re-watched but also rewritten. DVD/Blu-ray releases, Gilmore convincingly argues, discipline the multivalence of the franchise by strategically employing the rhetoric of brand fidelity via genre and authorship tropes. His use of the Spider-Man franchise is all the more compelling given that the Spider-Man films made between 2002 and 2014 were produced by Sony, not Marvel Studios. As such they offer a persuasive example of the discursive power of the Marvel brand.

Addressing the relationship between the comic books and films, Aaron Taylor scrutinizes the value of performance in portrayals of Spider-Man on film in chapter 10, "Playing Peter Parker: Spider-Man and Superhero Film Performance." In his close reading of Tobey Maguire and Andrew Garfield's interpretations of Marvel's most popular character, Taylor considers the intimate relationship between performer and role as mediated by the brand power of Marvel. This connection is particularly salient, he contends, given Spider-Man's status as the flagship character of a twenty-first-century transmedia conglomerate. Taylor cogently unpacks the ways in which larger economic, technological, and discursive forces exert unique influences on each actor. Foregrounding an inherent self-reflexive trope of the cinematic adaptations of comic books, Taylor explores the multiplicity of bodies on display and at play in superhero performance: namely, the actor's physical body and the fictional body of the character. The relationship between the actor and the character is complicated, he argues, by the star status of each actor in competition with the iconicity of Spider-Man (substantiated by the cultural archive of the character and audience memory). The integration of the two produces what Taylor regards as a third body, or a "body-too-much." Taylor concludes that the star is subsumed by the icon in a process that visually and affectively embodies for viewers the actual diminishment of star power. Within the Marvel Studios system, stars are generally more motivated by the promise of long-term exposure than by the promise of large paychecks to sign up for roles. As Taylor observes, the doubling of the star/superhero body denies viewer identification and instead requires that the viewer become a kind of partner with the actor, each hyperaware of the highly mediated and collaborative nature of the performance. In this way, Taylor offers us a fresh way to think about Marvel's long-standing strategy of encouraging a sense of participation by fans and how these films perhaps can actualize it.

Turning from Marvel's most iconic character, Dru Jeffries offers up a consideration of arguably its most iconic creator in chapter 11, "Spotting Stan: The Fun and Function of Stan Lee's Cameos in the Marvel Universe(s)." Analyzing the construction of Stan Lee's persona as the public face of Marvel, Jeffries explores how Lee is deployed within the Marvel Cinematic Universe as an authorizing link to the company's past (and its comic books), as a unifying symbol across various studio productions, as a playful signifier of the intermedial and intertextual connectedness of the comic book and film storyworlds, and as a primary architect of the Marvel Universe. Jeffries is most concerned with this last point, and his essay effectively illustrates how Lee's cameo appearances in Marvel films offer opportunities for fans to actualize their own relationship to Marvel via competing discourses regarding Lee. As Jeffries observes, these cameos themselves contain their own contradictions, as they validate the films in which they appear based largely on viewer recognition of Lee as a principal author of the Marvel Universe, even as this role is hotly contested by fans, and as they promote Lee as a tacit author of the films in which he appears. These complex significations actually serve to affirm the polysemic qualities of Lee's persona as, variously, a comic book visionary or a self-serving company shill. Ultimately, Jeffries compels us to reflect on the ways in which Lee is needed by fans as either—or, more tellingly, as both at the same time.

In a similar spirit of innovation, William Proctor completes this collection with his essay "Schrödinger's Cape: The Quantum Seriality of the Marvel Multiverse," chapter 12, in which he deploys both narrative theory and quantum physics in an analysis of the Marvel multiverse. Proctor's concern is with the ways in which Marvel manages its various narrative threads by means of what he calls "quantum seriality," the ordering of competing textualities within a shared storyworld. It is the very nature of the Marvel Universe as transmedial, Proctor argues, that allows for the management of a plethora of alternate realities and parallel narrative systems. This management has a twofold effect that echoes what Deron Overpeck sees as the value of NuMarvel: it potentially brings in new readers and inspires renewed dedication to the Marvel brand by long-term fans. For example, as Proctor aptly points out, the creation of the Ultimates Universe, a parallel to the canonical Marvel Universe, marks a strategy by which the company can attract new readers because the stories are not burdened by deep backstory; at the same time it reengages longtime fans by reworking familiar characters. Ultimately, Proctor says, all of this management of parallel worlds symbolically places the reader outside of time-and-space, where he or she can view the Marvel multiverse and appreciate its complex design. Consequently, as we have seen with Marvel from the very start of its world-building enterprise, the fan is a valued participant in the affirmation of the meaning of the Marvel Universe (and, by extension, the Marvel brand), something both diegetic and extra-diegetic, internal and external, personal and public.

As these essays make clear, the Marvel Universe is a richly complex construct, the product of a number of ever-shifting economic, industrial, technological, and artistic forces. Instead of the biblical-style genesis that Lee invoked in *Origins of Marvel Comics* back in 1974, these essays suggest that the Big Bang is a more apt metaphor. In the collision of artistic vitality, the superhero genre, and a more sophisticated readership, the Marvel comic book revolution of the 1960s incited the birth of a narrative universe and a media empire that continues to grow far beyond anything imagined back in 1961. In fact, this collection of essays could serve as a vital starting point for further academic explorations of this fascinating universe. 'Nuff said? This conversation's only beginning.

NOTES

1. Unless otherwise noted, emphasis in quotations is reproduced from the original.

2. The company was called Timely when it was founded in 1939, was rechristened Atlas in 1951, and began featuring the Marvel name on covers beginning in 1963.

3. In fact, both genres are neatly synthesized later in the run of *The Fantastic Four* when the Thing begins a romantic relationship with a blind sculptor, Alicia Masters, who, for the sake of further melodramatic angst, is the stepdaughter of the villainous Puppet Master.

4. Lee increasingly gave up his writing and editing duties over the course

of the 1960s and in 1972 named Roy Thomas editor in chief while, at the same time, beginning the practice of labeling every Marvel comic book opening credit page with "Stan Lee Presents." In 1981 Lee entirely removed himself from day-to-day operations when he relocated to Los Angeles to develop Marvel properties in the film and television industries.

WORKS CITED

"All-Time Casting Call." Thread at discussion board for Captain America. *Internet Movie Database* (IMDb), 1990. Web. www.imdb.com/title/tt0103923 /board/nest/145280780?d=145286179&p=1#145286179.

Cohen, Lizabeth. *A Consumers' Republic: The Politics of Mass Consumption in Postwar America*. New York: Vintage Books, 2004. Print.

Daniels, Les. *Marvel: Five Fabulous Decades of the World's Greatest Comics*. New York: Harry N. Abrams, 1991. Print.

Du Gay, Paul. "Introduction." In *Production of Culture/Cultures of Production*. Ed. Paul Du Gay. Thousand Oaks, CA: Sage Publications, 1997. 1–10. Print.

Hatfield, Charles. *Alternative Comics: An Emerging Literature*. Jackson: University Press of Mississippi, 2005. Print.

———. *Hand of Fire: The Comics Art of Jack Kirby*. Jackson: University Press of Mississippi, 2012. Print.

Howe, Sean. *Marvel Comics: The Untold Story*. New York: HarperCollins, 2012. Print.

Jenkins, Henry. *Convergence Culture: Where Old and New Media Collide*. New York: New York University Press, 2006. Print.

Lee, Stan. *Origins of Marvel Comics*. New York: Simon and Schuster, 1974. Print.

Sandvoss, Cornel. *Fans: The Mirror of Consumption*. Cambridge: Polity, 2005. Print.

Sciretta, Peter. "Interview: Director Joe Johnston Talks 'Captain America.'" *Slash Film*, 20 July 2011. Web. www.slashfilm.com/joe-johnston-interview.

Somigli, Luca. "The Superhero with a Thousand Faces: Visual Narratives on Film and Paper." In *Play It Again, Sam: Retakes on Remakes*. Eds. Andrew Horton and Stuart Y. McDougal. Berkeley: University of California Press, 1998. 279–294. Print.

Stam, Robert. *Film Theory: An Introduction*. Malden, MA: Wiley-Blackwell, 2000. Print.

Zakarin, Scott, dir. *Stan Lee's Mutants, Monsters & Marvels*. DHG Productions, 2002. DVD.

—

Reforming the "Justice" System

MARVEL'S *AVENGERS* AND THE TRANSFORMATION
OF THE ALL-STAR TEAM BOOK

MARK MINETT AND BRADLEY SCHAUER

When Marvel Studios released its blockbuster film *The Avengers* (Joss Whedon, 2012) in the summer of 2012, moviegoers were treated to a rare sight—the assembly in a single film of a group of superheroes, four of whom had already starred, independently, in their own features. As media scholars such as Derek Johnson and Matthias Stork have established, *The Avengers* represented the culmination of a years-long, multifilm strategy that differentiates the "Marvel Cinematic Universe," as it is described by Marvel Studios president Kevin Feige, from previous cinematic iterations of the superhero. Marvel's approach is based on the promise and promotion of a shared storyworld that reveals itself piecemeal through feature films, home-video bonus features, and television series. These texts encourage the audience to anticipate and construct a vast narrative continuity that was concretized in *The Avengers* (Johnson, "Cinematic Destiny"; Stork, "Assembling the Avengers").

As exciting as the "team-up" component of *The Avengers* was for movie fans who had enjoyed films like *Iron Man* (Jon Favreau, 2008) and *Thor* (Kenneth Branagh, 2011), in the realm of comic book superhero storytelling, this concept was old hat. Indeed, Marvel Comics has published *The Avengers* in one form or another, and sometimes in multiple simultaneous forms, since 1963, when Stan Lee and Jack Kirby first teamed up the Hulk, Iron Man, Thor, the Wasp, and Ant-Man, each of whom had starred or was starring in individual stories. Just as the *Avengers* film represented a breakthrough in the realm of franchise filmmaking, the original *Avengers* comic innovated a particular subgenre of the superhero comic, which we call "the all-star team book." These comics feature a group of superheroes who are already

---

familiar to readers from their own preexisting solo stories. For over three years before the launch of *The Avengers*, DC Comics' wildly popular *Justice League of America* (hereafter *JLA*) developed a distinctive formula for the all-star team book. With *The Avengers*, Marvel worked within this preexisting generic concept, but it also strategically revised, rejected, and elaborated upon key conventions employed by its rival publisher.

In this chapter we analyze *The Avengers'* innovative storytelling approach by concentrating on three central and interrelated aspects of the all-star team book: narrative formula (both in terms of single issues and multi-issue, serialized structure), approach to characterization, and relationship to continuity. We have adapted to comic studies an approach that film scholar David Bordwell has labeled "historical poetics." Historical poetics seeks to answer two primary questions: "1. What are the principles according to which [artworks] are constructed and by means of which they achieve particular effects? 2. How and why have these principles arisen and changed in particular empirical circumstances?" As a scholarly and critical project, poetics "studies the finished work as the result of a process of construction—a process that includes a craft component (such as rules of thumb), the more general principles according to which the work is composed, and its functions, effects and uses" (*Poetics* 12). For Bordwell, "the craft context can be understood as a situation posing problems that filmmakers must solve" (*Figures* 249). In this problem/solution paradigm, an artist is presented with "a repertory of schemas, those norms of style that experts can recycle, modify, or reject" (*Figures* 41–42). By applying this critical approach to *JLA* and *The Avengers*, we can better understand the ways in which Marvel innovated the all-star team book.

First, we focus on a specific historical period, offering a comparative analysis of *JLA* up to the debut of *The Avengers* in September 1963 and until *The Avengers* departs from the all-star team format in June 1965.[1] This group of comics offers a clearly delimited iteration and reiteration of the all-star team book subgenre. By focusing on a relatively small set of books, created under fairly consistent conditions of production, we are able to engage in close analysis that enables us to refine and fully support our claims about the processes of generic reinvention. This methodology also allows for a more accurate empirical account of the all-star team book during this period. The tendency of fans and critics to divide the superhero genre's history into decades-long ages can gloss over significant variation within periods and oversimplify generic development. As Steve Neale has pointed

—

out, a genre's history is likely to involve "discontinuities and breaks rather than smooth, organic development" (213–214). For Neale, genre is best understood as a process in which "the repertoire of generic conventions available at any one point in time is always *in* play rather than simply being *re*-played" (219).

Also motivated by historical poetics is our emphasis on proximate historical contexts, specifically the industrial and institutional environments in which *JLA* and *The Avengers* were produced during this period. The approaches to storytelling structure, characterization, and continuity elaborated here were developed neither out of whole cloth nor in isolation from pragmatic, artistic, and economic practices and imperatives. As Bordwell aptly puts it, poetics is "often assumed to aim merely at descriptions or classifications" of formal traits, when in fact it often seeks to also explain those traits using a variety of historically grounded "models of causation and change." We employ a "functionalist" model whereby the specific historical features of the institution (or institutions, here comics publishing at DC and Marvel) create constraints and affordances. These constraints and affordances play a significant role in articulating the goals or problems that creators formulate and then tackle as well as in guiding the storytelling strategies and solutions developed and employed by the publishers and their creative labor (*Poetics* 16).

In a roundtable discussion about the state of comics studies in 2011, Scott Bukatman argued that the field "needs more study of the poetics of comics, period" (qtd. in Smith 142). This essay is a gesture toward that research call. However, by employing the historical poetics approach, we do not mean to suggest that there is no theorizing at play in our account. Indeed, our first move has been to suggest a comic book superhero subgenre, the all-star team book, and to articulate its essential features. This approach leads us to certain historical questions: for instance, why did the all-star team book emerge as such an important publishing strategy of DC and then Marvel Comics in the late 1950s and early 1960s?

For a publisher, the all-star team subgenre offers a number of commercial appeals. In terms of marketability, it offers readers the novelty of seeing their favorite characters interacting, as well as the value of purchasing a single comic that contains all or most of their favorite characters. This aggregation of characters suggests an opportunity to attract an especially wide readership, as fans of the different characters each seek out the book. An all-star team book can also serve to promote lesser-known superheroes by placing them alongside more popular characters. Furthermore, its status as a hub in the elaboration of a shared narrative universe, or continuity, provides an exploitable attraction in and of itself, and might also be used to encourage or reinforce a completist mindset among readers, implicitly directing them to purchase all of the publisher's superhero publications in order to consume and master the entirety of the storyworld.

Given these general publishing incentives, it is easy to understand why DC and then Marvel would have been interested in producing all-star team books. As we shall see, though, they did so in significantly different ways, each offering an iteration of the all-star team book that was responsive to the specific constraints and affordances of their respective institutional organizations, practices, and objectives. JLA relied upon an intellectualized "theme and variations" approach to the form and content of all-star team storytelling that employed continuity fairly narrowly as a spectacle or special event. Marvel, on the other hand, fashioned a series that emphasized a more intensified emotionality and a more integrated approach to continuity while using a complementary storytelling style that was more fluid and serialized than the competition's.

Finally, we argue that both publishers' approaches were dynamic in ways not fully accounted for in previous studies. Derek Johnson has described superhero storytelling, and intra- and inter-industrial superhero franchising, in particular, as emblematic of the iterative cultural forms that dominate popular culture (*Media Franchising* 236–237). The notion of iteration here seems connected to the versioning of software, implying the successive reiteration, revision, and "refinement" of a product, or, in our case, a subgeneric storytelling stratagem, in response to feedback from the consumer and, more importantly, the needs of its producer. Johnson argues that creative agents "pursue textual strategies of difference that make the multiplication of franchising not a replication of sameness, but a more reflexive and iterative process" (*Media Franchising* 151). Understanding superhero storytelling as iterative in this sense accords with Neale's caution to understand genre as a messy, nonlinear process and with Bordwell's account of stylistic change. What our small-scale study demonstrates is that summarizing DC and Marvel's strategies, even during so short a period, runs the risk of obscuring significant shifts, and even reversals, in their approaches. Although there is some truth in binary accounts pitting DC's approach against "the Marvel Way," this study makes clear that both publishers displayed moments of significant and directed internal variation at

—

a time when approaches to the all-star team subgenre fluctuated not just from publisher to publisher, but from issue to issue.

INDUSTRIAL CONTEXT AND HISTORY

To understand the innovations found in *The Avengers*, it is essential to look beyond the stories themselves and establish the distinctive historical production contexts that can help to account for the divergent iterative strategies. Although Stan Lee's widely acknowledged preference for character-based storytelling may explain some of the dissimilarity between *JLA* and *Avengers*, key differences in Marvel's and DC's target audiences and divisions of labor, as well as the size and scope of their publishing lines, likely played a significant role as well. These differences set affordances and constraints that determined not just the variation in narrative strategies and approaches to continuity but also the casting of the companies' respective all-star teams.

The all-star team genre was pioneered twenty years before *JLA* and *Avengers* with All-American Comics' *All Star Comics*, starring the Justice Society of America (JSA), which ran from 1940 to 1951. The team was cast with characters appearing independently in anthologies published by All-American and its sister company, National Periodical Publications / DC Comics. At first, the primary function of *All Star Comics* was to promote the less visible characters in the All-American / DC roster. When a character proved popular enough to receive his own solo book, that character achieved "honorary" status and was replaced in the JSA by another minor character. After a falling out between All-American's Max Gaines and DC's Harry Donenfeld, the popular All-American characters the Flash and the Green Lantern returned beginning with issue no. 24 (Spring 1945) as substitutes for Starman and the Spectre, two DC characters (Thomas). All-American's headliners remained as part of the all-star ensemble, but the subsequent cancellation of the Flash and Green Lantern solo books in the late 1940s marked the declining fortunes of the superhero comic in the postwar period. Readers began to gravitate toward a variety of alternative genres, including romance, crime, horror, and western books. With the exception of nine titles starring Superman, Batman, and Wonder Woman, DC either canceled or changed the genre of all of its superhero books by 1952. The adventures of the JSA came to an unceremonious end when *All-Star Comics* was retitled *All-Star Western* for its fifty-eighth issue in May 1951.

The all-star team format lay dormant for nearly a decade until former *All-Star Comics* editor Julius Schwartz introduced the JLA in *The Brave and the Bold* no. 28 (Feb./March 1960). DC's publishing line was sufficiently large at the time that its editorial structure was the equivalent of mini-fiefdoms overseen by supervising editors. At the beginning of 1960, six editors were responsible for five to ten books each, for a total of forty-two books published monthly or bimonthly by DC. Editorial assignments were largely divided along genre lines; Schwartz's specialty was science fiction. Beginning with the Flash in 1956, he had found great success in reintroducing Golden Age superheroes in revised, science–fiction-inspired versions. His success in "rebooting" Flash and Green Lantern (in 1959) initiated the "Silver Age" of comics and reestablished the superhero as the publisher's dominant genre, a position it has obviously never relinquished.

Significantly, for Schwartz the JLA was not a Marvel Studios–style culmination of a shared universe and intra-industrial franchising, but simply another step in his revitalization of Golden Age properties. In his memoir, he writes, "Following the Flash, I successfully revived Green Lantern, The Justice League of America [sic], Hawkman, the Atom, and so on" (Schwartz 88). Under Schwartz's editorial direction, the creative team of writer Gardner Fox (who also authored the bulk of *All-Star Comics*) and artist Mike Sekowsky was responsible for the first eight years of *JLA*. The team was cast with all of DC's active superheroes circa 1959, including those whose exploits were limited to backup stories. The initial roster consisted of Superman, Batman, Wonder Woman, the Flash, Green Lantern, Aquaman, and Martian Manhunter. Green Arrow would join the team in *JLA* no. 4.

The success of *JLA* caught the attention of Marvel publisher Martin Goodman, who ordered editor in chief Stan Lee to create a competing superhero team. At the time, Marvel (known as Atlas Comics in the 1950s), specialized in science fiction and mystery books and had no existing superhero titles with which to cast an all-star team. Instead, Lee and artist Jack Kirby created a new superhero team book called *The Fantastic Four* (FF), which premiered in August 1961. Rather than revitalizing dormant superhero intellectual properties, the book famously revised the conventional superhero book by emphasizing character psychology and dysfunctional family dynamics that, as Bradford W. Wright explains, "often impede their work as a team," as the heroes "frequently argue and even fight with each other" (204).

The innovations of *The Fantastic Four* were partly rooted in Lee's personal dissatisfaction with the conventional superhero book (White 4). But beyond

—

aesthetic questions lie business considerations, such as the need for product differentiation from the DC juggernaut. The emphasis on characterization and interpersonal conflict, along with the Marvel book's self-aware, reflexive editorial approach, helped establish a new "reading community," to use Matthew J. Pustz's term, that was older and more sophisticated than DC's target audience (20–22). Months before the release of *The Fantastic Four* no. 1, Marvel had published *Amazing Adult Fantasy*, "the magazine that respects your intelligence." Lee aggressively promoted this older readership, publishing letters from college students (or, as has been suggested, writing some of the letters himself) and flattering his readers by praising their taste and discernment (53). Lee further stoked his readers' interest in Marvel comics by establishing a relatively tight continuity, or narrative interconnectivity, among his superhero titles. By collecting each book, readers could see a narrative world unfolding.

By 1963 Marvel had enough popular superheroes to create its own all-star team, which could help solidify the publisher's narrative continuity and also more directly challenge *JLA*. Although it seems likely that an all-star team book would have been created eventually, Marvel apparently first published *The Avengers* out of necessity and practicality. According to historian Will Murray, artist Bill Everett missed his deadline on *Daredevil* no. 1, and a replacement title was required. An all-star team book would be easy for Lee and series artist and co-creator Jack Kirby to quickly produce, as no new characters would need to be created (3–10). Thor's nemesis Loki was used as the team's first antagonist. The team consisted of all of Marvel's non-FF superheroes (Iron Man, Thor, Ant-Man, the Wasp, and the Hulk, whose book was canceled in early 1963), with the exception of Spider-Man. World War II–era hero Captain America was reintroduced in issue no. 4. Unlike Marvel Studios' cinematic strategy, then, Marvel's initial iteration of the all-star team genre was not cumulative so much as it was convenient and highly contingent.

Lee's innovations to the superhero comic were partly a function of the corporate and creative hierarchy at Marvel in the 1960s. As the lone editor of Marvel's superhero line, Lee was free to deviate from narrative tradition without facing the kind of burdensome intra-company negotiation found at DC. The scope of the DC line and its fragmented editorial organization hindered the intra-industrial synergy that might permit fuller exploitation of the publisher's assets. For instance, calling to mind *All-Star Comics'* de-emphasis of the more popular characters, Superman and Batman appeared only intermittently in the first twelve issues of the JLA's adventures, and only on five covers (usually minutely) in the first twenty-five. According to Schwartz, this marginalization was due to territorialism on the parts of Superman editor Mort Weisinger and Batman editor Jack Schiff, who feared that *JLA* would cannibalize sales of their heroes' solo titles (96).

In contrast to DC, which had an expansive line, Marvel was publishing only seventeen books regularly when *The Avengers* debuted, and only eight of these books were superhero titles, all edited by Lee. This small number was not a reflection of the limited popularity of the books, but instead of the artificial limits set by Marvel's distributor at the time, which in a deep irony was Independent News, owned by DC Comics (Cronin 160–161). Marvel's smaller number of books and one-man editorial department would have major ramifications for its own iteration of the all-star team genre. As editor and writer of the majority of Marvel's superhero titles, Lee had more control and fewer barriers to the conception and enactment of a coherent iterative strategy than JLA's Schwartz, Fox, and Sekowsky. Whereas Schwartz had to negotiate the use of characters like Superman and Batman with his fellow editors, Lee could assemble his Avengers and extend a line-wide continuity largely at his own discretion.

STORYTELLING AND CHARACTERIZATION

Given the considerable differences in industrial context, it should come as no surprise that Marvel's approach to the specific demands of all-star team storytelling in *The Avengers* varies significantly from the approach taken by DC in *JLA*. Comic book fans, critics, and scholars have asserted a set of broad differences between the two books, differences that usually restate the oppositional qualities that have served to characterize the two companies' approaches to the superhero. But in focusing on opposition, these accounts often underdescribe the precise nature of these variations and the distinct characteristics of DC's and Marvel's revisions, replications, and rejections of the all-star team formula. They also tend to flatten accounts of the iterative variation within each series from issue to issue, reserving a diachronic analysis for character and storyworld development rather than shifts in storytelling strategies.

Despite the numerous variations we will examine, the underlying structure of these superhero stories is similar and consists of the relatively standard progression found in much of popular storytelling. We begin with a more or less stable state of affairs, which is disrupted by an inciting incident in act one, move through some complication and development during which the hero confronts the challenge (be it a villain, natural disaster, etc.) in act two, and then proceed to the final confrontation, the eventual defeat of the threat, and the establishment of a new stable state of affairs in the third act. Our concern is the particular problem of executing this structure given the relatively unique qualities of the all-star team book.[2] In general, we can characterize the strategy employed by DC in the JLA's first twenty-five stories as consisting of highly rationalized (both in terms of form and content), largely episodic, pseudo-educational storytelling. Its most significant feature was its use of a "split-up" structure that was established through fairly strict repetition early on and then revised and elaborated in subsequent issues. The "theme and variations" approach allowed Gardner Fox to experiment with the parameters of narration and narrative formula in order to hold not just the reader's interest, but perhaps also his own.

JLA's split-up strategy was largely a carryover from All-Star Comics, the bulk of which were also written by Fox. In the typical All-Star issue, the group briefly assembled for a team meeting and then, when confronted with a challenge, dispersed into separate locales to individually face the multiple aspects or incarnations of the threat. They would later reassemble for a brief confrontation with the source of the threat and, finally, would then compare notes at another team meeting. For the final nineteen issues, writer John Broome took over from Fox and employed a condensed split-up strategy in which heroes typically worked in small groups rather than individually. This revision was at least partly a reflection of the reduced page count of later All-Star issues, from approximately sixty pages per issue to about thirty.

In their handling of the JLA, with stories running twenty-five or twenty-six pages, Fox and Schwartz replicated Broome's condensed split-up approach, using it as a basis from which to improvise experiments in narrative form. The split-up structure provided a solution to the problem of how to manage the all-star team book's large cast of nominal equals as they overcame the issue's threat. Rather than having a potentially calamitous team melee, smaller groups tackled distinct aspects of a threat that was itself divided in some manner. Extending the story across these distinct episodes allowed not only for a stable base of repetition along with novel variation but also for a convenient and plausible way to stretch the story across an entire issue (what threat could possibly resist the combined forces of DC's heroes for twenty-odd pages?). Choosing this model, then, precluded other options, such as including romantic or character-driven "B" plots found in other forms of popular storytelling, or developing more complex problem-sets requiring truly elaborate problem-solving that might confuse DC's young target audience.

The central position that the split-up holds for the early *JLA* formula is widely known, but the manner in which it was executed is more novel and flexible than has been previously acknowledged. For instance, Will Jacobs and Gerard Jones, employing an evaluative tone, suggest that "Fox fell short in the JLA's first ten adventures [*Brave and the Bold* nos. 28–30, *JLA* nos. 1–7], which followed a rigid formula. . . . [A] menace creates disasters in three exotic corners of the world; the JLA splits up into three teams, each of which overcomes a particular challenge; at the end the heroes rejoin to defeat the villain himself." The three parts in this formula account for each issue's three acts. After this initial ten-issue period, Jacobs and Jones claim, Fox "broke the bonds of habit and turned his great imagination to charting unique and devious plots that played endless variations on a single theme: that heroes must triumph by brain, not brawn" (Jacobs and Jones 36).

There are some important problems with this characterization of Schwartz and Fox's early run on the book. First, the emphasis on pseudo-scientific, pseudo-educational problem-solving is part of the *JLA* formula from the beginning. In *The Brave and the Bold* no. 28, which marked the JLA's first appearance, they defeat a starfish-shaped alien by covering it in lime after Aquaman observes that "oystermen use quick lime to fight starfish who prey on oysters in the sea" (25–26). This example serves as a primer for the rationalistic, deductive approach to problem-solving employed by the Justice League throughout this period. The scientific solutions are often highly dubious. But the emphasis on problem solving and the incorporation of a plethora of scientific trivia suggests that this thematic aspect of the *JLA* was driven by a publishing imperative—perhaps a superficial educational agenda directed at a young audience.

The second and more fundamental problem with Jacobs and Jones's description is that it overstates the extent to which the series adheres to a narrow formula while also misreading the trajectory of Schwartz and Fox's approach to formula in the early years of the *JLA*. The consistent presence of split-ups in all but two issues of the team's first twenty-six appearances provides a convenient descriptive hook, but it can distract from other sites of variation and from experiments with the core formula itself. The presence

—

of elaborations on and around the core split-up formula actually should not be much of a surprise, given the essential strategy of standardization and differentiation that characterizes much of genre storytelling. As Neale points out, though, the formulaic nature of genre and the attendant predictability of generic "story patterns" are often overstated, producing a flattened account of a genre and its iterations that fails to account for significant and nuanced differences (208–210). Here, emphasis on the formulaic quality of the split-up strategy has overshadowed the elaborative, almost permutational variation in storytelling from issue to issue.

As one form of issue-to-issue elaboration, we can see Schwartz and Fox varying the ways in which individual stories are set up in their first act. While almost every setup leads to a team meeting, the formula for arriving at this assembly can differ. Occasionally an individual hero is featured encountering the source of the problem and then bringing it to the team. In other issues, the setup consists mainly of establishing the challenge to the team, often through a villain's monologue. In *The Brave and the Bold* no. 30, Fox employs a third approach to the setup. Here, each of the team's members (with the exception of Superman and Batman) experiences the inciting incident individually over the course of four pages until, in the sequence's final two panels, Barry Allen sees a pattern in the crime reports and, as the Flash, signals the JLA to assemble (2–5). This kind of sequence, which provides readers with a display of some aspect of each character, constitutes what we will describe as an "individual display sequence," and while it is not a device that is specific to the all-star team book, it is employed in *JLA* and *The Avengers* so regularly that it is essential to understanding their storytelling strategies.

Instead of the stagnant storytelling that the standard account suggests, we can see instead the establishment of a formula and then a series of variations on and elaborations of that formula. After establishing the basis for reader expectations in the first six JLA stories, Fox begins to experiment. For instance, *JLA* no. 5 begins with the team members pondering their betrayal by their newest member, Green Arrow. When Green Arrow arrives, his teammates confront him, initiating a series of flashbacks that recount two split-ups, each of which ends with Green Arrow intervening to allow the team's foes to escape. Here Fox uses the split-up formula as the basis for formal experimentation, employing a narrative framework that plays with temporal order and varies viewpoint, incorporating flashbacks narrated by five separate team members. In the story's final segment, Fox replays the events of the first two split-ups from a new perspective, that of the accused Green Arrow, who recounts what really happened, filling in gaps of motivation and action that the previous all-star narrators, because of their limited perspectives, had missed. Schwartz and Fox have, then, revised the split-up structure to make room for a foregrounded shift in narrational perspective that uses temporal repetition as a vehicle for narrative revelation.

Beyond *JLA* no. 5, Schwartz and Fox initiate a series of permutational experiments around the split-up formula: they divide the team into two groups, but depict only one group's mission (*JLA* no. 7), shift the split-up to the stories' third act (*JLA* nos. 11 and 12), disperse it across the issue's acts (*JLA* no. 20), and include two rounds of split-up (*JLA* nos. 10 and 18). *JLA* nos. 21 and 22, which feature the first of what would become annual trans-universal team-ups between the JSA and the JLA, provide a kind of rococo zenith of the split-up formula. The final act of the two-issue story provides a climactic two-page split-up/display sequence hybrid consisting of six borderless horizontal "panels," each featuring a mixed trio of JSA and JLA members tackling a separate villain.

DC's intensely iterative strategy—a split-up formula that generates an internal episodic structure and is also repeated from issue to issue—is elaborated upon in a way that suggests not a lack of creativity but an interest in formal craftsmanship over expressivity through character or theme. It is an approach that conforms with Jean-Paul Gabilliet's account of the self-perceptions of the first and second generation of comic book creators, who valued "draftsmanship as craft" over a "sense of individualism" or self-expression (164–165). It also chimes with the self-perception and practice of other popular storytellers. For instance, David Bordwell has chronicled the work of celebrated mid-twentieth-century Japanese filmmaker Yasujiro Ozu, whose films demonstrate a similar, though arguably more sophisticated, attention to working with and within the strict parameters of formula. Bordwell relates a story told by film critic Tadao Sato in which Ozu gets angry with another filmmaker at a party "for maintaining that film was an art of self-expression rather than of rule-governed form" (*Ozu* 6). Adherence to formula, then, becomes not a constraint that precludes variation, but the basis for iterative elaboration and narrative experimentation.

It is against the backdrop of Schwartz and Fox's emphasis on pseudo-scientific rationality and their craftsman-like, intellectualized permutational experimentation with narrative form and formula that Marvel launched its all-star team book, *The Avengers*, in 1963. While Stan Lee has claimed that it was the popularity of DC's *JLA* that led to his creation of Marvel's *Fantastic Four*, he also asserts that he never read an issue of *JLA* (Eury 28). Whether he did or not, the *Avengers* formula is markedly different from that established in DC's all-star team book. Lee and his key collaborators, Jack Kirby and Don Heck, were tasked with reconciling the demands of the all-star team book genre with the qualities that made Marvel's books distinctive from its competitors: an emphasis on character psychology and emotionality, increased seriality, and an emphatic, integrated approach to continuity. Within this context we find a highly flexible approach to formula, and one that developed its own conventions, particularly the "splinter" storyline. Lee and company also revised key aspects of the all-star team book formula, such as the team meeting.

Upon opening their copies of *Avengers* no. 2, the first to feature a fully formed Avengers team, readers were immediately greeted with a key aspect of the book's revisionist strategy. The team meetings that in the pages of *JLA* had provided members with a (typically) act-one opportunity for rational discussion had been revised to serve as a forum for a trio of bickering, name-calling heroes. Thor insults the Hulk's purple shorts. The Hulk in return warns Iron Man to "get this yellow-haired yahoo off my back," before he decides to "boot him up to Asgard for good!" While not every team meeting in *The Avengers* was filled with confrontation and squabbling, such in-fighting did serve as a vehicle for the series' introduction of more complex characterization into the all-star team book formula. In *The Avengers* no. 7, for instance, the team discusses Iron Man's failure to respond to the "call to assemble" that was a trope of the Justice League's adventures. Iron Man solemnly declares that he "can offer no defense! I allowed a personal problem to affect my sense of duty!" It is a shortcoming to which no Justice Leaguer had ever admitted. In Marvel's iteration of the all-star team genre, then, a generic trope is revised: the Avengers' team meetings not only serve to assemble the team and showcase the superhero collective, as in *JLA*, but also display and motivate character conflict and emotion, qualities that could make the Marvel characters more identifiable to the publisher's reading community.

It was not just the convention of the team meeting that *The Avengers'* creative team had revised. The book also expanded the kinds of events that could play an essential role in the all-star team book's narrative formula. Most famously, *The Avengers* regularly employed (in a manner that complemented the "heroes bicker" trope found in the team's first meeting) the "heroes fight" event as an attraction in the book. Whereas readers could count on the spectacle of the all-star team-up and super-cooperation in JLA, in seven of the first sixteen issues of The Avengers they were treated to all-stars brawling with one another. The convention provided the grist for the bulk of the series' first three issues, and when the pristinely preserved Captain America is thawed out in The Avengers no. 4, his first act is to lash out wildly at his future teammates. His second is to convince the Avengers that he really is Captain America by challenging them to "try to conquer me"—an offer they eagerly accept. Here, Marvel's handling of the resurrection and reiteration of a Golden Age hero, immediately initiated into intra-team conflict and, as we shall see, primed for emotionality and character development, nicely contrasts with Schwartz's rationalized, science–fictionalizing, revisionist project.

Whereas JLA relies heavily on the split-up structure as the central component of its formula, The Avengers embodies an alternate approach that is much less dependent on a single formulaic element. The Marvel book does make use of the split-up in five of its first sixteen issues, four of which involved the Avengers combating the supervillain team the Masters of Evil. In these issues, the heroes split up to individually fight their respective villainous counterparts. Frequently, though, these split-up portions lasted no more than a page or two per hero. One of the reasons that Marvel was free to experiment with its storytelling formula was that it had fewer all-stars to incorporate into its stories. The smaller cast, just five heroes, could be more easily handled all at once than the more sprawling cast of all-stars available to DC. It was less necessary to create subgroupings because there were fewer heroes to trip over one another when they were jointly battling a threat. Likewise, one-at-a-time confrontations were more manageable, requiring fewer pages of a book that was already several pages shorter than JLA.

Even so, The Avengers does display the larger process of assembly, disassembly, and reassembly common to the JLA in many of the issues. But with so few characters to disperse and then bring back together, fewer pages were required, opening up narrative possibilities. One solution was what we might call the "N+1" strategy, used in some form in six out of the series' first sixteen issues, in which the heroes build their numbers over the course of an issue or act until the entire team is present and reassembled. The team has already initially been assembled and then dispersed in The Avengers no. 1, for example, when the third act displays the N+1 strategy: The Hulk's fight with Iron Man is brought to a halt by the arrival of Thor, with the villainous Loki in tow. When Loki escapes and threatens the heroes, a swarm of ants are shown pulling a lever that opens a trapdoor beneath his feet, heralding the arrival of Ant Man and Wasp to complete the reassembly of the newborn team.

Although the split-up and N+1 structures appear frequently throughout *The Avengers*, the core of the book's narrative formula is the deployment of the "splinter" strategy, which we find in all but one of the series' first sixteen issues. Here we see Marvel employing a branching approach to narrative that generates what can (sometimes only generously) be described as a "B" plot, a secondary plot that develops alongside the core narrative in which the larger group of heroes confronts the threat. Typically, one hero is given special attention and leaves the side of his or her teammates for a portion of the issue, sometimes for personal reasons and sometimes to pursue a goal that is important to the larger mission.

Over the series' first six issues, Thor proves to be a popular candidate for the splinter story. He serves as the featured hero in three of those issues. For instance, in *The Avengers* no. 1, Thor is lured away from the other heroes when he spots a vision of the Hulk that Loki has concocted as part of his larger plan to trick the Thunder God into returning to Asgard. Through fairly obscure logic, Thor deduces that Loki is behind the Hulk mirage and leaves for Asgard, and the storytelling moves away from the rest of the team's battle with the actual Hulk to show Thor's journey to the Isle of Silence to confront Loki. His return from Asgard with Loki unites the splinter story with the main storyline in a manner that is characteristic of the strategy.

Another distinct large-scale strategy employed by *The Avengers* is the negotiated serialization of the book's narrative. In some sense, comic book series, like television series, are by definition serial. That is, essential premises, such as the main characters' fight against evil, are repeated from issue to issue, and the narrative world is further elaborated. When individual installments provide a unified chain of cause and effect, and when a villain is introduced and overcome within a given issue, the narrative form is generally described as tilting toward the episodic. That said, individual issues may also contribute to a larger, serialized, causal chain that leaves some key questions unanswered, some causes dangling, to be picked up in subsequent issues or, more rarely, in a publisher's other titles.[3]

Storytelling in *The Avengers* intensifies the serialization of the narrative to an extent not seen in *JLA*, whose core split-up structure, as was discussed earlier, is so attractive in part because it provides a solution that works well with limited narrative development. The first three issues of *The Avengers* are episodic in the sense that each issue is unified around its own specific threat: Loki, the Space Phantom, and then the combination of the Hulk and Sub-Mariner. But they also trace a continuing story of the Hulk's "courtship" by, membership in, and then rejection of the team. *The Avengers* innovates upon *JLA*'s all-star team formula by integrating serialized character arcs as part of its storytelling strategy. While at the beginning of this three-issue arc the Hulk selflessly tries to save a train from a dynamited railroad bridge, by its end, through a series of misunderstandings and obnoxious comments made by his teammates (see Thor's criticism of his wardrobe), he is transformed into a villain who hates humanity, the Avengers, and his temporary ally, the Sub-Mariner. By contrast, the one moment of intra-squad conflict in the adventures of the JLA, Green Arrow's admittance to and then seeming betrayal of the team in *JLA* no. 5, is resolved by the end of the issue, through questioning and testimony rather than through the heroes fighting one another. As with its revisionist approach to the genre's narrative formula, Marvel's approach to the very conception of the all-star team incorporates flexibility and volatility as its underwriting principles.

Captain America, the Hulk's replacement, provides the subject for splinter stories in seven out of the thirteen issues of *The Avengers* in which he appears through issue no. 16. Famously thawed out in *The Avengers* no. 4, Captain America is immediately given the spotlight in a modified splinter story when the issue's second act begins. Here, the other members of the team are transformed into stone, and Captain America is left alone to wander and wonder at 1960s New York until the teenager Rick Jones, *The Avengers*' revision of the JLA's Snapper Carr, rouses him from a dream of his dead sidekick Bucky to request his help in saving them. Cap's initial confused belief that Rick is Bucky, and Rick's immediate fascination with Captain America, contribute to a character arc and serialized storyline that will continue with only brief intermissions through the recasting of the team in *The Avengers* no. 16. Baron Zemo, the Nazi villain responsible for Bucky's death and Captain America's imprisonment in ice, reappears six times throughout the initial run of the book, until his apparent death in *The Avengers* no. 15. Zemo is motivated by revenge against Captain America, whom he holds responsible for an errant shield toss that shattered a nearby vat of "Adhesive X" and permanently adhered his "hated hood" to his face (*The Avengers* no. 6, 4). Zemo's drive for retribution is counterbalanced by

Captain America's vendetta against Zemo, who is responsible for the death of Bucky. As with the issues detailing the Hulk's arc, each issue during this period stands more or less on its own, so *The Avengers* marks a revision to rather than a rejection of the episodic issue-to-issue narrative form found in *JLA*.

The story arc is resolved with the death of Baron Zemo and Captain America's subsequent return from the deceased Baron's South American jungle lair, and yet the individual installments of the arc serve more to reiterate the character dilemma than to push the plot toward an inevitable conclusion. Indeed, while scholars such as Charles Hatfield are right to emphasize Marvel's greater emphasis on characterization and emotionality, as opposed to the pseudoscientific rationalism central to Fox's *JLA*, we should be sure to qualify these claims (116–119). Lee and company's storytelling strategy does not depend on the kind of coherent character arcs we might find in contemporary comics or television. Instead, there is a decidedly ad hoc approach taken to Captain America's character arc. For instance, *The Avengers* no. 9 opens with a splash page featuring the hero hurling his shield toward a gigantic Zemo while his teammates look on. Cap declares, "You won't escape me again, Zemo! I'll get you this time!!" The page turn reveals that this image is not the metadiegetic splash-page preview that often opens comic books during this period (though much less frequently in *The Avengers* than in *JLA*), but instead part of the issue's first scene. Captain America's thirst for revenge is so profound that he has been hallucinating in the halls of Avengers Mansion.

Yet Captain America soon recovers, and this mental break has zero consequences for the character's psyche. Instead, it provides an extreme example of Marvel's strategy of augmenting its narratives not just with characterization per se but with moments of outsized emotionality. Here, the emotional display serves as a vehicle through which to reiterate the character's central tragedy—his feelings of guilt and anger at Bucky's death. Yet the display does not advance Captain America's characterization, even though the ensuing story features another encounter between Zemo and the Avengers. Captain America is denied his revenge and Zemo escapes, ensuring that the character dilemma can be reiterated once again. This employment of reiteration and the halting development of character act as cautions against idealizing or overgeneralizing Marvel's strategy. In these early issues of *The Avengers*, Lee and company are still navigating the demands of a form that is conventionally episodic and driven by action and spectacular display

—

rather than organic character development. Thus, they still rely on formula and repetition, even while incorporating emotional display and internal and external character conflict into their iterative formula.

CONTINUITY

The balancing act between repetition and development, as well as the role of emotion and characterization, are essential to understanding the special relationship between the all-star team book and continuity, which we narrowly define here as the consistency and interconnected quality of a serialized narrative world. We therefore discuss continuity in terms of the consistency of characterization between the team book and the solo books of the individual team members, and as the connectivity of narrative events that extend beyond the team book and throughout a publisher's entire line. JLA and The Avengers can largely be seen as extensions not just of the DC and Marvel narrative "universes," but also as distinct embodiments of and elaborations upon their publishers' approaches to continuity. Both found ways to limit and manage character continuity, though with different emphases. But more broadly, and more distinctively, whereas JLA initially served as a relatively isolated locus for the novel spectacle of continuity at DC, The Avengers was deployed as part of Marvel's line-wide campaign of intensified and integrated continuity.

Contributing to a continuity based on the consistency of characterization was relatively easy for JLA because of the homogeneous personalities of DC's all-star superheroes. As Bradford Wright notes, "DC superheroes 'spoke' in the same carefully measured sentences. Each reacted to situations in the same predictable manner. They were always in control, rarely impulsive, and never irrational. Most importantly, all of the DC superheroes were impossibly altruistic. Helping humanity was their only motivation" (185). In their home titles, DC's heroes exhibited a narrower range of character-based premises than Marvel's did. Secret identities were largely constituted by names, professions, romantic interests, and the summary of origin stories rather than their implications, which allowed DC to sidestep the kinds of tragic flaws and emotional needs and dilemmas that might be used to generate a character arc. Moreover, instead of the distinctive voices of Marvel characters, such as Hulk's bellicosity, the Wasp's strong libido, or Thor's grandiosity, DC's characters had powers, weaknesses, and villains that were foregrounded and mobilized as factors in problem-solving narrative

—

equations. Following this logic, character-based continuity in *JLA* only required consistently characterizing and differentiating the heroes though the repetition and display of their respective powers and weaknesses.

The consistency of each hero's powers was not always a priority for DC. Superman was considerably less powerful in his early Golden Age appearances when he fought gangsters and slumlords than in his 1950s science-fiction stories, when he was capable of pushing a planet out of orbit (as in *Superman* no. 110). But in 1958 Mort Weisinger took control of DC's Superman line and began constructing an elaborate, internally consistent world for the Man of Steel. The character received a revised origin that attributed his powers to the Earth's yellow sun. The powers themselves became practically unlimited, providing a novel solution to the problem of continuity. Rather than reiterating an essential power-set, Superman stories of the Silver Age would often highlight the character's two vulnerabilities: to kryptonite or magic. In general, a character's weakness (for instance, Green Lantern's helplessness against the color yellow, or Martian Manhunter's fear of fire) was often just as important to *JLA*'s character continuity as his or her powers. These premises from the home books became key to the problem-setting and -solving performed in the JLA's narratives.

Characterizing a superhero through his relationships, particularly his romantic relationships, was also common at DC during the 1960s. Along with their unique power-sets and weaknesses, superheroes were differentiated by the circumstances of their love lives: Ray Palmer (the Atom) helps his girlfriend lawyer Jean Loring with her cases so she will become successful and agree to marry him, while Green Lantern wants his boss Carol Ferris to love him as Hal Jordan, not as his super-powered alter ego. These romances, though, most often served as marginal, framing elements in the stories' narratives, sometimes appearing in the setup and then reappearing in a frequently humorous epilogue. They are reiterated without clear development and without shaping the superhero character in a way that would require special attention or care in *JLA*. Following, but condensing, the strategies found in the heroes' home books, the appearances of their romantic interests in *JLA* are almost wholly confined to concentrated individual display sequences, such as the one found in *JLA* no. 7, in which three horizontal panels at the story's end capture the heroes and their romantic partners enjoying a day at the "cosmic fun-house" featured in the story.

As in *JLA*, the characters' romantic relationships and love interests were generally excluded from *The Avengers*; for instance, the twists and turns of

Iron Man and Happy Hogan's strange love triangle with Pepper Potts in *Tales of Suspense* are absent from *The Avengers*. With romance removed from both team books, the remaining difference in character continuity consisted in quality rather than quantity. Whereas *JLA* emphasized the continuity of characters' powers and weaknesses, *The Avengers* focused on reiterating characters' unique internal struggles. This is not to say that *The Avengers* never deploys character weaknesses as obstacles in action-oriented conflicts: Iron Man's battery runs down, and Thor sometimes struggles to retrieve his hammer in time to prevent his reversion to his human identity. But once Lee decided upon a character's specific psychological conflict, he reiterated it frequently throughout both *The Avengers* and the character's solo book, tightening the continuity within the line.

In *The Avengers*, this kind of character continuity was frequently accomplished through revised versions of the kind of individual display sequences found in *JLA*. Although Lee and company show the heroes in their secret identities, as in *JLA*, they also frequently reiterate their character dilemmas. A four-panel individual display sequence in *The Avengers* no. 9 perfectly captures this approach. The first panel shows Iron Man thinking about the obstacle that his secret identity poses to his happiness. The second displays the "noble god of thunder . . . transforming himself into the lame Dr. Blake." The third shows the Wasp failing to pull scientist Hank Pym away from his experiment so they can go on a date. The fourth reiterates Captain America's aforementioned desire to "find Zemo—to avenge Bucky's death!" (5).

As established earlier, from an institutional standpoint narrative consistency was a simpler matter at Marvel, as Stan Lee edited all of the titles; along with his brother Larry Lieber, he wrote all of Marvel's early superhero books as well. This hands-on approach was particularly useful when it came to the intense narrative interconnectivity of its titles, the "Marvel Universe" for which the publisher would become famous. Even so, the concept of a shared narrative world in comics was not new; DC had already clearly established its own universe, dating back to the debut of the JSA in 1940. DC's version of shared continuity was enacted primarily through team-ups of two superheroes (and, often, their sidekicks). In 1952, Superman and Batman, who had co-headlined *World's Finest Comics* since 1941, joined forces for the first time; two years later, *World's Finest* became a Superman/Batman and Robin team book. Another innovation instituted by Weisinger upon taking control of the Superman books in 1958 was a much more frequent

—

use of superhero guest stars: for instance, Batman, Aquaman, and Green Arrow (all three edited by Murray Boltinoff and George Kashdan at the time) guest star in *Superman's Girl Friend, Lois Lane* no. 29 (Nov. 1961). By 1962, Schwartz's Flash and Green Lantern characters were also guest starring in each other's books. *JLA* can be considered simply a large-scale embodiment of the contained, "special" event, team-up approach to continuity. Its strategy, while undergoing moments of innovation and revision, seems likely to have been constrained by the publisher's balkanized editorial organization.

With his interlocking Marvel titles, Lee fashioned an intensely interconnected narrative world similar in some respects to Weisinger's "Super-verse," which featured its own set of recurring supporting characters, villains, and plot elements. Yet Weisinger's world was self-contained within his editorial fiefdom; although DC would occasionally publish two-parters that stretched across a pair of issues, the story was always confined to a single title. Readers could buy *Superman,* for example, without needing to read any of Weisinger's other five Superbooks. Likewise, DC's team-ups in the early to mid-1960s remained confined to the comic at hand and did not affect the narratives of any other book. In contrast, by weaving all of his company's superheroes into a complex latticework, Lee encouraged readers to purchase the entire Marvel superhero line, which in 1963 consisted of eight books.

Interconnectivity for Marvel was a more flexible principle that could take the form of guest appearances (major and minor) and overlapping narratives (major and minor). In a major guest appearance, a character from another book plays a key role in a story's events. A DC-style team-up would be considered a major guest appearance, but true to form, Marvel usually problematizes the traditional team-up by inserting conflict among the superheroes. For instance, *The Avengers* no. 11 is entitled "The Mighty Avengers Meet Spider-Man," but for most of the book the Avengers face an evil robot of Spidey who attempts to undermine their team unity. A minor guest appearance consists of a brief cameo that serves to remind the audience of the presence of the character in the shared Marvel Universe, but has no impact on the story. In *Tales of Suspense* no. 49, the X-Men try to contact the Avengers to ask for help. Three consecutive panels show Bruce Banner, Donald Blake, Hank Pym, and Janet van Dyne occupied in their everyday lives, and thus unable to reply. The Hulk, Thor, Giant Man, and the Wasp play no role in the events to follow, but the cameos remind us the characters are out there in the same narrative world as the X-Men.

In an overlapping narrative, a plotline is introduced in one title and continued in another. Lee is typically careful to have events in one book influence those in others. Sometimes the event is minor: in *Tales of Suspense* no. 56, a depressed Tony Stark briefly abandons his Iron Man persona and instructs Pepper Potts to tell the Avengers he is on vacation when they seek his assistance. *Avengers* no. 7, released less than a month after the *Tales of Suspense* issue, opens with a splash page and four panels in which Iron Man faces a one-week suspension from the Avengers for failing to answer their call. Sometimes, however, the overlapping event is a major crossover: for example, after the Hulk escapes the Avengers in issue 3, his story continues in *Fantastic Four* nos. 25 and 26, where the Avengers team up with the FF to tackle the green-skinned goliath. As Pierre Comtois points out, the Hulk's appearance in *Avengers* no. 5 serves as a kind of epilogue for this major crossover (64).

DC's version of continuity, rooted in the team-up, was based in the novelty of special events. For Marvel, this relentless interweaving of characters and plots was simply the status quo; continuity was understood as the continuous integration of narrative. But Marvel's emphasis on its shared universe would eventually result in fundamental changes to *The Avengers*, leading the company to reject the all-star team genre while retaining the "Avengers" brand. Throughout its first sixteen issues, the negotiation of continuity played a key role in shaping a core innovation of *The Avengers'* narrative strategy—the character arc. The book plays it safe and avoids conflict with other series in the Marvel lineup by assigning character arcs, and the serial storytelling that frequently goes with them, to the Hulk and Captain America, who were largely unaffiliated with a home book at the time. Although Captain America began appearing in *Tales of Suspense* seven months after his revival, only the first five issues were set in the present day. Subsequent issues were set during World War II, removing the possibility of interference with Captain America's characterization in *The Avengers*. Thus, the line-wide principles of intensely integrated continuity and character development butted up against the core features of the all-star team book, as the implementation of Marvel's revisions to the all-star team genre required a regular renegotiation of the company's other publications.

The shift in iterative strategy evident in *Tales of Suspense*, one that de-emphasizes integrated continuity, is particularly interesting because it came just two months before *The Avengers* replaced the original members with the "Cap's Kooky Quartet" cast of thawed-out hero and reformed villains (Captain America and Hawkeye, the Scarlet Witch, and Quicksilver) who would constitute the team's membership until the return of Hank Pym (as Goliath and now also without a home book) in *The Avengers* no. 28. With *The Avengers* no. 16, then, not only does Captain America complete his arc of loss and revenge, but the original team is traded out for a group of heroes who can be employed in their own character arcs with impunity. Lee would no longer need to coordinate their stories across titles, and *The Avengers* could serve as a means of showcasing these relatively new characters.[4]

Finally, and perhaps most importantly, the book now had the freedom to include more conflict and character development than before. As discussed earlier, in deference to the heroes' respective solo books, *The Avengers* served to display or reiterate character conflict more than to develop it. With "Cap's Kooky Quartet," not only could Lee develop his supporting characters, but he could amplify the intensity of the intra-team conflict (namely, Hawkeye's antagonism of Captain America, whom he considers outmoded and unsuited to lead) in a way that he could not with the original cast. *The Avengers'* potential for heightened emotionality, central to its revision of the JLA formula, would no longer be compromised by the demands of Marvel's heightened continuity.

This shift involved more than a simple recasting of the all-star team book. Its significance is underlined by the book's quick abandonment of Rick Jones, Marvel's revision of Snapper Carr, the Justice League's teen-aged honorary member. Whereas Schwartz and Fox employed Carr and his faux beatnik patois as a source of humor in JLA, the approach taken to Jones in *The Avengers* tended to focus on the character's desire to become a member of the team and to replace Bucky as Captain America's sidekick. Indeed, Rick's character arc is interwoven with Captain America's, but when Captain America's obsession with Bucky is temporarily resolved, with the elimination of Zemo in *The Avengers* no. 15, Jones is also quickly dispatched. In *The Avengers* no. 17, he makes his last appearance during Lee's run on the book. He stands to one side at "the first scheduled meeting of the new Avengers," a scowl on his face and his hands in his pockets, thinking, "It isn't fair! Those three Johnny-come latelies are now official members . . . and Cap still won't let me be a full-fledged uniformed Avenger!" The truth is that Rick Jones had become extraneous, not just to the fictional Avengers, but to *The Avengers'* storytelling stratagem. The fundamental problem-set of the series had been shifted away from the distinct set of affordances and constraints of the all-star team book.

CONCLUSION

The evident messiness of the process of generic iteration serves to reinforce Neale's caution against evolutionary and straightforward accounts of generic change. While the early, pre–"Kooky Quartet" version of the Avengers significantly revised the preexisting all-star team formula, it represents not a coherent step forward along a chain of innovation but a temporally limited generic experiment that was itself internally negotiated and seemingly constructed around the principle of flexibility. Likewise, the iteration of the all-star team book to which it directly or indirectly responded was itself committed to a formula that prescribed a narrower form of formal experimentation. These competing approaches are best conceived not in terms of the outdated past, the new present, or the visionary future of the genre, but as complex historical processes.

The careful formal analysis and contextualization that characterize the historical poetics approach enable us to nuance existing accounts of DC's and Marvel's practices. More specifically, the problem/solution critical paradigm allows us to situate Marvel's revisions to the all-star team book within a historical craft tradition. Marvel's creators faced the problem of how to successfully produce an all-star team book, a superhero format governed by a set of artistic norms, while also differentiating their product from that of their main competitor. To this end, we argue that they retained certain norms inherited from *All-Star Comics* and *JLA* and modified others. For instance, in some issues, *The Avengers* retains DC's "split-up" structure. But because of the small size of their superhero team, Lee and company did not face Schwartz and Fox's problem of giving roughly equal attention to a large number of heroes. The absence of this constraint allowed Lee to develop alternative structures, such as the "N+1" strategy, which DC could not have successfully executed. Likewise, rather than rejecting *JLA*'s episodic storytelling style, Marvel employed a kind of negotiated seriality in which character subplots were reiterated more than developed. Despite the standard story that Marvel's books were character-driven, we have found that the early issues of *The Avengers* were, like *JLA*, driven by action and spectacular display. Rather than marking an utter rejection of the DC model, *The Avengers* represents a process of negotiation with preexisting conventions.

The historical poetics approach argues that industrial structures are a proximate causal factor behind formal patterns, and industrial context is indeed important to understanding Marvel's revision of the all-star team book. First, as the leading publisher in the industry, DC had much less incentive to innovate than the upstart Marvel. However, within an established set of parameters, JLA exhibits a remarkable amount of formal variation and permutational experimentation. At the same time, large-scale change, particularly in terms of increased attention to continuity, was hindered by the editorial fiefdoms of DC. Stan Lee, in contrast, had wide latitude to fashion an innovative superhero line that appealed to a slightly older readership. His emphasis in *The Avengers* on heightened emotionality led to an unpredictable, volatile team that contested the more constrained JLA approach.

Of course, as the set of historically situated constraints and affordances shift—both over time within a given medium and across a variety of media—we should expect the iterative strategies of media-makers to shift as well. As we have demonstrated, historical poetics provides a useful tool for tracking the changing solutions to the problems posed by the all-star team genre. The kind of analysis conducted here, then, could be usefully extended to other influential and heretofore unexamined iterations of the all-star team comic. One could examine, for instance, the ways in which Marvel's approach to the all-star team book influenced DC in the early 1970s, when Marvel-inspired writers such as Mike Friedrich and Dennis O'Neil were hired to write JLA. Or one could examine Brian Michael Bendis's run on *The Avengers* (2004–2012) as an intensification of the norms established by Stan Lee and his collaborators in the mid-1960s, perhaps inspired by a shift in Marvel's industrial position and organization.

Further analysis of comics form can also assist the transmedia scholar who seeks to investigate, for instance, the similarities and differences among storytelling in comics, film, and television. As David Herman suggests, the intersections among media cannot be fully explored until we better understand "what sorts of constraints shape the communicative and representational properties of each storytelling medium" (68). As Marvel Studios, and more recently DC Entertainment and Warner Bros., move forward in creating arguably the most high-profile iterations of the all-star

—

superhero team subgenre, historical poetics can help us to more fully recognize the choices made in repeating, revising, and rejecting preexisting conventions and to situate these formal decisions within the context of concrete industrial strategies.

....

NOTES

1. The issues analyzed here include *The Brave and the Bold* nos. 28–30 (Feb./March 1960–June/July 1960), *Justice League of America* nos. 1–22 (Nov./Dec. 1960–Sept. 1963), and *The Avengers* nos. 1–17 (Sept. 1963–June 1965).

2. For one example of the application of the three-act structure to the comic book series, see O'Neil 32–45. The brief account of narrative structure presented here employs some of the specific terminology used by Thompson in her work on storytelling in Hollywood film and popular television.

3. For a discussion of episodic and serial storytelling structure, as well as character arcs, in television, see Newman.

4. For an account of Lee's recasting of *The Avengers* that emphasizes the burden of maintaining line-wide continuity, see Howe 56–57.

WORKS CITED

Bordwell, David. *Figures Traced in Light: On Cinematic Staging*. Berkeley: University of California Press, 2005. Print.

———. *Ozu and the Poetics of Cinema*. Princeton, NJ: Princeton University Press, 1988. Print.

———. *Poetics of Cinema*. New York: Routledge, 2008. Print.

Comtois, Pierre. *Marvel Comics in the 1960s: An Issue by Issue Field Guide to a Pop Culture Phenomenon*. Raleigh, NC: TwoMorrows Publishing, 2009. Print.

Cronin, Brian. *Was Superman a Spy? And Other Comic Book Legends Revealed*. New York: Plume Books, 2009. Print.

Eury, Michael. *Justice League Companion*. Raleigh, NC: TwoMorrows Publishing, 2005. Print.

Gabilliet, Jean-Paul. *Of Comics and Men: A Cultural History of American Comic Books*. Trans. Bart Beaty and Nick Nguyen. Jackson: University Press of Mississippi, 2010. Print.

Hatfield, Charles. *Hand of Fire: The Comics Art of Jack Kirby*. Jackson: University Press of Mississippi, 2012. Print.

Herman, David. "Toward a Transmedial Narratology." In *Narrative Across*

Media: The Languages of Storytelling. Ed. Marie-Laure Ryan. Lincoln: University of Nebraska Press, 2004. 47-75. Print.

Howe, Sean. *Marvel Comics: The Untold Story.* New York: HarperCollins, 2012. Print.

Jacobs, Will, and Gerard Jones. *The Comic Book Heroes.* Rocklin, CA: Prima, 1997. Print.

Johnson, Derek. "Cinematic Destiny: Marvel Studios and the Trade Stories of Industrial Convergence." *Cinema Journal* 52.1 (Fall 2012): 1-24. Print.

———. *Media Franchising: Creative License and Collaboration in the Culture Industries.* New York: New York University Press, 2013. Print.

Murray, Will. "Daredevil Vs. The Avengers." *Alter Ego* 118 (July 2013): 3-10. Print.

Neale, Steve. *Genre and Hollywood.* New York: Routledge, 2000. Print.

Newman, Michael Z. "From Beats to Arcs: Toward a Poetics of Television Narrative." *The Velvet Light Trap* 58 (Fall 2006): 16-28. Print.

O'Neil, Dennis. *The DC Comics Guide to Writing Comics.* New York: Watson-Guptill Publications, 2001. Print.

Pustz, Matthew J. *Comic Book Culture: Fanboys and True Believers.* Jackson: University Press of Mississippi, 1999. Print.

Schwartz, Julius. *Man of Two Worlds.* New York: HarperEntertainment, 2000. Print.

Smith, Greg M. "Surveying the World of Contemporary Comics Scholarship: A Conversation." *Cinema Journal* 50.3 (Spring 2011): 135-147. Print.

Stork, Matthias. "Assembling the Avengers: Reframing the Superhero Movie Through Marvel's Cinematic Universe." In *Superhero Synergies.* Eds. James N. Gilmore and Matthias Stork. Lanham, MD: Rowman and Littlefield, 2014. 77-96. Print.

Thomas, Roy. *All-Star Companion,* vol. 1. Raliegh, NC: TwoMorrows Publishing, 2004. Print.

Thompson, Kristin. *Storytelling in Film and Television.* Cambridge, MA: Harvard University Press, 2003. Print.

White, Ted. "A Conversation with the Man Behind Marvel Comics." In *Stan Lee: Conversations.* Ed. Jeff McLaughlin. Jackson: University Press of Mississippi, 2007. 3-13. Print.

Wright, Bradford W. *Comic Book Nation: The Transformation of Youth Culture in America.* Baltimore: Johns Hopkins University Press, 2001. Print.

Man Without Fear

DAVID MACK, DAREDEVIL, AND THE
"BOUNDS OF DIFFERENCE" IN SUPERHERO COMICS

HENRY JENKINS

The 2003–2004 release of David Mack's *Echo—Vision Quest* storyline for Marvel's *Daredevil: The Man Without Fear* (nos. 51–55) sparked intense debate wherever superhero fans gathered. The book challenged a number of entrenched, often unexamined assumptions about what a mainstream superhero comic book should look like and what kind of story it should tell. Today, we can find traces of those debates via the reader comments on Amazon. At one end of the spectrum, some loathe this book and everything it stands for. Says Amazon reviewer Redwolfsniper:

> This book is a sadistic deviation from thier [sic] storyline and is written and draw [sic] by David Mack. This is a . . . crap fest about a very minor character and her hippie like journey to discover her past. . . . He then further expresses his impotency in the field by using chicken scratch drawings and paintings to move the story along with hardly ANY dialog. THis [sic] book is an artsy load of crap that should not be affiliated with Daredevil or Marvel.

Whatever this reader wanted from a Daredevil comic, it was not, God forbid, art.

On the other end are readers who value its experimental qualities but also recognize that *Vision Quest* pushes against many fan expectations. For instance, from reviewer Stephanie Grant:

> If you'd like to see Daredevil swinging through New York City beating up bad guys, this is not the comic for you. Although this is technically Volume 8 of the recent Daredevil run, it isn't exactly part of the regular

continuity. . . . Daredevil subscribers expected more of the plot and action that had filled the series to that point, and this meditative break was frustrating, particularly considering the point that Bendis had halted the main plot. If you are a fan of *Alias* (the comic) or *Kabuki*, this is for you. If you would like to gaze in awe at the poetic writing, beautiful painting and stunning mixed-media art of one of the most creative men in comics, buy this comic. You won't regret it.

Vision Quest was written as a stand-alone book, but it was inserted at the last minute into the Daredevil series, due to a production delay, in the midst of a highly popular Brian Michael Bendis run. There, the story followed immediately after a gripping cliffhanger that would not get resolved for another six months. Even many fans who liked the book's aesthetics were angered by this badly timed interruption of the main storyline. For instance, reviewer Phillip Frangules writes:

> Imagine being engrossed in an intelligent, gritty fast-paced work and then being forcefed an elaborate, artsy character study on a relatively minor character. . . . This should have been a separate mini or graphic novel. Instead we get the equivalent of a documentary on Van Gogh between *Kill Bill* Volume 1 and 2.

There is much greater tolerance for works on the fringes of the continuity—such as an alternative "what if?" or "elseworlds" story, or works that are designated sites of auteurist experimentation. There is space for the moral inversion involved in telling the story from the point of view of the villain or a secondary character rather than the superhero: witness the popularity of Brian Azzarello's graphic novels about The Joker and Lex Luther, for instance. But, whatever his plans, Mack's experimental approach was inserted into the very heart of the Marvel superhero franchise; as a consequence, the book met with considerable backlash.

Vision Quest was not David Mack's only venture into the Daredevil universe: he wrote *Daredevil: Parts of a Hole*, which was illustrated by veteran artist Joe Quesada—then editor in chief for Marvel and only rarely tackling art assignments. Mack had also contributed art to *Wake Up*, written by Brian Michael Bendis, perhaps the most popular superhero scriptwriter of recent memory (Jenkins, "Best Contemporary Mainstream"). In both cases, Mack was coupled with someone more in the mainstream of contemporary superhero comics. But Mack, acting as both artist and author in *Vision Quest*, was now seeing how far he could push comic book form. As he did so, he also fit within a larger history of formal experimentation at the "House of Ideas," experiments that more often than not have centered around the "Man Who Knew No Fear."

COMICS AS POETRY

Most superhero comics are written in prose; more often than not, in purple prose. They tell larger-than-life stories that draw us into close identification with their characters and immerse us in their world. Their aesthetic goals are much like those of classical Hollywood cinema. The art serves the needs of the story, which typically centers on a goal-driven protagonist pursuing both a short-term (solve the case) and a long-term (create a better world) mission. The artwork must be legible; any narratively salient information must be presented in a way that can be easily deciphered by the most casual reader. There are no moments of confusion. As a second-order value, the artwork is also designed for immediacy and intensity—to shape our emotional response, so we keep flipping the pages and coming back for the next issue. Within these goals, there is some space for individual artists to develop distinctive styles. Many Marvel readers can trace its history in terms of the ways that key creatives worked within—and yet made contributions to—its stable of recurring characters.

David Mack (best known for his creator-owned comic series, *Kabuki*) creates comics that are closer to poetry. As he suggested to me during an interview at San Diego Comic-Con, the difference has to do with the process of condensation on the encoding side—trying to pack as much meaning into his images as possible—and decryption on the decoding side—inviting us to scrutinize the complexly layered images in search of hidden meanings:

> I want to get across what's actually happening in the story first and the clarity of that. But second, there are other things in the story that probably won't be revealed on the first read but hopefully will be very rewarding on repeated readings. You can get to those other levels in film and music, too, but I think it might be more nuanced in poetry because the images are so crystallized and concentrated. Every word is usually sparser but seems so much more packed with meaning next to another word also packed with meaning, next to another word packed with

meaning, that can unravel itself like DNA when you read it years later. ("Comics as Poetry" 694–695)

Mack began publishing *Kabuki* in 1994 while he was still completing a bachelor of fine arts degree in graphic arts at Northern Kentucky University. Mack's *Kabuki* comics are dazzling in their innovative techniques, including the incorporation of everything from tea stains to toy train tracks to origami to stamped letters. Across the story, his protagonist—a Japanese woman—is a paid assassin in a criminal network, the fictionalized character in a mass-media franchise, a prisoner trying to survive, a children's book author, and a leader in a resistance movement. Both Mack and his friend Brian Michael Bendis had been recruited by Marvel because of their accomplishments as indie comics artists known for distinctive styles, both visually (in Bendis's case, for an approach that involved rotoscoping and photocopying to transform photographs into graphic images) and in literary terms (Bendis's naturalistic dialogue; Mack's nonlinear storytelling and character subjectivity).

Mack had been recruited by Joe Quesada as he was starting his editorship over the Marvel Knights imprint, which was designed to appeal to older comics readers in part through its use of more mature subject matter (including more graphic sex and violence or more morally ambiguous characterizations) and experimental approaches. As Mack explained in a personal email, "he was given editorial and creative freedom on these, and possibly a bigger budget as well, and he was able to hire creators outside the norm for this project" (Sept. 13, 2014). Quesada had already hired filmmaker Kevin Smith to craft a Daredevil storyline, and Mack helped to convince him that Bendis might be another good recruit for this project.

Many experimental comics creators seek to escape the superhero tradition. In his work, Mack hopes to bring something back to it from his own independent practices. In 2004, Marvel assisted Bendis, Mack, and Michael Avon Oeming in forming the creator-owned imprint ICON, which published the later issues of *Kabuki* and of Bendis and Oeming's *Powers*, and has since supported a range of other independent artists who were doing work on the fringes of the superhero genre—for example, Mark Millar's *Kick-Ass*.

THE BOUNDS OF DIFFERENCE

With his collaborators Janet Staiger and Kristin Thompson, David Bordwell

introduced the concept of "the bounds of difference" in *The Classical Hollywood Cinema: Film Style and Mode of Production to 1960*, drawing on concepts
from Russian formalism to talk about the norms shaping Hollywood's production practices. By norms, they mean general ways of structuring artistic
works, not rigid rules. Norms emerge and grow through experimentation.
There is no great penalty for violating norms. The best art seeks to defamil-
iarize conventions—to break the rules in creative and meaningful ways and,
in the process, teach us new ways of seeing. Yet norms also work to ensure
the reader's comprehension, and thus popular art reverts back to its norms
much of the time. The norms thus are elastic. They encompass a range of
different practices, but they also have a breaking point beyond which they
cannot bend. This breaking point is what Bordwell describes as "the bounds
of difference."

Bordwell explores examples where the Hollywood style sought to absorb
other artistic traditions—for example, German Expressionist lighting or
Soviet montage—or dealt with the emergence of new technologies—the
coming of sound, the introduction of widescreen cinematography, and
so forth. He discusses a process of assimilation, in that the dominant system absorbs what it can from those outside influences, often making new
devices serve established artistic goals (such as incorporating the distorted
images of German Expressionism to represent the subjectivity of characters
suffering from madness or drunkenness, or using montages as a form of
narrative exposition).

Here, I am appropriating "bounds of difference" to discuss how a similar
set of visual conventions might operate in the context of mainstream comics
publishing—an industry also dominated by a small number of companies
that are similarly driven by tensions between standardization and innovation, and also likely to absorb and "mainstream" experimental work as it
seeks to sustain reader interest by presenting familiar characters through
new lenses. Marvel wants the difference Mack brings; but, at the same time,
its readers are often a conservative force constraining how much "WTF"
experimentation can be accepted within the industrial mainstream.

There is an important difference between Classical Hollywood Cinema
and mainstream comics, however. Hollywood tapped a structure of multiple competing (and sometimes overlapping) genres—each of which, by
Bordwell's account, allowed certain kinds of otherwise disruptive practices
as long as they fit within the conventions of that particular genre. Genres
are a complex balance of encrusted conventions and localized innovations

that make a work fresh and original. By contrast, the mainstream comics industry today has become overwhelmingly dominated by a single genre—the superhero saga (Jenkins, "'Just Men in Tights'"; Ford and Jenkins).

What happens when a single genre more or less takes over a medium and defines the way that medium is perceived by its public, at least in the American context? The superhero comic has absorbed a broad range of other genres—from comedy to romance, from mystery to science fiction—resulting in an ever-more-hybrid genre. The superhero comic becomes a site of aesthetic experimentation, absorbing energies from independent and even avant-garde practices. By looking more closely at the ways in which Mack's alternative style did or did not fit within Marvel, we can develop a deeper understanding of what constitutes the "bounds of difference" within contemporary industry practice. To do so, we will compare Mack to other artists who have worked within the Daredevil franchise and identify the different strategies through which Mack's style was integrated into the three Daredevil storylines to which he contributed.

QUESADA AND MACK

Some contrasts between "acceptable" stylistic choices and more challenging ones can be shown by looking at two images: the first (fig. 2.1) was drawn by Quesada based on a Mack script for *Parts of a Hole*; the second (fig. 2.2) was conceived and drawn by Mack for *Wake Up*. Both images combine multiple layers of texts to convey Echo's fragmented perspective as she confronts her sometimes lover (Matt Murdock), sometimes foe (Daredevil). The use of bold primary colors and a more realist style in Quesada's version pulls him closer to mainstream expectations, whereas Mack's more variegated hues and collage-like aesthetic stretches our sense of what a superhero comic looks like. The subject matter is more or less the same, but the mode of representation is radically different.

Most mainstream superhero comics follow a logic of decoupage—breaking down a larger narrative space; framing specific actions, reactions, and details; and deploying a grid-like structure to give a familiar shape to the page. Will Eisner explains these practices: "In sequential art, the artist must, from the outset, secure control of the reader's attention and dictate the sequence in which the reader will follow the narrative. . . . The most important obstacle to surmount is the tendency of the reader's eye to wander" (40). For Eisner, the breakdown of the action into discrete segments through

2.1. *Parts of a Hole*, story by David Mack, art by Joe Quesada (1999).

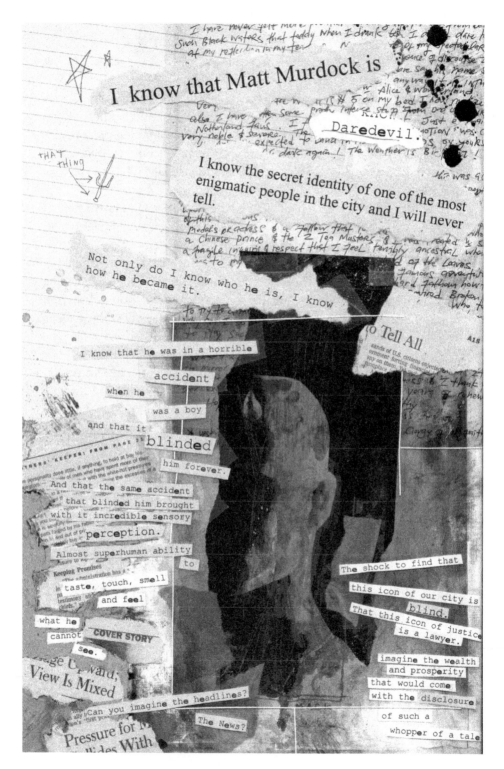

2.2. *Wake Up*, story and art by David Mack (2004).

framing results in the "containment of thoughts, ideas, actions, and location or site" (38).

Mack's aesthetic, in contrast, is based on principles of collage: various elements are pasted onto a canvas, creating layers and unexpected juxtapositions that the reader works through as a visual puzzle. Historically, collages foreground the materials as much as the content. Decoupage treats images as windows into a world, whereas collage treats the page as a surface.

The painted image of Daredevil in figure 2.2 becomes simply one element in an assemblage that also includes a yellow legal pad, newspaper scraps, and cutout words. This comic should still be read left-to-right, top-to-bottom, but we are encouraged to absorb the page as a whole before focusing on any individual element. The bright red of Daredevil's costume may draw the eye to the page's lower center before our vision is dispersed again. If Eisner celebrates decoupage as a means of controlling the reader's wandering eye, Mack offers in this collage a playground we can explore.

Quesada's art in figure 2.1 starts with similar design principles—for example, the absence of a grid. There are multiple kinds of representations here: a fight scene involving Daredevil, a framed portrait of Maya, the Kingpin depicted as a partially constructed puzzle, and a detail of a hand holding a syringe. Daredevil's thoughts are represented through layered snippets of text, with only one word bubble, from Kingpin, at the bottom of the page. Yet the consistent drawing style smooths out these elements, giving a greater unity to the page. As Mack explained, "Joe would take my layouts and use the best parts or the parts he connected with. He would marry that to his own unique graphic sensibilities and create a hybrid art style, using some of the things I was putting into the layouts and his own natural vibrancy—how he drew" (qtd. in Jenkins, "Comics as Poetry" 682). In a textbook example of aesthetic assimilation, Marvel veteran Quesada had developed an intuitive grasp of how far he could push his readers.

Maya, a new character developed by Mack, is the daughter of Crazy Horse, a longtime Kingpin lieutenant who was murdered at the hands of his boss. Born deaf, she has a photographic memory that allows her to perfectly reproduce the skills she observes from other people or from media representations. Despite their contrasting disabilities, the deaf Maya and the blind Matt fall for each other. However, the relationship is disrupted when Echo, Maya's alter ego, is misled by Kingpin to think Daredevil was responsible for her father's death, and she does battle with "the man who knows no fear." *Parts of a Hole* takes us through this complex relationship—all of the love and hate, tragedy and loss.

In *Vision Quest*, Maya tries to heal her wounds and think through what has happened to her. The result is a character study, told in stream of consciousness, which circles through her memories and her visions and is often depicted in a highly iconic manner.

Figure 2.3 depicts the moment in *Parts of a Hole* when Kingpin kills Maya's father even as he promises to take care of his daughter; figure 2.4 shows how *Vision Quest* depicts the same event.

Mack duplicates specific Quesada images, some of which are marked over and crossed out. Quesada uses a jumbled composition—including one panel that is a block of red with a sound effect rendered in a jolting manner—to convey Crazy Horse's violent end, but the borders between panels still establish a clear separation between the images. Mack's page combines multiple modalities—multiple ways of depicting the world—with highly iconic and abstract images existing alongside realistic representations of the same characters. This radical mixing of styles is a hallmark of Mack's work. Says Mack: "For me, contrast is everything. Contrast with color. Contrast with panel layout. . . . You might render something a little bit more realistic in one image or use some photo reference in a close-up so it feels like a real human, but you don't want to do that in every panel because it'll just cancel itself out. So for contrast, you want the other things that are read more quickly to be more abstracted" (qtd. in Jenkins, "Comics as Poetry" 677). Mack's interest in multimodality extends into Quesada's artwork for *Parts of a Hole*, which includes children's drawings, puzzle pieces, photographs, television screens, musical notations, blueprints, shadows, and printed theatrical programs, not to mention various textual strategies—mixing typeset words with personal handwriting (rendered in both crayon and pencil), for example, often on the same page.

One of the most powerful icons across the two books is the handprint that Echo paints on her face. At first glance, the handprint functions a bit like the bull's-eye on the face mask of the villain who is named Bullseye: an identity marker. But the handprint accrues other layers of meaning linked to her Native American ethnicity and also reminding us of a traumatic moment: the death of her father. As Maya explains in *Vision Quest*, "I remember being in the ambulance. He puts his hand on my face. Then it falls lifeless, and he leaves me with only his echo." Quesada uses the open palm, fingers spread wide, as a recurring visual motif—for example, Kingpin's open hand just

2.3. *Parts of a Hole*, story by David Mack, art by Joe Quesada (1999).

2.4. *Vision Quest*, story and art by David Mack (2004).

after he has shot her father (fig. 2.3); Maya's childhood drawings of the hand; Matt's palm pressed against the window of a cab as Maya drives away; Maya's hand as she lets go of a swing, abandoning another date with Matt in order to tend to "family matters"; or Maya's portrait framed within a handprint on the cover of the first issue of *Vision Quest*. Mack's appropriation and reworking of such icons assumes a reader who has read and can recall the earlier work.

Consider figure 2.5's rendering of key plot events. The Kingpin is reduced to his big feet and legs, much as a child might see him, while the breakup is represented by the figure of the child ripping the couple's portrait in half. Once the book has established these rich icons, they can be recycled and remixed for further emotional impact.

In figure 2.6, Mack juxtaposes a more mature version of Maya with her child self, and the childlike drawings are repeated to evoke key emotional moments. She is no longer a vulnerable child victim but someone who can strike back at those who caused her pain. Part of what gives these images their traumatic impact is a kind of repetition or compulsion that forces Maya (and the reader) to re-experience these moments again and again. All of this detail furthers understanding of what Mack means when he suggests that his images hold the "crystalized and concentrated" meaning achieved by poets through their word choices (qtd. in Jenkins, "Comics as Poetry" 694).

DAREDEVIL AND THE MARVEL HOUSE STYLE

Quesada's work on *Parts of a Hole* represents innovation within what we might describe as the Marvel "house style" as it has taken shape across five decades of ongoing production. Charles Hatfield has documented the ways in which Jack Kirby and his contemporaries were influenced by classic adventure comics artists, such as Milton Caniff, Hal Foster, Burne Hogarth, and Alex Raymond, with their commitments to illustration, realism, and "dynamic anatomy." Over time, their heavily detailed style was streamlined. Their renderings of the human figure become more intuitive than studied; such choices give the artwork immediacy and dynamism but also allow the artists to reproduce characters and settings more efficiently under industrial conditions. As Hatfield writes, "Something punchier and more assaultive has taken over" (62).

If Kirby helped to establish the classicism we associate with the Marvel house style, he also modeled the ways in which this style might absorb

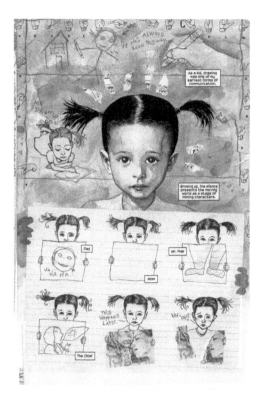

2.5. *Vision Quest*, story and art by David Mack (2004).

2.6. *Vision Quest*, story and art by David Mack (2004).

aspects of experimental or modernist art practice. As Steven Brower reminds us, Kirby was repeatedly drawn toward collage techniques in his comics—often in his efforts to represent altered states of consciousness or the kinds of cosmic storylines that would run through his work on the Fantastic Four and the New Gods in the late 1960s and 1970s. In most cases, the collage involved juxtaposing his protagonists, drawn in classic cartoon style, across a background that was constructed from one or more photographic images. He had at one time, as Brower notes, intended to depict all of the Negative Zone sequences in this manner, though it proved too labor intensive for him to maintain, given the page-rate demands he faced from the publisher. Brower links this approach to Marvel's efforts to attract college-age readers at a time when such looks were associated with psychedelic artists such as Victor Moscoso, Stanley Mouse, and Wes Wilson. As with Mack's later experiments with collage in *Daredevil*, these experiments were not always well received by his fans. During an exchange in *The Comics Journal*, Glen David Gold writes, "As a reader I felt the same way about Kirby's collages as I did the harp solos in Marx Brothers movies—they were things I didn't like but put up with because they made an artist I revered feel happy, and besides, the good stuff would start again in a moment" (Heer).

Andrei Molotiu uses Steve Ditko's work in *The Amazing Spider-Man* no. 23 to illustrate how comics scholars might use a conceptual vocabulary developed for talking about abstract comics to understand the visual choices made in more mainstream books. In particular, he is interested in two core concepts—sequential dynamism ("the formal visual energy, created by compositional and other elements internal to each panel and by the layout" shaping the reader's movement across the page [89]) and iconostasis (the page layout as "a unified composition" [91]). Molotiu suggests:

> To introduce a sense of sequential dynamism into a representational comic is to acknowledge that the medium's purpose is not only narrative and mimetic, basing its sense of sequence on the logic of a represented storyline, and therefore on the progression of diegetic time; rather, it is to understand comics as a means of providing the viewer with a visual aesthetic satisfaction that is not the static satisfaction of traditional painting or drawing, but a specifically sequential pleasure, achieved by putting the eye into motion, and by creating specific graphic paths, speeds of scanning, and graphic rhythms to enliven its aesthetic experience. (89)

Kirby and Ditko helped not only to define many of the core characters within the Marvel Universe but also to set Marvel's house style. They were stylistic innovators seeking a distinctive look and feel for their comics that would be defined through how they borrowed from and how they broke with the earlier generation. As a result, their work established criteria by which subsequent Marvel artists would be judged.

Daredevil's 1964 introduction places him after the first wave of innovation and its A-list superheroes. Bill Everett, who had been working in the comics industry since the 1930s and was best known for shaping the Sub-Mariner, was brought in to assist in developing Daredevil in response to the Silver Age resurgence of Batman. Historians dispute how active Kirby was in the development of this character, with some (Evanier) suggesting that the legendary artist had already designed the costume and sketched some of the first issue before Everett was assigned to the project, while others (Quesada) dispute that claim. Regardless, Everett was working in Kirby's shadow, developing a B-list character; he was also informed by Ditko, given how many of Daredevil's rogue's gallery were hand-me-downs from Spider-Man. Everett's visual style is workmanlike but hardly distinguished. His pages offer few formal surprises.

MILLER AND JANSON: AN INTENSIFIED STYLE

The first Daredevil writer-artist team to really excite readers was that of Frank Miller and Klaus Janson in the early 1980s. Gerard Jones and Will Jacobs describe this run as "the comic book where it came together—the sophisticated and the visceral, the daring and the familiar" (246, stressing the inspiration Miller and Janson took from Samuel Fuller and Anthony Mann). In a 1981 interview, Miller discussed how those film noir borrowings impacted their pages:

> I see the city as a series of rectangles encasing organisms. We are soft
> little creatures that walk around these big concrete rectangles. One
> of the things I do is to use the shape of the page and the shape of the
> panels to emphasize that, often to make it more claustrophobic. . . . Part
> of what makes the art successful is that the rectangles get so extreme
> and they so dominate the overall look of the book, that that says many
> things about the city and how the characters relate to it that don't have
> to be in words or illustrations. (Sanderson 300)

You can see this focus on elongated rectangles as compositional elements in figures 2.7 and 2.8, part of an extended battle between Daredevil and Bullseye in *Daredevil* no. 170 (Miller et al.).

Figure 2.7 shows the villain kicking the protagonist out the window, with a high-angle depiction of the horn-head looking straight down toward the street below. A horizontal panel spans the top of the next page (fig. 2.8), followed by five vertical panels, stretching down three-quarters of the page, that show Daredevil grabbing a flag for support while falling earthward. We might see this illustration as an amped-up version of Ditko's sequential-dynamism and iconostasis techniques. The shape of the page conveys a strong sense of verticality, and the hero's movement, ending with the flag ripping and Daredevil falling out the bottom of the final panel, conveys his desperation. Both of these pages break with the classic grid, but their exaggerated framing works toward clearly defined narrative goals.

Miller described his visual rhetoric in terms of pulls toward abstraction: "I wanted to do a style where the reader had to do a great deal of the work, where a pair of squiggles and a black shadow became an expressive face in

2.7. *Daredevil* no. 170, story by Frank Miller, art by Frank Miller and Klaus Janson (May 1981).

2.8. *Daredevil* no. 170, story by Frank Miller, art by Frank Miller and Klaus Janson (May 1981).

—

2.9. *Daredevil* no. 167, story by David Michelinie, art by Frank Miller and Klaus Janson (Nov. 1980).

the reader's mind" (Jones and Jacobs 247). Figure 2.9 uses silhouettes during a key action scene (from no. 167), here again coupled with extreme angles looking straight down onto the action: we can easily read this scene because the Daredevil costume, especially his horns, makes him such a recognizable figure, whereas the henchmen are interchangeable units.

Above all, the emphasis is on action and on the protagonist's acrobatic movements, as we see in figure 2.10, where the artist renders the superhero's full workout regime in a single image. Everett uses this technique sometimes, but few artists took it to the extremes that Miller and Jansen do here. Miller trusts his collaborator's visual storytelling enough that Janson may go several pages with wordless action scenes, yet he may also use multiple panels to depict fairly simple actions—for example, a series of panels in *Daredevil* no. 164 (Miller et al.) explores the flicker of light on reporter Ben Ulrich's face as he lights up a cigarette (fig. 2.11). Such quiet moments contrast with the accelerated action elsewhere.

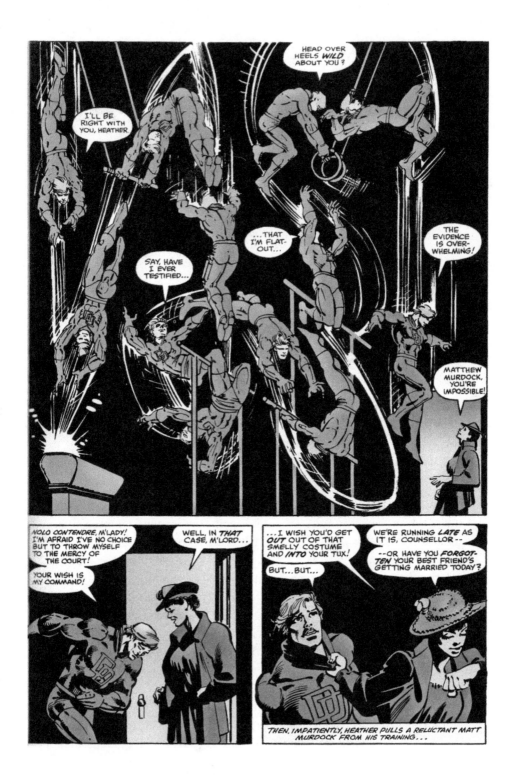

2.10. *Daredevil* no. 166, story by Roger McKenzie and Frank Miller, art by Frank Miller and Klaus Janson (Sept. 1980).

2.11. *Daredevil* no. 164, story by Roger McKenzie, art by Frank Miller and Klaus Janson (May 1980).

We should flag two other commonly used devices, both illustrated in figure 2.12 (from *Daredevil* no. 161 [Miller et al.]), as Daredevil and Bullseye duke it out on the Coney Island Cyclone.

The first is the self-conscious use of sound effects as an active compositional element (another device Everett deploys from time to time); the second is how characters are allowed to burst out of the frame and, in some extreme cases, cut across the gutters, to suggest actions so intense that they cannot be fully contained. Miller and Janson's approach is bold and even brutal. They expanded the visual vocabulary of the superhero comic, but ultimately what they did was still consistent with the logic of superhero storytelling that had been mapped out by Kirby, Ditko, and others of their generation. David Mack recalls being deeply impressed by Miller and Janson's Daredevil stories when he read them as a child and has said that they planted the seeds for his own subsequent contributions to the series.

2.12. *Daredevil* no. 161, story by Roger McKenzie, art by Frank Miller and Klaus Janson (Nov. 1979).

SIENKIEWICZ: A MORE PAINTERLY APPROACH

Mack's run on Daredevil is most often compared with Frank Miller's collaboration with Bill Sienkiewicz on the 1986 projects *Daredevil: Love and War* and *Elektra: Assassin*. Jones and Jacobs sum up some of the innovations this artist-writer pair brought: "Paint splashed and flowed and splattered, photos were scanned and collaged in, Elektra's childhood memories were drawn like a first-grader's crayon pictures, slammed alongside airbrushed and hyper-rendered paintings of the present. Miller apparently started with a plot, but Sienkiewicz ignored it and let the pictures—more than that, the media and the materials—lead him. . . . The result was a mess, but it was an invigorating mess" (298).

No doubt, part of what had prepared the way for Marvel to embrace such a wildly experimental style was the enormous popularity and critical acclaim surrounding Jim Steranko's work in the 1960s around the character of Nick Fury, Agent of S.H.I.E.L.D. Steranko's approach drew heavily on surrealism, pop and op art, and contemporary graphic design, resulting in unexpected juxtapositions, characters who seemed to pop off the page, highly self-reflexive compositions, and dynamic plays with framing. Steranko had succeeded in taking a B-list character and developing a cult following around him while at the same time focusing more fan attention on the pleasure of visual style as an end unto itself. Steranko helped to establish Marvel's ongoing fascination with pushing the "bounds of difference" while working in the mainstream of the superhero genre. He had also been an early mentor for David Mack, writing the introduction for the first *Kabuki* graphic novel.

Like Mack, Sienkiewicz brought a painterly aesthetic that stood out in terms of its vivid color palette after decades of inked primary color images. M. J. Clarke has documented the many institutional, commercial, and technological factors that paved the way for Marvel to embrace a more artistically ambitious approach in the early 1980s. This shift occurred in conjunction with the introduction of the direct market and, with it, a consumer base willing to pay more for books published with high-quality paper and enhanced color—tastes sharpened by the growing American awareness of the *Metal Hurlant* series in France. As Clarke explains, "The full color process also embodied an editorial concession to the increasing importance of the work of the comic artist and his or her ability to express his or herself through all the features of the medium as well as artists' corresponding eagerness to obligingly experiment formally with structural and textural uses of coloring."

One of the most basic ways in which superhero comics ensure clarity is through the distinctive color-coding of key characters, especially the hero and the villain. Daredevil in the Everett era wore a yellow and black costume with a large red "D" on his chest; the Frank Miller–era Daredevil wears mostly red, and Elektra, his lover, was also designed with a dominant use of red, accenting their relationship. Sienkiewicz and Mack, by contrast, like the *Metal Hurlant* artists, deploy color for its expressive potential to create a mood or tone.

In figure 2.13, from *Daredevil: Love and War*, Sienkiewicz is seemingly as interested in abstract patterns—in this case, the contrast between the blue, green, and purple wallpaper and the red, black, and yellow suit the Kingpin is wearing—as he is in what the characters are doing. Aside from the use of color and pattern, this page takes us well beyond the techniques that Kirby and Ditko borrowed from earlier adventure comics illustrators. The figures are highly stylized, in this instance to emphasize Kingpin's heft, with the villain rendered with his head in the middle of a square body. Elsewhere in *Love and War*, Sienkiewicz uses extreme close-ups—or even a full splash page—of the rotund criminal mastermind, so that his plump, rosy flesh overwhelms the frame.

Figure 2.14 shows how Sienkiewicz deals with an action sequence: Daredevil is reduced to expressive lines and blurs of color rather than with the dynamic anatomy that characterizes the Marvel house style. *Love and War* offers a more abstract version of many of the techniques developed through Miller's collaborations with Janson—the silhouetted and multiple figures of the hero in action, sound effects as compositional elements, rectangular compositions. Sienkiewicz may use collage techniques in individual panels, but there is still a grid structuring the page. For all of this focus on technique, the emphasis is still on externalized action rather than internalized reflection—which contrasts with Mack's work, at least in *Vision Quest*, and the way in which it broke with the tradition.

Whereas most superhero artists convey intense action in almost every frame, Mack often empties his images, suspending time. The splash page traditionally either emphasizes a particularly significant action or offers a highly detailed image (classic Kirby technique), both moments of heightened spectacle. Mack instead often strips down his splash pages to focus on the character's emotional state.

We might contrast all of the action-oriented representations of Sienkiewicz's Elektra in *Elektra: Assassin* (fig. 2.15) with Mack's contemplative

—

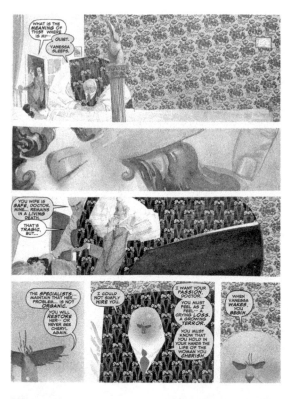

2.13. *Daredevil: Love and War*, story by Frank Miller, art by Bill Sienkiewicz (Dec. 1986).

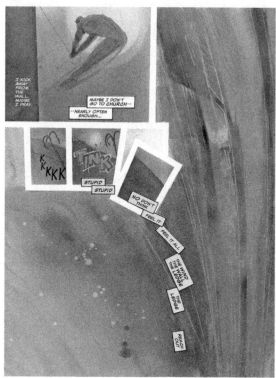

2.14. *Daredevil: Love and War*, story by Frank Miller, art by Bill Sienkiewicz (Dec. 1986).

full-page image of the same character in *Wake Up* (fig. 2.16). Mack doesn't even show the character's face, focusing instead on her posture. He shows us Elektra's death, but stripped of its larger narrative context, and focusing primarily on her physical vulnerability. Mack deploys similar techniques throughout *Vision Quest* to render the comic's usual protagonist unknowable: Daredevil's face is covered in shadows. He looks away from us. He blocks his face with his hands. The deaf woman cannot understand his words if she cannot read his lips (fig. 2.17).

This representation of Daredevil contrasts sharply with the Marvel house style, which normally seeks to give us immediate physical and emotional access to the series' protagonist so that we know his thoughts (through monologue) and feel what he is feeling as he swoops through the air. Sienkiewicz would return to Daredevil in 2013, when he collaborated with Mack, Bendis, and Janson on *Daredevil: End of Days*.

Few other artists who have worked on Daredevil pushed their stylistic experiments as far as Miller and Sienkiewicz did, but they brought their own sensibilities to bear on the shared materials Marvel allowed them to play with.

2.15. *Elektra: Assassin*, story by Frank Miller, art by Bill Sienkiewicz (1987).

2.16. *Vision Quest*, story and art by David Mack (2004).

2.17. *Vision Quest*, story and art by David Mack (2004).

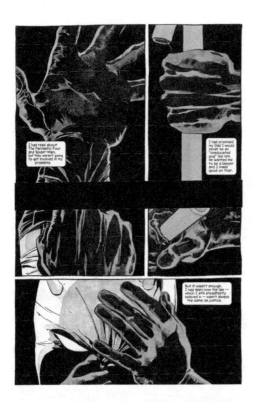

2.18. *Daredevil: Yellow*, story by Jeph Loeb, art by Tim Sale (2002).

2.19. *Daredevil Vol. 4: Underboss*, story by Brian Michael Bendis, art by Alex Maleey (2002).

Figure 2.18 shows Tim Sale and team depicting only fragments of Daredevil's body. Figure 2.19 shows Alex Maleev and team creating a much more muted palette and a scratchy/grainy image. There has been far greater range for visual experiments within the Daredevil series precisely because the character has rarely been a top seller. The risks of backlash are relatively low, and the publisher is constantly seeking to draw more reader attention to the series.

THE POETICS OF PERCEPTION

From the start, superhero artists have enjoyed much greater freedom from the constraints of realist representation when depicting their protagonist's powers than when illustrating more mundane types of scenes. So, for example, Everett uses concentric circles radiating from Daredevil's face to convey his heightened sense of hearing.

In this tradition, Mack's fascination with subjective experience motivates his conceptualization of Echo. According to Mack:

> Because the Echo character is deaf, most of her understanding of the world is through sight. Her focus on visuals really translated very well to comics for me, and she gave me something to push against how Daredevil sees the world. They're both detectives in a way, deciphering—like we all are—all of their input, but in very different ways than most people are. . . . Her skill-set comes from this kind of pattern recognition in terms of her growing up, trying to pay so much attention to every nuance of visual stimuli from body language to facial expression to lip reading.[1] (qtd. in Jenkins, "Comics as Poetry" 685)

Vision Quest opens and closes with the same passage, as Maya tells us:

> My name is Maya Lopez. This is my story. The story is called Echo.
> It doesn't happen in words. It happens in movements and memories, shapes and feelings. When it does happen in words, it doesn't happen in the sound of words, but in the color of them. The mood and texture and mystery of their crossword puzzle meanings. My story happens in music, sometimes slow and awkward, like little fingers on the worn out keys, searching for meaning. My story doesn't happen in the sound of the notes but in the silence between them. This is where the magic happens.

Vision Quest's first issue shows how Maya comes to make sense of the world around her, sorting out what environmental elements make meaningful sounds, drawing to communicate with other people, and categorizing gestures: "When you've never heard your father's voice, you learn to decipher every shade of expression that moves over his face. His lips mouth to you the silent secrets of the universe. . . . Body language, too, begins to whisper its meanings."

Mack takes the reader through a similar process—of learning a new way to read this comic. This includes sorting the jumble of different signs and symbols, which make extensive use of musical notes, Scrabble tiles, and Native American sign language. It also requires interpreting different representations, including realistic and symbolic renderings, full images of the body in action, and detail shots of specific facial expressions. For those readers who felt frustrated or angered by Mack's experiments, it was as if the artist was expecting too much from them in terms of their decipherment and discernment skills. They reacted with confusion or incomprehension rather than with enthusiasm for the rewards of epistemaphilia that such techniques promise.

Maya—the artist, the sign reader, the storyteller, the performer, the director and playwright—becomes a stand-in for Mack himself. Her emphasis on the meanings that come in the gaps between notes highlights the central role of the gutter in comics (McCloud). Maya's search for a stable identity justifies the shifting modalities; she is represented through a range of different pastiches of modern artists, including one borrowing from Gustav Klimt (fig. 2.20).

Mack, Quesada, and team's *Parts of a Hole* similarly starts as Daredevil's memoir of the senses: "Somehow I cross the line—a blurring one, where the scents, echoes and chills come less from outside my head and more from inside it. Memory and Dreams—the only places where I'm not blind." Mack encourages us to think about how Matt Murdock processes the world around him, including a sequence where he plays the piano and reads the sheet music from its "raised texture": "For me, music is the closest thing to seeing. I don't mean knowing where you are going, I mean seeing the way you'd look at a painting. Every chord has color—the way memory has color—the way memory has a scent." Late in *Parts of a Hole*, Mack, Quesada, and team juxtapose the different ways in which Matt and Maya perceive the world face to face within panels and side by side in a sequence of panels on the same page (fig. 2.21.) What draws them together—and holds them apart,

2.20. *Vision Quest*, story and art by David Mack (2004).

2.21. *Parts of a Hole*, story by David Mack, art by Joe Quesada (1999).

preventing Maya from fully understanding their confusing relationship—is their distinctive modes of perception.

In *Wake Up*, reporter Ben Ulrich is seeking ways to communicate with an emotionally disturbed child who can talk only through crude drawings and a repeated monologue, both memory traces of a rooftop struggle he witnessed between Daredevil and his father, a B-level baddie named The Frog. This focus on the mental life of a disturbed child motivates the shifts in visual style, with the child's mental images depicted in the Marvel house style, while other aspects of the story are rendered through a range of other techniques (fig. 2.22).

The boy's constant monologue sounds like classic Stan Lee prose, and the visual iconography of the superhero gets parodied through the boy's crayon drawings and his scattered and broken action figures. Ulrich functions here as an editor to the boy's artistic vision, putting the panels in order and, through this process, allowing the boy to express what it was he did and saw that night. We can see the focus on the subjective experience of an emotionally disturbed character as being in line with the historical motivations of modernist style—starting perhaps with the film *The Cabinet of Dr. Caligari*, which frames German Expressionism in terms of the world as seen through the eyes of an asylum inmate, or, for that matter, Alfred Hitchcock's *Spellbound*, another film set at a mental hospital, which absorbs Salvador Dali's surrealism into a dream sequence.

Mack's use of children's drawings (fig. 2.23) evokes a long tradition of modern artists who have sought inspiration by mimicking what they saw as the simple, more direct ways in which children engage with their perceptions and emotions through art (Fineberg). This focus on children's art takes its place alongside a number of other modernist frames that help to justify the use of abstraction across Mack's Daredevil books: altered states of consciousness (mental illness, disability, the dream quest), references to "primitivism" (however problematically, the references to Native American culture in *Vision Quest*), and animalism (the deconstruction of Wolverine, who may be understood as a human shaman or an animal guide depending on how you read the sequence). Each of these themes has a long history across multiple modern art movements, yet Mack also finds a way to reconcile them to the genre conventions of the superhero comic.

Parts of a Hole introduces isolated moments of abstraction, where we see how the two characters perceive their worlds, within an otherwise classical narrative. In *Wake Up*, abstracted and incoherent images come to make

2.22. *Daredevil Vol. 3: Wake Up*, story by Brian Michael Bendis, art by David Mack (2002).

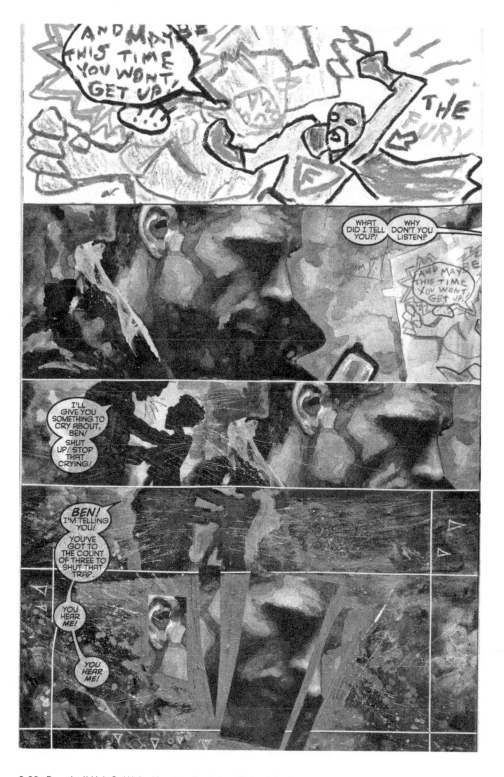

2.23. *Daredevil Vol. 3: Wake Up*, story by Brian Michael Bendis, art by David Mack (2002).

sense through the reporter's therapeutic intervention. *Vision Quest* remains inside Maya's head from start to finish. As a result, there is no classically rendered world to which we can return between more stylized segments.

CONCLUSION: FROM ARTIST'S BOOK TO GRAPHIC NOVEL

In this essay, I have privileged one moment in Mack's overall creative cycle, reading Mack's images in relation to the norms of the Marvel house style. In doing so, I've explored how these pages fit within or push against the "bounds of difference," the range of acceptable experimentation within the superhero genre, as policed by Marvel's editorial decisions and the collective judgment of hard-core fans.

But it's important to remember that Mack also deals with these pages as individual works of art when he reproduces them in various printed portfolios of his works, displays them on gallery walls, or sells them to collectors. *The Alchemy of Art*, a 2007 documentary about Mack directed by Greg Juris, shows the artist creating one of the more elaborate *Vision Quest* pages. He's working on this massive page, deploying various objects, such as individual Scrabble tiles, bits of ribbon or wood (which he uses to literally frame his images), feathers and leaves, and old newsprint. Mack explains how he assembles these resources: buying them at local craft shops, receiving them as gifts from readers, finding them on the roadside. Each of these objects can be used only once, unlike, say, the drawings (like Quesada's image of Kingpin shooting the gun), which get reproduced multiple times across the books. Mack's physical pages are precious artworks on their own terms.

Mack works within the modernist tradition of the artist book. In defining this tradition, Johanna Drucker writes, "It's easy enough to state that an artist's book is a book created as an original work of art, rather than a reproduction of a preexisting work. And also, that it is a book which integrates the formal means of its realization and production with its thematic or aesthetic issues" (2). The first trait transforms the book into what Drucker calls an "auratic object" (93), building on Walter Benjamin's notion of "the aura" as that which gets broken down via mechanical reproduction, and the second forces us to think about the book as a physical object. Drucker also describes such books as "private archives" (96), because the materials used often carry personal meanings for the artists that readers may not

———

fully access; the documentary allows the artist to narrate and annotate his sources.

Mack had done many handmade books as an art student and remains fascinated with their "texture," agreeing that his original comics pages have the look and feel of other such experiments (Jenkins, "Comics as Poetry" 689). But their character changes when they are mass-produced by Marvel, first in floppy comics and later in graphic novels. Even the most advanced processes for color reproduction lose some of the nuances that Mack achieves through his innovative uses of washes and stains; only visual traces remain of what once was a much more tactile experience.

Bart Beaty (*Unpopular Culture*) has coined the term "unpopular culture" to describe some of the creative tensions shaping contemporary European comics that tap vernacular traditions while seeking art-world recognition (see also Beaty *Comics Versus Art*). In that vein, there are great contrasts in how Mack's work is evaluated as an "artist book" versus as a mass-produced comic. These images may be understood and interpreted quite differently depending on whether they are read as stand-alone pieces of art or as part of a narrative "whole." And Mack is also moving between the commercial mainstream of superhero comics and the more experimental space of independent comics, making such tensions even more pronounced.

David Mack is certainly not the only comics artist straddling the superhero/indie comic realm; more and more, the walls between them are breaking down, either because the mainstream publishers are inviting indie artists to play with their characters (DC's *Bizarro World* series) or because indie artists are experimenting with iconic images of the superhero (*Project Superior*). Such works may well be understood as "unpopular," not simply in the sense of the distaste or disappointment expressed by some fans (such as some of the comments that introduced this essay), but also because they encourage reflection upon the norms that structure popular narratives.

Perhaps, then, it is David Mack, the artist, who might best be described as "the man without fear."

....

NOTES

1. I am bracketing the sometimes problematic ways in which superhero comics depict issues of disability and ethnic identities. They are topics worthy of serious critique, but peripheral to my focus here.

WORKS CITED

The Alchemy of Art: David Mack. Dir. Greg Juris. Hero Video Productions, 2007. DVD.

Azzarello, Brian. *The Joker.* New York: DC, 2011. Print.

———. *Luther.* New York: DC, 2013. Print.

Beaty, Bart. *Comics Versus Art.* Toronto: University of Toronto Press, 2013. Print.

———. *Unpopular Culture: Transforming the European Comic Book in the 1990s.* Toronto: University of Toronto Press, 2007. Print.

Benjamin, Walter. "The Work of Art in the Age of Mechanical Reproduction." In *Illuminations.* Author Walter Benjamin. Trans. Harry Zhan. Ed. Hannah Arendt. New York: Harcourt, Brace and World, 1968. 219–253. Print.

Bordwell, David, Janet Staiger, and Kristin Thompson. *The Classical Hollywood Cinema: Film Style and Mode of Production to 1960.* New York: Columbia University Press, 1985. Print.

Brower, Steven. "Jack Kirby's Collages in Context." *PRINT,* April 17, 2012. Web. www.printmag.com/illustration/jack-kirbys-collages-in-context.

The Cabinet of Dr. Caligari. Dir. Robert Wiene. 1920. Kino Video, 2004. DVD.

Clarke, M. J. "The Production of the Marvel Graphic Novel Series: The Business and Culture of the Early Direct Market." *Journal of Graphic Novels and Comics* 5.2 (2014): 192-210. Print.

Ditko, Steve, pencils, inks, and cover art. *The Amazing Spider-Man* 1.23 (April 1965). Written by Stan Lee. Lettered by Artie Simek. Print.

Drucker, Johanna. *The Century of Artists' Books.* New York: Granary Books, 1994. Print.

Eisner, Will. *Comics and Sequential Art: Principles and Practices.* New York: W. W. Norton, 1985. Print.

Evanier, Mark. "The Jack FAQ: 'What Did Jack Do on the First Stories of Iron Man and Daredevil?'" *P.O.V. Online,* n.d. Archived from the original on 19 July 2007. Web. www.webcitation.org/5QR8165hr.

Fineberg, Jonathan. *The Innocent Eye: Children's Art and the Modern Artist.* Princeton, NJ: Princeton University Press, 1997. Print.

Ford, Sam, and Henry Jenkins. "Managing Multiplicity in Superhero Comics: An Interview with Henry Jenkins." In *Third Person: Authoring and Exploring Vast Narratives.* Eds. Pat Harrigan and Noah Wardrip-Fruin. Cambridge, MA: MIT Press, 2009. 303-313. Print.

Frangules, Phillip. "Disappointing." Customer Review for *Daredevil Vol. 8: Echo—Vision Quest. Amazon,* 31 October 2004. Web. www.amazon.com /review/R24RAIQX87RV99/ref=cm_cr_pr_perm?ie=UTF8&ASIN=0785112324.

Grant, Stephanie. "For David Mack Fans, Not Superhero Fanboys." Customer Review for *Daredevil Vol. 8: Echo—Vision Quest. Amazon,* 25 November 2006.

Web. www.amazon.com/review/R1PEK05I1TQNS4/ref=cm_cr_pr_perm?ie
=UTF8&ASIN=0785112324.

Hatfield, Charles. *Hand of Fire: The Comics Art of Jack Kirby*. Jackson: University
Press of Mississippi, 2012. Print.

Heer, Jeet. "Jack Kirby: Hand of Fire Roundtable (Part One)." *The Comics Journal*,
30 April 2012. Web. www.tcj.com/jack-kirby-hand-of-fire-roundtable-part-1.

Jenkins, Henry. "Best Contemporary Mainstream Superhero Comics Writer:
Brian Michael Bendis." In *Beautiful Things in Popular Culture*. Ed. Alan
McKee. Malden, MA: Blackwell, 2007. 15–32. Print.

———. "Comics as Poetry: An Interview with David Mack." *Amerikastudien
American Studies* 56.4 (2011): 669–697. Print.

———. "'Just Men in Tights': Rewriting Silver Age Comics in an Era of Multiplicity." In *The Contemporary Comic Book Superhero*. Ed. Angela Ndalianis.
London: Routledge, 2009. 16–43. Print.

Jones, Gerard, and Will Jacobs. *The Comic Book Heroes: The First History of
Modern Comic Books from the Silver Age to the Present*. Rocklin, CA: Prima,
1997. Print.

Mack, David, writer and cover art. *Daredevil Vol. 2: Parts of a Hole*. Pencils and
co-cover art by Joe Quesada. Inks and writing by Jimmy Palmiotti. Pencils
and inks by Rob Haynes. Pencils by David Ross. Inks by Mark Morales.
Colors by Richard Isanove and David Self. Letters by Richard Starkings and
Comicraft. New York: Marvel, 2002. Print.

Mack, David, pencils and painted art. *Daredevil Vol. 3: Wake Up*. Written by
Brian Michael Bendis. Inks by Mark Morales and Scott "Pond Scum" Elmer.
Colors by Richard Isanove. New York: Marvel, 2002. Print.

Mack, David, story and art. *Daredevil Vol. 8: Echo—Vision Quest*. Letters by Cory
Petit. New York: Marvel, 2004. Print.

Maleev, Alex, pencils, inks, and cover art. *Daredevil Vol. 4: Underboss*. Written
by Brian Michael Bendis. Colored by Matt Hollingsworth. Lettered by Richard Starkings, Wes Abbott, and Comicraft. New York: Marvel, 2002. Print.

McCloud, Scott. *Understanding Comics: The Invisible Art*. New York: William
Morrow, 1994. Print.

Miller, Frank, pencils, cover art, and writing. *Daredevil by Frank Miller & Klaus
Janson Volume 1*. Inks and cover art by Klaus Janson. Writing by Roger
McKenzie, David Michelinie, and Bill Mantlo. Colors by George Roussos,
Glynis Wein, Bob Sharen, D. R. Martin, and Mario Sen. Co-cover art by Josef
Rubinstein, Wally Wood, Bob McLeod, George Roussos, Danny Crespi, Dave
Cockrum, Al Milgrom, and Keith Pollard. Inks by Frank Springer. Letters
by Joe Rosen, Jim Novak, Diana Albers, John Costanza, Denise Wohl, and
Elaine Heinl. New York: Marvel, 2008. Print.

Molotiu, Andrei. "Abstract Form: Sequential Dynamism and Iconstasis in Abstract Comics and Steve Ditko's *Amazing Spider-Man*." In *Critical Approaches to Comics: Theories and Methods*. Eds. Matthew J. Smith and Randy Duncan. New York: Routledge, 2012. 84–100. Print.

Quesada, Joe. "Joe Fridays Column #4," *Newsarama*, n.d. Archived at *Internet Archive: Wayback Machine* from the original on 21 May 2005. Web. http://web.archive.org/web/20050521232116/http://www.newsarama.com /JoeFridays/JoeFridays4.htm.

Redwolfsniper. "!!!!!!!!!," Customer Review for *Daredevil Vol. 8: Echo— Vision Quest*. *Amazon*, 7 August 2005. Web. www.amazon.com/review /R2M9GS5M6IME4D/ref=cm_cr_pr_perm?ie=UTF8&ASIN=0785112324.

Sale, Tim, pencils, inks, and cover art. *Daredevil: Yellow*. Written by Jeph Loeb. Colors by Matt Hollingsworth. Letters by Wes Abbott. New York: Marvel, 2002. Print.

Sanderson, Peter. "The Frank Miller / Klaus Janson Interview." In *The Daredevil Chronicles*. Albany, NY: FantaCo, 1982. 9–27. Rpt. in *Daredevil Volume 2*, by Frank Miller and Klaus Janson. New York: Marvel, 1981–1982. Print.

Sienkiewicz, Bill, pencils, inks, colors, and cover art. *Daredevil: Love and War*. Written by Frank Miller. Letters by Jim Novak. New York: Marvel, 1986. Print.

———. *Elektra: Assassin*. Written by Frank Miller. Letters by Jim Novak and Gaspar Saladino. New York: Marvel Epic Comics, 1987. Print.

Spellbound. Dir. Alfred Hitchcock. 1945. Fox Searchlight, 2008. DVD.

CHAPTER 3

"This Female Fights Back!"

A FEMINIST HISTORY OF MARVEL COMICS

ANNA F. PEPPARD

"**B**eware . . . The claws of *The Cat!*" (fig. 3.1). Beneath the jagged letters of this title, a shapely female form in a canary yellow unitard and navy blue, cat-eared mask lunges forward, her raised hands ending in long, sharp claws. All around her, bold fonts declare the introduction of "*Marvel's newest action bombshell!*" and ask, "How did a *beautiful girl* gain the uncanny powers of a *killer beast*??" *The Cat* no. 1 represents a rare instance in which a comic book cover's typical surfeit of colorful adjectives and frantic punctuation actually underestimates the uniqueness of its story and star. *The Cat* was not only Marvel's first ongoing superhero comic starring a female protagonist, but also its first to be both written and drawn by women, with a script by Linda Fite and pencils by Marie Severin. The year was 1972. It would be another forty years before Marvel would repeat this particular milestone.[1]

Many of Marvel's iconic superheroes can be considered monstrous in the ways they literally and graphically blur certain seemingly natural boundaries. Iron Man, for instance, is part man and part machine; Spider-Man is part man and part arachnid; and the Thing is part man and part rock. The cover of *The Cat* no. 1, however, situates the female superhero as a particularly gendered monster. The Cat blurs the boundaries separating masculine activity from feminine passivity; she is both an "action" hero and a "bombshell," both a "killer beast" and a "beautiful girl." Inside her skin-tight costume, the Cat also embodies these "unnatural" combinations, her razor-sharp claws contrasting, both visually and ideologically, with the soft curves of her hourglass figure. Even before her story begins, the Cat is beset by struggles familiar to many female action heroes before and since. As Jeffrey Brown explains,

3.1. *The Cat* no. 1 (Nov. 1972).

within male-dominated action genres, the female protagonist's status as "heroic subject" is typically threatened by her status as "sexual object" (7). Although the female action hero "represents a potentially transgressive figure capable of expanding the popular perception of women's roles and abilities," her persistent sexualization also "runs the risk of reinscribing strict gender binaries" by suggesting that she is "nothing more than sexist window-dressing for the predominantly male audience" (Brown 43).

Superhero comics objectify and idealize both male and female bodies. Yet this idealization almost always "reinforces the dichotomy between the masculine and the feminine body" (Behm-Morawitz and Pennell 87). Whereas male superheroes tend to display exaggerated power characteristics, such as muscles, female superheroes tend to display exaggerated sexual characteristics, such as breasts and buttocks, which their bodies are frequently contorted to display at the same time (in what is colloquially known as the "broken back pose"). The sexual objectification of female superheroes has long been a convention of the superhero genre, to the point where, as Aaron Taylor observes, "the general rule of thumb seems to be that any panel featuring a female character must always depict her from the bust up" (354). None of this, however, should negate discussion of female superheroes as complex figures in their own right. Despite several pioneering histories and critical analyses of female superheroes (see Madrid, Robbins, Robinson), and several more of female action heroes (see Brown, Heinecken, Inness, Stuller), much of the existing scholarship on superheroes dismisses the meaning and function of female superheroes as too simplistic or obvious to warrant nuanced examination or analysis. For example, there is a dangerous neglect in Scott Bukatman's assertion that "the spectacle of the female body in these titles is so insistent, and the fetishism of breasts, thighs, and hair is so complete, that the comics seem to dare you to say anything about them that isn't redundant. *Of course*, the female form has absurdly exaggerated sexual characteristics; *of course* the costumes are skimpier than one could (or should) imagine; *of course*, there's no visible way that these costumes could stay in place; *of course*, these women represent simple adolescent masturbatory fantasies (with a healthy taste of the dominatrix)" (65). Bukatman's "of course" evinces a double-oppression, an oppression in which the complexity of female superheroes is undercut both within the superhero genre itself and within an academic discourse that dismisses them as nothing more than masturbatory fantasies for "a nearly exclusive male gaze" (Avery-Natale 72).

The scholarly neglect of female superheroes goes hand in hand with scholarly neglect of the fact that superhero comics can and do have female readers. This neglect is inexcusable. Although the production and consumption of superhero comics is indisputably dominated by men and boys, there is very little reliable hard data on readership demographics. As Suzanne Scott observes, while estimates that girls and women make up 5 to 10 percent of the total readership of superhero comics are routinely invoked as "common knowledge," these statistics are often little more than assumptions based on informal Internet polls or anecdotal observation of comic book stores. This reliance on assumptions is partly the result of "a lack of transparency from publishers who, when they do conduct surveys, do so to 'maximize profits' within the existing system, rather than seeking to extend the readership of comics across barriers of sex, age, and race" (Scott 7). In general, readership statistics compiled and released by the "big two" American comic book publishers, Marvel and DC, should be taken with a grain of salt, as these companies have a vested interest in emphasizing their appeal to what is widely considered the most desirable advertising demographic: young men aged eighteen to thirty-four. Case in point, a 2011 Nielsen survey of DC Comics readers reported 93 percent male readership, with more than 50 percent of respondents within the eighteen to thirty-four age range. However, these figures, which were widely distributed in a press release that appeared on many different pop culture and general news outlets, represented a survey of 793 customers completed in-store and through digital comics retailers. A survey of 5,336 respondents that was completed online through a link distributed on social media reported very different numbers: 77 percent male readership and 23 percent female readership. Although this second set of figures does appear in the full report of the survey (Newsarama), it is not mentioned in the press release.[2]

Ultimately, though, even if girls and women do make up less than 10 percent of the total readership of superhero comics, this is still not an insignificant amount. Consequently, as Karen Healey observes, when scholars completely ignore this demographic, "they suggest, perhaps unconsciously, that superhero comics are inherently uninteresting to the female reader" (145). While it is relatively easy to understand why some girls and women might be turned off by the superhero genre's often egregious sexism, most obviously manifested in its sometimes extreme sexualization of female characters, it is less clear why all girls and women would be turned off by its themes of action, heroism, and identity-formation. At worst, neglecting female readers implies their "natural" dislike of action-based, heroic narratives, an assumption that exonerates both critics and the comic book industry from any in-depth interrogation of the superhero genre's politics of representation. As Scott writes, "scholarly accounts of comic book publishers' attempts to reach out to female readers and expand their current fan base tend to stress that these attempts invariably fail, . . . with minimal examination of why" (6). Too often, privileging the *fact* of such failures at the expense of their possible *reasons* reflects an underlying, essentialist assumption that "women simply don't like superhero comics."

Of course, *The Cat* notwithstanding, very few mainstream superhero comics starring female protagonists have been created, written, or drawn by women; this has meant that even when female superheroes are intended to appeal to female readers, they often reveal more about how men view women than about how girls and women view themselves. Nonetheless, as Yvonne Tasker and Diane Negra observe, because post-1970s popular culture in particular has been produced, at least in part, in response to feminism, performing a feminist analysis of this era's texts requires interrogating their politics of both marginalization and incorporation (5). In this chapter I offer a brief, and admittedly incomplete, history of Marvel's female superheroes, focusing specifically on the ways in which they have incorporated evolving interpretations of feminism. Throughout, I will argue that developing a more nuanced understanding of Marvel's attempts to appeal to female readers through female superheroes requires appreciating these characters as complex negotiations between female (and/or feminist) needs and male (and/or patriarchal) expectations. Owing to space limitations, I will not be discussing Marvel's various attempts to appeal to female readers through male characters (as in the recent series *Loki: Agent of Asgard*, which partly aims to capitalize on actor Tom Hiddleston's considerable female fan following). Nor will I be discussing female comics characters in non-superheroic settings, some excellent histories and analyses of which can be found elsewhere (see Chute, Nolan, Robbins). Instead, my primary focus is the major themes and marketing strategies informing female superheroes who have starred in their own ongoing series, as these characters and publishing contexts especially highlight the intense contradictions that female superheroes, and female action heroes in general, have commonly negotiated and embodied from the 1970s to the present. My goal is not to offer a definitive history or analysis, but rather to begin a conversation about the neglected complexity of female superheroes and the female readers they have often infuriated, but sometimes inspired.

The Claws of the Cat was one of three ongoing series starring female characters that Marvel debuted in 1972, all of which were written by women; the others were Night Nurse (an action-romance written by Jean Thomas) and Shanna the She-Devil (a throwback to the "Jungle Girl" comics of the 1940s and 1950s written by Carole Seuling). The "Marvel Bullpen Bulletin" from November of that year foregrounds the female writers of these series as a potential selling point while also emphasizing the titles' wide appeal: "That's right, effendi—three great new comic mags, all written by gals—yet aimed neither at girls *nor* at guys, but at true lovers of comix literature everywhere!" Nonetheless, The Cat, the only superhero title of the three, can and should be viewed as Marvel's first attempt to appeal to female readers by adapting superhero conventions to the context of second-wave feminism.

In issue no. 1, the Cat, aka Greer Nelson, begins her heroic journey after her policeman husband Bill, in a clear reference to the origin story of Batman, is shot and killed by a mugger while the couple are leaving a movie theater. The feminist twist on this familiar tale is that Bill's death does not motivate Greer to vengeance so much as liberate her. Before his death, Bill actively limited Greer's independence, refusing to allow her to finish her college degree or drive a car. On their wedding day, Bill had told Greer, "You're *my* little girl now—and that's the way it's gonna be *forever*!" The narration also states that after the wedding, "Bill cherished and protected her—and she felt more helpless than ever before, because he seemed to *like* that in a woman." In this comic, Bill is an exaggerated patriarchal lover/father, treating his wife/daughter as an object of exchange rather than a fully fledged individual. The Cat's first villainous opponent, Mal Donalbain, is also an exaggerated patriarch; Donalbain is a health-club owner whose evil scheme involves creating an army of superwomen whom he plans to control. He will do this by using a "will-nullifier" that "renders the wearer *helpless* against the superior wishes of [his] *superior mind*." In the final pages of the issue, the Cat provokes Donalbain's death in a scene redolent with rape imagery. Knowing that the maniacal Donalbain has an intense phobia of being touched, Greer corners him in a dark room and slowly advances on him while uttering suggestive threats. This scene can be read as both a connotatively female revenge fantasy and an implied critique of patriarchal masculinity; because Donalbain prefers death to being touched by the active (or phallic) woman, his masculine need for dominance and control proves literally self-destructive.

In its very first issue, *The Cat* revises several key tropes related to female action heroes. One of the most significant revisions involves the introduction of a female mentor. After being turned down for all of the jobs she applies for after Bill's death—a state of affairs that causes "women's lib . . . to have new meaning"—Greer is finally hired as a lab assistant by Dr. Tumolo, a kindly, gray-haired female scientist who nurtures Greer's intellectual talents, and whose experiments are the source of Greer's superheroic transformation. As Jennifer Stuller has elaborated, female action heroes, mirroring the motherless Athena, generally have male mentors, sending the message that such characters "can only be as independent as they are because they lack a mother's womanly—almost always implied as passive—influence" (*Ink-Stained Amazons* 107).[3] Yet Greer's enriching relationship with Dr. Tumolo, especially when contrasted with her destructive relationship with Bill, situates the Cat's superheroism outside of, and even in opposition to, male authority and/or the quest for male approval. Many of Marvel's female superheroes of the 1960s, including the Invisible Girl, the Wasp, and Marvel Girl, become and remain superheroes primarily to stay close to their male love interests; Greer's heroism is instead inspired by a surrogate mother figure. Thinks Greer: "Dr. Tumolo really makes me *proud* to be a woman. I can't let her—or *myself*—down" (*The Cat* no. 1).[4]

The Cat also revises tropes related to the physicality of female superheroes. As Trina Robbins observes, almost all of Marvel's female superheroes from the 1960s have "hands off" powers, exemplified by the force fields of the Invisible Girl (later the Invisible Woman) and the telekinesis of Marvel Girl (later Phoenix) (*The Great Women Super Heroes*, 113). Mike Madrid similarly notes that female superheroes commonly possess "'strike a pose and point' powers," which allow them to "keep their looks intact in the heat of battle" (292). In contrast, the Cat is an explicitly physical superhero, using her razor-sharp claws and advanced acrobatic skills to scale buildings and engage in hand-to-hand combat. However, the way the Cat comes by her physicality is, at best, problematic. She is empowered via a scientific experiment whose reputed goal, as Dr. Tumolo states in issue no. 1, is to "someday make it possible for any woman to totally fulfill her physical and mental potential—despite the handicaps that society places on her." As Stuller observes, "While the message resonates with consciousness-raising politics of Women's Liberation in the 1970s . . . [u]sing a machine to amplify women's abilities excuses them from the responsibilities of empowering themselves" (*Ink-Stained Amazons*, 40). It is worth noting, too, that aspects of the Cat's power-set essentialize her femininity. In issue no. 1, the narration states that "[Greer's] intensified perceptions were like an *embodiment* of that mythical quality known as *woman's intuition*." Greer's "superpowered intuition" allows her to both instinctively solve mechanical problems and feel the pain in the paw of an injured squirrel; as such, her power-set heightens stereotypically feminine qualities of empathy and emotionality alongside, or perhaps in compensation for, more stereotypically masculine capabilities related to engineering and problem solving.

After several convoluted plots that often strayed from the feminist purpose of its first issue, *The Cat* was abruptly canceled at issue no. 4. Yet despite its short existence, *The Cat* established a paradigm for adapting superhero narratives to female experiences and desires. This series crystallized, but left unresolved, the major contradiction that the next several decades of female superheroes would be compelled to negotiate. The Cat invokes this contradiction in the last panel of issue no. 1, after the death of Donalbain and the near-death of Dr. Tumolo: "All our plans for the *betterment* of womankind—! I did what I set out to do, and I did it *well*—but have I *misused* my powers? Did I become a stronger *woman*—only to become a *poorer* human being?" Since *The Cat*, designing female superheroes that can appeal to female readers without alienating the traditionally male fan base has meant negotiating the meaning and consequences of female strength; in general, female superheroes created during and after second-wave feminism represent attempts to devise ways of empowering female lives and bodies that seem liberating to girls and women, while not being threatening to boys and men (or, more broadly, patriarchal gender norms). To repurpose a timeworn antiperspirant ad: during and since the era of *The Cat*, the commercially perfect female superhero has needed to be strong enough for a woman, while still being made (primarily) for a man.

In the decade following the cancellation of *The Cat*, ongoing titles starring newly created female superheroes Spider-Woman, She-Hulk, and Dazzler, related to feminism largely by default rather than design. In general, the titles starring these newly created female superheroes lacked a clear vision, which is unsurprising given their origins. Spider-Woman and She-Hulk were created out of necessity, to preserve Marvel's legal right to their names, while Dazzler was originally commissioned by Casablanca Records as part of a planned cross-promotion with a recording artist. Although her creation was also the result of a mandate from publisher Stan Lee to "come up with another female hero who can use the Marvel name" (qtd. in Boney 24), Ms. Marvel, who debuted in her own ongoing series in 1977, would ultimately be Marvel's most focused effort since *The Cat* to appeal to female readers by incorporating feminist themes.

Compared to the Cat, Ms. Marvel, aka Carol Danvers, a former security chief with the United States Air Force, enjoys a significant increase in physical power: the first scene of *Ms. Marvel* no. 1 shows her flying through the sky, delivering roundhouse punches, and throwing a car full of escaping bank robbers. While the Cat's introduction included a comparison to Batman, Ms. Marvel's introduction establishes her similarity to history's first and most famous superhero, Superman, who also made a memorable first impression by throwing a car. Ms. Marvel's physical power is also immediately foregrounded as an aspirational ideal for girls and women. In the aforementioned opening scene of issue no. 1, a little girl, wide-eyed by Ms. Marvel's physical display, points to her and says, "Mommy, I've never seen a woman like *that*—have *you*?" The little girl's mother replies, "No, Suzy— *never!*" The girl then exclaims, "Wow! When I grow up—I wanna be just like *her!*" This scene emphasizes the intention—or perhaps the conceit—that Ms. Marvel could become a hero for a new generation of women, serving as both a model and a metaphor for women's liberation.

Importantly, however, this increase in physical power is accompanied by an increase in sexualization. While the Cat's costume and figure undoubtedly conjured dominatrix fantasies, Ms. Marvel's original costume is a much skimpier affair, a "cut-out" design featuring bare legs and an exposed back and midriff. Although this costume is demure compared to the outfits many female superheroes (including Ms. Marvel) would sport in coming years, it nonetheless reflects what was then a growing trend. As Madrid observes, beginning in the late 1970s, superhero comics exploited the sexual revolution to assert that female superheroes could "be liberated and still sport a sexy and revealing costume." During the era that introduced Ms. Marvel, sex appeal was increasingly justified as a symbol of female empowerment while also providing "the 'spoonful of sugar' that helped the 'medicine' of feminism go down" (155).

Epitomizing this compromise, Ms. Marvel is not only more powerful and more sexualized than her predecessors, but also more explicitly aligned with feminism. In issue no. 1, Danvers is hired by *Daily Bugle* publisher J. Jonah Jameson to edit a new magazine called *Woman*. In creating this magazine and hiring Danvers, Jameson is, like Marvel, attempting to attract new female readers to an erstwhile male-dominated media empire. However, *Ms. Marvel* no. 1 emphasizes Marvel's and Jameson's different goals and strategies. In describing the content of his previous publications aimed at women, Jameson, a stereotypical "male chauvinist pig," vehemently rejects feminism: "Articles on *women's lib*, interviews with *Kate Millet*, stories about *careers for women—yecch*." Jameson wants *Woman* to be a more traditional women's magazine, offering "*new diets*, and *fashions*, and *recipes*," and, of course, a scathing condemnation of Ms. Marvel. Danvers (and by extension Marvel) subsequently demonstrates a heroic commitment to feminism by refusing to write about diets, fashions, or recipes, and, of course, by producing a pro–Ms. Marvel piece. This scene and context is a crucial site of negotiation; it allows Marvel to criticize a patriarchal publishing industry while privileging itself above such criticism—because, after all, it publishes the (purportedly) feminist *Ms. Marvel*. Ms. Marvel's feminist credentials are further bolstered by the first splash page of *Ms. Marvel* no. 6, which features a close-up of *Woman* no. 1 with an image of Ms. Marvel on the cover (fig. 3.2). This image explicates Marvel's effort to connect Ms. Marvel and Carol Danvers to feminist icon Gloria Steinem, cofounder of *Ms.* magazine, which featured the world's most iconic female superhero, Wonder Woman, on the cover of its 1972 debut issue.

This alignment of Steinem with Ms. Marvel against the extravagant chauvinism of J. Jonah Jameson represents a significant acknowledgment of institutionalized sexism as a problem worth addressing. However, the writers and editors of *Ms. Marvel* would often struggle to understand or admit their own implication in this sexism, as exemplified by writer/editor Gerry Conway's[5] introductory letter at the end of *Ms. Marvel* no. 1. In his letter, Conway exploits the notion of gender equality to assert a man's ability—and right—to create a feminist-inspired female superhero: "If the women's liberation movement means anything, it's a battle for equality of the sexes. And it's my contention that a man, properly motivated and aware of the pitfalls, can write a woman character as well as a woman." Although this statement is not untrue, it also serves as a convenient excuse for the absence of a female writer from this and so many other titles.

Conway similarly invokes feminism in his defense of Ms. Marvel's naming. Ms. Marvel's name can be considered problematic inasmuch as it links and arguably subordinates her to the male superhero Captain Marvel, whose name, unlike that of Ms. Marvel, connotes institutional authority.

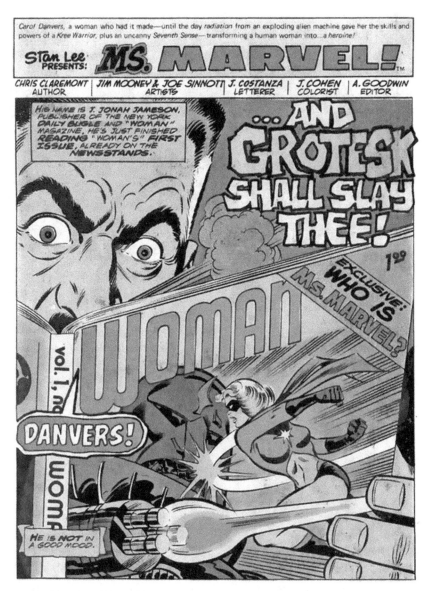

3.2. *Ms. Marvel* no. 6 (June 1977).

This subordination is furthermore suggested by the fact that Captain Marvel is also the source of Ms. Marvel's imagery and superpowers; like Eve created from Adam's rib, Ms. Marvel gains her superpowers when her DNA is merged with that of Captain Marvel in a super-scientific accident. In his

115

letter, Conway ignores these issues in favor of asserting the importance of the "Ms." prefix as a statement of female independence. Writes Conway: "Her name, if nothing else, is influenced, to a great extent, by the move toward women's liberation. She is *not* a Marvel Girl; she's a woman, *not* a Miss or a Mrs.—a *Ms.* Her own person. Herself." Though seemingly well-intentioned, Conway's letter emphasizes Ms. Marvel's feminism in ways that downplay, and even dismiss, possible feminist criticisms.

In spite of, or perhaps in response to, its problematic invocations of feminism, Conway's letter spurred a debate about the representation of female superheroes that would continue in *Ms. Marvel*'s letter pages until the title's cancellation at issue no. 25. Many readers, including "Miss (and proud of it) Mary-Catherine Gilmore," whose letter appears in issue no. 4, felt that the creation of *Ms. Marvel* provided an "opportunity . . . to comment on . . . the blatant sexism running rampant among the pages of Marvel and your Distinguished Competition." Significantly, girls and women were a consistent presence in the letter pages of *Ms. Marvel*, averaging 50 percent of the total published letters.[6] Although it is impossible to know whether this percentage came close to reflecting the title's actual readership, it does confirm a mandate to make it *seem* as though girls and women were reading the title—though not, importantly, in greater numbers than boys and men. As Matthew Pustz observes, because fan letters are strategically selected and edited by the publishing company, "they are a part of the self-image of the comic. They present that self-image, and help to encourage the right kind of future response from readers" (166). Based solely on its letter pages, *Ms. Marvel*'s self-image involved encouraging female and even feminist involvement while also demonstrating that this encouragement did not conflict with, or come at the expense of, Marvel's traditionally male fan base.

It is beyond the scope of this chapter to detail all the fascinating debates that play out within *Ms. Marvel*'s letter pages. However, it is worth noting that these debates reveal female-identified readers' deep awareness of the prejudices and contradictions informing Ms. Marvel's representation of female strength. For instance, in issue no. 8, a letter from "Debbie Lipp" succinctly articulates the troubling implications of the tagline that appeared on the cover of *Ms. Marvel* until issue no. 4: "'This female fights back!' is blatantly sexist, in that it implies that other females don't fight back—that it is, in fact, unusual and entertaining that a female should fight back." *Ms. Marvel*'s letter pages also highlight serious disagreements among female-identified readers concerning how female strength should ideally be depicted. The "Ms." prefix alone proves very controversial. The aforementioned "Miss (and proud of it) Mary-Catherine Gilmore," as well as "Cynthia Walker (Mrs., not Ms.)" (*Ms. Marvel* no. 3), and "Ms. (and bubbling with pride over it) Adrienne Foster" (*Ms. Marvel* no. 7), all identify themselves in relation to their support for, or dissent from, the version of feminism they read into the naming of Ms. Marvel. These disagreements effectively illustrate that the contradictions informing the creation and depiction of female superheroes also appeared within feminism itself, as well as in real women's lives and imaginations.

Overall, *Ms. Marvel*'s plots and imagery mirrored and no doubt substantiated the dissonance of its letter pages. For the first dozen issues of her series, Danvers suffers from a highly gendered personality disorder. For the first several issues of her series, she is not even aware that she and Ms. Marvel are the same person, her transformations into her superheroic alter ego being triggered, as Alex Boney explains, by "fainting spells and blackouts, which had been used to signal female hysteria and instability for centuries" (24). Although some of Marvel's male superheroes, most notably the Hulk, could also be said to suffer from hysteria, there are specific meanings and consequences to depicting a female superhero as hysterical. Mary Poovey observes that the nineteenth-century discourse of hysteria situated the female body as "always lacking and needing control"; because hysteria was viewed as both a normal state of womanhood and a pathology, it defined women as essentially pathological—as somehow inherently "abnormal" or "disturbed" (qtd. in Balsamo 27). Consequently, using the signs of hysteria to signal Danvers's transformations into Ms. Marvel suggests either that women are inherently pathological, abnormal, and disturbed, or that they become this way when they become superheroes.

Both readings are supported by an initial storyline in which Danvers's male psychiatrist, Michael Barnett—who is also a potential love interest—learns her dual identity before she does, which places him in a position of superior knowledge and control. During the scene in which Danvers exposes her dual identity to Barnett under hypnosis, her vulnerability and dependence on men is strongly emphasized; in this scene, which is partly a series of flashbacks, Danvers is shown fainting three times in four pages, twice into the hands of a more capable man—first Captain Marvel, and then Barnett. This foundational storyline presents Marvel's most overtly feminist superhero as not only sick, but actually torn apart emotionally and

3.3. *Ms. Marvel* no. 20 (Oct. 1978).

physically; it furthermore suggests that this sickness can only be managed or controlled by a male authority figure who is both doctor and lover.

Ms. Marvel's constantly changing costume reflects and compounds her uncertain identity. In issue no. 9, Ms. Marvel's exposed back and midriff are covered up, making her costume less sexualized and more practical; yet in issue no. 20, she is flagrantly re-sexualized as she swaps her bright primary colors for a shiny black ensemble consisting of a backless bathing suit, thigh-high heeled boots, and long gloves. Here, she is also given a much longer, fuller mane of blonde hair (see fig. 3.3). Arriving so close to the title's cancellation, it is difficult not to read this final costume change as a last-ditch effort to save the title by abandoning a demonstrably fickle female readership in favor of a franker appeal to the more dependable male gaze. In the end, however, *Ms. Marvel*'s commercial failure almost certainly says less about female consumers than it does about the ambivalence and confusion of male producers, who saddled themselves with the admittedly impossible task of devising one woman, and one version of female strength, to stand for, appeal to, and represent all girls and women.

In the era following the cancellation of *Ms. Marvel*, female superheroes were often depicted as "bad girls." At Marvel, this trend was perhaps best exemplified by the Frank Miller–created character Elektra, a deadly assassin dressed in a red, one-shoulder thong bathing suit, armed with a pair of sai (a traditional Japanese weapon) and a massive daddy complex. In their book *Reel Knockouts: Violent Women in the Movies*, Martha McCaughey and Neal King argue that bad girls can serve a feminist purpose: "Visions of sexually attractive women skilled with weaponry, licensed to kill, beating up men might rather take the wind out of the sails of the culture in which sex difference seems unalterable. Such images might challenge smug oppressors" (6). However, in terms of their ability to signal and enact political critique or change, bad girls tend to be limited by their often apolitical self-centeredness. Most bad girls, including Elektra, are brutal and generally emotionless killers who are motivated primarily by money, revenge, or a quest for personal power.

Amid the bad girl trend, a re-vamped She-Hulk emerged as an alternative representation of female strength. She-Hulk's first solo series, *The Savage She-Hulk* (1980–1982), established the character's basic origin story: when mild-mannered attorney Jennifer Walters is gunned down by a vengeful mobster, she accepts a blood transfusion from her cousin, Bruce Banner, which transforms her into a considerably more sexualized version of the Hulk. However, it was She-Hulk's second solo series, *The Sensational She-Hulk*, that developed the self-aware sense of humor that has since come to truly define the character and distinguish her from her more famous male cousin. Debuting in 1989, *The Sensational She-Hulk* would last sixty issues, making it one of Marvel's longest-running series starring a female superhero.[7]

She-Hulk has several things in common with her feminist-inspired predecessors. Like the Cat and Ms. Marvel, she is explicitly physical, but more so: she is a 6'7", 650-pound, virtually indestructible green-skinned Amazon who always leads with her fists. In her *Sensational* iteration, She-Hulk also has a female companion and sometime-mentor in the form of Golden Age heroine the Blonde Phantom, now middle-aged, overweight, and known as "Weezie." The inclusion of Weezie is important not only because her age and body type make her an atypical female protagonist within the superhero genre,[8] but also because she helps to foreground the rejuvenation of She-Hulk as a gesture of recovery, resurrecting female superheroes and demonstrating these heroes' untapped potential.

However, the revamped She-Hulk is also different from her predecessors in several important ways. First, in both her *Sensational* iteration and in subsequent solo series (vol. 1, 2004–2005; vol. 2, 2005–2009; vol. 3, 2014–present), She-Hulk's sense of humor can be a double-edged sword. On the one hand, the humorous tone of her comics enables her to satirize superhero conventions, including those related to the representation of female characters; for instance, She-Hulk often complains about her own sexualization, sometimes by "breaking the fourth wall" to speak directly to the reader. On the other hand, her sense of humor is just as often a justification for her sexualization. As a case in point, in an infamous scene from *The Sensational She-Hulk* no. 40, She-Hulk jumps rope "naked" for five full pages because, as she says, "Marvel will do just about *anything* to make a sale."[9] That She-Hulk is sexualized at all is obviously notable. While Bruce Banner transforms into a muscle-bound version of Universal Studios' Frankenstein's monster, Jennifer Walters's transformation includes exaggerated feminine features such as longer hair and much larger breasts. A story from 2007 also suggests that her transformation includes a heightened sex drive (*She-Hulk* vol. 2, no. 19). Furthermore, while the Hulk generally fights in torn purple shorts, She-Hulk often finds herself fighting in lacy lingerie. Importantly, however, She-Hulk's sexualization is generally presented as a personal choice. In the "Sensational She-Hulk" graphic novel (*Marvel Graphic Novel* no. 18), for instance, She-Hulk gives the following explanation for wearing a Playboy-esque white bustier bodysuit and bow tie to dinner with her boyfriend, Wyatt Wingfoot (fig. 3.4): "It's pointless for me to try to wear conventional clothes. Besides, I'm *six foot seven and bright green!* People are gonna *stare* no matter how I dress!" As Lillian Robinson observes, in this scene and in general, She-Hulk's liberated sexuality is as double-edged as her sense of humor. Although her "exuberant sexual subjectivity may be read as a declaration of women's right to the assertion of desire . . . [i]t is rather disquieting . . . that that assertion coincides so seamlessly with mainstream commercial representations of male sexuality" (Robinson 101).

In foregrounding She-Hulk's sexualization as a "choice and for her own enjoyment" (McRobbie 33), *The Sensational She-Hulk* is decidedly postfeminist. In brief, postfeminism is situated in opposition to the supposed rigidity and extremism of second-wave feminism; it purports to offer "the pleasure and comfort of (re)claiming an identity uncomplicated by gender politics,

3.4. *Marvel Graphic Novel* no. 18 (Nov. 1985).

postmodernism, or institutional critique" (Negra 2). Frequently operating "through 'stylistic alibi' or irony" (Harzewski 9), postfeminism embraces feminist gains while rejecting second-wave feminist politics rooted in sisterhood, organizing, and protests. As Tasker and Negra argue, "postfeminist culture involves an evident erasure of feminist politics from the popular, even as aspects of feminism seem to be incorporated within that culture" (5). Although She-Hulk's assertion of agency over (and through) her body evokes feminism, she is postfeminist inasmuch as her empowerment is largely individualistic, severed from any larger political movement or message. As Robinson observes, despite the presence of Weezie, *The Sensational She-Hulk* ultimately locates female strength less in sisterhood than in a woman's ability to embody connotatively male forms of physical strength and sexual aggressiveness (104). In fact, Weezie's mentorship could be read as supporting this sexy individualism: although Weezie is considerably more complex than the average sidekick, her age and body type nonetheless disqualify her from being a true hero or central protagonist, roles she willingly cedes to her protégée, She-Hulk, an ideally modern (or postmodern) woman who is, unlike herself, strong enough to be eternally sexy, and thus, desirable and popular.

Unlike its feminist-inspired predecessors, *The Sensational She-Hulk* makes few (if any) overt attempts to directly solicit female readers, as evinced by the near-total absence of female letter writers from *Sensational*'s letter pages. This shift again reflects the logic of postfeminism, wherein part of women's liberation is their transformation from a politically or experientially united group into a collection of individual consumers. When and where the representation of women is addressed in *The Sensational She-Hulk*'s letter pages, individual power is often presented as a cure for the perceived inadequacy of feminist politics. A typical example occurs in issue no. 40, in which "Robert H. McGregor" writes: "She-Hulk is a sly parody of sexist attitudes. She punches large holes in the brick walls such attitudes construct. More so than picket signs and angry letters."

Significantly, most of the letters that appear in *The Sensational She-Hulk* are written not to the writer or editor, but to She-Hulk herself, who also answers them. Although these letters and responses often poke fun at the male gaze—as She-Hulk sarcastically (but always sympathetically) rejects numerous marriage proposals and pleas to pose naked—the ironic tone also maintains barriers between consumers and producers. "She-Hulk's" response to a letter from "Don Schenk" in *The Sensational She-Hulk* no. 46 illustrates the political consequences of these barriers. In his letter, Schenk criticizes what he calls the "beanpole-look" popular in women's fashion magazines, while telling "She-Hulk," "you'd never get into the women's magazines because you're too, uh, bountiful. Maybe as a service to the women of America you should sell SHE-HULK at the supermarket." This letter effectively blames real women for cultivating unrealistic ideals while upholding She-Hulk, a fictional character written and drawn by men within a male-dominated and conventionally sexist industry, as the true feminist. The response from "She-Hulk" (which is actually written by series editor Renée Witterstaetter) offers a slight corrective to Schenk's argument but nonetheless embraces a very similar postfeminist logic. While acknowledging that she has also been criticized as an unrealistic ideal, "She-Hulk" argues that healthy self-image is ultimately a matter of personal responsibility. "We'll all be better off, . . ." she says, "when we finally start making the best of what we are, instead of trying to look or act like somebody else's idea of what we should be." In effect, by affirming She-Hulk's gravity-defying, cantaloupe-sized breasts and propensity for fighting crime in her underwear as an expression of individuality rather than institutionalized sexism, *The Sensational She-Hulk* attempts to transform the stereotypical objectification of women into a celebration of diversity. In the end, the key to *The Sensational She-Hulk*'s (comparative) commercial success may also be its key feminist failure, inasmuch as its depiction of female strength results in, and even depends upon, diminishing the realities of institutionalized sexism.

In the past decade, in particular, the increased mainstream relevance of superheroes—generated in large part by the success of superhero films—has both coincided with and aided the increased visibility of feminist websites and blogs specializing in comics and "geek culture." Following in the footsteps of Gail Simone's 1999 "Women in Refrigerators" blog, which compiled a list of female characters who had been "depowered, raped, or cut up and stuck in the refrigerator," projects such as "The Hawkeye Initiative," a website launched in 2012 that "uses Hawkeye and other male comic characters to illustrate how deformed, hyper-sexualized, and impossibly contorted women are commonly illustrated in comics, books, and video games," have disseminated feminist critiques of the superhero genre well beyond both academia and the traditional confines of superhero fandom. "The Hawkeye Initiative" alone has been prominently featured on popular entertainment sites such Bleeding Cool and BuzzFeed, as well as major news outlets such as the BBC. This type of exposure has almost certainly played a role in Marvel's recent efforts to reinvigorate its roster of female superheroes as well as in its renewed interest in promoting the visibility of female readers and creators.

Carol Danvers's well-publicized relaunch as *Captain Marvel*, a title established in 2012 under the reign of writer Kelly Sue DeConnick, notably resurrects several important aspects of Danvers's original introduction as Ms. Marvel. The first story arc of DeConnick's *Captain Marvel* foregrounds female mentorship and community, with Danvers helping Tracy Burke, the former editor of *Woman*, as she begins cancer treatment, while also time-traveling to World War II to fight alongside a squad of female pilots led by Danvers's lifelong idol, a fictional flying ace named Helen Cobb. In this series, Danvers's updated name and costume are at least as important as her stories in terms of recovering and updating the character's feminist aspirations. Danvers's adoption of a non-gender-specific, institutionally powerful moniker once again makes her naming a political statement, while her updated costume restores her original bright colors and adds more practical features, being much less revealing and incorporating flat boots and a shorter hairstyle (fig. 3.5). This renaming and re-costuming is also a very important rebranding, not just for Danvers, but for Marvel as a purveyor of female superheroes aimed at girls and women. The vast majority of *Captain Marvel*'s advance press chose to foreground the significance of Danvers's costume change. In an interview on popular comics news site Newsarama, the costume's designer, Jamie McKelvie, describes it as "a result of us trying to create something that came out of her character and background in the military. I think the best and strongest costumes arise from the character's personality, backstory and so on" (Ching).

Interestingly, while McKelvie characterizes Danvers's costume change as a function of good storytelling, DeConnick's interviews suggest a more explicitly feminist purpose. For instance, in an interview with Comic Book Resources, DeConnick cajoles the reader, saying, "C'mon now, people. . . . Show me that a female-led book about the power of the human spirit, about the many guises of heroism, a book wherein no one gets raped or puts her cervix on display, can break six issues, won't you?" (Richards). In this instance, the advance marketing of *Captain Marvel* negotiates the ever-supposed conundrum of female strength by balancing the voice of a male artist defending a female superhero's pants as a matter of artistic integrity with the voice of female writer defending the same pants as an important protest against a history of marginalization and exploitation.

A similar balancing act is present in the letter pages of *Captain Marvel* no. 1, which features an introductory address not from writer DeConnick, but from series editor Stephen Wacker. In his letter, Wacker only tentatively addresses the politics of the costume change, limiting himself to saying that although Danvers's black latex look "was definitely titillating . . . it wasn't always the attention we wanted for arguably our strongest female character." Wacker's letter is followed, however, by an entire page of fan art depicting the new costume, which Wacker says he received, unsolicited, in advance of the series' debut. Significantly, all four pieces of art are attributed to female fans. In these letter pages, the authoritative voice of the male editor serves to reassure the traditionally male fan base, while the female artists do the work of reaching out to female readers—with their artwork, and even the simple fact of their presence. Taken as a whole, these letter pages establish and legitimize *Captain Marvel* as a female-friendly (but still male-supervised) space. Ultimately, the marketing of *Captain Marvel* tries to balance male (and/or patriarchal) expectations with female (and/or feminist) desires by asserting that good art and design can also serve and reflect good politics (and, in turn, good business sense).

Significantly, however, *Captain Marvel*'s relatively direct solicitation of female readers was, at the time, somewhat of an anomaly. Despite certain surface similarities to the rejuvenation of Carol Danvers, including the

3.5. Ms. Marvel's feminist aspirations are revived with a new costume and moniker (Captain Marvel) in 2012.

design of a less revealing, more character-driven costume for the previously thong-clad Psylocke, the 2013 relaunch of *X-Men* (a subsidiary of that franchise's main title, *Uncanny X-Men*) as an all-female team makes no such appeal. In an interview with *Wired* magazine prior to *X-Men*'s release, series writer Brian Wood[10] claimed that the title's all-female team would "transcend gender lines." Says Wood: "When you approach the page with the thought, 'Okay, so what should this *woman* do now,' you start off from a place of stereotype and bad writing, and there's no fixing it because that is now your foundation. . . . I'm not approaching this new *X-Men* as a 'female book,' but I'm writing it as a high action X-Men comic, and with some luck that will nullify some of these poisonous critics who go looking for something to feel angry/uncomfortable/threatened by" (Hudson).

In this quote, it is difficult to determine whether the "poisonous critics" Wood refers to are misogynists who do not like reading comics about powerful women, or feminists who believe that sex and gender do, in fact, meaningfully inform social experience. At any rate, the series' title magnifies the gender bias implicit in Wood's universalism, wherein "transcending" gender means assuming a masculine pronoun, and women have all the same privileges as men only if they do not refer to themselves—or even think about themselves—as women. Within the comic itself, the characters describe their all-female team as a simple coincidence; this fact corroborates the suggestion, already present in Wood's above statement and in the title's naming, that *X-Men* is not intended to critique past exclusions, but rather to celebrate and congratulate the X-Men franchise, and by extension Marvel, for its supposed historical and continued inclusiveness.[11]

Marvel's 2010 "Women of Marvel" celebration, based around the thirtieth anniversary of the creation of She-Hulk, sings a similar tune. The "Women of Marvel" celebration featured the release of several limited series and print and digital "One-Shots" starring female superheroes. Its flagship release, however, was *Girl Comics*,[12] a three-issue comics anthology produced entirely by female writers, artists, and editors. In an interview entitled "Comics by Women, for Everyone," that appeared in the commemorative *Women of Marvel Magazine*, *Girl Comics*' editor Jeanine Schaefer states that the goal of the anthology is to "make good comics, not woman-centric comics." Schaefer also asserts that where female readers are concerned, "we're not asking for special stories geared toward us. . . . Make good comics and we will come" (Jaffe 47).

In the service of this purportedly inclusive message, *Girl Comics* features a mix of male and female protagonists. The stories in the anthology are also interspersed with both biographies of female creators (including *The Cat*'s Linda Fite and Marie Severin) and several highly sexualized pinups of female superheroes. One of these pinups, by Sana Takeda, shows a nearly naked She-Hulk tied up and bound by a jump rope (in reference to the aforementioned "naked" jump rope scene from *The Sensational She-Hulk* no. 40) (*Girl Comics* no. 1) (fig. 3.6); another pinup, by Sho Murase, depicts Elektra clothed only in unraveling ribbons, and framed by the much larger body of her sometimes-lover Daredevil (*Girl Comics* no. 3). The nature and placement of this imagery seems to disavow the disempowering and even violent aspects of female superheroes' sexualization in favor of celebrating the supposedly empowering fact that female creators are able to participate in it. The She-Hulk image,

3.6. *Girl Comics* no. 1 (May 2010).

in particular, which is paired with a "Happy Anniversary" caption, celebrates the female superhero to whom the anthology is dedicated less for her heroism than for her ability to appeal to, and even humble herself for, the male gaze. In this image, the emphasis is on the female superhero's willingness to make herself more consumable by binding her strength, an act that also actively and graphically limits her ability to "fight back."

Similar to *X-Men, Girl Comics'* celebration of female characters and creators seems to come at the expense of exposing and critiquing their long-standing and continued (narrative) marginalization and (visual) exploitation. This effect is foregrounded by the "introduction" pages of each issue. Written and drawn by Coleen Coover, these pages feature the friendly, smiling faces of Marvel's female superheroes describing their motivations and the nature of their heroism. From the introduction to *Girl Comics* no. 2:

> Scarlet Witch: "We don't do it to shake things up."
> Hellcat: "We're not trying to move the Earth."
> Rogue: "Or start a ruckus."
>
> . . .
>
> Araña: "We don't do it to get ahead of the pack."
> Psylocke: "Or inspire awe."
> Firestar: "But we move forward."
> Katie Power: "And we are awesome."
> She-Hulk: "We do it because it's *fun.*"

By having each of Marvel's prominent female superheroes state that she is *not* trying to "shake things up," or "get ahead of the pack"—that is, that she is *not* trying to be critical, different, or "better"—this introduction can be read as an attempt to diffuse the potentially destabilizing presence of female characters and creators within a traditionally male space. Significantly, these pages very directly echo the logic of postfeminism inasmuch as they position "progress" as the ability to have "fun," which is in turn defined as the opposite of large-scale change. At worst, both *Girl Comics* and *X-Men* suggest that girls and women who do "start a ruckus" are traitors to inclusiveness. At best, these series sanction specific, direct appeals to male experiences and desires while characterizing specific appeals to female experiences and desires as divisive and thus politically and commercially undesirable.

However, one of Marvel's most high-profile recent attempts to directly solicit female readers is, from a feminist standpoint, arguably even more problematic. In 2013, Marvel partnered with Hyperion Books to release a series of romance novels starring female superheroes. The release of the partnership's two initial offerings, *Rogue Touch* and *The She-Hulk Diaries*, was widely reported; interviews with the authors and editors appeared in mainstream media outlets such as *The Guardian*, *USA Today*, and *Publishers Weekly*. Each of these interviews emphasizes that the novels are intended to lure female readers to Marvel's male-dominated publishing empire. According to the *Publishers Weekly* article, Hyperion editor in chief Elisabeth Dyssegaard "acknowledged that the novels are intended to attract women by adding the narrative elements of commercial women's fiction. . . . 'Marvel has had tremendous success with recent hit movies,' Dyssegaard said, 'and we think it's a great time to explore what happens to super heroines when they are dropped into traditional women's novels'" (Reid).

Unfortunately, this "traditional" setting requires a significant loss of agency for the characters featured in the book versions, even compared to their already-problematic comic book counterparts. For instance, while the comics version of Rogue discovers her heroism within the family context of the X-Men, in *Rogue Touch* she becomes a hero primarily to earn the love and respect of a man, a prince from the distant future who goes by the name of "Touch." In the book's final lines, Rogue says: "So I knew I had to watch myself—make sure my choices landed toward good rather than evil—so if Touch ever did decide to come back, I'd still be worthy of him" (Woodward 273). *The She-Hulk Diaries* similarly revises comic book canon in some troubling ways. Most notably, while the comics version of Jennifer Walters prefers to be She-Hulk, the version of Walters in *The She-Hulk Diaries* considers She-Hulk a separate entity altogether. Walters's disavowal of her superpowered self also disavows her participation in the liberating and gender-deviant aspects of She-Hulk's body and behavior. In addition, the decision to depict Marvel's strongest female superhero as suffering from a multiple personality disorder rather uncomfortably echoes the original *Ms. Marvel*. As in the original *Ms. Marvel*, *The She-Hulk Diaries* places the physically strong but mentally "sick" female superhero in the hands of a male psychiatrist; although Walters initially resists the advice of this psychiatrist, she eventually learns to accept and respect his judgment. Both *The She-Hulk Diaries* and *Rogue Touch* were packaged with enthusiastic pull-quote endorsements from established male comics creators, such as Chris Claremont and Peter David, that seem to sanction a new, "female take" on traditionally male spaces. In the end, however, the decreased agency of the female protagonists, combined with the fact that these novels are set outside of the regular comics universe, severely limits their ability to comment on or critique the past or present sexism of the superhero genre or industry.[13]

For better or worse, the feminist history of Marvel continues to grow and change. At the end of 2011, Marvel had no ongoing titles starring female superheroes; as of March 2016, they have fourteen (*A-Force*; *All-New Wolverine*; *Angela: Queen of Hel*; *Black Widow*; *Captain Marvel*; *Mighty Thor*; *Mockingbird*; *Ms. Marvel*; *Patsy Walker, A.K.A. Hellcat!*; *Scarlet Witch*; *Silk*; *Spider-Gwen*; *Spider-Woman*; *The Unbeatable Squirrel Girl*), eight of which have at least one women in a regular role as writer or penciller. At the very least, Marvel's current strategy of appealing to female readers through female superheroes seems to acknowledge the need for different and diverse depictions of female strength. In the past year alone, Marvel has offered female superheroes who fought both on their own and teamed up with other women within the context of both action and romance, in convenience stores in Jersey City and the furthest reaches of outer space. It has also offered three solo series (*Ms. Marvel*, *Silk*, and the now-canceled *Storm*) starring women of color; although this number is hardly great, it is notable given the extreme rarity of female protagonists of color within mainstream action-adventure genres.[14]

At this juncture, however, female superheroes are still making most of their gains on the margins; male superheroes continue to dominate best-selling team comics and crossover events, such as the 2015 installation of *Secret Wars*, which primarily centered on the all-male members of the Marvel "Illuminati." There have also been plenty of missteps when it comes to marketing this minor explosion of female superheroes to female readers. For instance, the 2014 relaunch of *Spider-Woman* was marred by a controversy surrounding a variant cover drawn by Milo Manara that depicted the title character in a very sexually charged position, the suggestively spread butt cheeks of her extremely exaggerated rear end thrust high into the air above the New York cityscape. Jill Pantozzi of TheMarySue.com wrote of this cover, "Although it appears Marvel is attempting to draw in women with a slew of new female-led titles, this does not instill confidence" ("Marvel"). The relevance of female superheroes for female readers and fans also continues to be undermined by voices with considerable institutional power. As a case in point, in a now somewhat infamous 2014 interview with the podcast Scriptnotes, David S. Goyer, the screenwriter for the 2016 film *Batman v Superman: Dawn of Justice* (which features the filmic debut of Wonder Woman), described She-Hulk as "a giant green porn star that only the Hulk could fuck" (qtd. by Kistler), effectively reducing one of mainstream comics' most complicated female characters to the sole domain of male sexual fantasy.

On a more positive note, the 2014 relaunch of *Ms. Marvel*, starring a Pakistani American, Muslim teenager named Kamala Khan, and the rebirth of Thor as a woman (later revealed to be the male Thor's longtime love interest, Jane Foster), were reported by nearly every major news outlet in North America, including CNN and the *New York Times*, as well as major entertainment outlets such as *Variety* and *The View*. The newsworthiness of these publishing endeavors shows just how fashionable female strength is in art and entertainment today; the months and years ahead will determine whether what is fashionable is also marketable, and whether Marvel's increasing diversity is a momentary trend or part of a significant and potentially meaningful transformation. Significantly, several of Marvel's current female-led titles, including *All-New Wolverine*, *Mighty Thor*, and *Spider-Gwen*, involve women taking over "legacy" titles usually held by men, and historically, legacy titles tend to revert back to their original owners within a few years' time. Yet the success of the new *Ms. Marvel*, the only current legacy title to feature a female superhero taking over from another female superhero, does inspire belief in the possibility of sustained change. Upon its launch, *Ms. Marvel* was Marvel's best-selling digital comic (Gerding), and Kamala Khan is currently appearing twice monthly, in her own series and in the team comic *All-New, All-Different Avengers*. On the whole, signs point to more big changes ahead at Marvel and in the superhero comics industry more generally. At present, however, the newsworthiness of female superheroes proves that it is still far too unusual to see superpowered girls and women doing what real girls and women are doing every day: fighting back, and saving the world.

NOTES

1. Marvel would not have another issue of an ongoing comic book starring a female superhero that was both written and drawn by women until Kelly Sue DeConnick and Emma Rios worked on *Captain Marvel* nos. 5–6 in 2012.

2. DC's presentation of the full results of the survey indicates that the online responses carried less weight because such surveys are statistically less reliable (Newsarama). However, DC's decision to discount the online responses entirely remains conspicuous. In an interview with *Publishers Weekly*, DC Comics marketing executive John Rood had this to say about the discrepancy in the online survey: "So was there a glut of activity specific to wanting to register certain feedback? I can't say whether females found their voice in [the online survey] or whether they had specific female related issues to report on, but this is something that stood out" (MacDonald). Rood does not, however, speculate further on why this discrepancy stood out; nor does he offer any explanation as to why it was excluded from the press release.

3. An important exception to this rule is Wonder Woman, who, in her 1942 origin story, in *Sensation Comics* no. 1, is built out of clay by her mother and imbued with life by Aphrodite. However, even Wonder Woman's superhero-ism is to some extent prompted by a man; originally, Wonder Woman leaves Paradise Island only after Steve Trevor crash lands there and she falls in love with him.

4. The Cat spends issue no. 2 and the beginning of issue no. 3 fighting to save Dr. Tumolo's life. Although the doctor ends the series in a catatonic state, it is unclear whether she would have recovered had the series continued.

5. On the first page of *Ms. Marvel* no. 1, the words "Conceived, written & edited by Gerry Conway" are accompanied by an asterisk with a note that reads, "With more than a little aid and abetment from Carla Conway." Making reference to the involvement—and approval—of Conway's wife may be read as an attempt to both include a female perspective and sanction the male writer's authority.

6. This 50/50 split between male and female letter writers is also likely meant to emphasize the title's commitment to "equality."

7. To date, the only Marvel title starring a female superhero to run for more than sixty consecutive issues is the "alternate universe" title *Spider-Girl*, starring May Parker, the daughter of retired Spider-Man Peter Parker, and his wife, Mary Jane Watson. *Spider-Girl* reached one hundred issues from 1998 to 2006.

8. Although Weezie's weight is often a subject of humor, the fact that Weezie sometimes functions as a "point-of-view" character suggests that the reader is intended to identify with her imperfection rather than ridicule it.

9. In the scene in question, She-Hulk is finally revealed to be wearing a skimpy bikini, meaning she was never "actually" naked. However, the pages preceding this reveal strongly suggest She-Hulk's nudity, her nipples and crotch being barely obscured by the blurred lines of the jump rope.

10. Brian Wood was replaced on the title in January 2015 by female writer G. Willow Wilson, co-creator and writer of the current *Ms. Marvel* series.

Wood's departure may have been influenced by accusations of sexual harassment publicly leveled against him by several female comics professionals (Pantozzi). The series has since been canceled.

11. Notably, while *X-Men* enjoyed a nearly three-year run, another all-female team, *Fearless Defenders*, which had also been launched in 2013, was canceled after just twelve issues. In contrast to *X-Men*, *Fearless Defenders* incorporated female voices and perspectives by showcasing female cosplayers, artists, and crafters in its letter pages; it also featured a new lesbian character as a potential love interest for the female superhero Valkyrie. Although it is possible that *Fearless Defenders* failed because it spotlighted queer characters or because it more overtly solicited female readers, this possibility must be weighed against the title's much less high-profile cast of characters.

12. The company that would become Marvel published the original *Girl Comics* in the 1940s; it was aimed at female readers and featured the superhero Miss America as well as magazine-style content related to beauty, fashion, and dating.

13. To date, there have been no further installments in this romance novel series. The 2015 novel *Black Widow: Forever Red*, by Margaret Stohl, takes a different tack, being marketed as "YA fiction" rather than romance. Set within the Marvel Cinematic Universe, *Forever Red* also has more overt feminist aspirations, centering on the mentor-student relationship between Black Widow and a teenage girl with super abilities. In an interview with EW.com, Stohl said she hoped the novel would inspire girls, including her own daughter, to "speak up and demand more, demand better" (Towers).

14. To illustrate this rarity: a recent (2014) study by children's book publisher Lee and Low found that just 8 percent of the one hundred top grossing US science-fiction and fantasy films had female protagonists, and none of those were women of color (McNally).

WORKS CITED

Acosta, Marta. *The She-Hulk Diaries*. New York: Hyperion, 2013. Print.

Avery-Natale, Edward. "An Analysis of Embodiment Among Six Superheroes in DC Comics." *Social Thought and Research* 32 (2013): 71–106. Print.

Balsamo, Anne. *Technologies of the Gendered Body: Reading Cyborg Women*. Durham, NC: Duke University Press, 1996. Print.

Behm-Morawitz, Elizabeth, and Hillary Pennell. "The Effects of Superhero Sagas on Our Gendered Selves." In *Our Superheroes, Ourselves*. Ed. Robin S. Rosenberg. New York: Oxford University Press, 2013. 73–96. Print.

Boney, Alex. "Flashback: Ms. Marvel: A Binary Life." *Back Issue!* February 2012, 21–33. Print.

Brown, Jeffrey A. *Dangerous Curves: Action Heroines, Gender, Fetishism, and Popular Culture*. Jackson: University Press of Mississippi, 2011. Print.

Bukatman, Scott. *Matters of Gravity: Special Effects and Supermen in the 20th Century*. Durham: Duke University Press, 2003. Print.

Byrne, John, writing and pencils. "The Sensational She-Hulk." Inks by Kim DeMulder. *Marvel Graphic Novel* 1.18 (November 1985). Marvel Comics. Print.

Byrne, John, writing, pencils, and inks. *The Sensational She-Hulk* 1.40 (June 1992). Marvel Comics. Print.

———. *The Sensational She-Hulk* 1.46 (December 1992). Marvel Comics. Print.

Ching, Albert. "Jamie McKelvie Details His Captain Marvel Redesign." *Newsarama*, 22 March 2012. Web. www.newsarama.com/9263-jamie -mckelvie-details-his-captain-marvel-redesign.html.

Chute, Hillary L. *Graphic Women: Life Narrative and Contemporary Comics*. New York: Columbia University Press, 2010. Print.

Claremont, Chris, writer. "The All-New Ms. Marvel." Pencils by Dave Cockrum. Inks by Bob Wiacek. *Ms. Marvel* 1.20 (October 1978). Marvel Comics. Print.

———. "And Grotesk Shall Slay Thee!" *Ms. Marvel* 1.6 (June 1977). Marvel Comics. Print.

———. "Call Me Death-Bird!" Pencils by Keith Pollard. Inks by Joe Sinnott. *Ms. Marvel* 1.9 (September 1977). Marvel Comics. Print.

———. "Death Is the Doomsday Man!" Pencils by Jim Mooney. Inks by Joe Sinnott. *Ms. Marvel* 1.4 (April 1977). Marvel Comics. Print.

———. "The Lady's Not for Killing!" Pencils by John Buscema. Inks by Joe Sinnott. *Ms. Marvel* 1.3 (March 1977). Marvel Comics. Print.

———. "The Last Sunset . . . ?" *Ms. Marvel* 1.8 (August 1977). Marvel Comics. Print.

———. "Nightmare!" *Ms. Marvel* 1.7 (July 1977). Marvel Comics. Print.

Conway, Gerry, writer. "This Woman, This Warrior!" Pencils by John Buscema. Inks by Joe Sinnott. *Ms. Marvel* 1.1 (January 1977). Marvel Comics. Print.

Coover, Coleen, writing, pencils, and inks. "Introduction." *Girl Comics* no. 2 (July 2010). Ed. Jeanine Schaefer. Marvel Comics: [1–2]. Print.

Fite, Linda, writer. "Beware the Claws of the Cat." Pencils by Marie Severin. Inks by Wallace Wood. *Claws of the Cat*, no. 1 (November 1972). Marvel Comics. Print.

Fieffer, Jules. *The Great Comic Book Heroes*. Seattle: Fantagraphics Books, 2003. Print.

Gerding, Stephen. "'Ms. Marvel' Rockets to the #1 Slot on Marvel's Digital Sales Chart." *Comic Book Resources*, 10 February 2014. Web. http://robot6

.comicbookresources.com/2014/02/ms-marvel-rockets-to-the-1-slot-on
-marvels-digital-sales-chart.

Harzewski, Stephanie. *Chick Lit and Postfeminism*. Charlottesville: University
of Virginia Press, 2011. Print.

Hawkeye Initiative. "About THI and FAQ." N.d. Web.
http://thehawkeyeinitiative.com/faq.

Healey, Karen. "When Fangirls Perform: The Gendered Fan Identity in Superhero Comics Fandom." In *The Contemporary Comic Book Superhero*. Ed.
Angela Ndalianis. New York: Routledge, 2009. 144–163. Print.

Heinecken, Dawn. *The Warrior Women of Television: A Feminist Cultural Analysis
of the New Female Body in Popular Media*. New York: Peter Lang, 2003. Print.

Hudson, Laura. "*X-Men* to Relaunch as All-Female Superhero Team." *Wired*, 15
January 2013. Web. www.wired.com/underwire/2013/01/x-men-relaunches
-as-all-female-superhero-team.

Inness, Sherrie A. *Tough Girls: Women Warriors and Wonder Women in Popular
Culture*. Philadelphia: University of Pennsylvania Press, 1999. Print.

Jaffe, Sarah. "The Marvel Q & A: Comics by Women, for Everyone." *Women of
Marvel Magazine*, Spring 2010, 45–50. Print.

Kistler, Alan. "Man of Steel Sequel Writer David S. Goyer Calls Marvel's She-
Hulk 'A Giant Green Porn Star,' Insults Geeks." *The Mary Sue*, 21 May 2014.
Web. www.themarysue.com/david-goyer-calls-she-hulk-sex-fantasy.

MacDonald, Heidi. "DC's Rood Breaks Down Reader Survey." *Publishers Weekly*,
14 February 2012. Web. www.publishersweekly.com/pw/by-topic/industry
-news/comics/article/50633-dc-s-rood-breaks-down-reader-survey.html.

Madrid, Mike. *The Supergirls: Fashion, Feminism, Fantasy, and the History of
Comic Book Heroines*. Minneapolis: Exterminating Angel Press, 2009. Print.

McCaughey, Martha, and Neal King. *Reel Knockouts: Violent Women in the
Movies*. Austin: University of Texas Press, 2001. Print.

McNally, Victoria. "This Chart Graphs Diversity in Science Fiction and Fantasy
Films: Guess How Wide the Gap Is." *The Mary Sue*, 30 July 2014. Web.
www.themarysue.com/diversity-in-scifi-and-fantasy-films.

McRobbie, Angela. "Postfeminism and Popular Culture: Bridget Jones and the
New Gender Regime." In *Interrogating Postfeminism: Gender and the Politics
of Popular Culture*. Eds. Yvonne Tasker and Diane Negra. Durham: Duke
University Press, 2007. 27–39. Print.

Melrose, Kevin. "ComiXology Is Connecting with Female Audience."
Comic Book Resources, 10 October 2013. Web. 8 August 2014. http://robot6
.comicbookresources.com/2013/10/comixology-is-connecting-with
-female-audience.

Murase, Sho. "Elektra and Daredevil." *Girl Comics* no. 3 (September 2010). Ed. Jeanine Schaefer. Marvel Comics: [32] (pinup image). Print.

Negra, Diane. *What a Girl Wants? Fantasizing the Reclamation of Self in Postfeminism.* New York: Routledge, 2009. Print.

Newsarama Staff. "The Full Nielsen: DC's Complete NEW 52 Consumer Survey." *Newsarama*, 12 April 2012. Web. www.newsarama.com/14637-the -full-nielsen-dc-s-complete-new-52-consumer-survey.html.

Nolan, Michelle. *Love on the Racks: A History of American Romance Comics.* Jefferson, NC: McFarland, 2008. Print.

Pantozzi, Jill. "Comic Creator Harassment Claims Met with Response from Alleged Harasser." *The Mary Sue*, 15 November 2013. Web. www.themarysue .com/comic-creator-harassment.

———. "Marvel, This Is When You Send an Artist Back to the Drawing Board." *The Mary Sue*, 19 August 2014. Web. www.themarysue.com/marvel-spider -woman-variant-butt.

Pustz, Matthew. *Comic Book Culture: Fanboys and True Believers.* Jackson: University of Mississippi Press, 1999. Print.

Reid, Calvin. "Marvel, Hyperion Plan Women's Fiction Starring She-Hulk and Rogue." *Publishers Weekly*, 7 February 2013. Web. www.publishersweekly .com/pw/by-topic/industry-news/book-deals/article/55862-marvel-hyperion -plan-women-s-fiction-starring-she-hulk-and-rogue.html.

Richards, Dave. "DeConnick Soars with 'Captain Marvel.'" *Comic Book Resources*, 18 March 2012. Web. www.comicbookresources.com/?page =article&id=37616.

Robbins, Trina. *From Girls to Grrrlz: A History of Women's Comics from Teens to Zines.* San Francisco: Chronicle Books, 1999. Print.

———. *The Great Women Superheroes.* Northampton, UK: Kitchen Sink Press, 1996. Print.

Robinson, Lillian S. *Wonder Women: Feminisms and Superheroes.* New York: Routledge, 2004. Print.

Scott, Suzanne. "Fangirls in Refrigerators: The Politics of (In)visibility in Comic Book Culture." *Transformative Works and Cultures* 13 (2013). Web. http://journal.transformativeworks.org/index.php/twc/article/view/460/384.

Simone, Gail. "Women in Refrigerators." Updated 2000. Web. www.lby3.com /wir.

Slott, Dan, and Ty Templeton, writers. "The Gamma Defense." Pencils by Rick Burchett. Inks by Cliff Rathburn. *She-Hulk* 2.19 (July 2007). Marvel Comics. Print.

Stuller, Jennifer K. "Feminism: Second-Wave Feminism in the Pages of *Lois*

Lane." In *Critical Approaches to Comics: Theories and Methods*. Eds. Matthew J. Smith and Randy Duncan. New York: Routledge, 2012. 235–251. Print.

———. *Ink-Stained Amazons and Cinematic Warriors: Superwomen in Modern Mythology*. New York: I. B. Tauris, 2010. Print.

Takeda, Sana. "Happy Anniversary, She-Hulk!" *Girl Comics* no. 1 (May 2010). Ed. Jeanine Schaefer. Marvel Comics: [24] (pinup image). Print.

Tasker, Yvonne, and Diane Negra. "Introduction: Feminist Politics and Postfeminist Culture." In *Interrogating Postfeminism: Gender and the Politics of Popular Culture*. Eds. Yvonne Tasker and Diane Negra. Durham: Duke University Press, 2007. 1–16. Print.

Taylor, Aaron. "'He's Gotta Be Strong, and He's Gotta Be Fast, and He's Gotta Be Larger Than Life': Investigating the Engendered Superhero Body." *Journal of Popular Culture* 40.2 (2007): 344–360. Print.

Towers, Andrea. "Margaret Stohl Talks *Black Widow: Forever Red*." *Entertainment Weekly*, 28 May 2015. Web. www.ew.com/article/2015/05/26/margaret-stohl -talks-about-black-widow.

Wacker, Stephen. "Introductory Letter." In *Captain Marvel* 7.1 (September 2012). Written by Kelly Sue DeConnick. Pencils and Inks by Dexter Soy. Marvel Comics: [23–24]. Print.

Woodward, Christine. *Rogue Touch*. New York: Hyperion, 2013. Print.

"Share Your Universe"

GENERATION, GENDER, AND THE FUTURE OF MARVEL PUBLISHING

DEREK JOHNSON

In May 2014, rumor held that Marvel Comics would soon cut off its nose to spite its face. As reported on fan sites like *Bleeding Cool* and *Comic Book Resources*, Marvel would soon cease print publication of its *Fantastic Four* titles. Meanwhile, these reports claimed to identify new corporate policies rendering the *X-Men* franchise "no longer the focus of internal promotion," despite titles like *All-New X-Men* and *Uncanny X-Men* being written by star creative talent, including Brian Michael Bendis and other top sellers (Ching "Fantastic Four"; Johnston). Some fans went further, predicting that *X-Men*, too, would be canceled: 20th Century Fox held the film rights to *The Fantastic Four* and *X-Men* through a licensing deal made during Marvel's late 1990s bankruptcy, and few compelling reasons existed for Marvel to continue producing legacy comics that fed external rather than internal film and television projects (the bankruptcy was before the formation of Marvel Studios as an in-house film production arm and the subsequent purchase of Marvel by Disney). Although Marvel owned *The Fantastic Four* and *X-Men* properties, their use by Fox in a crowded blockbuster market posed competition for still unlicensed properties such as *Iron Man, Thor, Captain America*, and *The Avengers* to which Marvel Studios had exclusive claim. The Fox film *X-Men: Days of Future Past* (Bryan Singer, 2014) had brought revenues of $302 million globally during its Memorial Day weekend opening just days before these rumors surfaced (Stewart), offering a tangible example of why Marvel might have become disgusted by its licensing relationship with Fox. Marvel's license fee entitled it to only a small percentage of those revenues, and the success of the film more generally legitimated Fox's continued creative control of Marvel property. Observers speculated that Marvel might lash out at

Fox by marginalizing *The Fantastic Four* and *X-Men* in the comics world in the hope that doing so might bolster the company's creative and promotional emphasis on superheroes that more directly fed Marvel's cinema profits.

Although these rumors may have had some elements of truth in them, it is more likely that they exaggerated or misread Marvel's strategic position. *All-New/Uncanny X-Men* writer Brian Michael Bendis, for one, spoke from within the industry to deny the rumors, characterizing them as "outlandish" claims by "frustrated" fans feeling "persecuted" by Marvel management. Furthermore, as fan sites reporting the rumors acknowledged, the pending "cancellation" of *The Fantastic Four* could ultimately prove to be a mere hiatus prior to one of Marvel's frequent relaunches of popular titles. Canceling a best-seller like *X-Men* would thwart the bottom-line interests of Marvel's publishing division while having a negligible potential impact on Fox, which depends only marginally on the tiny comics market to provide promotional support for its tentpole films (Ching, "Fantastic Four"; Johnston). The point in discussing these far-flung rumors, therefore, is not to validate them or suggest their potential veracity.

The existence of the rumors, however—and the efforts that Bendis and others made to deny their accuracy and assert Marvel's continued publishing interest in *X-Men* and *The Fantastic Four*—does bring into sharp relief the tensions, contradictions, and corporate negotiations currently defining a comics publishing industry embedded in the relations of branded media franchising and conglomeration. On the one hand, Marvel has become fully integrated into a transmedia industrial landscape. Its most profitable and most high-profile projects no longer lie in the world of comic book publishing specifically; instead, Marvel Studios' film productions have become the point of strategic focus. Marvel's relationships with other Disney subsidiaries, such as ABC and Disney XD, have also become more important. On the other hand, Marvel does maintain its publishing interests. The company has not abandoned comic book publishing, even as the market contracts, and the publishing division remains a crucial site of legacy and identity for the company as well as a source of ongoing employment for many managers and creators. At the heart of the "new" Marvel under Disney, therefore, is a dilemma: both a contradiction and a question about the persistence of the old in the face of new opportunities. These fan rumors (however inaccurate)—and the professional denials of them—reflect the uncertainty and anxiety about the future of comic books and the comic book readership amid corporate metamorphosis.

Much scholarship has explored Marvel's transformation in this time of change. Robert Brookey has examined Marvel as a company under transformation as it has expanded from comic books into other markets such as video gaming. In my own work, I have studied the impact of Marvel's transmedia branding strategies on the management of characters across comics and film ("Will the Real Wolverine"), the struggles over identity and meaning that emerge in the use of Marvel properties across different contexts of labor and production ("A Knight"), the changing logics in Marvel's overall franchising outlook ("Franchise"), the stories circulated by Marvel executives to legitimate its attempts to seize control of comic book film production from licensed Hollywood partners ("Cinematic Destiny"), and the persistence of licensed partnerships in Marvel's moves beyond cinema (*Media Franchising*). Outside of Marvel specifically, much of the research on the comic book industry over the past decade has similarly been concerned with this transformation away from traditional print comic book publishing and toward cinema, the digital marketplace, and transmedia efforts. Sam Ford and Henry Jenkins, Kimberly Owczarski, and James Gilmore and Matthias Stork have all considered what happens to comic books in an age of convergence, media multiplicity, franchising, and synergy, producing many insights into the industrial negotiation of transforming comic book cultures. Nevertheless, in attempting to understand a company like Marvel as a film studio, a video game developer, a digital distributor, and more, there remains significant room to consider how the company remains a comic book publisher and how that comic book division negotiates the changing and contradictory priorities, identities, and market emphases that constitute "Marvel" as a company.

To explore these issues, I will examine in this chapter the launch (and eventual failure) of a specific Marvel marketing initiative aimed at recentering the comic book publishing market in this industrial and cultural context. At the heart of this campaign was a concern about generational marketing and the potential—or lack thereof—for comic book reading practices to be passed down to a new generation only familiar with comic superheroes from appearances in other media. Although Marvel's recent film, television, and gaming successes had certainly attracted the attention of children, that visibility had not translated to increased comic book sales (with adults or children), and this failure created a challenge for the very future of the publishing market. Marvel created the 2013 "Share Your Universe" campaign to attract young readers to the comic book publishing market, aiming to enlist adults to secure this new readership. With its core audience growing consistently older, Marvel sought to cultivate a new generation of comic book readers, addressing the existing audience frequently (but not always) as parents who could pass on consumer interests to their children.

Campaigns like "Share Your Universe" suggest a crucial articulation between industrial anxieties about the reproduction of cultural product across media lines and industrial assumptions about children, adults, and social reproduction across generational lines. To more clearly explain the factors at work, I will first analyze the state of the comic book market, both in terms of its overall contraction and aging readership and in comparison to other markets where comic-themed heroes increasingly thrive. Trade reports and other primary documents reveal the generational pressures tied to the industrial processes of transmedia expansion within organizations like Marvel under Disney. Second, I will analyze the "Share Your Universe" campaign, explaining what it was, how it worked in Marvel's promotional spaces, and how it ultimately petered out without much fanfare. Of central concern here will be how older comic book readers were constructed and imagined as variously aged and gendered agents of industrial promotion who would share comic books with a new generation to ensure the continuation of the line. Ultimately, this research offers insight into how a comic book publisher works to stay a comic book publisher in the context of shifting media markets, tastes, and industrial priorities; at the same time, the research emphasizes the combined, intersectional power of gender and generation in imagining that continuity of industrial structure and identity. Marvel's continued investment in its legacy publishing market has depended upon both a calculated intergenerational marketing strategy and the construction of gendered audience identities that both facilitate cultural reproduction and enable claims to authority over it.

GENERATION X

To understand Marvel's transgenerational marketing, we have to first consider its industrial status in a transmediated entertainment economy. Paradoxically, the market for comic book superheroes has grown steadily over the past two decades, thanks to intertextual, promotional, and organizational relationships with the film, television, gaming, and merchandising industries, while the fortunes of the comic book publishing industry itself have remained comparatively meager. According to market data offered by the website *Comichron* and compiled from reports by the distributor Diamond Comics and the trade publication *Internal Correspondence*, the number of comics shipped at wholesale to North American comic book retailers has been in overall decline since the late 1990s. In September 1996, these retailers ordered 11 million comic books from their suppliers. Sales dropped precipitously soon after, hovering around 7 million units per month in September 1998 and reaching a low point of under 5 million in March 2001 (Miller, "Comics Sales to Comics Shops"). *Comichron's* numbers paint a rosier picture in that the number of overall dollars in the market has steadily increased in this time. Although March 2001 would see a low point in retail dollars as well, at under $14 million, the market's value gradually grew from that time forward, with $25 million per month in early 2013 matching the peaks of 1996 and 1997. Moreover, if we look beyond periodical distribution to comic book shops and include newsstands and bookstore sales of trade paperback compilations, we find that the 2013 estimated market of $780 million dwarfs the 1997 market of $300 million to $320 million (Miller, "Comic Book Sales by Year"). The new market of digital distribution adds another estimated $90 million to that overall market (up from $25 million and $70 million in 2011 and 2012, respectively).

Of course, inflation and increasing cover prices skew these increases. Market growth has not been the result of selling more comics so much as the result of selling the same comics repeatedly (re-collected and in new digital formats) and at higher prices. The 1991 debut of *X-Men* no. 1 sold a record 8 million copies; the years since, however, have seen far lower sales ceilings for individual titles. Since 1997, the most orders for a single issue came for *The Amazing Spider-Man* (vol. 3, no. 1), at 532,586 copies in April 2014. Perhaps more tellingly, outside of these debut issues, top-selling comics for any given month frequently sell less than 100,000 copies; in February 2011, the top-selling comic of the month (DC's *Green Lantern* no. 62) sold only 71,517 copies (Miller, "Comics Sales Records"). Compare this to May 2001—the month with the lowest dollar volume ever—where each of the ten top-selling comics still outsold this low point. Although comic book "hits" now reach far fewer initial readers than ever before, this is characteristic of shifts in the culture industries more generally, where logics of market fragmentation and niche marketing make for more choices and smaller audiences for individual products. The difference here is that the two major publishers have not lost their market share to new distribution outlets; instead their overall market has decreased. From a market share of around 25 percent in 1997, Marvel now consistently hovers around 35 to 40 percent, as does its major competitor, DC (Miller, "Market Shares"). By contrast, television networks that have lost the bulk of their market share to new cable channels can still build record-setting viewerships for major events like the Super Bowl. Where the comparison to maturing industries like post-network television might be more apt is in industrial anxieties about continued relevance amid threats from online entertainment experiences. While claims about the death of television have been greatly exaggerated (Lotz), the uncertain imagined future of television extends in part from perceptions that an emerging, digitally savvy generation of young Internet users have waning interest in its old-fashioned broadcast model.

Gloomy economic forecasts in the cultural industries have thus frequently taken on the hue of a generational conflict across different forms of media industry. For Marvel, specifically, comparative success in generating massive hits outside of comic book publishing calls attention to the declines in unit sales and changes in the perceived generational identity of the company's readership. Several industry reports give us a sense of the identities ascribed to comic book readers by companies like Marvel. A 2012 DC Comics report, for example, suggested that readers of its highly promoted New 52 campaign were anything but "new," despite the campaign seeking to attract first-time consumers. Nielsen market research suggested that only 5 percent of readers were completely new to buying comics, with 93 percent of readers being male and only 2 percent being under eighteen years old.

Commenting at the Comics Alliance website, Laura Hudson suggested that these "troubling" findings represented "serious questions about DC's ability to expand their audience base, and the accessibility of their content to both women and younger readers." At stake in her analysis was the very future of the industry: this study, she said, "should worry anyone who cares about the future of superhero comics, and its ability to sustain an audience into the future." Lest we assume that DC faces these challenges alone, other industry reports confirm "panic" about the increasing age of comics readers more broadly (Hauman). Digital distribution offers the possibility of reaching younger readers, and the emergence of applications for online comics, such as ComiXology, suggests some success in that regard. ComiXology reported in 2013 that in addition to its "core customer" group of longtime male comic readers aged twenty-seven to thirty-six, a "new customer is emerging" understood as female, "newer to comics," and aged seventeen to twenty-six. However, while digital distribution seems to have helped slow the aging of the comic book readership, it provides little indication that a critical mass of children aged sixteen and under has yet re-embraced the medium. Despite stereotypes about comics being "for kids," only a very few children participate in the comic book publishing economy.

Yet Marvel's transmedia success affirms the more general appeal of comic book heroes to children in other venues. The most visible evidence of this market is the runaway success of Marvel's films, as produced both by licensed studios and Marvel itself. According to figures compiled at Box Office Mojo that track overall box-office numbers for ongoing film franchises, as of the summer of 2014, approximately a year after the launch of "Share Your Universe," *Spider-Man* and *X-Men* were the seventh- and eleventh-highest-grossing franchises in film history, at $1.580 and $1.297 billion, respectively. These figures put Marvel's licensed comic book characters just below Hollywood heavyweights like *Star Wars*, *Harry Potter*, James Bond, and *The Lord of the Rings*, and above *Pirates of the Caribbean*, *Star Trek*, *Indiana Jones*, *Toy Story*, and *The Hunger Games*. Yet Marvel saw even greater success in its self-produced films, with the *Iron Man*, *Captain America*, *Thor*, and *Avengers* contributions to the "Marvel Cinematic Universe" making it the single highest-grossing franchise in film history, with a recorded domestic box-office gross at that time of $2.621 billion. Only the second-place *Harry Potter* series could boast a higher per film average, at $299 million compared to $291 million ("Franchise Index—Series"). In the tentpole world of blockbuster cinema, Marvel's characters were, if not the biggest, then one of the biggest draws for mass audiences. In total, Box Office Mojo ranked the total Marvel oeuvre (licensed and unlicensed) as the single most successful production brand in the history of Hollywood cinema. These thirty-four films had averaged by that time $190.3 million in domestic box-office gross each, for a total of almost $6.5 billion, significantly ahead of second-place DreamWorks Animation's twenty-nine-film total of just over $4.5 billion total and $159.2 million average. Only fourteen films of fourth-place Pixar had a higher per picture average at that time, at $252.6 million ("Franchise Index—Brands"). Trade reports thus refer to Marvel as "the only live-action brand that matters to most audiences," suggesting that this clout gives the company power in the Disney conglomerate disproportionate to its status as a relatively new acquisition, and that Marvel CEO Isaac Permutter has a strong influence over executive culture and personnel decisions at Disney (Masters). Theatrical exit polling additionally suggests that the success of Marvel's signature tentpole *The*

Avengers (Joss Whedon 2012) "played evenly across all demographics," inclusive of families with children. This audience was estimated to be 40 percent female ("surprisingly," to some analysts). Moviegoers under the age of twenty-five made up 50 percent of the audience, and 24 percent of the audience came with their families (Pereira).

Yet against these all-inclusive box-office numbers, the greatest evidence of a disconnect between transmedia success with children and a culture of comic readership can be seen in smaller niche markets such as cable television, console video games, and toy merchandising. One of the major rationales for Disney acquiring Marvel came from the potential for superhero properties to appeal to young male television viewers; having already succeeded in securing a young female viewership on The Disney Channel, the company could rely on Marvel as a way of serving a specialized boys market in the new channel space of Disney XD (launched in 2009, just months before the purchase of Marvel). By 2014, Marvel Television productions served as a staple of the cable channel: the new *Avengers Assemble* series averaged 699,000 total viewers, making it the top-ranked animated series in the Disney XD lineup, with *Hulk and the Agents of S.M.A.S.H.* bringing in another 480,000 (Hutchins). Of course, many of those viewers could be adult fans of the Avengers franchise—but even discounting adult viewers, the *Assemble* series remained the top-ranked animated series in the Boys 6–14 demographic, as well as the second highest in the Boys 2–11 demographic (Disney XD's stated target market in press releases is an audience of Boys 6–11) (Kondolojy). In 2013, Marvel's *Ultimate Spider-Man* sat in a similar position as the top animated performer in the target demographics of Boys 2–11 (197,000 viewers), Boys 6–11 (138,000), and the gender-inclusive Kids 2–11 (265,000) ("Avengers & Hulk"). In this boy-targeted niche, therefore, Marvel has proven itself a consistent television draw, but it lacks similar appeal in the publishing market.

Although Marvel's successes with mass audiences and child niches in video games are less dramatic compared to film and television, here, too, we can see a disconnect with the flatter children's market for superhero comics. In 2013, the most visible Marvel game title was the co-branded *LEGO Marvel Super Heroes*, which was released across all major consoles and several mobile and PC gaming platforms. The game was not among the best-selling titles of the year, but the pre-order campaign in the United States, coordinated with Wal-Mart, spoke to Marvel's status as a game tentpole worthy of being heavily promoted on the physical and virtual shelves of "the biggest retailer in the world" (Berfield). Wal-Mart anticipated sales great enough to justify paying LEGO and Marvel for exclusive rights to sell an "Iron Patriot" LEGO minifigure unavailable anywhere else in a campaign to provide an added incentive for pre-order consumers to buy from Wal-Mart and ignore other mass market retailers such as Target, Gamestop, and Amazon. Here, too, we can expect the actual consumer base to have been a mix of children and adult fans, who might have been equally drawn to the exclusive, collectible giveaway. Still, the game's content rating of E-10 ("for everyone" over ten years old) by the Entertainment Software Rating Board suggests that the designers and marketers behind the game perceived its market as being far younger than that of the M (mature) and A (adult) games that dominate software sales—half of the top ten best-selling 2013 games in the United States carried an M or A rating (*Grand Theft Auto V, Call of Duty: Ghosts, Battlefield 4, Assassin's Creed IV, Call of Duty: Black Ops*) (Crossley). One could therefore wonder whether Marvel actually offers a more powerful draw for kids in a video game market geared toward older consumers than it does in a comic book market that similarly skews much older.

In 2014, Marvel also played a new role in the ongoing marketing and production of the tenth game on the 2013 best-sellers list: *Disney Infinity*. An action-adventure sandbox experience, the game is unique both for giving players the opportunity to mix characters from across the Disney house of brands (playing *Fantasia*'s Sorcerer Mickey alongside *Toy Story*'s Buzz Lightyear and *Frozen*'s Elsa, for example) and for supporting future purchases beyond the software itself: players can add new elements to the game by purchasing related toy figures. These add-ons bring the potential to play as (or with) Disney princesses, but at the same time the default characters packaged with the core game (male heroes like *Pirates of the Caribbean*'s Captain Jack Sparrow, *Monsters Inc.*'s Sulley, and *The Incredibles*' Mr. Incredible) situated the game alongside Disney XD as part of Disney's targeted outreach to boys. With the game's sequel figured as *Disney Infinity 2.0: Marvel Super Heroes*, the E-10 title's continued development hinged upon the Marvel characters dominating blockbuster film and niche boys' television. This endeavor marked a significant vote of confidence in the potential for Marvel properties to attract the attention of boys in the video game market. Until 2016, the Disney Interactive division focused "all of its efforts" on the *Disney Infinity* platform, framing Marvel's ongoing film and television appeal as a way to "[keep] things fresh" in the E-10 video game market (Gaudiosi).

——

In their emphasis on material playthings, both of these video games call additional attention to Marvel's standing in the toy merchandising market. Outside of Disney-conglomerate relations proper, Marvel has licensed its property to several toy manufacturers that find consistent success in connecting superhero product with children. Marvel licenses Hasbro to handle action-figure lines based on its characters. Although some of these products clearly appeal to adult collectors as well, lines such as Marvel Legends, offering super-articulated action figures in the $15 to $22 range, have stagnated and suffered "brand fatigue," leading retailers to refuse to offer sufficient support ("Toy Fair 2014"). By contrast, the more basic toy lines aimed at boys continue to perform quite well for Hasbro: alongside brands like Transformers, the trade journal *Kidscreen* credits Marvel product with driving a 32 percent year-to-year increase in second-quarter 2014 revenue for Hasbro in its "boys category" US market (Fisher). In addition to its co-branding arrangement with Marvel in the video game market, the LEGO Group has licensed the right to produce construction toys from Marvel superhero properties since 2012. "Super Heroes" are just one "theme" of construction play among many marketed by LEGO, but at the 2014 London Toy Fair, LEGO representatives named it as an "evergreen" line, suggesting that it will remain as integral to LEGO's future marketing strategy as its best-selling City or Star Wars themes (and thereby unlikely to experience production hiatuses in the way that the Castle and Pirates lines have) ("London Toy Fair Report"). These toy merchandisers' attempts to connect product with children increasingly revolve around characters borrowed from Marvel.

Marvel properties have proven to have greater potential for transgenerational marketing in film, television, video games, and toy merchandising than in the legacy market of comic book publishing. The impact of this appeal on the day-to-day world of comic book publishing itself is unclear, however. Responding to the rumors of the pending cancellation of *The Fantastic Four* and *X-Men*, Marvel editor in chief Axel Alonso argues, "whether we own the media rights to a character informs so little of what we do in editorial. Our job—my job—is to tell stories that sell comics. And we want all our comics to sell. . . . It's important that we maintain and grow the popularity of characters that are already popular, and that we elevate characters we want to make popular—like Guardians of the Galaxy, Ant-Man, Inhumans and Doctor Strange" (Ching, "Axel-in-Charge"). As much as he allows for the possibility of strategically elevating comic books with upcoming films, Alonso positions the work and culture of publishing as separate from Marvel's other media markets. Yet in wanting to "sell comics," Marvel's publishing branch must necessarily confront the challenges of the future: the aging market for comic book readers, the lack of young readers waiting in the wings, and the frustration of seeing other divisions within Marvel thrive in appeals to a new generation. It is in this contradictory context that we might situate Marvel's promotional initiatives in publishing as an attempt to manage the generational tensions underlying an industrial success story.

THE INITIATIVE

Over the past fifteen years, the comic book industry has taken steps to try to proactively regenerate younger readership. Since 2002, retailers, distributors, and publishers have supported an annual Free Comic Book Day designed to expose new readers to comic books, typically timed with the release of a blockbuster superhero film to maximize potential awareness. Although the event does encourage former comic book readers to return to specialty shops to sample the free titles on offer (often special editions highlighting the properties that publishers most want to promote), the official Free Comic Book Day website suggests a specific interest in improving the appeal of comic books to children. In the summer of 2014, the site featured a number of images of customers participating in the event at shops around the United States, thanking customers for their participation. Of fifteen photos immediately visible, at least ten were of children (both boys and girls and even babies) who were dressed up in superhero costumes and proudly displaying their comic book hauls ("Free Comic Book Day").

As a visual representation of organizers' priorities and desired perceptions of the event, these images suggested that the event's "success" rested in reaching children. At the same time, however, images of children with their parents—or rather, more exclusively, their fathers—showed that the organizers figured the event as an opportunity for transgenerational marketing, a day on which fathers specifically might bring their children into the space of the comic book shop to help introduce a new generation to the medium. Recent attempts by conference organizers to hold "Kids Days" at major sites of industry-reader interface—such as New York's Comic Con, Wizard World, Chicago Comics, and Entertainment Expo (and many more)—suggest a similarly concerted attempt by the industry to improve appeals to children. Tellingly, the need for specific Kids Days suggests that comic conventions are not regularly sites made friendly to children on other days, and that being inclusive of younger audiences requires special promotional efforts.

In 2013, Marvel launched its own internal publishing campaign within this context. Announced via publicity releases and a conference call to the entertainment press on July 9, the new "Share Your Universe" strategy was promised as a way of more effectively leveraging Marvel's success in children's cable television as an asset for the publishing division. This feat would be accomplished through transgenerational marketing, whereby Marvel's existing adult readers would usher young television viewers into the publishing market. The announcement on Marvel's website described "Share Your Universe" as "a landmark new initiative encouraging fans to share their favorite Super Heroes with the next generation who will make theirs Marvel. . . . [T]here's never been a better time for parents—or anyone with young fans in their lives—to pass on the timeless lessons of power, responsibility and heroism to a new generation" ("Marvel: Share Your Universe"). The strategy hinged on the idea of older fans extending superhero print culture to the children in their lives, which implied that fans had stewardship of an inheritance and the responsibility to "pass on" comic reading practices.

This transgenerational transfer further centered on the transmedia relationships in which Marvel's superhero properties circulated. As understood by one writer in the comics press, the campaign was "designed as a bridge between the animated programming available on Disney XD and all-ages comics." Although this bridge could support two-way traffic, Marvel's aim seemed to be encouraging more traffic from animated cable television in the direction of comics: "At heart, it serves as a way for parents and older readers to share their love of Marvel Comics and their characters with younger generations through modern platforms" (Montgomery). As another member of the press understood it, "this program is meant to turn fans of that material back to the comics from which all those ideas spring" (Phegley). In a show of solidarity and interest in the legacy of the Marvel organization, Vice President of Television Animation Jeph Loeb stated: "We want everyone to realize that it all starts with publishing. It all starts with comic books" (Montgomery). The growth of the television division was certainly outpacing that of comic publishing, and the new campaign aimed to publicly re-center comics as the linchpin of overall corporate strategy.

In this reframing, Marvel acknowledged the challenges involved in connecting children with comic books specifically. As publisher and president of the company's print, animation, and digital divisions, Dan Buckley explained to the press that "sometimes it's hard for us to refer a younger kid to content in the Marvel Universe easily, because our comics have grown up" (Ching, "Marvel Reveals"). Marvel admitted that the need for the campaign was based on barriers to entry for children, given the company's (and more broadly, the industry's) long-standing focus on adult readers. Claiming knowledge about children's tastes and reading strategies from focus group testing, moreover, Buckley told the press that the campaign would need to negotiate the greater difficulty children supposedly face in parsing multiple interpretations of a single superhero across different comic titles, films, and television series. When character models did not match, Buckley reported, children began to ask, "Which Spider-Man is the real one?" (Montgomery). The "Share Your Universe" campaign meant to mitigate that perceived challenge by coordinating appeals across media in a more strategic way, using greater visual consistency to dissolve existing barriers to transmedia and transgenerational comic book consumption.

It was far easier to state these goals than to accomplish them, however; many entertainment journalists expressed concern about the implications for existing markets and the feasibility of building bridges across market and age gaps. For commentators at *iFanboy*, the campaign prompted concerns about whether a "house style" that unified different creators' takes on a character across various comic and television projects would produce excessive homogenization (Montgomery). Unstated here seemed to be a concern about kid appeals overtaking the interests of an older fanbase. *Hollywood Reporter* also took a skeptical tone, calling the viability of the campaign into question: "Sure, the entire world has become overrun by superhero culture . . . but that doesn't mean that it's been easy to get kids into reading about their favorite fictional heroes on a regular basis." Acknowledging that Marvel hoped to get "new readers into the habit of supporting what used to be the company's core product," this analysis predicted a need for new kinds of product more suitable for six- to ten-year-olds, which should be "clearly marked and marketed as such to make it easier for parents to know what their kids are reading." The trade journal concluded on a less than confident note: "The question is, will any of this make the kids any more eager to actually read the comics . . . ?" (McMillan). Playing into assumptions about both the hostility of contemporary children to reading and the perception of comics as a fading industry, *Hollywood Reporter* suggested that "Share Your Universe" faced an uphill generational battle.

With its work cut out for it, Marvel began using the specific components of the new campaign to create opportunities for cross-promotion, and, more crucially, to hail the adult comic book fan as an integral participant and partner in the project of recruiting children to comics readership. At its launch in July, "Share Your Universe" was supported with free print samplers distributed to comic book shops that existing customers could acquire and pass on to other, younger readers. The Marvel comics mobile app offered digital giveaways of all-ages comics to reach readers without access or interest in comic shop patronage. A new Marvel Kids website, branded with the "Share Your Universe" imprint, simultaneously drew linkages between different platforms in Marvel's superhero empire. This site featured four clearly labeled menus for "shows," "games," "comics," and "activities," inviting users to toggle between these different modes of engagement with Marvel properties. While the simple puzzles, mazes, coloring tasks, and other interactive experiences offered as activities seemed designated for use by children in particular, these were matched by parallel call-outs that hailed adults as important participants in transgenerational interactivity with comics. "Marvel is YOUR Universe. Now, make it THEIRS," the site commanded. "This is the place to get the latest information on family-friendly Marvel comics, movies and TV series to help you share your passion for Marvel characters and stories with the next generation of fans" ("Share Your Universe" *Marvel Kids*). The idea of this space as a bridging point was driven home by the "Share Your Universe" logo and key art, which featured on the left side a lineup of superheroes drawn in comic book styles evocative of the 1980s, and on the right side mirror renderings of the same superheroes in the style of Disney XD animation.

Outside of kid-specific web spaces, "Share Your Universe" also became a tag in the online catalogs of comics on Marvel.com, identifying almost twenty different first-issue offerings that would give younger readers pleasurable entry into Marvel publications ("Share Your Universe!"). This tag thus offered a guideline to inform and encourage adult readers' purchases on behalf of children. Along with putting all this energy into bringing children to comics from television, the campaign also worked to encourage television viewing of Marvel shows in the first place, offering basic promotion of the company's television series on Disney XD. For the first week of the campaign, Xbox Live and Windows 8 users could access free episodes online. These attempts at cross-promotion came together in the space of the campaign's Facebook page, where from July to November users could get regular updates, suggestions, and strategies for bridging the divide between television and comics, childhood and adulthood ("Share Your Universe" *Facebook*). The Facebook page proved to be the most dynamic component of the campaign, as it continually reminded viewers of upcoming episodes on Disney XD, encouraged viewers to "check in" with GetGlue to earn virtual reward stickers, and prompted fans to transition their viewing into comics reading experiences. In the first week of the campaign, for example, the Facebook feed inquired, "How often do you visit your local comic book store with your kids?" Adult fans were thus urged to attest to their dedication to transgenerational transmission, and perhaps to feel guilty for not pursuing that responsibility with more frequency.

Beyond comic shops and web spaces, the "Share Your Universe" campaign extended into public events like comic book conventions. At the San Diego Comic-Con just days after launch, for example, Marvel held a costume contest in conjunction with the campaign, calling attention to and rewarding child engagement with its characters (the event was both announced and then reported upon in the Facebook feed). Yet these opportunities for public outreach to children maintained an emphasis on transgenerational marketing and the role that adult fans might play as intermediaries between children and Marvel. At New York Comic-Con in October, Marvel held a contest to "Be the Face of Share Your Universe," framed as a search for the perfect transgenerational evangelist: "Are you the ultimate Marvel fan? Do you share the Marvel Universe with your friends and family? And do you want to bring the world of Marvel to the next generation?" ("NYCC 2013"). Although the campaign focused on children, the face of that campaign was to be the adult who could best help Marvel reach that younger audience. Video entries recorded in a special booth at the convention could "include children with parental permission," but the rules explicitly called for a winner over the age of eighteen who could be envisioned as a fan spokesperson for Marvel in future promotional videos.

Altogether, these components demonstrate an attempt not just to achieve cross-promotion, but also to strike a specific set of generational relationships surrounding superhero-themed transmedia culture. Moreover, as idealized in industrial discourse, these generational relationships took shape in relation to invocations of family that often—but not always—hinged on gendered assumptions about comic reading as a masculinized experience to be passed down from fathers to sons. First and most generally, Marvel engaged in a very concerted effort to frame the "share" of this campaign as a family experience. Regardless of the exact cross-promotional strategy and invitation to interactivity in the Facebook feed, invocations of family were ever-present: "Will you and your family be attending NYCC Kids at New York Comic-Con on Sunday?"; "Celebrate Halloween early with your family by checking out this special episode on October 5!"; "Where would your family like to go on vacation: Asgard, Stark Tower, or somewhere else?"; "Help Captain America defeat the Red Skull with your family in this online game!"; "Hawkeye is super skilled in archery, but what does the young Marvelite in your family have a super skill in?"; "Take a family trip to your local comic book store and pick up the latest issue of Marvel Universe Ultimate Spider-Man (2012) #17, out tomorrow!" ("Share Your Universe" *Facebook*). Diminutive mentions of the "youngest Marvelites" sometimes offered a less limited imagination of this transgenerational relationship, where "you and your little Thor fans" could allow for a broader range of adult-child relationships. But far more frequently, Marvel framed "Share Your Universe" as a consumer relationship occurring within a family unit.

Within that family narrative, Marvel concretely framed the transgenerational sharing of comic books as a gender-inclusive activity. To Marvel's credit, it overtly presented "Share Your Universe" as a way of inviting young girls into comic reading culture as well. Managed statements about the campaign's goals deployed gender-equal language that made this desire for inclusiveness clear: as Buckley, publisher and president, sold it, "every Marvel fan has a unique story for how these heroes, their stories and the experience of entering the Marvel Universe helped shape their childhood—and we want to make it easy to continue that tradition with your kids, nieces, nephews, and loved ones" ("Marvel: Share Your Universe"). In this initial press conference, shrewd Marvel representatives also identified as the campaign's inspiration four-year-old girl Mia Grace, who had gained some notoriety that spring on YouTube and *Jimmy Kimmel* for her vast knowledge of Marvel trivia (Phegley; Ching, "Marvel Reveals"). In doing so, Marvel deflected accusations that it sought to extend a comic book boys' club to a new generation, recognizing that its future rested in the hope of broader appeal. Through the execution of the campaign, moreover, Marvel took advantage of opportunities to model young girls as its new generation. From the San Diego Comic-Con costume contest, for example, the "Share Your Universe" Facebook page presented the image of a young girl participating with the caption: "What do you think of this little Captain America?" ("Share Your Universe" *Facebook*). Other group photos of cosplayers from conventions similarly highlighted young girl fans. The "Share Your Universe" campaign thus imagined its transgenerational family relationships as ones that crossed gender lines.

Nevertheless, slippages in promotional discourse and marketing logics contradictorily privileged the role of an idealized father in building this bridge to the next generation. It may not be surprising, given the disproportionate number of men working in management positions at Marvel, that company representatives speaking at the initial press announcement framed the initiative specifically around father-son relationships when invoking their personal histories and identities to sell the concept. Despite Buckley's strategic gender inclusiveness, other personal narratives reframed the transgenerational dynamic as fatherly. Chief Creative Officer Joe Quesada explained in the press conference that for him "it gets down to the core of what it was that got me into the Marvel Universe at first. It brings back memories of my dad buying me my first comics. It was just that sharing experience where one person leads to another to another" (Ching, "Marvel Reveals"). Quesada leaves open the possibility that this "one person" behind the sharing need not be a father, but this notion of the Marvel fan passing on a comic book inheritance becomes tangible through fatherhood imagery. Vice President of Television Animation Jeph Loeb reinforced that imagery by imagining the generational exchanges of "Share Your Universe" to occur between men and their male offspring, where "the interpersonal stuff of whether you're a father or a son and wanting to talk about this stuff is amazing" (Phegley).

This tendency to frame the adult fan responsible for Marvel's generational transfer as a father continued in the execution of the campaign. In addition to sharing Marvel's promotional messages about television airdates and comic book availability, for example, the Facebook feed linked to episode reviews that came "straight from a Marvel Dad" ("Share Your Universe" *Facebook*). To be clear, Marvel did not imagine the adult "Sharer" in exclusive terms of fatherhood, and more often than not succeeded in strategically framing "Your Universe" as something to be shared with both boys and girls in the imagined family. However, in laying out a number of different idealized fan subject positions throughout the campaign—the family, the Youngest Marvelites, and the Marvel Dad—the potential for a Marvel Mom remained unexplored. The idea of a mother passing "her universe" on to her sons and daughters rarely, if ever, seemed to surface, suggesting that while the inheritors of the Marvel Universe might be of any gender, that inheritance was imagined as the gift of a father.

A major exception to this imagination of sharer-as-father came in the announcement of the winner of the New York Comic-Con "Be the Face of Share Your Universe" contest. Over six months after the convention, a May 2014 blog post appeared on the Marvel website declaring Constance Katsafanas, a thirty-one-year-old woman studying neurology, and Marvel fan for twenty-five years, as the ideal embodiment of the "Share Your Universe" principle. Describing her lifelong relationship with Marvel, Katsafanas said: "I didn't like to read. So my grandmother, in her infinite wisdom, when I was six years old, bought me an X-Men comic book from one of those spinner racks in the gas station. That was it. I was completely hooked" (Stevens). Her story contrasted with Marvel's more masculinized rhetoric about transgenerational inheritances, locating the origins of her fandom in the cultural intervention of a grandmother rather than of a father, uncle, or even another beneficent individual of indeterminate gender. As the new face of the campaign, Katsafanas also contradicted its single-minded focus on sharing the Marvel Universe within the context of "family." Katsafanas described her experiences as a Marvel sharer as occurring in the context of friendships rather than familial relationships: "[My] friends have young children—which is bizarre, that I'm at the point of my life where my friends have kids—and I get to share [comics] with them," she said. This statement disarticulated Katsafanas from the family world of childrearing to which Marvel had previously hitched its campaign. The emphasis on her professional life in residency further differentiated her from the parental role—she played more of the role of a parent's cool friend, perhaps. When Marvel quoted her as saying, "My husband says that I am like a little kid whenever I talk to him about this," Katsafanas could be imagined to be more in touch with the young Marvelite than she was with the adult parent otherwise so frequently emphasized in the campaign.

Marvel's selection of Katsafanas was both surprising and refreshing. Although there is little evidence that Marvel was interested in imagining mothers as responsible for cultural transmission to the next generation beyond the grandmother figure she invoked, her story worked to de-articulate the "Share Your Universe" campaign from normative ideas about transgenerational inheritance of comic book culture via masculine authority over Marvel and traditional notions of family reproduction. What may be even more radical, however, would be to imagine those transgenerational relationships as lying outside of reproductive familial relationships (perhaps revealing new ways for Marvel's invocation of "family" to be understood). It is with much irony, then, that the selection of Katsafanas as the face of the campaign occurred after the campaign became essentially defunct. As of November 2013, the "Share Your Universe" Facebook feed ceased its regular updates, and no further announcements or related news stories on Marvel.com preceded the reveal of Katsafanas. In the campaign's initial announcement, publisher Dan Buckley had claimed that the "success" of "Share Your Universe" would be measured by "the general response we get on the Internet, Facebook likes, people engaging with us in general, how they actively respond to this activity at the various cons that we go to with this initiative" (Ching, "Marvel Reveals"). Having retreated from spaces like Facebook, and not announcing the results of a convention activity until some sixth months later, Marvel's overall pursuit of the strategy had met with failure by its own definition. At best, Katsafanas may have represented a strategic rethinking of the initiative prior to a relaunch under a different set of principles, goals, and tactics. As of this writing, however, Katsafanas had only been strangely revealed as the face of a campaign that was apparently no longer operational. Although winning meant "the opportunity" to record six promotional videos to be featured on Marvel.com ("NYCC 2013"), there is no guarantee that any strategy remains to support those videos (if and when they are ever made public).

These contradictions and apparent failures can offer us important insights about Marvel and "Share Your Universe." In trying to concretize a transgenerational transmedia marketing strategy, Marvel identified a core audience of adult fans and worked throughout the campaign to provide a set of generational and familial identities for those fans to inhabit. As Buckley put it, the initiative was meant "to do something that was very unique and took advantage of the very unique network of fans we have through social media and through comic shops." For all of its slippages in privileging a core fandom based in familial relationships, reproduction, and fatherhood, while at the same time allowing for the (belated) possibility of single female professionals as ideal transgenerational spokespeople, the "Share Your Universe" campaign was, significantly, a site of shifting industrial tactics and discourses by which Marvel ascribed meaning and power to its audience. This meaning and power, moreover, centered on the company's struggle to construct bridges not just between adults and children, but also between its different corporate divisions. The oscillation in the campaign between a tactical drift toward fatherly relationships and a strategic commitment to exploring a wider range of possible transgenerational engagements with comic books reflected the company's overall dilemma of trying to hold on to the old and the new. On the one hand, "Share Your Universe" represented recognition that building a new generation of comic book readers might mean expanding appeals beyond boys and men. On the other, the contradictions and ultimate failures of the campaign suggested resistances to such shifts.

Greater gender inclusivity may be the way forward for comic books, but when that medium is promotionally linked to a realm of cable television focused exclusively on boys, the potential for change is limited. When asked if the "Share Your Universe" campaign would be used to justify greater promotion of female characters and outreach to female fans, Vice President of Animation Development and Production Cort Lane replied with a comment about how the appeal of "strong female lead[s]" like Black Widow and She-Hulk to boys would indeed enable that kind of outreach to occur in the future (Phegley; Ching, "Marvel Reveals"). Here, gender inclusiveness becomes practical only because of its compatibility with a focus on boys. In that context, it seems like the imagination of Marvel Comics as a transgenerational practice of exchange will continue to depend on the logic of gender in addition to that of age, regardless of the degree to which more radical imaginations of the audience might better serve the needs of a single division of the company.

CONCLUSION

Although it appears that "Share Your Universe" has reached an end—or at least a phase of significant reconsideration—Marvel will likely continue to pursue some set of strategies for both constructing a new generation of comic book readers and imagining transgenerational roles for audiences to play in helping to realize that corporate goal. In that process, rumors and speculation will continue to abound about how Marvel will sustain its print-based legacy and its older audiences as it moves forward into newer media sectors.

In this chapter I have therefore considered transmedia strategies in relation to transgenerational audience appeals, focusing on how Marvel has imagined its ideal core audience while laying out identities for them to take up in relation to the next generation. From the Marvel family to the young Marvelite and the Marvel Dad, and only later the single female professional outside of these filial relationships, the "Share Your Universe" campaign gave Marvel a way to conceive their construction of a transmedia audience in transgenerational terms. This promotional effort constantly negotiated the intersections between age and gender that came along with notions of how culture is passed down from generation to generation. Much of my analysis depends upon a political economic assessment of the relationships between the different Marvel divisions invested in markets of unequal value. Nevertheless, this exploration of transgenerational transmedia marketing gives us valuable insight into a culture of production in which Marvel and perhaps other media industries and companies construct meaningful audience subject positions that offer popular participatory roles in the transmission and inheritance of popular media.

At its core, this project may also be most about ownership of the Marvel Universe. The command "Share Your Universe" depends on understanding who has claim on it. Within Marvel itself, the initiative grew from industrial tensions and anxieties over where the center of the superhero universe might rest—within emergent markets like film, television, and new media, or in the legacy market of print? And as the campaign reached out to potential audiences, the construction of ideal Marvel families, fathers, and friends offered claims about who might have power (and with it, great responsibility) over that world to pass it on through time.

From this perspective, we might productively return to the rumors of Marvel's potential cancellation of fans' favorite titles amid its increasingly transmediated corporate outlook. Marvel management reads some of its fan base as having a "persecution" complex, and much additional discourse exists to similarly construct the existing comic book readership as one threatened by change, especially insofar as the privilege of white, male, heterosexual masculinity in comic book culture is concerned. In 2011, Marvel faced significant negative reaction when killing off white hero Peter Parker in the *Ultimate* comic book line to pass on the Spider-Man mantle to newcomer Miles Morales, a new mixed-race African American and Latino character. As fed by conservative pundits like Glenn Beck and Lou Dobbs, this response claimed that Marvel had violated the racial essence of Spider-Man in favor of kowtowing to political correctness; other news outlets took this resistance to representational diversity as an opportunity to explore the anxious soul of the comic book reader (Hartmann, Macnicol, Petri).

No fan response is univocal, and many readers embraced Miles Morales—but this narrative resurfaced. Many fans called foul again in 2014 when Marvel announced plans to make a new female version of the Thor character and relaunch the *Captain America* comic book with African American character Sam Wilson in the title role (Tracey). Similar unrest followed announcements that the 2015 *Fantastic Four* film would star African American actor Michael B. Jordan in the role of otherwise assumedly white hero Johnny Storm (Zakarin). Add to this a critical mass of popular reporting and criticism on issues such as the harassment of female cosplayers at comic book conventions (Zara, Cohen), and more broadly the desire of privileged white male fans to police the legitimacy of women who participated in that fandom (from comic books to #gamergate in video games), and it is easy to see how Marvel might imagine its existing market core of male readers as a double-edged sword: ideally intense in its fandom, but potentially volatile in response to strategies meant to generate new markets and greater inclusivity of other readers. In this light, "Share Your Universe" worked to manage the threat of change by positioning the existing readership as an ally in the project of seeking out new readers. Rather than be threatened by the terms of a more inclusive future, readers were invited to become the indispensable agents by which that new generation would be produced.

WORKS CITED

"Avengers & Hulk Animated Series Get Premiere Dates." *Marvel*, 8 March 2013. Web. http://marvel.com/news/tv/2013/3/8/20256/avengers_hulk_animated _series_get_premiere_dates.

Bendis, Brian Michael. "Bendis!" *Tumblr*, 24 June 2014. Web. http:// brianmichaelbendis.tumblr.com/post/89801714582/outside-of-the-cbr -rumor-ive-been-hearing-quite-a-bit.

Berfield, Susan. "Where Wal-mart Isn't: Four Countries the Retailer Can't Conquer." *Business Week*, 10 October 2013. Web. www.businessweek.com /articles/2013-10-10/where-walmart-isnt-four-countries-the-retailer-cant -conquer.

Brookey, Robert Alan. *Hollywood Gamers: Digital Convergence in the Film and Video Game Industries.* Bloomington: Indiana University Press, 2010. Print.

Ching, Albert. "Axel-in-Charge: In-Depth on 'Avengers NOW!' and New Takes on Captain America, Thor, and Iron Man." *Comic Book Resources*, 18 July 2014. Web. www.comicbookresources.com/?page=article&id=54183.

———. "'Fantastic Four' May Live On-Screen, Disappear from Comics." *Comic Book Resources*, 30 May 2014. Web. www.comicbookresources.com/?page =article&id=53158.

———. "Marvel Reveals SHARE YOUR UNIVERSE." *Newsarama*, 9 July 2013. Web. www.newsarama.com/18305-marvel-reveals-share-your-universe -live.html.

Cohen, Sandy. "Sexual Harassment at Comic-Con Leads to Call for New Cosplay Policy." *Huffington Post*, 28 July 2014. Web. www.huffingtonpost .com/2014/07/27/sexual-harassment-at-comic-con_n_5625686.html.

Crossley, Rob. "NPD: Best-selling US Games of 2013 Revealed." *Computer and Video Games*, 17 January 2014. Web. www.computerandvideogames.com /445780/npd-best-selling-us-games-of-2013-revealed.

Fisher, Daniela. "Action Toys Transform Hasbro's Second Quarter." *Kidscreen*, 21 July 2014. Web. http://kidscreen.com/2014/07/21/action-toys-transform -hasbros-second-quarter/?utm_source=newsletter&utm_medium =email&utm_campaign=action-toys-transform-hasbros-second -quarter&_u=238834.

Ford, Sam, and Henry Jenkins. "Managing Multiplicity in Superhero Comics: An Interview with Henry Jenkins." In *Third Person: Authoring and Exploring Vast Narratives*. Eds. Pat Harrigan and Noah Waldrip-Fruin. Cambridge, MA: MIT Press, 2009. 303–312. Print.

"Franchise Index—Brands." *Box Office Mojo*, n.d. Web. www.boxofficemojo .com/franchises/?view=Brand&sort=sumgross&order=DESC&p=.htm.

"Franchise Index—Series." *Box Office Mojo*, n.d. Web. www.boxofficemojo.com /franchises/?view=Franchise&sort=sumgross&order=DESC&p=.htm.

"Free Comic Book Day." *Free Comic Book Day*, n.d. Web. www.freecomicbookday.com/Home/1/1/27/992.

Gaudiosi, John. "Disney Powers New Infinity Game with Marvel Super Heroes." *Fortune*, 24 June 2014. Web. http://fortune.com/2014/06/24/disney -infinity-marvel-super-heroes.

Gilmore, James N., and Matthias Stork, eds. *Super Hero Synergies: Comic Book Characters Go Digital*. New York: Rowman and Littlefield, 2014. Print.

Hartmann, Margaret. "Glenn Beck Thinks Michelle Obama's Behind the New Biracial, 'Gay' Spider-man." *Jezebel*, 4 August 2011. Web. http://jezebel.com /5827942/glenn-beck-thinks-michelle-obamas-behind-the-new-biracial -gay-spider-man.

Hauman, Glenn. "Yet Another Reason for Comics to Go Digital: 40 Is the New 15." *Comic Mix*, 8 June 2011. Web. www.comicmix.com/2011/06/08/yet -another-reason-for-comics-to-go-digital-40-is-the-new-15.

Hudson, Laura. "DC Comics Survey Reports 'New 52' Readership 93% Male,

Only 5% New Readers." *Comics Alliance*, 10 February 2012. Web. http://mediadecoder.blogs.nytimes.com/2012/05/03/nielsen-reports-a-decline-in-television-viewing.

Hutchins, Aaron. "The Avengers and Hulk Smash into Second Seasons on Disney XD." *Kidscreen*, 28 July 2014. Web. http://kidscreen.com/2014/07/28/the-avengers-and-hulk-smash-into-second-seasons-on-disney-xd/?utm_source=newsletter&utm_medium=email&utm_campaign=the-avengers-and-hulk-smash-into-second-seasons-on-disney-xd&_u=238834.

Johnson, Derek. "Cinematic Destiny: Marvel Studios and the Trade Stories of Industrial Convergence." *Cinema Journal* 52.1 (2012): 1–24. Print.

———. "Franchise Histories: Marvel, X-Men, and the Negotiated Process of Expansion." In *Convergence Media History*. Eds. Janet Staiger and Sabine Hake. London: Routledge, 2009. 14–23. Print.

———. "A Knight of the Realm vs. The Master of Magnetism: Sexuality, Stardom, and Character Branding." *Popular Communication* 6.4 (2008): 214–230. Print.

———. *Media Franchising: Creative License and Collaboration in the Culture Industries*. New York: New York University Press, 2013. Print.

———. "Will the Real Wolverine Please Stand Up? Marvel's Mutation from Monthlies to Movies." In *Film and Comic Books*. Eds. Ian Gordon, Mark Jancovich, and Matthew McAllister. Jackson: University Press of Mississippi, 2007. 64–85. Print.

Johnston, Rich. "Would Marvel Really Cancel Fantastic Four to Snub Fox?" *Bleeding Cool*, 29 May 2014. Web. www.bleedingcool.com/2014/05/29/would-marvel-really-cancel-fantastic-four-to-snub-fox.

Kondolojy, Amanda. "'Marvel's Avengers Assemble' & 'Marvel's Hulk and the Agents of S.M.A.S.H.' Renewed by Disney XD." *TV by the Numbers*, 26 July 2014. Web. http://tvbythenumbers.zap2it.com/2014/07/26/marvels-avengers-assemble-marvels-hulk-and-the-agents-of-s-m-a-s-h-renewed-by-disney-xd/286747.

Kraft, Amy. "ComiXology: The Changing Face of Comic Book Readers." *Geek Mom*, 10 October 2013. Web. http://geekmom.com/2013/10/comixology-comic-book-readers.

"London Toy Fair Report." *Brick Fanatics*, 21 January 2014. Web. http://brickfanatics.co.uk/london-toy-fair-report.

Lotz, Amanda D. *The Television Will Be Revolutionized*, 2nd ed. New York: New York University Press, 2014. Print.

"Marvel: Share Your Universe." *Marvel*, 9 July 2013. Web. http://marvel.com/news/tv/2013/7/9/20847/marvel_share_your_universe.

Masters, Kim. "How Marvel Became the Envy (and Scourge) of Hollywood."

Hollywood Reporter, 1 August 2014. Web. www.hollywoodreporter.com
/print/720363.

Macnicol, Glynnis. "Jon Stewart on Why New, Biracial Spiderman Is
Lou Dobbs' Worst Nightmare." *Business Insider*, 5 August 2011. Web.
www.businessinsider.com/jon-stewart-spiderman-lou-dobbs-2011-8.

McMillan, Graeme. "Marvel Invites Fans to 'Share Your Universe' with Next
Generation." *Hollywood Reporter*, 9 July 2013. Web. www.hollywoodreporter
.com/heat-vision/marvel-invites-fans-share-your-582376.

Miller, John Jackson. "Comic Book Sales by Year." *Comichron: The Comics
Chronicles*, n.d. Web. www.comichron.com/yearlycomicssales.html.

———. "Comics Sales Records in the Diamond Exclusive Era." *Comichron:
The Comics Chronicles*, n.d. Web. www.comichron.com/vitalstatistics
/diamondrecords.html.

———. "Comics Sales to Comics Shops." *Comichron: The Comics Chronicles*, n.d.
Web. www.comichron.com/vitalstatistics/alltime.html.

———. "Market Shares." *Comichron: The Comics Chronicles*, n.d. Web.
www.comichron.com/vitalstatistics/marketshares.html.

———. "May 2001 Comic Book Sales Figures." *Comichron: The Comics Chronicles*,
n.d. Web. www.comichron.com/monthlycomicssales/2001/2001-05.html.

Montgomery, Paul. "Marvel's Next Big Thing: 'Share Your Universe.'" *iFanboy*,
9 July 2013. Web. http://ifanboy.com/articles/marvels-next-big-thing-share
-your-universe.

"NYCC 2013: Marvel Wants You to Be the Face of Share Your Universe." *Marvel*,
9 October 2013. Web. http://marvel.com/news/tv/2013/10/9/21316/nycc_2013
_marvel_wants_you_to_be_the_face_of_share_your_universe.

Owczarski, Kimberly. "*Batman*, Time Warner, and Franchise Filmmaking in
the Conglomerate Era." PhD dissertation: University of Texas at Austin,
2008.

Pereira, Reuben. "Weekend Box Office: 'The Avengers' Grosses $200 Million
in Three Days." *Examiner*, 7 May 2012. Web. www.examiner.com/article
/weekend-box-office-the-avengers-grosses-200-million-three-days.

Petri, Alexandara. "Sorry Peter Parker: The Response to the Black Spiderman
Shows Why We Need One." *Washington Post*, 3 August 2011. Web.
www.webcitation.org/614Q5Z5z2.

Phegley, Kiel. "Marvel Announces 'Share Your Universe.'" *Comic Book Resources*,
9 July 2013. Web. www.comicbookresources.com/?page=article&id=46512.

"Share Your Universe!" *Marvel*, n.d. Web. http://marvel.com/comics/list/698
/share_your_universe.

"Share Your Universe." *Facebook*, 1 November 2013. Web. www.facebook.com
/ShareYourUniverse.

"Share Your Universe." *Marvel Kids*, n.d. Web. http://marvelkids.com/activities.

Stevens, Tim. "Meet the New Face of Share Your Universe." *Marvel*, 15 May 2014. Web. http://marvel.com/news/tv/2014/5/15/22523/meet_the_new_face_of_share_your_universe.

Stewart, Andrew. "Box Office: Fox's 'X-Men: Days of Future Past' Powers Up with $111 Mil Domestic Start." *Variety*, 26 May 2014. Web. http://variety.com/2014/film/news/box-office-foxs-x-men-days-of-future-past-powers-up-with-111-mil-domestic-start-1201192788.

"Toy Fair 2014: Hasbro Marvel Legends Report." *Action Figure Pics*, 16 February 2014. Web. www.actionfigurepics.com/2014/02/toy-fair-2014-hasbro-marvel-legends-report.

Tracey, Janey. "Best and Worst Fan Reactions to Female Thor and Black Captain America." *Outer Places*, 17 July 2014. Web. www.outerplaces.com/buzz/news/item/4901-fan-reactions-to-female-thor-and-black-captain-america.

Zakarin, Jordan. "Michael B. Jordan on 'Fantastic Four' Racist Backlash: It Was Expected." *The Wrap*, 7 March 2014. Web. www.thewrap.com/michael-b-jordan-fantastic-four-racist-backlash-expected.

Zara, Christopher. "San Diego Comic-Con: Cosplay Sexual Harassment Takes Center Stage at 2014 Fan Convention." *International Business Times*, 28 July 2014. Web. www.ibtimes.com/san-diego-comic-con-cosplay-sexual-harassment-takes-center-stage-2014-fan-convention-1641202.

Breaking Brand

FROM NUMARVEL TO MARVELNOW! MARVEL COMICS IN THE AGE OF MEDIA CONVERGENCE

DERON OVERPECK

Since its inception in the early 1960s, Marvel Comics' line of superhero titles has been known for its emphasis on continuity—the sense that its characters and their experiences existed within a shared universe and thus would have a lasting impact beyond any one specific title. The storylines this approach generated were presented across several issues and in multiple titles. The interconnections helped the company to develop devoted readers who felt as though they were reading stories that "counted" (Wright 218-225; Howe 44-47, 156-157). After several decades, however, Marvel's continuity began to prove daunting to new readers, who did not necessarily want to wade into several decades' worth of accrued backstory (Howe 404, 410).[1] Additionally, the editors and marketing executives who dictated these crossovers often designed them to encourage readers to buy multiple titles that they would not necessarily have intended to buy (Wright 278-281; Howe 362-366, 381). Thus, to some eyes, Marvel's detailed continuity had become as much a hindrance as an essential, defining feature of the company.

At the turn of the twenty-first century, Marvel shifted its emphasis away from continuity and began to develop new narrative strategies that its executives believed would better position it to survive in an entertainment marketplace that offered many more options than it had from the late 1960s to early 1990s. The company was just coming out of the mid-1990s collapse of the comic book and trading-card market and its subsequent bankruptcy.[2] Determining that the company needed a new direction, its de facto publisher, Bill Jemas, and editor in chief, Joe Quesada, replaced long-time writers and artists at the company with new talent drawn from the ranks of independent comics and the entertainment industry. These moves signaled a shift in both the "House of Ideas" storytelling policies and in how the company marketed its products—changes that were drastic enough that the company was given the nickname "NuMarvel." Creators were now given the leeway to ignore continuity and develop the characters to be more in line with their own thematic interests and tastes. These writers began to rely on the narrative style known as "decompression," in which storylines are expanded to cover six or more issues through the use of "widescreen" panel layouts that offered fewer actions per page. Although its proponents assert that decompressed narratives allow for greater character development or artistic storytelling, the style's detractors point out that it dilates storylines so that they better fit the minimum length of trade paperback collections, a market that Quesada aggressively pursued ("Comics 101"; "Joe Quesada"). Additionally, Marvel began to place more promotional emphasis on its artists and writers than on its characters through branding campaigns such as Young Guns and Marvel Architects. These moves aggravated longtime readers even as they drew renewed attention to the company as a creative entity (rather than home to an impenetrable thicket of backstories), bringing increased sales to some of the publisher's flagship titles, such as *The Amazing Spider-Man*, *The Avengers*, and *X-Men* (Howe 417–418).[3] These developments played out as Marvel's characters finally made the successful transition to the big screen in films like *X-Men* (Bryan Singer, 2000) and *Spider-Man* (Sam Raimi, 2002), providing the members of the comic book line's creative team with both the chance to see their works translated to the big screen and renewed pressure to publish stories that were accessible to new readers and an increasingly interested Hollywood.

Herein, I analyze how, at the beginning of the twenty-first century, Marvel the publishing company effectively renewed its brand as the "House of Ideas," with its parent company, Marvel Entertainment (ME),[4] in the words of a 2002 press release, "transform[ing itself] to a licensing-driven business" ("Marvel Releases"). In so doing, Marvel adopted marketing techniques and aesthetic policies influenced by the larger entertainment industry that it was seeking to join. Its promotion of writers and artists can be understood as a form of the commercial auteurism theorized by Timothy Corrigan, in which the concept of a central creative, guiding visionary functions to legitimate and promote commercial art (101–136). The employment of auteurism provided Marvel with responses to critics who alleged that the company was denigrating the stories that fans had become invested in through the decades. Later, it allowed the company to introduce legitimacy to the massive crossover events that continued to be central elements of Marvel's publishing plans. Furthermore, Marvel's adoption of decompression as its primary aesthetic model better positioned it to exploit its comic book properties beyond their initial appearance in monthly magazines. My goal here is to examine how Marvel has continued to function—thrive, even—in its core business as a comic book company even as its parent company attracted more attention by transforming its characters into cinematic brands.

WHICH BRAND ARE WE TALKING ABOUT, ANYWAY?

Marvel's activities as a licensing-driven business have been the primary focus of recent scholarship on the company, and with good reason. Since the release of the first *X-Men* film, Marvel Enterprises has either licensed characters for use in—or itself produced—films that, as of this writing, have collectively grossed more than $5 billion domestically and $12 billion internationally.[5] Derek Johnson has detailed how ME repositioned itself in the early twenty-first century in order to better exploit its characters for film properties. In "Cinematic Destiny: Marvel Studios and the Trade Stories of Industrial Convergence," he analyzes how Marvel Studios, the film production subsidiary of Marvel Entertainment, has used interlocking filmic storylines and canny trade-press narratives to promote the business savvy and comic bona fides of its executives in order to "organize the production and consumption of its comics content across media platforms" (8). This consumption includes not only the films themselves but also "Easter eggs," such as inter-credit sequences or throwaway images. Such elements reward faithful fans who search DVD, Blu-ray, or streamed versions of the films for clues to future Marvel storyline developments, helping to tie the films together into a shared universe. Johnson refers to "Marvel" throughout his essay—but he's always referring to Marvel Studios, the film production company, not to Marvel the comic book publisher.

In an earlier piece, "Will the Real Wolverine Please Stand Up? Marvel's Mutation from Monthlies to Movies," Johnson does address the comic book publisher—but only as a company in the process of refashioning itself into "an intellectual property production company" (72). Johnson details how Marvel has revised characters like Wolverine so that they more closely resemble their cinematic counterparts, making them more attractive to

Hollywood (73, 77–81), while also adopting the practice of repackaging monthly comics into collections that "make available to a general audience the recent reimaginings, restructurings and relaunchings of its comic book titles" (75). In this view, Marvel has moved away from primarily addressing its traditional audience of comic book readers toward attracting various cinematic audiences, general and industrial alike. That the extant comic book fan base might also be interested in purchasing trade paperback collections is minimized in Johnson's analysis. The important story regarding Marvel, it seems, is how it has facilitated ME's plans to create film franchises out of its thousands of characters.

In structuring his studies in this way, Johnson follows other recent scholarship on ME that prioritizes the company's nonpublishing activities. In his examination of the corporate structure of the comic book industry as a whole, Matthew McAllister has argued that Marvel's publishing is less important to ME's bottom line than is its licensing businesses (15–38). Similarly, Matthew Pustz and Dan Raviv each have asserted that, in the wake of the company's bankruptcy in 1996, film ventures provided ME with a more secure platform on which to profit from its intellectual property (Pustz 16–17; Raviv 277–278). Broadly speaking, these scholars and writers focus on Marvel as a potential cinematic brand. Following Janet Wasko's approach to studying Disney, Johnson explicitly argues that Marvel is best treated as an organized network of texts and properties that establish a conglomerate identity ("Will the Real Wolverine" 69). This frame—Marvel's characters as brandable merchandise—was even reflected within ME. As Bill Jemas told Marvel employees:

> Let's talk about the Spider-Man brand. Whether Spider-Man is on a
> T-shirt or in a TV show, he's Spider-Man. He's our way of communicat-
> ing a particular set of characteristics and a spirit and a liveliness. There's
> an ethos, an emotion, and a *brand* captured in Spider-Man. That's what
> Spider-Man is. And don't get lost in questions like "Is that a T-shirt? Is it
> a license? Is it a fast-food tie-in?" It's Spider-Man! (Raviv 267)[6]

Interestingly, Jemas doesn't specify that Spider-Man might be in a Marvel comic book; he conceives of the character and its attributes solely within the context of licensed merchandise. Such a conception of Marvel's characters, within both the scholarly and corporate communities, is certainly understandable, given the enormous box-office grosses generated by films based on Marvel characters compared to the generally anemic comic book market—the best-selling comics issues currently sell approximately a third of what top-sellers did in the 1960s and 1970s.[7] However, it is worth emphasizing that Marvel has licensed its comic book characters for animated series, live-action films, and television series, posters, T-shirts, and other paraphernalia since the mid-1960s. According to Sean Howe, the company's creative staff was told throughout the 1970s not to introduce any meaningful changes to Marvel's characters because they might upset licensing deals, and the very successful mid-1980s miniseries *Marvel Super Heroes Secret Wars* had been developed solely in order to market Mattel's new line of toys. Similarly, Marvel had been pursuing live-action film and television deals in Hollywood since the late 1970s.[8]

Unfortunately for Marvel, for years its forays into live-action film and television were disappointments. Prior to the success of the *X-Men* and *Spider-Man* films, the only Marvel character-based property to have any lasting success was *The Incredible Hulk* television series (CBS, 1977–1982). Far more typical were such regrettably bad misfires as *The Punisher* (Mark Goldblatt, 1989), *Captain America* (Albert Pyun, 1990), *Fantastic Four* (Oley Sassone, 1994), and the Fox television movie *Generation X* (Jack Sholder, 1996), which was actually a failed series pilot. (The company has had more success with animated series, from *Spider-Man and His Amazing Friends* [NBC, 1981–1983] to the *X-Men* series in the 1990s and the *Avengers* series in the 2000s.) Given the company's lengthy history of licensing its trademarked characters, what is perhaps most notable about ME's transformation into a licensing powerhouse is not that it is now so focused on exploiting its characters in other media, but that it has finally become successful at it.

What sustained ME throughout its awkward attempts at establishing itself in Hollywood were the comic books for which it first became well known—and which first helped create Marvel itself as a brand, as the sum of its specific properties. And even if much of the attention that ME receives is generated by the success of Marvel Studios' films, the company's publishing division continues to publish comics successfully; its titles dominate the top ten of the sales charts, even if a DC title might take the overall number-one position in a given month. Marvel's share of the comic book publishing market (comprising Marvel, DC, Image, IDW, and a clutch of smaller independent publishers) is 40 percent ("Marvel Entertainment LLC"), and the publishing division accounts for approximately 20 percent of ME's profits; recent figures have been difficult to come by—attempts to get an official statement from

Marvel were unsuccessful—but in 2008, publishing accounted for 18 percent of the company's sales ($125.4 million of $676.2 million) (Brady). It has been the industry's leader since the early 1970s, maintaining that dominance throughout the periodic industry-wide downturns in sales, including the bust of the speculator-driven bubble that contributed to the company's bankruptcy in 1996. It has been the core of the parent company's survival as well as the source of its exploitable characters; indeed, Marvel Studios has borrowed elements from Marvel comic books for the narratives of its films, including *Marvel's The Avengers* (Joss Whedon, 2012) and *Captain America: The Winter Soldier* (Anthony and Joe Russo, 2014). This reality makes an examination of Marvel Comics as a publishing entity essential for understanding the overall success of ME as a diverse media conglomerate.

AUTEURISM AT MARVEL

Auteurism has long been a controversial theoretical model within media studies. Originally developed by the editorial board at *Cahiers du cinema*, the French film journal, as an analytical tool to explain the seemingly personal styles of filmmakers within the Fordist Hollywood studio system, it soon came to signify a critical position that treated the director as someone whose singular vision guarantees the importance and quality of the film. Although this later form of auteurism may retain some currency in mainstream public film criticism, scholarly studies of the media industries problematized, if not outright abandoned it, decades ago.[9] By placing such emphasis on the director as author of a film, classical auteurism minimized the important contributions of other skilled and unskilled laborers in the film production process, production, and reception contexts as well as the constraints of dominant storytelling methods. Indeed, the modern comic book itself serves as a demonstration of the drawbacks of the classic definition of auteurism. Since 2001, Marvel has placed the names of the writer, penciller, and inker on the cover of the comic book, as well as prominent credits for colorists, letterers, and editors on the title page. Some hierarchy does exist: the writer, the penciller, and sometimes the inker are considered the more important members of the creative team, and will most likely be presented first and in a larger font than the other talent, and this practice has fostered a tendency among readers to follow these creators more closely. However, all creator credits will appear on the same page in a comic book, unlike those for film and television programs, where directors, writers, producers, editors, et alia, are listed individually. The more-or-less equal credit given to all of the creative staff on a comic book underscores the collaborative nature of the medium.

The auteur, however, can serve as more than just a means of assigning an idealized legitimation to a work of art. As Timothy Corrigan has argued, a more complete theory of auteurism incorporates the "the increasing importance . . . of the auteur as a *commercial* strategy for organizing audience reception, as a critical concept bound to distribution and marketing aims that identify and address the potential cult status of the auteur" (Corrigan 103). The auteur in this model becomes a marketable symbol, a means of asserting a film's coherence through promotional material that presents it as the work of a central vision. Following Meaghan Morris, Corrigan notes that trailers, interviews, and critical reviews are used to establish a film as an auteurist work even before the film is released (106).

He then divides the commercial auteur into two categories. The first is filmmakers-as-celebrities: "What defines this group is a recognition, either foisted on them or chosen by them, that the celebrity of their agency produces and promotes texts that invariably exceed the movie itself" (107). The filmmaker, of course, is not the author of the film in any legal sense; the status as auteur is merely a promotional fiction that legitimizes the industrial nature of the text by obscuring it. In effect, commercial auteurism is a strategy by which the capitalist-conglomerate nature of media production effaces itself in order to assert its privilege. Corrigan's second category is the auteur of commerce, in which the filmmaker attempts to push back against the film industry, to reshape it to his purposes even as it reshapes him to its bottom line. Corrigan uses Francis Ford Coppola as an example of the auteur of commerce, citing how his struggles to create a new, artist-friendly film industry effectively bankrupted him in the early 1980s (ibid.).

The second category of auteur is not of interest here, although one could find examples of it within the comic book industry; the careers of Steve Ditko, Neal Adams, Jim Starlin, and Robert Kirkman are at least partially defined by their calls to fellow creators to work outside of the traditional industrial structure in order to protect their own creative rights. Instead, my focus is on the first category, commercial auteurs—writers and artists who are positioned by Marvel as unique creators whose narrative and rendering talents are as central to the success of the company's titles as are the characters themselves. Although the first marketing push focused on Marvel's prominent pencillers, its promotion of a core group of writers as the Marvel Architects most clearly exemplifies how the company has adapted the commercial auteur model to promoting its talent. As will be demonstrated below, the Architects promotion has been used to create the sense that stories set in the Marvel Universe have been parts of one overarching narrative that has been designed by a team of important writers, reflecting Corrigan's insight that auteurism is used as a metatext that elides the commercial origins and function of popular works of art.

To an extent, a kind of commercial auteurism has always been a part of Marvel's brand. For example, Stan Lee cultivated a sense of celebrity in the late 1960s and 1970s when he made speaking appearances on college campuses and sat for print, radio, and television interviews to promote Marvel Comics. These appearances helped to establish the popular belief that he was the primary creator of Spider-Man, the Incredible Hulk, and the X-Men—a belief that Lee has not always discouraged. In the early 1980s, he moved to Los Angeles to guide the development of live-action projects based on Marvel properties, further cementing the sense of Lee as larger than the comics themselves. He also has made cameo appearances in every Marvel film since 2000. However, Lee's celebrity should not be confused with the kind of auteurist presentation described below.

Although Lee was the writer and editor on many of the classic Marvel comics, he consistently worked with Jack Kirby, Steve Ditko, and John Romita, whose distinct visual styles were as crucial to the popularity of Marvel's comics as Lee's storylines and florid prose. Indeed, Kirby and Ditko have both claimed that they were more responsible than Lee for the comics, further blurring Lee's status as auteur (Howe 262–263, 400–401). Furthermore, Lee had largely ceded control of the writing and editing of Marvel's comics in the early 1970s in order to write a screenplay with art-house film director and avowed Marvel fan Alain Resnais (a project that never came to fruition) (ibid. 113–114); for the past forty years of Marvel history, he has been a figurehead more than an active creator. Some writers and artists prior to the Quesada era also had a certain celebrity status: John Byrne, Chris Claremont, Frank Miller, and Walt Simonson were "fan favorites" who brought with them devoted followers, and thus increased sales, to particular titles. However, none of these creators ever received the kind of organized marketing that Marvel has bestowed on its writers and artists in the twenty-first century. The characters and comics were still the primary foci of Marvel's promotional efforts.

Marvel's move toward commercial auteurism is best understood in light of the company's reputation at the end of the 1990s. Throughout the decade, Marvel had specialized in crossover events that required fans to purchase issues of multiple series in order to receive the full "story"; some of these tie-in issues were, at best, only tangentially related to the idea behind the crossover. Gimmick covers with holograms, die-cut figures, gilded letters, et cetera, were offered, as were multiple variant covers of one issue. New series were created to capitalize on apparently popular characters like Gambit and Bishop, while established series were canceled just to be restarted with a new issue no. 1. These new titles and crossover events were mandated by executives and editors more interested in cash flow than creative vision; one assistant editor on the *X-Men* said "we see writer-driven comics as an experiment that's failed" (Howe 362–366, 381). And at least during the early 1990s, it seemed like this strategy worked. When Marvel re-vamped its *X-Men* line to include a new title featuring the core heroes, and canceled *New Mutants* to relaunch it as *X-Force,* the titles sold millions of copies: *Uncanny X-Men, X-Men,* and *X-Force* each had variant covers. The skyrocketing sales on these titles attracted speculators to the comic book market, and they purchased multiple copies of each variant cover, expecting to realize a tidy profit when they resold them on the collectors market. However, once it became clear that such profitable resales would not happen—the fact that so many speculators were in the market buying comics kept those issues from becoming rare enough to be valuable—sales began to drop precipitously. At the same time, Marvel began to lose some of its top writers and artists. The industry's most popular pencillers left to form their own company, Image Comics. Others decamped for DC Comics, which offered royalties when Marvel would not, published off-beat titles like *Animal Man* and *Suicide Squad,* and, in 1993, created the Vertigo line of creator-owned comics.[10]

According to comics writer Kurt Busiek, throughout this period the comics line remained profitable for the company. All the same, the drop in sales and simultaneous profligate spending by CEO Ron Perelman forced ME into bankruptcy.[11] Three years later, as part of the process of reorganization, Bill Jemas was appointed as Marvel's president of publishing and new media, which made him the company's de facto publisher. Displeased with the continuity-heavy storylines the company had been publishing, Jemas hired artist Joe Quesada as Marvel's new editor in chief. Quesada's Marvel Knights imprint had had recent success with rejuvenating *Daredevil,* and his relationships with independent comic book writers, including Brian

Michael Bendis, as well as with Hollywood writers such as Kevin Smith, promised inroads to new, dynamic talent on Marvel's comics. Quesada handed Bendis the reins of *Ultimate Spider-Man*, the new Ultimate line's flagship title, and hired Axel Alonso away from DC's Vertigo imprint to serve as senior editor with responsibilities for *The Amazing Spider-Man*, *The Incredible Hulk*, the X-Men titles, and other high-profile books.

As editor in chief, Quesada worked to repair much of the creator-unfriendly, insular reputation that Marvel had developed in the 1990s. He canceled series that he felt were redundant, discontinued gimmick covers, and limited the scope and number of crossovers. To reward longtime readers, he also restored the original numbering to several titles that had been rebooted over the previous decade, providing a renewed sense of continuity and history to the titles even as many of the writers and artists who had been working on those titles were pushed off the books and even out of the company. This nod to the company's lengthy past was one of the few concessions Quesada was willing to offer to long-term readers, though. He and his editorial team quickly began to cultivate a company atmosphere that prioritized newness over tradition and authorial personality over narrative continuity. "We took a concentrated look at putting the best talent on the best books," he would later tell the entertainment website Ain't It Cool News, regardless of whether or not that "best talent" embraced the recent storylines of the books ("AICN Comics").

Quesada and Alonso sought to rejuvenate the comics with writers who had made their reputations through their works for independent publishers or for DC's edgy, less editorially driven Vertigo imprint. These writers included Garth Ennis, Neil Gaiman, Mark Millar, and Grant Morrison. New artists, including anime star Kia Asamiya, French artist Olivier Coipel, David Finch, and Frank Quitely, were given their first high-profile Marvel jobs at this time. Although Quesada prioritized the recruitment of writers who had not been previously associated with Marvel, he did reach out to legendary comic writer Alan Moore, who had refused to work for Marvel since the mid-1980s in a dispute over royalties; in the intervening years, Moore had become famous for groundbreaking graphic novels such as *Watchmen* and *From Hell*. Although he was unable to persuade Moore to work for Marvel, Quesada's efforts signaled his commitment to establishing Marvel as a company that would be more respectful of the rights and talents of its creators.

Quesada also reached outside of the comic book industry for new writers. As an independent publisher himself, Quesada had cultivated connections with Hollywood writers and producers since the mid-1990s (Howe 393), and once he became editor in chief at Marvel, he recruited many of them to work on Marvel's top titles to position Marvel as a comic book company that had "matur[ed] and grow[n] up." Quesada described the talent as "important and prominent authors who write novels, movies, and TV shows of significance, who are now jumping onto the comics' bandwagon to provide readers with that same experience, and maybe in some cases, a better experience" (Koller). These people included Allan Heinberg (*Party of Five* [FOX, 1994–2000], *The O.C.* [FOX, 2003–2007]), Reginald Hudlin (*House Party* [1990], *Boomerang* [1992]), Damon Lindelof (*Lost* [ABC, 2004–2010]), J. Michael Straczynski (*Babylon Five* [TNT, 1994–1998]), and Joss Whedon (*Buffy the Vampire Slayer* [WB, 1997–2001; UPN, 2001–2003]). Bruce Jones, who had written comics in the 1970s but had found more success as a writer for mystery- and horror-themed shows (such as *The Hitchhiker* [HBO, 1983–1987]) and thriller novels, was hired to write *The Incredible Hulk*. Jeph Loeb had written for previous Marvel regimes as well, but he had also had an extensive career in Hollywood, including as screenwriter for *Teen Wolf* (Rod Daniel, 1985) and *Commando* (Mark L. Lester, 1985); he later would serve as producer on *Lost* and such superhero-themed shows as *Smallville* (CW, 2001–2011) and *Heroes* (NBC, 2006–2010).

Other than Lindelof, who wrote a miniseries featuring the Ultimate Universe versions of Wolverine and Hulk, and Heinberg, who developed a series featuring new teenage characters based on the Avengers, most of the Hollywood-connected writers worked on established Marvel properties. Hudlin reworked *The Black Panther* during a controversial three-year run from 2005 to 2008; Straczynski wrote *The Amazing Spider-Man*, *Fantastic Four*, and *Thor*; and Whedon received a new *X-Men* title that featured mutantdom's most popular characters. By and large, the bold directions that Quesada initiated attracted readers back into Marvel's fold; books written by talent from outside of the comic book industry sold well by the somewhat depressed standards of the time. In 2002, his first year on the title, Straczynski doubled the sales on *The Amazing Spider-Man* ("Aggregated 2002"),[12] and Whedon's first twelve issues of *Astonishing X-Men*, published over fifteen months in 2004 and 2005, averaged nearly 140,000 copies sold ("Aggregated 2004"; "August 2005"). Jones's tenure on *The Incredible Hulk* saw improvements in sales, although the book never entered the top ten.[13] However, not every Hollywood hire succeeded. Ron Zimmerman, who had written for numerous sitcoms and appeared on *The Howard Stern Show* radio program, produced the dismally received *Rawhide Kid: Slap Leather* (2003), which used the classic western hero as an excuse for a series of juvenile jokes about homosexuality.

Although these hires did seem to breathe fresh life into the Marvel properties, and occasioned upticks in sales, fans of the company's continuity-based stories complained. Many of the writers took the series in unexpected directions that seemed to fly in the face of established characterization or continuity. Hudlin wrote the Black Panther as a supremely confident warrior, ignoring that the previous writer had established the character as relying on his intelligence more than his strength. Straczynski introduced the concept that Spider-Man, rather than being a teenager accidentally bestowed with superhuman powers that he had to learn to use heroically, was actually part of a long line of mystical arachnid-themed warriors.[14] Under Jones, *The Incredible Hulk*'s Bruce Banner (and green-skinned alter ego) resembled his peripatetic version in the television series of the late 1970s more than the psychologically driven character found in the previous decade of the series. In *Thor*, the title character materialized the mystical city of Asgard over New York City, where it remained for nearly a year's worth of issues—yet no mention was made of it in any other Marvel comic.

Even as sales for many of Marvel's titles rose, longtime readers complained about the loss of a sense of cohesion among or even within titles. Jemas and Quesada responded that Marvel continuity had become cumbersome. The company, according to Quesada, had not seen a rise in sales following the first *X-Men* movie because the comics themselves were too convoluted for new readers.[15] Furthermore, the fact that the writers involved in such revisionism came from other fields provided Marvel with a measure of insulation from the complaints of longtime fans. Straczynski, Whedon, and Hudlin all carried a kind of celebrity that comic book writers could not—the kind that came from success outside of the comic industry and that made their names familiar to non-comics readers: Marvel's changes could now be presented as bold new directions guided by respected artists who understood that good stories were defined by more than devotion to the past.

Marketing campaigns that began in 2004 placed further emphasis on the creators over the books they worked on. These campaigns formalized the commercial auteurist bent the company had taken since Quesada's accession to the editorship. Perhaps reflecting Quesada's background as a penciller, the first promotion touted artists who Marvel felt would make a dramatic impact on the industry. The "Young Guns" initiative ran biannually from 2004 to 2008. In the press release announcing the first class of Young Guns, Marvel described the pencillers, including Jim Cheung, Adi Granov, and Trevor Hairsine, as "young artists laying down the law and defining the future of comic books" ("Marvel's Young Guns"). In 2006, for its second Young Guns push, the company trumpeted Clayton Crain, Billy Tan, and Leinil Francis Yu, among others, as "artists on the precipice of scorching the entire comic book industry with their bombastic art" ("Marvel's Young Guns Assemble"). Such blandishments recall the alliterative nicknames that Marvel's first editor, Stan Lee, would bestow on writers and artists (e.g., Gentleman Gene Colan, Rascally Roy Thomas) to create a sense of community on Marvel's staff. But the Young Guns marketing campaigns effectively placed these artists as having a greater influence on Marvel and the industry than other creators. To be selected as a Young Gun, an artist already had to be working on a high-profile title that was worthy of such a high-profile marketing push. In an interview regarding the second Young Guns promotion, Quesada noted:

> We work very hard at managing creators. We chose these six particular artists because they . . . are working on projects that are going to be breakthrough career projects for them. . . . There were people we had to say 'next year' to who are certainly worthy of the honor. I think it's the best way to market their careers. There's no sense in saying Joe Smith is one of the Young Guns and yet he's on a very small project right now. It doesn't serve them as well as if they're on a big mainstream mover. ("WWC")

Quesada here clearly prioritizes the marketing of talent over the marketing of Marvel's characters or titles. Rather than using these star artists to promote smaller titles, the larger titles would be used to market the star artists. Readers were encouraged to follow the creators, not necessarily what they created.

In 2010, Marvel began to promote its top writers; however, this campaign did more than offer the hottest artists on the hottest properties. By this time, the writers the company had recruited from the film and television industries had by and large ceased to work for the company, and the Marvel Architects campaign allowed the publisher to generate the same kind of attention to them that had come with the high-profile hires a decade earlier. The Marvel Architects were five scribes whose ideas were changing "the very fabric of the Marvel Universe"—Jason Aaron, Brian Michael Bendis, Ed Brubaker, Matt Fraction, and Jonathan Hickman ("Marvel Unveils"). Although Marvel named six artists as Architects the next year—Mark Bagley, Mike Deodato, Stuart Immonen, Salvador Larroca, Humberto Ramos, and John Romita Jr., who had all worked at Marvel before Quesada assumed the editorship—the promotion was limited to a small panel at a convention in Chicago and a handful of variant comic book covers in September 2011 (Esposito). It would be the initial group of writers who would receive ongoing attention as the stewards of the Marvel Universe.

The Architects campaign was initiated with a featurette about the writers that was published in several titles in April 2011 along with a panel dedicated to them at the 2011 Emerald City Comicon in Seattle ("ECCC"). The featurette included an interview with Bendis, who had been writing for Marvel for the longest period of time. It also provided a list of titles that the Architects wrote and suggested that future featurettes would include interviews with the other four writers. Although no future featurettes appeared, the five writers continued to be framed as the guides to Marvel's future stories—multiple trade press stories reported on the annual creative retreats the Architects and their editors took to map out the future of the comics line (Sunu, Johnston, Khouri, Sava).

Marvel has emphasized its core writers much more than it has its artists. The Young Guns campaign was put on hiatus—no new class was introduced between 2008 and 2014—and replaced by the Architects. The titles of these campaigns are telling. Dubbing the company's hot pencillers as "Young Guns" suggested that they were, in effect, fighters for hire, callow shooters looking to make their mark in the world—the comic book world's equivalents of Billy the Kid, José Chavez y Chavez, or Doc Holliday. And as it happened, several of the Young Guns did not necessarily make the mark that Marvel expected they would. Some of them were never attached to high-profile ongoing series—Clayton Crain, for example, has drawn only miniseries and covers,[16] while Adi Granov has done primarily covers and the occasional guest appearance on a title ("Adi"). In fact, some of the artists no longer work for Marvel: David Finch signed an exclusive contract with DC Comics in 2010 (Phegley, "Exclusive"), which was also the last year that Trevor Hairsine produced art for Marvel;[17] Crain has not worked for the company since 2012. In contrast to the Young Guns, however, the Architects have been models of stability. Indeed, the sobriquet given to the group of writers itself suggests greater maturity: architects are designers with long-range visions about how to transform empty spaces into functional, masterly works of art—think Frank Lloyd Wright, Mies van der Rohe, or I. M. Pei. Even though the architect does little, if any, of the actual construction work him or herself, he or she is still treated as the "builder" of the edifice. The bestowal of "architect" status on these writers thus implied that they had developed a blueprint for the structure of the Marvel Universe and would be responsible for it regardless of who did the actual creative work. And while all of the writer Architects have published creator-owned works through Image and other independent presses, their work-for-hire titles have only been at Marvel.

The Architects program also has provided the metatext that is essential to Corrigan's concept of the commercial auteur. Since 2005, Marvel has increasingly returned to large crossover events as a cornerstone of its narrative plans. The events have included *House of M* (2005), *Civil War* (2006–2007), *World War Hulk* (2007), *Secret Invasion* (2008), *Dark Reign* (2009), *Siege* (2010), *Fear Itself* (2011), and *Avengers vs. X-Men* (2012). Unlike the crossover events of the 1990s, which were perceived as mandated by marketing executives and written by editors, the events of the past decade have been presented as organic developments from previous storylines and the brainchildren of Marvel's most respected writers. Quesada and Alonso have claimed that these crossovers were part of a larger interconnected narrative (Khouri). Brian Michael Bendis was largely responsible for these narratives, writing the central miniseries for *House of M*, *Secret Invasion*, *Dark Reign*, and *Siege*, and co-writing *Avengers vs. X-Men*. His impact was indirect as well: the crossover events in which he did not have a direct hand still developed from *Avengers Disassembled*, his 2003 work on the Avengers titles. By bestowing on him the Architect title, Marvel acknowledged his role in shaping the company's titles, even those he did not write. By the time of *Avengers vs. X-Men*, Marvel was presenting the crossover as the creation of the Architects as a group—all of five of the writers wrote at least two issues of the core miniseries and were heavily featured in promotional material for the series. This material included a series of webisodes for Marvel Television that explained the genesis of the crossover event and each writer's expectations for it and its aftermath.

Avengers vs. X-Men led into the MarvelNOW marketing push, in which several series were canceled only to be restarted with first issues—another throwback to the 1990s, when series were canceled and restarted solely to cause sudden sales spikes. The newly rebooted titles included the core

X-Men and *Avengers* titles as well as titles featuring characters that are members of one or both of those teams, including Captain America, Hulk, Iron Man, Thor, and Wolverine. Some of the new titles directly arose in the aftermath of *Avengers v. X-Men,* but other titles, such as *Indestructible Hulk* and *Thor: God of Thunder,* merely piggy-backed on the branding campaign to generate more interest in what amounted to changes in the creative teams assigned to those books. The series became associated with a specific Architect—Hickman became the guiding force behind the *Avengers* books, while Bendis began to write the core *X-Men* titles. Twenty years ago, the transparently venal motivation behind the ever-expanding crossovers and constant restarts of titles drove away readers. The Marvel Architects campaign, however, provided Marvel with insulation from similar charges of profiteering; it presented the writers as responsible for these crossovers—the events were generated organically through the narrative, not through marketing demands. In effect, Marvel Architects is a marketing campaign designed to draw attention away from the centrality of marketing to Marvel's line.

AESTHETICS AT MARVEL

At the same time that Marvel adopted an auteurist approach to marketing, the art in its comics began to mimic the cinematography of Hollywood action films. The traditional grid layout, in which the positioning of individual panels both presented narrative information and guided the reader's eye across the page to follow that material, was replaced with one that emphasized page-wide panels, including more common use of splash panels. This became known as "widescreen" presentation, a reference to such film formats as 70mm or IMAX. The link between comics and films is not entirely apt—in many cases within the realm of film, the cinematic format expanded the size of the individual frame, the screen, and the running time; in comics, it has expanded only the individual panel. Indeed, individual Marvel issues have gotten shorter, going from twenty-two to twenty pages of story, since Alonso became editor in chief. The format has nevertheless become a selling point for Marvel. Since 2010, Alonso has championed the widescreen format for both miniseries (the "Age of X" and *Infinity* crossover events) and ongoing series (*Guardians of the Galaxy, Bucky Barnes: The Winter Soldier*). To be sure, Marvel comics have used page-wide panels and splash pages for decades, as evidenced by Kirby's work on *The Fantastic Four* and *Thor,* or Ditko's work on *Dr. Strange.* However, such panels were not as prominent in plotting as they currently are, and in any event, they did not have a specific term to identify them.

When the widescreen format was paired with the narrative technique known as "decompression," individual plot points were doled out sparingly and individual moments drawn out. Anthony Smith has referred to this narrative style in comic books as "incremental action." Because comic books traditionally have had fixed page counts, economy in presentation was at a greater premium than in films with longer running times. Decompression rejected this economy, presenting one action from a variety of perspectives or using multiple panels to present the completion of a single action. For example, rather than presenting a helicopter landing in one panel, the first issue of *The New Avengers* (vol. 1) presented the event over two mostly word-free pages, showing the helicopter's approach, descent, and landing, and then the characters emerging from the craft. Similarly, in *Astonishing X-Men* (vol. 1, no. 14), writer Joss Whedon takes one page of five widescreen panels, three of which are virtually identical, to tell one brief joke about Wolverine approving of the romance between Kitty Pryde and Colossus.

Marvel's cinematic influence has had an impact on Marvel's aesthetics on comic book credits as well. Beginning in 2013, Marvel began to incorporate cinematically influenced title sequences into its books. Rather than have an issue's title incorporated into the artwork, as had been standard in comic books for decades, Marvel began to devote one or even two pages to presenting the title and creators of an issue. The new title style would sometimes be included on the recap page that opens every Marvel comic, but in other cases it was a separate one- to two-page spread. The story's title and credits are presented in fonts and formats that mimic those used on movie promotional posters. In a particularly striking example, an issue of *The New Avengers* (vol. 3, no. 1), written by Hickman, placed the title toward the end of the issue, after a particularly striking moment of action. Its placement resembled the opening sequence and title card of *Marvel's The Avengers*, which had been released the previous year. Other credit pages, often presented as two-page spreads, have included design elements identical to those used in promotional posters.

In addition to its impact on the narrative pacing and visual presentation of Marvel's comics, the widescreen format also furthered the publisher's goal of strengthening its trade paperback market. Quesada considered the cultivation of that market a priority when he assumed the editorship and was open about the fact that Marvel comics would have to change to fit this format. When he took over Marvel, he and his staff looked for past story-lines to release as trade paperbacks but couldn't find any—"because none of the stories ever end," he told the online site Millionaire Playboy ("Interview with Joe Quesada"). In order to attract newsstand customers in the 1960s, Stan Lee had developed ongoing storylines that featured overlapping plots and characters and ended each issue on a cliffhanger. "Our business is more with direct sales these days, in comic shops. So we have to change the way we tell stories," Quesada explained. "We have to create a story, and that's what we're doing with story arcs. . . . [Y]ou can't have someone pick up the [trade paperback] and read on the last page that there's another cliffhanger. It's not a satisfactory read." Storylines were to be self-contained into five- to six-issue arcs that could be easily repackaged into a single volume. The use of widescreen layouts and decompressed plotting meant fewer panels per page, which stretched storylines out to the required length.

As Johnson notes, the collected-edition market gave Marvel better access to mainstream retail bookstores and thus to a larger audience.[18] However, it also places Marvel more in line with the expectations that media conglom-erates have for their properties; that is to say, it allows Marvel to realize profits from a single storyline across multiple formats. Prior to its aggressive move into collected editions, Marvel usually realized profits from a particu-lar issue only once, at the time of its original release; collected editions were offered infrequently and often contained reprints of issues that were years or even decades old. However, since the 1980s—roughly concurrent with the time that they were bought up by international conglomerates—film studios and television networks have catered to the sizable home video market by releasing both recent and classic movies and series in a variety of formats. This development can be understood as being part of a kind of media-based parsimony principle: the miserly but widespread use and reuse of films and television shows in order to wring as much money out of them as possible. By pursuing the trade paperback market, Marvel not only adopted this policy but began to organize its narratives around what in other industries is a secondary market. Under Quesada, Marvel began to release collected editions of recent storylines, in some cases only a month after the last individual issues hit the stands. Hardcover editions were released first, followed by paperback editions several months later.

The expectations of the collected-edition market have furthered the development and scope of Marvel's annual crossover events. Although Que-sada has admitted that the crossovers become exhausting for both readers and creators ("Joe Quesada Talks"), they have nevertheless increased both in frequency and in terms of the number of issues devoted to them. Although one could argue that the stories behind the crossovers warranted more issues in more titles, it is also easy to see that they generate more product for the collected-editions market. *Avengers vs. X-Men*, for example, not only appeared in a core twelve-issue miniseries, but also was featured in *AvX*, an accompanying six-issue miniseries that highlighted individual heroes facing off in battles apparently too massive to be presented in the main series, as well as five special "prelude" issues and fifty-one tie-ins to regular Marvel titles. Almost all of these issues were in some way republished in one of the eleven collected editions dedicated to the event. Similarly, the 2013 event, *Infinity*, included a six-issue miniseries and forty-one separate tie-in issues that appeared in seven different collected editions.

Widescreen, decompressed plotting seems to have become a permanent part of Marvel's house style, particularly as it facilitates the expansion of the company's collected-edition sales. At this writing, the role of auteurist marketing is still important, though perhaps not as prominent as it once was. The Architects took a somewhat lower profile at the company in 2014. Marvel introduced a larger line of new titles and reboots with the "All New Marvel NOW!" branding campaign in the beginning of 2014. House advertisements for "All New Marvel NOW!" carried banners reading "The BIGGEST creators. The BEST characters," and although this formulation still prioritizes creators over characters, writers' and artists' names were not as prominently placed as in the Architect-era advertisements. None of the new titles were written by the Architects. And although other writers, including Cullen Bunn, Kelly Sue DeConnick, and Rick Remender, have been mentioned as potential members of a new Architects group, they have never been described as such in Marvel press material. And yet Marvel did announce a new Young Guns campaign in June 2014. Like the former promotions, this one included artists who were already working on high-profile titles, including Nick Bradshaw and Sara Pichelli—the artists on *Guardians of the Galaxy*, the film adaptation of which was Marvel Studios' big release for the summer—and Valerio Schiti, who was part of a semi-regular rotation of pencillers on Hickman's *Avengers* titles (Phegley, "SENYC"). The campaign suggests that, even as its characters continue to attract audiences to movie theaters, Marvel will continue to promote its creators to bring readers to its comics.

———

NOTES

1. For a general analysis of the benefits and drawbacks of continuity-driven comics, see Pustz 129–134.

2. For a history of Marvel's mid-1990s collapse and bankruptcy, see Raviv.

3. Sales information for specific titles will be provided below.

4. Since 2010, the company's comics line has been published by Marvel Worldwide, LLC; it was named Marvel Comics (with slight variations) from 1949 to 2006 and Marvel Publishing from 2006 to 2010 (Marvel Indicia/Colophon). Marvel Entertainment is the parent company that controlled Marvel Comics, the publishing division, and Marvel Studios, the production company initially formed as Marvel Films in 1993 (it changed its name to Marvel Studios in 1996). In 2009, Marvel Entertainment, Inc., became a wholly owned subsidiary of Disney, which transformed it into a limited liability company. In this essay, I use "Marvel" to refer to the publishing division and "ME" to refer to the parent company.

5. Box Office Mojo provides domestic grosses (see "Marvel Comics"). The chart does not include international grosses, but they were computed using figures from the individual pages for Marvel films.

6. It's unclear, either from the text or from the notes appended to the book, exactly when Jemas said this.

7. Compare, for example, the sales on titles from 1968 and the same from 2008 ("1968 Comic Book Sales Figures"; "2008 Comic Book Sales Figures").

8. For 1970s-era injunction and attempts at making live action adaptations, see Howe 171, 215–216. For *Secret Wars*, see Howe 263–265. For details on Marvel's licensing deals, see Howe 61, 76–77, 101–102, and 293–295, and Raviv 34–41.

9. Important examples of scholarship problematizing traditional concepts of the film auteur include Wollen 77–105; Schatz; and Caldwell.

10. On DC offering royalties, see Howe 246; on creation of Vertigo, see Itzkoff.

11. On Marvel's bankruptcy, see Raviv 25, 37–39; on Busiek's claim, see Comic Book Resources forum, http://forums.comicbookresources.com /showthread.php?280192-Worst-Editor-in-Chief/page8.

12. *The Amazing Spider-Man* had averaged 50,000 copies (and frequently fewer) in the months before April 2001 when Straczynski began his run.

13. Jones was writer on the book from November 2001 to August 2004; monthly sales figures can be found at Comichron, www.comichron.com /monthlycomicssales.html.

14. Straczynski's first arc, covering nos. 30–35 of *The Amazing Spider-Man Vol. 2*, is reprinted in *The Amazing Spider-Man Vol. 1: Coming Home* (2001).

15. See www.aintitcool.com/node/9362.

16. See catalog of Clayton Crain's work at www.comics.org/penciller/name /clayton%20crain/sort/alpha.

17. See catalog of Trevor Hairsine's work at www.comics.org/penciller /name/trevor%20hairsine/sort/alpha.

18. See McAllister.

WORKS CITED

"Adi Granov—Chronological Listing." *ComicBookDB*, n.d. Web. http://comicbookdb.com/creator_chron.php?ID=2845#year_2013.

"Aggregated 2002 Comic Book Sales Figures." *Comichron*, n.d. Web. www.comichron.com/monthlycomicssales/2002.html.

"Aggregated 2004 Comic Book Sales Figures." *Comichron*, n.d. Web. www.comichron.com/monthlycomicssales/2004.html.

"AICN Comics. Part III: Marvel.Comics + an Interview with Joe Quesada!" *Ain't It Cool News*, 19 June 2001. Web. www.aintitcool.com/node/9362.

"August 2005 Comic Book Sales Figures." *Comichron*, n.d. Web. www.comichron.com/monthlycomicssales/2005/2005-08.html.

Brady, Matt. "Marvel Sets Revenue Record for 2008." *Newsarama*, 2008. Web. www.newsarama.com/2295-marvel-sets-revenue-record-for-2008.html.

Caldwell, John. *Production Culture: Industrial Reflexivity and Critical Practice in Film and Television*. Durham, NC: Duke University Press, 2008. Print.

"Comics 101: What Is Decompression?" *Examiner*, n.d. Web. www.examiner .com/article/comics-101-what-is-decompression-part-2-of-4.

Corrigan, Timothy. *A Cinema Without Walls: Movies and Culture After Vietnam*. New Brunswick, NJ: Rutgers University Press, 1991. Print.

"ECCC: Marvel's 'The Architects' Panel." *Comic Book Resources*, 6 March 2011. Web. www.comicbookresources.com/?page=article&id=31178.

Esposito, Joey. "C2E2: Marvel's Artist Architects." *IGN*, 29 March 2011. Web. www.ign.com/articles/2011/03/19/c2e2-marvels-artist-architects.

George, Richard. "Marvel's Young Guns Assemble." *IGN*, 9 November 2006. Web. www.ign.com/articles/2006/11/09/marvels-young-guns-assemble.

Howe, Sean. *Marvel Comics: The Untold Story*. New York: HarperCollins, 2012. Print.

"Interview with Joe Quesada." *Millionaire Playboy*, n.d. Web. www.millionaireplayboy.com/comics/joeq.php.

Itzkoff, Dave. "Comics' Mother of 'the Weird Stuff' Is Moving On." *New York Times*, May 30, 2013, C1. Print.

"Joe Quesada." *Dynamic Forces*, n.d. Web. www.dynamicforces.com/htmlfiles /infodatabase.html?showInfodatabase=NS03220788364.

"Joe Quesada Talks Captain Britain, Event Fatigue." *Comic Book Resources*, 17 June 2009. Web. www.comicbookresources.com/?page=article&id=21638.

Johnson, Derek. "Cinematic Destiny: Marvel Studios and the Trade Stories of Industrial Convergence." *Cinema Journal* 52:1 (Fall 2012): 8. Print.

———. "Will the Real Wolverine Please Stand Up? Marvel's Mutation from Monthlies to Movies." In *Film and Comic Books*. Eds. Ian Gordon, Mark Jancovich, and Matthew McAllister. Jackson: University of Mississippi Press, 2007. Print.

Johnston, Rich. "Marvel Architects Panel at Emerald City Comic Con." bleedingcool.com, 5 March 2011. Web. www.bleedingcool.com/2011/03/05 /marvel-architects-panel-at-emerald-city-comic-con.

Khouri, Andy. "Marvel Executives Joe Quesada, Axel Alonso and Tom Brevoort on MarvelNOW!" *Comics Alliance*, 6 July 2012. Web. http://comicsalliance .com/marvel-now-interview-joe-quesada-axel-alonso-tom-brevoort.

Koller, Brock. "Marvel's Joe Quesada Talks Big Events." *ABC Action News*, 1 June 2008. Web. http://abc30.com/archive/6178207.

"Marvel Comics." *Box Office Mojo*, n.d. Web. www.boxofficemojo.com/franchises /chart/?id=marvelcomics.htm.

"Marvel Entertainment LLC Company Information." Hoovers, n.d. Web. www.hoovers.com/company-information/cs/company-profile.Marvel _Entertainment_LLC.18676ea3c3585a26.html.

Marvel Indicia/Colophon Publishers. *Grand Comics Database*, n.d. Web. www.comics.org/publisher/78/indicia_publishers.

"Marvel Releases 4Q numbers, 2002 Income." *Comic Book Resources*, 4 March 2003. Web. www.comicbookresources.com/?page=article&id=1875.

"Marvel Unveils the Architects." *Marvel*, 6 December 2010. Web. http://marvel .com/news/comics/14759/marvel_unveils_the_architects.

"Marvel's Young Guns." *Marvel*, 3 November 2010. Web. http://marvel.com /news/comics/3/marvels_young_guns.

McAllister, Matthew. "Ownership Concentration in the U.S. Comic Book Industry." In *Comics and Ideology*. Eds. Matthew McAllister, Edward H. Sewall Jr., and Ian Gordon. New York: Peter Lang, 2001. Print.

"1968 Comic Book Sales Figures." *Comichron*, n.d. Web. www.comichron.com /yearlycomicssales/1960s/1968.html.

Phegley, Kiel. "Exclusive: David Finch Signs with DC Comics." *Comic Book*

Resources, 5 June 2010. Web. www.comicbookresources.com/?page=article &id=24289.

———. "SENYC: Marvel's All New Young Guns." *Comic Book Resources*, 14 June 2014. Web. www.cbr.com/senyc-marvels-all-new-young-guns.

Pustz, Matthew. *Comic Book Culture: Fanboys and True Believers*. Jackson: University of Mississippi Press, 1999. Print.

Raviv, Dan. *Comic Wars: How Two Tycoons Battled over the Marvel Comics Empire—and Both Lost*. New York: Broadway Books, 2002. Print.

Sava, Oliver. "Jason Aaron interview." *avclub.com*, 27 February 2012. Web. www.avclub.com/article/jason-aaron-69883.

Schatz, Thomas. *The Genius of the System: Hollywood Filmmaking in the Studio Era*. New York: Pantheon, 1988. Print.

Smith, Anthony. "Action by Increment: Marvel Comics, Decompressed Narratives and the Collected Edition Market." Paper presented at Society for Cinema and Media Studies Annual Conference, New Orleans, Louisiana, March 2011.

Straczynski, J. Michael, story, John Romita Jr. and Scott Hanna, art. *The Amazing Spider-Man Vol. 1: Coming Home*. New York: Marvel Comics, 2001. Print.

Sunu, Steve. "HeroesCon '11: Matt Fraction's Fear Itself Panel." Web. www.comicbookresources.com, 5 June 2011. http://staging.cbr.com /heroescon-11-matt-fractions-fear-itself-panel.

"2008 Comic Book Sales Figures." *Comichron*, n.d. Web. www.comichron.com /monthlycomicssales/2008.html.

Wollen, Peter. *Signs and Meaning in the Cinema*. Bloomington: Indiana University Press, 1972. Print.

Wright, Bradford W. *Comic Book Nation: The Transformation of Youth Culture in America*. Baltimore: Johns Hopkins University Press, 2001. Print.

"WWC: Marvel's Young Guns II." Comic Book Resources, 5 August 2006. Web. www.comicbookresources.com/?page=article&id=7800.

CHAPTER 6

Marvel and the Form of Motion Comics

DARREN WERSHLER AND KALERVO A. SINERVO

omics have always been an "intermedial" form. That is, in the sense of Dick Higgins's classic definition of the term, as a medium, comics occupy a space between visual art and literature (49). But what happens when comics fuse with media that produce moving images? Douglas Wolk provides the following caveat:

> The most thoroughly ingrained error in the language used to discuss comics is treating them as if they were particularly weird, or failed, examples of another medium altogether. Good comics are sometimes described as being "cinematic" (if they have some kind of broad visual scope or imitate a familiar kind of movie) or "novelistic" (if they have keenly observed details, or simply take a long time to read). Those can be descriptive words when they're applied to comics. It's almost an insult, though, to treat them as compliments. Using them as praise implies that comics *as a form* aspire (more or less unsuccessfully) to being movies or novels. (13)

Fair enough. But if comics as a form do not aspire to anything, the communities that form around comics and create a sense of what comics are *for them*—including marketing departments—definitely have aspirations, and those aspirations are always motivated by particular ideological agendas. Wolk claims that we "pretty much" know what comics are, and that that is good enough (17). While this approach avoids having to attribute any sort of essence to comics, it also skirts around the need for critical analysis in the interest of getting on with describing the stuff that we like. However, it is entirely worth taking the time to look at discourse about comic forms in order to see what sorts of claims are being made about them and to think about what motivates those claims.

This chapter concerns the history of one major formation in Marvel's digital repertoire: the motion comic. Over the past two decades, Marvel has rolled out a new iteration of the motion comic on a surprising number of occasions, making claims each time for its innovative status, only to scrap it entirely and begin again within the space of a few years, claiming once more that what is produced is unprecedented. What is it about the form of motion comics that produces this constant churn, and how do we begin to trace it? What sort of audience does Marvel imagine for motion comics? Does it resemble the traditional comics audience, or even support the things that readers have always valued about print comics? And what contributions, if any, has the motion comic form made to the celebrated content of the Marvel Universe?

The larger point that emerges from a study of Marvel's various adventures in digital publishing is that in a networked digital culture, circulation outstrips continuity and preservation. In the name of increasing circulation, Marvel has produced a discontinuous series of mutually incompatible forms of digital comics. Digital technologies have also altered the physical form of print comics and, as a result of the new business models that accompany digital content, have transformed the histories and continuities of the characters on which their brands are based. Digital media excel at cheaply and shamelessly promulgating information across the globe. When they are used for storage, archiving, and preservation, however, they work against the grain, often producing uneven results.

Embracing circulation, then, occurs at the expense of duration, and this has been the case as long as writing and publishing have been industrialized. In 1942, Joseph Schumpeter coined the term "creative destruction" to describe "the essential fact about capitalism": in the very process of creating a new version of itself, its economic structure never ceases to destroy itself from within (83). It is simply not in the ethos of most companies, let alone contemporary companies, to carefully archive what they do.

Perhaps there is something specific about the production of superhero comics as a genre that accentuates this general tendency toward reinvention and the disavowal of older forms. In "Baroque Mutants in the 21st Century? Rethinking Genre Through the Superhero," Saige Walton argues for a "baroque" model of the superhero genre. For Walton, the superhero is "a mobile sign, historically dispersed across an array of media" (97). From this perspective, individual texts in the superhero genre function as components of immense transmedia networks, in which changes are not "evolutionary and discrete" but perpetually in flux (99). Crucially in these networks, Walton observes, "renewal occurs at a technological level, by maintaining connections with its Marvel comics past while drawing attention to media reframings, through temporally heightened, filmic, and digital metamorphoses of the superhero" (87). By this logic, if there is a specific recipe for "making Marvel," it will involve efforts to make Marvel's superhero narratives proliferate across any and every emerging media form, with little heed to *how* they connect to what came before, as long as there is always a connection. Moreover, says Walton, we should also be looking for claims about the ways in which a given superhero text in one of these emergent media forms "asserts the precedence of its own articulation" despite its reliance on Marvel's stock images, characters, and narratives (97)—in other words, that text will assert that its value lies precisely in the novelty of the appearance of superheroes in this new form. In Marvel's superhero media, then, both form and content exhibit a tension between the static idea of the superhero, on the one hand, and a constant formal and generic churn, on the other.

Part of the problem, then, is how and where to begin thinking about motion comics. The arrival of digital comics has altered our sense of the comic's efficacy as a storage medium. As Vilém Flusser notes in his writing about newspapers (the ancestral home of the print comic), digital media have changed the cultural context in which print appears, recontextualizing it into its exact opposite: "Paper, which is an ephemeral memory in comparison to marble or metal, becomes a durable one in the context of electromagnetic media—until tapes and records take over this role" (112). In comparison to their digital cousins, as Flusser suggests, print comics appear more sturdy, but this is a tenuous status at best. For most of their history, print comics had low production values to match their low cultural status. Even after the rise in popularity of variant covers and prestige-format trade editions in the late 1980s, comics are still more likely to be venerated by collectors rather than distributors or casual readers. Although the print quality of contemporary comics is markedly better than that of comics from the 1970s and earlier, most mainstream monthly comics today are still produced relatively cheaply, in large quantities—and official comics archives, especially public ones, are a rarity. Marvel's history of archiving its own materials, whether in the form of reference copies of their own publications or as original art, was patchy from the company's earliest days (Wershler 127). As a result, scholars and historians interested in the history of digital comics are facing significant forensic work if they wish to reconstruct that history.

One important, ongoing component of that work will be the development of a schema of the various *formations* of digital comics. In *The Form of News*, Kevin G. Barnhurst and John Nerone describe "form" as follows:

> By *form* we mean the persisting visible structure of the newspaper.
> . . . Form includes the things that are traditionally labeled layout and design and typography; but it also includes habits of illustration, genres of reportage, and schemes of departmentalization. *Form* is everything a newspaper does to present the look of the news.
>
> Any media form includes a proposed or normative model of the medium itself. Put another way, the form includes the way the medium imagines itself to be and to act. In its physical arrangement, structure, and format, a newspaper reiterates an ideal for itself. (3)

This definition is explicitly ideological and post-Althusserian (3): form is how the medium imagines itself to be for another, not "as it is." In other words, formal choices are far from neutral, because they always do some kind of ideological work. Any explanation of media form has to take its ideological aspects into account in order to be effective.

Barnhurst and Nerone expand their analytical framework by suggesting that for any medium in its historical context, forms can be bundled together into a series of different *formations*. Each formation combines a system of production and "a broader cultural configuration" (the ideological component) with a "look" (4). Barnhurst and Nerone also use the word "format" in a way that is more or less interchangeable with "look," but "format" has several advantages over "look" as a term of reference. Recent influential work by Jonathan Sterne ("The MP3"; *MP3: The Meaning*), Lisa Gitelman (*Paper Knowledge*), and John Guillory ("The Memo") has refined the traditional site of analysis in communication and media studies from media writ large to include more finely detailed studies of format and genre. For Sterne, as for Barnhurst and Nerone, the notion of format always includes social context: digital format is a "crystallized set of social and material relations" that includes both a set of technological specifications and the various authorized and unauthorized ways that people make use of them ("The

MP3," 826). Not even genre escapes the connection to the social. Rather than seeing genre as a collection of conventions or literary attributes, Gitelman describes it, too, as a dynamic yet historically and culturally specific "mode of recognition" that takes its shape as a result of social practices of reception and expression (2). In *Comics Versus Art*, Bart Beaty contends that comics should be conceptualized as "the products of a particular social world, rather than as a set of formal strategies" (43). In Barnhurst and Nerone's formulation, as well as Sterne and Gitelman's more recent and complementary work, form—including the triad of media, format, and genre—always includes the social world from the outset.

These distinctions are necessary because it is far too easy to collapse genres, formats, and media into each other. Say "comic," and most people think "superhero comic," because we have a habit of mistaking formats for the genres that they express. But even the exclusively superhero-branded Marvel digital offerings contain a few surprises, such as the award-winning adaptations of Jane Austen novels by Nancy Butler with Hugo Petrus (*Pride and Prejudice*), Sonny Liew (*Sense and Sensibility*), and Janet Lee (*Emma*). Even when "comics" referred to print alone, there was always a wide range of formats, some standardized (comic strips, comic books, collected trade editions, and so on) and some unorthodox (very large or very small books, unbound books, comics on materials other than paper, comics as installations or architectural spaces). The problem is that the history of forms, especially digital forms, is messy.

Marvel has a strong interest in building its brand, and, odd as it might seem, this has everything to do with the fragmentary nature of its historical archive. Harold Innis, one of the foundational thinkers of communication studies, articulated an approach to understanding media and power based around the ratio of two forces that are always in tension with one another: time and space (Heyer 61). Innis argued that in a given culture, a concentration of one of these forces necessitates compromising attention to the other. This is what Innis famously referred to as "the bias of media"—not "bias" in the sense of a lack of objectivity, but in the same way that wood or cloth has bias (Heyer 33). For Innis, a given culture in a specific time and place always has a grain to it; actions that follow that grain will go smoothly, while things that rub against it will be more difficult. Digital media are space-biased, better at circulation than at storage, and that circulation often occurs in the name of building and maintaining a media empire. As opposed to the various forms of digital media on disk or the Web, contemporary mobile digital media formats are a walled garden. They make it possible to maintain centralized control of intellectual property, expand rapidly, and maintain uniformity through inexpensive methods of access and translation. The cost of propagating information over space is preserving it over time.

Marvel's various and sometimes contradictory digital distribution strategies have rarely followed a single track, and they have certainly not "evolved"—old ideas keep reappearing, in many cases despite their repeated (commercial and aesthetic) failure. Newer forms are not necessarily better adapted to their cultural contexts than older ones, or more aesthetically satisfying, but it is difficult to tell, because they often completely erase their predecessors, which makes comparison problematic. As a result, the only practical way of studying the history of Marvel's electronic media forms is in terms of ephemera and refuse. This is not a new problem for media history; from Walter Benjamin to Erkki Huhtamo, Jussi Parikka, and Bruno Latour, media history often begins its investigations in the wreckage. Aside from the obvious pragmatism of this approach, it has the further advantage of avoiding the sense that technological change is a triumphant series of advances into the future (Huhtamo and Parikka 6). Latour clarifies how to do such work, noting that construction and demolition sites are places where the processes that make objects work (and fail to work) actually become visible (79–82). Marvel's early adventures in digital distribution are a graveyard of aborted experiments and unceremoniously abandoned products. When unveiling a new product, Marvel focuses on its features and its potential to reach new audiences or give loyal readers a new way to experience the comics they love. Rarely does the company draw attention to moves away from particular products, formats, or strategies.

It is helpful to think of Marvel's adventures in digital comics in terms of three different formations: interactive comics, digitized comics, and augmented print comics.[1] Each formation includes (or has included) several different forms, each of which has its attendant set of implications about what digital comics are supposed to be. As Beaty argues, trying to reduce this multitude down to an essence is beside the point. Thinking about the social world that each one imagines itself to be addressing, though, might tell us something useful about the sort of work that these forms do for Marvel.

Of the various digital formations, Marvel's motion comics appeared first, perhaps because, as Scott McCloud suggests in *Reinventing Comics*, most of the media windows in the contemporary environment are filled with moving images. Here is our first example of the ideology of form at work: when digital windows arrive in our lives, they bring with them the expectation that what fills them should be in motion. McCloud contends that digital comics offer us the possibility of "diversifying our perceptions" (19)—but that will only occur if the producers of digital comics do not accept the expectation that motion is the most interesting option for them or the only possibility.

In 1996, in the early days of popular interest in the Internet, Marvel began its digital efforts by producing custom-made content for America Online's (AOL's) services. Cybercomics, a hybrid, "slightly interactive" form that fell somewhere between comics and animation, produced with Macromedia (now Adobe) Director, a complex and notoriously difficult multimedia authoring tool better suited for producing CD-ROMs than web pages, were probably the first entirely digital Marvel product (Chichester; Wershler 129). Like most emergent technologies, Cybercomics were, at the moment of their appearance, marginal, clunky, and at odds with the print comics that at that point were still the sustaining technology of the Marvel media empire. AOL users received free access to Cybercomics as part of their subscription package. Beginning in 1997, Cybercomics were available on the Marvel Zone website, which required only a free registration for access. In 1999, the site Next Planet Over republished a dozen previously released Cybercomics.

Cybercomics writer D. G. Chichester still maintains some of his works in the area on his personal website as of this writing, but this is where the digital forensics need to begin. No doubt the interface of these works has changed a great deal since the days of AOL and first-generation graphic web browsers, but it is difficult to tell *how much* it has changed because of the many layers between the contemporary reader and the files salvaged from AOL, as well as the impossibility of checking the versions that now exist against earlier versions. Indeed, the stark reality of working with the textual environment that Alan Liu dubs "Discourse Network 2000" (50) is that the appearance of the Cybercomics is now potentially different *for each reader*. The display resolutions and color gamuts of user hardware can vary greatly; the operating systems and browser display conventions (forward, advance, and pause buttons, image lightboxing, etc.) have changed; title cards and menus have been added to the comics; the framing of the Cybercomic content appears inside a web page rather than an AOL page; and so on. Chichester notes that he translated the Cybercomics into the form in which

—

193

they currently appear because the Director plug-in that originally powered them was late to be ported to Macs with an Intel processor (that update was only first announced in 2005). However, more than a decade online is a long time, and Chichester's own website has also been subject to digital decay. Although it offers visitors two versions of the Cybercomics, "Panel by Panel" and "Video" (in the ".flv" Flash video format,[2] embedded in the page with JW Player, a multi-format video player), the links to the latter return a 404 "File not found" error.

The content of the "Panel by Panel" option, which still functions as of this writing, is similar to what can be found in Marvel print comics of the late 1970s and early 1980s. Chichester's site includes Cybercomics featuring Spider-Man ("Sandblasted"), Captain America and Iron Man ("Invasion Force"), the X-Men ("Twisted History"), Nick Fury, Agent of S.H.I.E.L.D. ("Jungle Warfare"), Daredevil ("Protection Racket"), and Blade (an early example of what would now be termed a transmedia tie-in with the first *Blade* movie). The Cybercomic form is specifically digital, though in true McLuhanesque fashion, the large speech balloon inside the browser lightbox that frames the Cybercomic alludes to its print ancestry. Inside the speech balloon is a rectangular frame that serves as the Cybercomic's cognate of a comic book page (in the Blade Cybercomic, vestigial nonfunctioning text, presumably from previous online locations of these panels, displays the message "NEXT PAGE LOADING" on the bottom of the last frame [Chichester]). Along the bottom of the frame-page is a thin gray strip, which indicates the frame number in the sequence in the left-hand corner; of the examples Chichester provides, the typical number of pages in each Cybercomic part is eight. As one mouses over the Cybercomic page, a popup navigation panel appears that (from left to right) consists of a thumbnail view of the entire Cybercomic part, a "back" arrow, an autoplay arrow, and a "forward" arrow. Clicking the forward arrow either causes a change in state in the current panel (such as a change in speech balloons, or a fade-in of a different graphic or audio element, as when, in the second panel of page 6 of "Twisted History," Professor X thinks of Magneto, Blob, Wolverine, and Storm, and each appears faintly in the background) or advances to the next panel in the frame (some panels are initially blacked out but faintly visible; some appear against a black background). In the lower right corner of the frame is a circular pie chart that indicates the progress through each frame's sequence of states. Some Cybercomics also included responsive audio tracks.

Cybercomics did not appear to be part of anything as organized as a

digital strategy; nor did they have a particular model for revenue generation attached to them. In his brief explanatory text "About Cybercomics,"
Chichester downplays his own role and emphasizes their ephemerality:
"Although these weren't 'real' comics, they were terrific to work on and I
was very pleased with the relatively solid story arcs. These had a limited
exposure and short run. Since then, they've occupied a lonely corner on
various hard drives I've cycled through. Before there's a crash and I lose the
whole collection to the digital graveyard, I figured I'd float 'em back out to
whomever would like a read." Marvel stopped producing Cybercomics in
early 2000, though the form bears a strong resemblance to later efforts such
as motion comics and Guided View technologies.

At the same time that Marvel halted production of Cybercomics in 2001,
it expanded its digital presence with the creation of Marvel dot.comics.
Dot.comics were Flash-based motion comics that functioned much like
Cybercomics, suggesting that the minimally interactive form still dominated the notion of what digital comics might be at the House of Ideas. The
few dot.comics that can still be located are available exclusively through
one of Marvel's own domains (http://dotcomics.marvel.com, no longer live),
but readers of the first dot.comics also could access them on DVD-ROM or
download them to their hard drives to be played through a piece of software
called the Marvel dotComics Player, which can still be found in the backwa-
ter corners of the Web. Three exclusive dot.comics were also bundled with
the DVD release of the two-disc special edition of Sam Raimi's *Spider-Man 2*
(2004), so the notion of motion comics as part of the transmedia marketing
mix was gaining traction.

As with Cybercomics, readers of dot.comics clicked their way through
panels to reveal word balloons and transitions between frames, with the
occasional cinematic effect like a pan added for splash pages or action
scenes. In many respects, though, dot.comics were *less* interactive than
their predecessors. Dot.comics were silent affairs, and their thumbnails
represented entire pages of the original print comic, sans word balloons,
rather than the individual animated states of the digital frame, as with the
Cybercomics. For the reader willing to squint at his or her screen, this format did offer a rare chance to view the completed artwork of a comic page
without any of the image being covered by word balloons or text boxes.
At the same time, technical quality was low. Dot.comics panel transitions
and visual effects were poorly animated, eliciting display errors and fuzzy
resolutions when readers attempted to move backward through the comic.

Clicking on the panels of a motion comic to activate them is only the most visible and least important way in which the form engages the participation of the consumer audience. Transmedia is at least as much a business model as it is a creative form (if not more). Motion comics are attractive components of a transmedia assemblage because they are relatively cheap and easy to produce from existing properties, yet still smack of novelty, so we should expect to see more of them tied to Marvel events and major cinematic releases in the coming years. Moreover, they are highly amenable to the four "forms of participatory culture" that Henry Jenkins identifies as the milieu for the appearance of transmedia: affiliations, expressions, collaborative problem-solving, and circulations (Jenkins xi–xii). Both fan-made and professional animations and motion comics circulate across the Web, organized, cataloged, described, and debated passionately by fans, who often invest significant chunks of their time into these activities. The collaborative work of fans preserves such objects where even the publisher appears disinterested in doing so; further, their online writing is a huge component of what makes academic histories such as this one possible.

With the dot.comics, Marvel also began to develop a digital business model. Some of the content was drawn from back issues and some came from recent releases. In both cases, for dot.comics the added labor of producing original content from scratch was gone—another important difference from their Cybercomic predecessors. Marvel monetized dot.comics in a fashion similar to the early 1990s shareware model, where the first few levels of a video game might be available free of charge as a demo, and players had to purchase the full product to continue the games they had begun to enjoy (Allen). Individual dot.comics appeared and disappeared from the site to complement Marvel's print publishing schedule: for example, the first few back issues of a new series like *Ultimate Spider-Man* would be available in dot.comic format, but never the current issue. Further, the entire run would disappear for a time if the publisher reprinted a storyline in a collected edition (Allen). This practice is typical of the "bricks-and-clicks" marketing model that publishers of many types of print media were trying around the turn of the millennium: if readers wanted to keep reading, they had to go out and purchase the print comic (or follow a link from the dot.comics site to order it online).

Shortly after Marvel began making Cybercomics, in 2003, it doubled down on a different version of the motion comic form by penning a licensing deal with Intec Interactive, a digital entertainment company (now primarily a video game accessories manufacturer) based in Florida, to produce Digital Comic Books (DCBs). These were DVDs that used Chameleon, a cross-platform (DVD, Xbox, Playstation 2, Mac PC) software viewer with its own digital rights management (DRM) system, to display "digitally enhanced" versions of classic Marvel titles (Reid). In this case, the digital enhancements in question included "professional voice-overs, original music, stunning effects and high-end sound design," according to a description published at the time. "Plenty of extra material is packed in as well, like previews, character biographies, original sketches, a documentary about how comics are made, and bonus chapters (including classic first appearances of the main characters)"—more than one hundred minutes of content per DVD (Wieland). Although their name suggests that DCBs were most closely related to comic books, Intec's own press releases repeatedly used the language of cinema to describe them: "a new digital format on DVD that retells some of these heroes' timeless tales in a cinematic style"; "they play like mini-movies"; and "because they play more like a movie than a comic book, each story delivers an amazingly immersive experience, even for those people who have never opened a comic book in their lives" (Intec Interactive, Inc.). The reason behind this repeated positioning of the intermedial comic as cinematic has everything to do with that last quotation.

It is the people who have never opened a comic book in their lives that are the imagined audience of the motion comic. By 2003, the rise to market dominance of the superhero blockbuster film was well underway, and the plans to sell digital comics followed suit. The places that Intec planned to market DCBs were not comic book stores, but "Toys R Us, GameStop, Hastings, SamGoody.com, SunCoast.com and other video/DVD retailing outlets" (Reid)—general retailers, game stores, and video media retailers. Given the amount of content they contained, the suggested retail price for DCBs was a bargain, at $9.99 each (Wieland). However, DCBs met the same fate as all of their predecessors—they were ignored by that coveted general audience. Today, searching YouTube for the string "Intec Read Along" reveals some of the contents of those DVDs, which are closer in the aesthetics of the dialogue and voiceovers to the 1963 animated *Spider-Man* series than to Sam Raimi's version.

By 2009, it should have come as no surprise that Marvel was making yet another foray into motion comics, this time under the Marvel Knights Animation banner. The press release for the first title, *Spider-Woman: Agent of S.W.O.R.D.*, completely ignores Cybercomics and dot.comics, claiming that "this is the first time an original Marvel motion comic will be made available for fans to download and own!" (Marvel Motion Comics). Rather than hosting the content itself, Marvel chose to distribute it through iTunes, which initially had an exclusive right to it. Episodes were released biweekly, and the first episode of the series was initially priced at $0.99 to entice readers. The price rose to $1.99 per episode after two weeks, and that price stayed the same through all subsequent episodes. (Marvel would later use this same pricing scheme for its initial in-app purchasing system for static digital comics.) Marvel also went to pains to emphasize that these new motion comics were "true to the heritage of panel-by-panel graphic storytelling" (Marvel Motion Comics)—they used original art from the print versions of the stories, and the writers and artists of the print versions received full credit. The use of original art requires compromises somewhere, though: animation and voice acting are nearly as wooden as they are in Marvel's earlier attempts at motion comics, relying on sliding static figures across backgrounds, minimal movements of mouths and other facial features, fade-ins and outs, and so on. The second title in the series, an adaptation of Warren Ellis and Adi Granov's acclaimed *Iron Man: Extremis*, arrived with similar amnesiac hyperbole from Marvel editor-in-chief Joe Quesada: "Just as the *Iron Man: Extremis* comic book forever changed how we see Iron Man, the motion comic adaptation represents the next evolution of the medium" (Marvel, "New Motion Comic"). With *Extremis*, Marvel expanded its circulation beyond iTunes to include the Zune and Xbox networks. It also penned a licensing deal with reissue specialists Shout! Factory, who continue to distribute DVD and Blu-ray versions of these titles. Interestingly, Shout! Factory refers to these works as "films"—"a wonderful hybrid" whose "line remains true to the heritage of panel-by-panel graphic storytelling incorporating smart storytelling, groundbreaking graphics and incredible action." The logic of marketing trumps formal innovation.

In March 2012, the publisher announced the development of Marvel Infinite, yet another foray into motion comics that functioned like streamlined Cybercomics. Once again, in the official press release, a new iteration of Marvel's ongoing experiments in digital comics is described as if the previous ones had never appeared. This latest version of the intermedial comic form is touted as both innovative and faithful, "a new technique in comics storytelling that is built specifically for the digital world [and] yet in a very elegant way manages to keep the purity of what makes a comic a 'comic.'" The quotation is attributed to none other than Chief Creative

Officer Joe Quesada. Within three sentences, Queseda reiterates this balancing act three times. It's an implicit dismissal of Marvel's previous efforts along these lines. The press release also quotes writer Mark Waid, who says: "What we're doing isn't bargain basement animation or print pages simply transcribed to the screen" (Morse).

What is *actually* new about this press release is that it provides a reasonably detailed description of some of the ways that the formal possibilities of motion comics are finally beginning to affect genre, particularly in terms of the decisions that writers and artists make about narrative technique. Waid describes his collaboration with illustrator Stuart Immonen on *Avengers vs. X-Men #1 Infinite* (the first Marvel Infinite title) as follows: "It's a lot more labor-intensive than your garden variety 10-page story, that's for sure; a lot more 'what if we tried this rack-focus effect?' or 'what if this frame stretched across multiple screens?' but it was so rewarding," and, "We're no longer confined by the limitations of the page. While we still are confined in a way by the size of a tablet screen in the same way that we have to deal with the physical size of a page, the screen is capable of so much more. You can layer your story in ways that are impossible with a physical comic" (Morse).

At the same time as the announcement of the Marvel Infinite initiative, the publisher launched a complementary project adding motion and meta-content to its print comics through special software tools—augmented reality (AR) apps for smartphones. Marvel AR launched in 2012 as a free app (developed in partnership with Aurasma) on iOS and Android devices (Hutchings). Certain print comics, such as Warren Ellis, Mike McKone, and Jason Keith's *Avengers: Endless Wartime* (tellingly, the first of Marvel's Original Graphic Novels line, which requires no knowledge of Marvel continuity other than what might be derived from Hollywood films), now arrive with icons marking their covers and certain pages. When the reader holds the camera of his or her phone or tablet over a marked page, the app scans the entire page as if it were a QR code and launches a short video or audio segment "enhancing" the page's content (Marvel, "The Marvel ReEvolution"). These segments range from full animated sequences with sound, dialogue, and narration to adaptive audio tracks, drawings animating the transition from pencil roughs to full-color artwork, or the author or penciller walking across the screen and offering commentary on the production of the comic.

AR features change the comic book experience in more than just the obvious ways. For example, when using the app, the reader must reorient the way a print comic is read, holding the mobile device an appropriate distance away from or above the comic. Accessed this way, even a print comic is now read through a practice of digital mediation and network access (as the AR app must be on a working phone connected to the Internet in order to function). The features also layer the comic in question with extra dimensions of ephemeral temporality; just like the smart-panel system of Marvel's digital comics, the AR content changes the experience of reading a comic from interpreting fixed images into interpreting moving images, and often transforms comic reading from a silent activity into an auditory one. Finally, the AR pushes against expectations of the materiality and mobility of comics. While the migration from the page to the phone or tablet screen meant that readers could take more comics with them in smaller and lighter packages (after all, an iPhone can potentially hold thousands of comics on a device that fits into a pocket), using the AR app with a print comic is far more cumbersome than either holding the print comic or squinting at the smartphone screen. Certainly, the app is not optimized for use on the bus. Perhaps this is why some of the content of Marvel AR has recently begun to migrate onto Marvel Digital Comics Unlimited (Rosenblatt), showing up in comics on the subscription service here and there. This move suggests that adding multimedia content to the printed page will also be a passing phase. Amalgamating all the content onto a digital device provides an easier reading experience for the consumer than hybridizing the print comic and the mobile device. And, given the rate with which companies render consumer technology obsolete, the probability that any of the AR content in books like *Endless Wartime* will be accessible to anyone in even five years approaches zero (unless, perhaps, someone captures it and uploads it to YouTube or another video hub).

At this time, the narrative of Marvel's digital strategies is becoming increasingly tangled as the publisher's transmedia tactics begin to bear fruit. Marvel's digital products are difficult to track not only because the company keeps so few publicly accessible organized records, but also because the products move and mutate quickly. Interfaces change with no warning and frenetic frequency; features available with other products appear and disappear; and tie-ins to other branches of Marvel's successful transmedia empire spring up everywhere. Context is now harder than ever to trace, and there is no cataloging allowing users to coordinate their reading experience. The current state of affairs is a far cry from the GITCorp DVD archives of entire Marvel print runs, where the reader was able to see even the peripheral content of ads, letter pages, and editorial notes, all as they appeared at the original time of printing. Now, even accessing the same comic through the same digital avenue twice results in different contexts, as sidebar ads, menus, and interface tools are continually updated as part of the product's cloud-based status. Reading a Marvel digital comic tomorrow may offer a completely different experience than it offered today, owing to a totally different interface aesthetic, with new or absent features. Tomorrow, the same comic you read today may have a soundtrack, or it may have had a soundtrack removed. For scholars seeking to track and describe these objects, the difficulties are clearly multiple and solutions are rare.

The subtext running through this entire fragmented narrative is deeply embedded in discursive frameworks of control. Such discourses run through these products on a level that becomes most apparent when the user pushes up against the boundaries of these controls. The sense of "shared ownership" over the product that both comic book scanners ("pirates") and readers have in a transmedia environment may have led Marvel to move toward cloud-based intermedia libraries laced with DRM tools. While the tactics relating to access and control are obvious in the case of online-only, DRM-locked comics, the contents that come through augmented reality apps, while copyable, are much harder to reproduce and pirate than when pirating involves simply extracting image files. For readers, there is more to experience when accessing comics via Marvel's official proprietary services than when reading scanned print comics in CBR or CBZ format via independently created software—but only in the short term. And, given the number of iterations that motion comics have already seen, Marvel's basic refusal to even acknowledge their existence, and the tendency of new hardware and software in both home computing and mobile platforms to lack any kind of backward compatibility, digital comics readers who might be interested in any sort of long-term relationship with the products they purchase should remain skeptical.

These trends point toward Marvel's focus on market expansion and control rather than fan values or communities. The comic book store was long the local center of fan-based commerce and casual interaction among comic book readers (Wright), although the annual convention was the gathering place for more formalized and spectacular fan interactions—cosplay, swag bags, etc.—and for interactions between fans and creators. By selling DVDs online and alongside movies and music, Marvel was attempting to reach new markets, but in neglecting to ensure wide placement on comic book store shelves, the publisher ignored the established readers who sustained its business. Fans interested in purchasing the DVD collections generally had to do so outside of the comic book store, and therefore not within their local communities. This development may have had less to do with Marvel's intentions than it did with the established circulatory networks of Marvel's licensees. Regardless, neglecting the local comic book shop was reflective of Marvel's prioritization of market expansion over fan values. It was a first tiding of things to come as the publisher's increased focus on digital products moved Marvel comics farther and farther outside the local communities fostered by the comic book store, and farther as well from the interests of comic book collectors.

In his writing on computerized networking, Darin Barney claims that the imbalance of space-biased media in the modern age (embodied by digital technologies) lessens our culture's sense of community. He points to the capacities of digital networks for storage and retrieval, explaining that they devalue the preservation of communicated information, enforcing a cultural priority of speed over continuity (52–53). Traditions and shared values flounder under the weight of digital nowness, a nowness, according to Barney, that negates collective, communal memory and replaces it with unmoored communications between individuals (60). This thesis fits comfortably with Marvel's shift from products (ownable removable media) to services (subscription-based networked media). The company's lack of organized, publicly accessible documentation of its own strategies further elaborates Barney's point, as it constitutes an absence of history. But the even greater loss of history and documentation will come when (not if) Marvel discontinues a given service, changes a given interface, or stops offering a given special feature.

A reader who buys a Marvel print comic owns that content for as long as the paper stock lasts or the reader keeps track of it. A reader who purchases the same comic digitally has it for as long as Marvel maintains its own servers, services, and records. The purchase of a particular digital product may entitle the customer to a digital copy, but only until a certain date, beyond which it may no longer be available (Ellis and McKone 120). Due to the cloud-based nature of Marvel's contemporary digital offerings, accessible only through approved Marvel web portals and apps, the reader's "ownership" of his or her purchases depends on Marvel's continued success (or, at the very least, existence). Extra content, such as AR features and adaptive audio tracks, are even more ephemeral, because proprietary methods do not yet exist for pinning this content down locally. Perhaps eventually,

Marvel will monetize these features in a fashion that is distinct from Marvel Digital Comics Unlimited (perhaps in the same way one can purchase a standard DVD or an edition loaded with special features). Until such a time, it is effectively impossible to track or capture these digital objects in any kind of coherent fashion. The target is not only moving; it is also blurring, flickering, splitting apart, and reforming in versions that are oddly similar, but apparently unaware of their own recent past.

From Cybercomics to Infinite Comics and AR, all of Marvel's iterations of the motion comic form are predicated on the same basic notion: animating the static comic page. The reinvention and relaunching of intermedial motion comics every few years demonstrate that the ideology of that form operates according to the familiar logic of creative destruction. Various combinations of special features and digital-only content, as well as the ever-changing interfaces for accessing such content and the constant rhetorical claims of innovation, provide ample evidence for this contention. The circulatory methods and business models of a space-based, networked, digital milieu favor endless permutation, not preservation for posterity. The only way to stay profitable in such an environment is to stay on the cutting edge of distribution methods, attempting to maintain accessibility across devices and formats, while viewing content as something to be remixed rather than preserved. Off the page, ads can be replaced, terms of service can be updated, editorial content can be rewritten. Locks might be placed on content as well, but focusing on preservation is beside the point, because Marvel's business is now based on anything but time-biased media.

This overriding concern with circulation is not promising for the development of the comic form. Formal innovations remain at a minimum when brand is king. From a creator's perspective, the obsession with motion is particularly odd, because it is only one possibility for making comics digital. The list of possibilities that Scott McCloud presents in *Reinventing Comics* could remain as a set of moribund futures betrayed by the actual course of events, much like Ted Nelson's *Computer Lib/Dream Machines*, first published in 1974, was for a more sophisticated form of hypertext than the World Wide Web. But the ongoing obsession with motion has more to do with the lucrative nature of motion pictures and the desire to build an audience for Marvel films than with a general interest in formal innovation. As Jennifer Daryl Slack and J. Macgregor Wise point out, one of the linchpins of modern ideology was that progress—which is really just forward movement—somehow equaled evolution toward something better (10, 17).

Marvel invokes that rhetoric constantly with its motion comics, but all that changes, really, is the digital resolution, the soundtracks, and the commentary, changes that have rarely, if ever, made for better art. Perhaps we've even given up on the notion of progress in favor of the convenience of having short-term access to comics on our mobile devices (Slack and Wise 19). We cannot be certain about the characters, the storylines, and the continuity of any fictional universe: the only thing we can be certain of when we try to predict the future of the Marvel brand in digital media is that the iconic capital "M" logo on the cover of every issue, the masthead of every website, and the opening shots of every film will remain.

NOTES

1. This chapter does not address the introduction of digital production techniques to print comics, a subject broad enough for many other papers on a number of topics, including the use of digital typefaces, colorization, the influence of drawing tablets and Photoshop on illustration style, digital layout and prepress methods, the "widescreen aesthetic" of writers like Warren Ellis and its influence on framing and storytelling, and so on.

2. A logical choice because Macromedia had purchased Flash from its original manufacturer and developed it as an export option from Director.

WORKS CITED

Allen, Todd. "Dot-comics Lure New Readers." *Chicago Tribune*, 24 June 2002. Print.

Barney, Darin. "The Vanishing Table, or Community in a World That Is No World." *Topia* 11 (2004): 49–66. Print.

Barnhurst, Kevin G., and John Nerone. *The Form of News: A History*. New York: Guildford Press, 2001. Print.

Beaty, Bart. *Comics Versus Art*. Toronto: University of Toronto Press, 2012. Print.

Chichester, D. G. "About Cybercomics." *Capitalist Fiction*, 2010. Web. http://capitalistfiction.com/web/cybercomics/comics_carousel.html.

Ellis, Warren, Mike McKone, and Jason Kieth. *Avengers: Endless Wartime*. New York: Marvel Worldwide, 2013. Print.

Flusser, Vilém. *Does Writing Have a Future?* Trans. Nancy Ann Roth. Minneapolis: University of Minnesota Press, 2011. Print.

Gitelman, Lisa. *Paper Knowledge: Toward a Media History of Documents*. Durham, NC: Duke University Press, 2014. Print.

Guillory, John. "The Memo and Modernity." *Critical Inquiry* 31.1 (2004): 108–132. Print.

Heyer, Paul. *Harold Innis*. New York: Rowman and Littlefield, 2003. Print.

Higgins, Dick, with an Appendix by Hannah Higgins. "Intermedia." [1966] *Leonardo* 34.1 (2001): 49–54. Print.

Huhtamo, Erkki, and Jussi Parikka. "Introduction." In *Media Archaeology*. Berkeley: University of California Press, 2011. Print.

Hutchings, Emma. "Marvel Launches Augmented Reality Comics." *PSFK*, 14 March 2012. Web. www.psfk.com/2012/03/marvel-augmented-reality -comics.html#!F5OtK.

Intec Interactive, Inc. "Intec Interactive Partners with Marvel Comics to Release Digital Comic Books On DVD: New Product Line Augments Classic Comics with Voice, Music, Sound Effects and Special DVD Features." *PRNewswire*, 9 December 2003. Web. www.prnewswire.com/news-releases /intec-interactive-partners-with-marvel-comics-to-release-digital-comic -books-on-dvd-73251257.html.

Jenkins, Henry, with Ravi Purushotma, Margaret Weigl, Katie Clinton, and Alice J. Robison. *Confronting the Challenges of Participatory Culture: Media Education for the 21st Century*. John D. and Catherine T. MacArthur Foundation Reports on Digital Media and Learning. Cambridge, MA: MIT Press, 2009. Print.

Latour, Bruno. *Reassembling the Social: An Introduction to Actor-Network Theory*. Oxford: Oxford University Press, 2005. Print.

Liu, Alan. "Transcendental Data: Toward a Cultural History and Aesthetics of the New Encoded Discourse." *Critical Inquiry* 31 (2004): 49–84. Print.

Marvel. "The Marvel ReEvolution Is Here." *Marvel*, last modified 15 March 2012. Web. http://marvel.com/news/comics/2012/3/11/18265/the_marvel _reevolution_is_here.

———. "New Motion Comic: IRON MAN: EXTREMIS." *Marvel*, 25 March 2010 (updated 12 April 2010). Web (Google cache version). http://webcache .googleusercontent.com/search?q=cache:D412K23lvqEJ:marvel.com/news /comics/2010/3/25/11770/new_motion_comic_iron_man_extremis.

Marvel Motion Comics. "Spider-Woman: Available Now on iTunes." *Marvel*, 19 August 2009 (updated 14 October 2009). Web (Google cache version). http:// webcache.googleusercontent.com/search?q=cache:_joG8bBLIEYJ:marvel .com/news/comics/2009/8/19/9237/spider-woman_available_now_on_itunes.

McCloud, Scott. *Reinventing Comics*. New York: HarperCollins, 2000. Print.

Morse, Ben. "Marvel Infinite Comics Unveiled." *Marvel*, 11 March 2012. Web.

http://marvel.com/news/comics/2012/3/11/18266/marvel_infinite_comics
_unveiled.

Nelson, Theodore. *Computer Lib/Dream Machines*, 2nd ed. Redmond, WA:
Tempus Books / Microsoft Press, 1987. Print.

Reid, Calvin. "Digital Comics from Intec." *Publishers Weekly*, 22 December 2003.
Web. www.publishersweekly.com/pw/print/20031222/36251-digital-comics
-from-intec.html.

Rosenblatt, Seth. "Finally, Marvel's Ready for You to Hear Its Comics." *CNET*,
9 March 2014. Web. www.cnet.com/news/finally-marvels-ready-for-you-to
-hear-its-comics-scoop.

Schumpeter, Joseph A. *Capitalism, Socialism, and Democracy*. 1942. New York:
Harper, 1975. Print.

Shout! Factory. "Marvel Knights: Collection." *Shout! Factory*, 22 November 2011.
Web. www.shoutfactory.com/product/marvel-knights-collection.

Slack, Jennifer Daryl, and J. Macgregor Wise. *Culture + Technology: A Primer*.
New York: Peter Lang, 2005. Print.

Sterne, Jonathan. "The MP3 as Cultural Artifact." *New Media & Society* 8.5
(2008): 825–842. Print.

——. *MP3: The Meaning of a Format*. Durham, NC: Duke University Press, 2012.
Print.

Walton, Saige. "Baroque Mutants in the 21st Century? Rethinking Genre
Through the Superhero." In *The Contemporary Comic Book Superhero*. Ed.
Angela Ndalianis. Routledge Research in Cultural and Media Studies.
New York: Routledge, 2009. 86–106. Print.

Wershler, Darren. "Digital Comics, Circulation, and the Importance of Being
Eric Sluis." *Cinema Journal* 50.3 (2011): 127–134. Print.

Wieland, Jonah. "Eagle One Media to Distribute Marvel and CrossGen
Digital Comic Books." *Comic Book Resources*, 13 April 2004. Web.
www.comicbookresources.com/?page=article&id=3377.

Wolk, Douglas. *Reading Comics: How Graphic Novels Work and What They Mean*.
New York: Da Capo Press, 2007. Print.

Wright, Frederick. "How Can 575 Comic Books Weigh Under an Ounce?
Comic Book Collecting in the Digital Age." *Journal of Electronic Publishing*
11.3 (2008). Web. http://dx.doi.org/10.3998/3336451.0011.304.

Transmedia Storytelling in the "Marvel Cinematic Universe" and the Logics of Convergence-Era Popular Seriality

FELIX BRINKER

When the Marvel Cinematic Universe (MCU) kicked off with the release of *Iron Man* in 2008, few suspected that Jon Favreau's movie would end up being the first installment of one of the most profitable media franchises of our time. During the preceding twelve months, cinemagoers had witnessed the release of *Spider-Man 3* (Sam Raimi, 2007), *Fantastic Four: Rise of the Silver Surfer* (Tim Story, 2007), and, shortly afterward, *The Dark Knight* (Christopher Nolan, 2008). When *Iron Man* premiered, it seemed to do little more than follow the same tried-and-true model, which, coincidentally, *Superhero Movie* (Craig Mazin, 2008) had spoofed just weeks earlier.

Nine years in, Marvel Studios' project to build a franchise around a series of self-financed, interconnected film and television releases is still in progress. Currently comprising the films *Iron Man* and *The Incredible Hulk* (Louis Leterrier, 2008); *Iron Man 2* (Jon Favreau, 2010); *Captain America: The First Avenger* (Joe Johnston, 2011) and *Thor* (Kenneth Branagh, 2011); *The Avengers* (Joss Whedon, 2012); *Iron Man 3* (Shane Black, 2013) and *Thor: The Dark World* (Alan Taylor, 2013); *Captain America: The Winter Soldier* (Anthony and Joe Russo, 2014) and *Guardians of the Galaxy* (James Gunn, 2014); *Avengers: Age of Ultron* (Joss Whedon, 2015) and *Ant-Man* (Peyton Reed, 2015); *Captain America: Civil War* (Anthony and Joe Russo, 2016) and *Doctor Strange* (Scott Derrickson, 2016); plus the ABC television series *Agents of S.H.I.E.L.D.* since 2013 and *Agent Carter* since 2015; the Netflix shows *Daredevil*, *Jessica Jones* since 2015, and *Luke Cage* (since 2016); and a number of associated short films called "Marvel One-Shots" (included as bonus content on DVD and Blu-ray releases) and tie-in comic books, the MCU has made Marvel characters a ubiquitous presence on the screens of our media environment and raked in staggering profits for its parent company. At the time of writing, three of these titles—the two *Avengers* films and *Iron Man 3*—list among the top ten of highest-grossing films ever made ("All Time"). With several new installments currently in production, the competition over dominance at the box office against DC-based properties (and competing Marvel films produced by other majors) seems to be settled in favor of Marvel Studios, at least for the time being.[1]

However, it is not only the commercial success that sets recent Marvel Studio releases apart from other cinematic and televisual takes on the comic book superhero. The MCU also constitutes an unprecedented attempt to transfer logics of serial storytelling, in this case established in the medium of superhero comics, to film and beyond. Like the comic book properties on which it is based, the MCU is organized in a number of separate subseries whose narratives all take place within a shared diegesis. Within this common "universe," events in one film or episode are continuous with others, producing lasting impacts for succeeding installments, and characters and objects move easily from one subseries to the other. The result is a rapidly expanding, complex narrative universe whose scope already surpasses those of the *Star Trek* and *Star Wars* film franchises.

What further distinguishes the MCU from other successful series is its relationship to earlier incarnations of the superheroes who populate it: each of its entries effectively presents itself as a cross-medial remake or reimagining of preexisting Marvel properties and reinterprets established characters, themes, stories, and iconographies for the big or the small screen. As a result, the MCU not only tells stories about established superhero figures who are already known to avid comic book readers, but also fills its shared diegesis with countless (more or less oblique) references to the existing comic book lore. Interestingly, and contrary to what one might assume, neither the MCU's complex overall narrative structure nor its open appeal to specialized fan-knowledge has so far detracted from its mainstream success—in fact, these aspects seem to represent one of the MCU's primary advantages over competing film and television series, a circumstance that prompts us to reflect on the narrative logics of the franchise and the medial preconditions for its emergence.

Along these lines, in this chapter I will suggest that the commercial success of Marvel Studios' recent film and television releases is closely related to its combination of different modes of serial narration: the (multi-)linear serial storytelling typical of comic books and television series, a transmedial serialization of content across different media formats, and the nonlinear narrative seriality characteristic of reboots, remakes, and adaptations. Charting the confluence of these different types of serialization, I argue that it is the MCU's situatedness within a digital media environment—whose economic logics call for a spread across media, and whose countless legal and illegal online archives and services allow for a constant access to all things Marvel—that makes it possible for the franchise's complex relationships of reference and continuity to come into existence in the first place. As I will show, those at the helm of Marvel, and especially those who have been charged with guiding the cinematic entries of the franchise, are acutely aware of the role of each installment in this respect and self-consciously thematize each one's embeddedness in multiple serial trajectories. Finally, I argue that the MCU's multidimensional seriality partakes in broader cultural shifts responding to the digitization of our media environment, and that it constitutes a model for a new, emergent logics of popular seriality that is also at work elsewhere, in other genres and media.

MEDIA CONVERGENCE AND TRANSMEDIA STORYTELLING

In many ways, the MCU presents itself as a prime example of transmedia storytelling, or, in other words, as a media franchise designed to operate smoothly within the competitive environment of what Henry Jenkins has called "convergence culture." For Jenkins, the technological convergence of formerly separate, analogue media in the supra-medium of digital code has had far-reaching consequences for the production, distribution, and reception of popular narrative texts—in particular for film and television, which, after having lost their former status as cultural dominants, are now faced with the "migratory behavior of media audiences" that can choose from an abundance of different entertainment options (Jenkins, *Convergence* 2, cf. 1-25). In addition, the unprecedented availability of content on the Internet, along with a proliferation of media outlets that cater to ever more fragmented audiences and specialized niche markets, has increased the competition among producers, whose outputs now compete more directly over the attention of easily distracted viewers (cf. 74-79). Media conglomerates like the Walt Disney Company—which has owned Marvel Entertainment and its subsidiaries since 2009—respond to this situation with a two-pronged strategy designed to secure their standing within the industry: a business model based on the horizontal integration of different markets under the banner of shared brands, and an emphasis on the production of content that provides intensified, long-term immersive experiences to diverse audiences (cf. Grainge 54–60; Jenkins, *Convergence* 95–96). The goal of such efforts, as Paul Grainge points out, is the creation of "total entertainment," that is, "an expansive entertainment and communication environment in which [media conglomerates] have a . . . near total stake in terms of ownership and control," and in which revenue streams are maximized across a range of media channels (54). What Jenkins terms "transmedia storytelling"—defined as the unfolding of a narrative "across multiple media platforms, with each new text making a distinctive and valuable contribution to the whole"—is a cultural form specifically tailored to meet these goals that capitalizes on the combined strength of different media in order to establish long-term and sustained relationships with a large group of diverse consumers.[2]

The MCU's reach across cinema, television, short films, comic books, and digital games can thus be understood as both a commercial and a textual strategy. On the level of industrial practice, the individual installments of the franchise contribute to the cultural visibility of the Marvel "megabrand" and serve to produce synergistic effects for all kinds of products that feature the company's iconic characters and logos (from comic books to T-shirts, coffee mugs, and action figures) (Grainge 58, cf. 59–60). On the level of textual practice, the MCU "integrates multiple texts to create a narrative so large than it cannot be contained within a single medium" and attempts to "sustain a depth of experience that motivates more consumption" (Jenkins, *Convergence* 95, 96). Within the franchise, the various media formats serve as "points of entry for different audience segments" (Jenkins, "Transmedia"): blockbusters like *Avengers: Age of Ultron* or *Guardians of the Galaxy*, for example, periodically attract a broad audience of cinemagoers and find a profitable afterlife in ancillary markets, while shows like *Agents of S.H.I.E.L.D.* target a smaller demographic of television viewers on a more regular basis. Tie-in comic books like *Ant-Man: Prelude* address an even smaller circle of readers, and the "One-Shot" short films, in their function as digital bonus content, serve to promote the sale of DVDs and Blu-ray discs. In order to be functional for the franchise's broader narrative architecture, each of these installments must promote the reception of other parts of the franchise and also be self-contained enough to function outside of the larger context (cf. Jenkins, "Transmedia"). Accordingly, the MCU's feature films, the One-Shots, and the individual seasons of the TV shows all provide a high degree of narrative closure; but at the same time, all of them connect to other parts of the franchise by means of shared storylines, characters, events, and motifs. Taken together, as the result of what one might call a medial division of labor, the MCU is simultaneously open to various different media audiences and still able to integrate disparate viewers into a steadily growing base of loyal fans and followers.

Although Jenkins's conception helps us to understand the commercial imperatives of transmedia storytelling—Marie-Laure Ryan characterizes it as "a way to get us to consume as many products as possible" ("Transmedial" 384)—it remains vague when it comes to the ways in which a franchise's individual texts and media relate to each other. Trying to fill this gap, Ryan has turned to the concept of the "storyworld," suggesting that transmedia storytelling serves to construct a common diegesis (whose setting, events, characters, objects, physical laws, and social rules are shared by more than one text) across all of the installments of a franchise, irrespective of the medium in which these appear (cf. Ryan, "Story/World/Media"; "Transmedial" 363–365). As she points out, transmedial storytelling in this sense is a "special case of transfictionality," that is, a "migration of fictional entities across different texts," in which succeeding works either expand the storyworld of a source text by adding characters and plots, modify it by reimagining an alternate version of the same story with different outcomes, or transpose the basic elements of a story into a new setting ("Transmedial" 366, 365, cf. 366). From this perspective, we can understand the MCU as a seemingly straightforward example of transfictional expansion, in which *Iron Man*, as the first installment of the franchise, establishes the central elements and rules of the storyworld that are subsequently expanded on in succeeding films, One-Shots, TV shows, and other transmedia extensions in order to create the immersive experiences referred to by Jenkins and Grainge.

Such an understanding of the MCU, however, remains plausible only if we consider *Iron Man* as the source text of the franchise—a position that cannot account for the MCU's relationships to the rest of the Marvel oeuvre. In fact, I would argue that the MCU's location within the long history of Marvel productions demonstrates the limits of Ryan's understanding of transmedia storytelling as a form of transfictionality, which hinges on the notion of a stable and clearly identifiable source narrative that the succeeding installments then expand, modify, or transpose into a different setting (cf. Ryan, "Transmedial" 366–367). Any attempt to identify a singular source narrative for the MCU, however, is bound to fail, as the franchise's storyworld is only one among many succeeding incarnations of the Marvel Universe and, accordingly, relates to multiple different earlier incarnations of its superhero protagonists in comic books, film, television, and elsewhere.

Already in the 1970s, Marvel licensed the production of several television programs (most prominently the *Incredible Hulk* series, two made-for-TV movies about *Captain America*, and the *Amazing Spider-Man* TV show) and diversified its roster of comic book titles in order to address different audience segments—with titles like *Spidey Super Stories*, as Frank Kelleter and Daniel Stein note, "targeted specifically at young readers," for example (Kelleter and Stein 274—my translation, cf. Johnson 7). This "multiplication of serial formats" during the Bronze Age of comic books, they point out, "coincide[d] with a diversification of serial storytelling": "Mostly episodic and oneiric narrative structures are now accompanied by longer plotlines spanning several issues, as well as ever more complex constellations of characters. In order to be able to follow the overall development of a character, readers now have to buy other superhero- or team-up titles as well, since all events are located within an overarching Marvel Universe (located in New York) that extends across several synchronized series and allows characters to move freely between titles" (274–275, my translation). The MCU, in other words, is based on a multiplicity of source materials that, to complicate things, are themselves already transfictional (as well as serial) in character, and similarly spread out across several media.

The difficulty of singling out individual source texts for the MCU increases further if we take another fact into account: the franchise still coexists with several alternate incarnations of its superhero protagonists in other media, each of which constructs a storyworld separate from that of the MCU—like those of Marvel Animation's direct-to-video films, the *Avengers Assemble* and *Hulk and the Agents of S.M.A.S.H.*, or the multiple ongoing comic book titles. Depending on what we consider to be the source text, the MCU, in Ryan's terms, could thus not only be understood as a transfictional extension of *Iron Man*, but also as a transposition of classic comic book stories and characters into a new setting as well as a reimagination of stories from other media that retells established plots (for example, the origin stories of Captain America or Iron Man) with minor or major modifications. But each of these claims would be based on a highly selective foregrounding of some connections between the MCU and other parts of the Marvel

Universe. Although Ryan's focus on the expansion of storyworlds is helpful, her conception of transmedia storytelling as transfictionality seems to be too schematic to account for the fact that most entries of the MCU can be understood as an adaptation or remake of not just one, but many different source texts from the large back-catalog of Marvel properties.

The long history of Marvel productions in other media also problematizes aspects of Jenkins's more general conception of transmedia storytelling, most obviously his claims about the novelty of the phenomenon, as the company's properties adhered to similar industrial and narrative logics well before the onset of the digital age. Jenkins's take on the concept also does not tell us a lot about the specific narrative appeals of the MCU. Drawing on Umberto Eco's discussion of cult movies, Jenkins locates the allure of transmedia texts in their intertextuality, arguing that successful franchises would foreground a wealth of "archetypes, allusions, and references drawn from a range of previous works" as a central narrative attraction (Jenkins, *Convergence* 98). By displaying such "endless borrowings" from all kinds of popular culture, transmedia texts would frame themselves as inexhaustible reservoirs of information and foster ongoing and open-ended practices of comprehension and interpretation on the part of the viewer (ibid.). Although references to contemporary popular culture can certainly be found in Marvel Studios' latest in-house productions (*Guardians of the Galaxy*'s soundtrack of 1960s and 1970s pop rock songs comes to mind), a focus on intertextuality in this general sense misses the crucial point that sets the MCU apart from other transmedia narratives: the fact that the majority of the MCU's narrative elements—from the titular heroes of the films and their iconic looks to fictional agencies like S.H.I.E.L.D. and magic artifacts like the "cosmic cube" or Thor's Hammer, right down to details like Nick Fury's eyepatch—have already been introduced in the pages of Marvel comics or in other incarnations of the Marvel brand.

Rather than foregrounding what Eco has termed "intertextual frames" and "archetypes" ("*Casablanca*" 5), the MCU thus repurposes very specific, well-defined, instantly recognizable (and copyrighted) characters, iconographic elements, and even storylines from a range of earlier Marvel texts. How can we make sense of this specific form of intertextuality? And how can we conceptualize the relationships among the individual installments of the franchise, if not we do not want to subscribe to a definition of transmedia as a form of transfictionality that seems to be too narrow to account for the MCU's multiple borrowings from other Marvel texts? To come to terms with these questions, I argue, we have to engage with an aspect of the MCU that is implicit in both Jenkins's and Ryan's conceptions of transmedia storytelling, but that deserves a more detailed consideration: its inherent seriality.

MULTILINEAR AND TRANSMEDIAL SERIALIZATION IN THE MARVEL CINEMATIC UNIVERSE

In the most basic sense, the terms "series" and "serial" refer to a narrative with a stable and recurring set of main characters that unfolds over more than one installment (cf. Kelleter, "Einführung" 18).[3] Roger Hagedorn argues that serialization in this sense has been a mainstay in, and perhaps even a dominant form of, popular culture since the first serialized novels appeared in the newspapers of the 1830s and 1840s—a success story that can be attributed to the fact that series represent "an ideal form of narrative presentation under capitalism" (12, cf. 5–7). Serial texts promote themselves as well as their carrier media: when a story is told in installments, each part of the series "functions to promote consumption of later episodes of the same serial," prompting the audience to return to the media channel that disseminates them as content (for example, a magazine, radio station, television channel, movie theater, or video-on-demand provider) (5). Series thus have the capacity to convert casual audiences into regular followers, and thus to build and expand a base of viewers, readers, or listeners over a long period of time.

What further sets serial narratives apart from other cultural forms is their recursivity, that is, their openness to audience response, which is made possible by an overlap of production and reception (cf. Kelleter, "Einführung" 19–25; Jahn-Sudmann and Kelleter 207). Since the later installments of serial texts are typically still in production while preceding ones are already being distributed and consumed, producers can respond to the popular reception of their works as expressed, for example, in online fan forums, sales figures, Nielsen ratings, returns from the box office and ancillary markets, and reviews and other journalistic discourse, as well as in the textual production of fans. Frank Kelleter and Ruth Mayer, among others, have argued that the recursivity of serial texts and their potential to bind audiences to specific media channels over time allow us to understand serialization as a social practice rather than as just a specific mode of narration. Serial narratives, in other words, constitute "Actor-Networks" or "machinic assemblages" that "conjoin . . . living beings and technological apparatuses into intricately layered arrangements," and that reproduce themselves over time through the productive interactions of producers, institutions, media, audiences, and, last but not least, the serial texts themselves (Mayer 12; cf. Kelleter and Stein 260-263; Kelleter, "Einführung" 20; Kelleter, *Serial Agencies* 3-5).[4] Put differently, we can understand serial narratives as cultural forms that weave connections not only among different texts (such as the installments and episodes of a series) but also between producers and their viewers, audiences and media channels, media channels and serial texts, and so on.

Serial narratives unfold thanks to the interactions of these different entities—and, centrally, because they manage to encourage audiences to consume them repeatedly and on a regular basis (cf. Brinker). On a very basic level, serial narratives try to accomplish this ongoing consumption by balancing familiar and well-known elements with new material over the course of their unfolding. Each installment of a series has to tell "*the same* [story] *again, but in a new way,*" in order to be both recognizable as part of an ongoing narrative and different enough to warrant the consumer's return to the text (Kelleter, "Einführung" 27—my translation).[5] Since serial narratives are unashamedly commercial forms, they depend on their audiences' willingness to consume them; once they fail to draw in sufficient numbers, they are promptly discontinued, but series rarely end as long as they are profitable (cf. Kelleter, "Einführung" 26). Due to this potential open-endedness of serial narration, series challenge many of the assumptions that academics schooled in the study of literary texts might bring to their material, as the series, especially in film and television, are almost invariably multiauthored and lack a strict adherence to classical norms of closure, coherence, and plausibility. Instead, popular serial texts exhibit a drive toward enabling their own continued serialization as well as a tendency to leave plotlines unresolved and open for development in future installments (cf. Kelleter, "Einführung" 27).

While serial narratives classically unfold their narratives linearly, mono-medially, and according to media-specific parameters of serialization, serialization might take a variety of different forms. Along these lines, we can understand transmedia storytelling as a form of serialization that unfolds horizontally, across several media instead of just a single medium, and that comes to full prominence only in an environment in which the participating channels are equally accessible to a broad audience.[6] Such a conception seems congruent with Jenkins's and Ryan's understandings of the term, which stress the commercial orientation of transmedial franchises and their drive toward the expansion of an existing storyworld (although it would hold that it unfolds in a dynamic interaction with the audience and its demands, and not as something that is centrally planned and executed, as both Jenkins and Ryan seem to suggest) (cf. Jenkins, *Convergence* 93–130; Ryan, "Transmedial" 363). But this redefinition still does not explain the relationship between the MCU and the other parts of the Marvel oeuvre. As I will argue below, the MCU, in terms of its relationship to earlier incarnations of its protagonists, is best understood as the effect of yet another nonlinear form of seriality, one typically associated with practices of rebooting or remaking. For the moment, however, I would like to discuss the MCU's seriality as a combination of linear serial storytelling within the medium of film and a transmedial serialization of content across different formats.

The MCU's take on serial storytelling is perhaps best understood as an attempt to translate what Kelleter and Stein have called the "multi-linear" seriality of Marvel comics into the medium of cinema (as well as, subsequently, across media) (cf. Kelleter and Stein 274–282). As I have mentioned above, Marvel set its comic titles and series in a shared storyworld (later expanded into a "multiverse" of several interconnected, but nominally separate storyworlds) from the 1970s onward. Accordingly, the adventures of its superhero figures unfolded and developed in parallel and occasionally overlapping storylines that shared a narrative continuity (Kelleter and Stein 274–282). The films of the MCU similarly take place within a shared storyworld separate from the several continuities of the company's other titles, and are similarly organized in a number of interconnected subseries—that is, the *Iron Man, Hulk, Thor, Captain America, Avengers, Guardians of the Galaxy,* and *Ant-Man* films—whose narratives occasionally overlap and intersect. Each entry of the franchise nonetheless shares narrative elements with other films in the larger series, and each relates to the preceding and following installments within a relatively straightforward, linear temporal sequence. The diegetic events of *Iron Man* (2008), for example, are followed by those of *The Incredible Hulk* (released later that same year), and have an impact on the plot of *Iron Man 2* (2010), which in turn foreshadows events from *Thor* (2011); *The Incredible Hulk* similarly introduces plot elements that would resurface in *Captain America: The First Avenger* (2011). Finally, all the protagonists join forces in 2012's *The Avengers,* followed by individual adventures in *Iron Man 3, Thor: The Dark World* (both 2013), and *Captain America:*

The Winter Soldier (2014). *Guardians of the Galaxy* (2014) adds the eponymous cosmic superhero team to the franchise, and so on.[7] Within this order, several characters, as well as objects and events, routinely cross over from one film and subseries into the next—the character Agent Carter, for example, who is introduced in the first *Captain America* film, reappears in 2013's *Agent Carter* One-Shot, 2014's *Captain America: The Winter Soldier*, and several episodes of *Agents of S.H.I.E.L.D.*'s second season (2014/2015); becomes the protagonist of ABC's *Agent Carter* in 2015; and afterward cameos in *Avengers: Age of Ultron*, *Ant-Man*, and the *Ant-Man: Prelude* tie-in comic. In contrast to Marvel's traditional comic book continuities, then, the MCU's storyworld also reaches across media, in the process constructing what Ruth Mayer calls a "serial cluster," that is, a narrative unit or set with "a fictional logic and continuity of its own" (*Serial* 9, cf. 25).

Although the serial unfolding of the MCU within the medium of film is relatively linear, the franchise's expansion into television and short films complicates this linearity by introducing additional, media-specific models of serialization (each with its own norms of episodic closure or openness, rhythms of publication, and demands for audience engagement), a movement that gives rise to a complex transmedial chronology and hierarchization of series and installments. For example, the MCU's film premieres are typically slated to occur several months apart from each other; *Agents of S.H.I.E.L.D.*, however—which relates the adventures of a group of investigators working for Marvel's fictional intelligence agency—follows the schedules of the American television season and consequently releases its installments in far quicker succession. As an example of what Jason Mittell has called "narratively complex television," the show relies heavily on ongoing storylines that unfold over the course of several episodes as well as across seasons (cf. "Narrative" 29–33), but nonetheless also connects directly to the films of the franchise.

Accordingly, the alien invasions, government conspiracies, and character deaths that occur in the movies produce lasting consequences for the protagonists of the television show, whose adventures frequently involve dealing with the fallout from these and other world-shaking events. The episode "F.Z.Z.T.," for example, thematizes the long-term effects of the Chitauri invasion that occurred in *The Avengers*; similarly, "The Well," which aired less than two weeks after the premiere of *Thor: The Dark World*, has the protagonists on cleanup duty in London after an attack by the film's

Dark Elves. The show's pilot episode, which premiered shortly after the theatrical release of *Iron Man 3*, even takes up a central plot element from this film—the superhuman-generating "Extremis" biotechnology that villain Aldrich Killian used to exact his revenge against Tony Stark—and turns it into a crucial part of the ongoing conspiracy plot that the series develops over the course of its first season. Almost all of the following episodes subsequently develop this storyline as an ongoing subplot, which soon becomes entangled with the mystery of Agent Coulson's unexplained resurrection, and eventually leads to the uncovering of an even greater conspiracy involving the terrorist organization HYDRA. Starting with the episode "Turn, Turn, Turn," the show eventually develops this season-long story arc into an extended crossover event with *Captain America: The Winter Soldier*, which was released to theaters internationally just four days before. For the remaining six episodes of the season, the events of the show are set within the timeframe of the movie, in which a terrorist plot results in the dissolution of S.H.I.E.L.D. and the disavowal of its agents by the US government. This development forces the show's protagonists to react to the film's shocking events, and the confrontation with HYDRA eventually culminates in the season finale.

Along with the storylines, characters, too, become intertwined in the various media representations. During these same episodes (for whose duration the series added the word "Uprising" to its title), the minor characters Maria Hill, Nick Fury, and Jasper Sitwell cross over from the movie and the TV series into the respective other medium, each time playing a central role in the unfolding of events. In having these characters cross over, the MCU effectively presents its own version of the type of crossover that Marvel introduced into superhero comics during the mid-1980s, when event series like "Secret Wars" brought the protagonists of different titles together to confront an all-star cast of villains for a number of special issues.

The logics of multilinear serial narration in Marvel comics, however, are somewhat different from the logics of such narration in TV and film. Whereas crossovers in comics could, and frequently did, go in both directions, there is often an asymmetric relationship between the events of blockbuster movies and those of weekly TV episodes. The examples given above reflect this point. Although the television show reacts and responds to the dramatic events depicted in the films, those that occur in the show itself (which tells its stories on a much smaller scale and with a much smaller budget) do not reverberate through the rest of the MCU in the same way. If significant events occur within the episodes of *Agents of S.H.I.E.L.D.*, these play into and fuel the unfolding of the season-spanning story arc rather than radiating out into the rest of the franchise. The show thus directs more energy to the development of its own narrative trajectory while remaining subordinated to, and affected by, the more significant events of the feature films. The same is true for the other television shows of the franchise, whose plots, at least so far, have not overlapped significantly with those of the movies—*Daredevil* and *Jessica Jones* connect to the rest of the franchise mostly through their shared setting in the MCU's version of Manhattan, and otherwise tell their stories on a more local scale than the films. In a similar fashion, *Agent Carter*'s 1940s time frame put the show at a remove from other entries of the franchise.

In contrast, the One-Shot short films tell small stories about the fate of minor characters and tie up plotlines that were left dangling by the movies. Originally included on the home video releases of the MCU's feature films (but also circulating informally via online video portals), the plots of these shorts are presented in the form of brief vignettes set in the aftermath of the feature films.[8] Understood as a separate subseries, the One-Shots connect to each other only loosely and function like an anthology of episodic stories rather than as a continuous serial narrative. As such, they are typically released out of the established chronological order of the MCU: *The Consultant*, which comments on the fate of villain Emil Blonsky from the 2008 *Hulk* movie, for example, is set sometime between the events of the former film and *Iron Man 2*, but appears on the *Thor* home media release. Similarly, the *Agent Carter* short was released as bonus material for *Iron Man 3*, but is set in the 1940s time frame of *Captain America: The First Avenger*. *All Hail the King*, the most recent One-Shot as of this writing, grants a look into the prison life of the *Iron Man 2* and *Iron Man 3* villains Justin Hammer and Trevor Slattery, but was first released as a bonus feature of the *Thor: The Dark World* digital download.

The television series and the One-Shots thus each expand the MCU's storyworld in different ways, but are similarly subordinated to the core narrative that unfolds in the big-budget feature films. The shows add to the MCU by weaving complex serial narratives across several episodes and seasons, but their plots otherwise relate only tangentially to the events of the feature films. The One-Shots expand the shared diegesis in a more episodic and less linear fashion than the TV series, and might sprawl off into all kinds of unexpected directions (although their stories remain similarly inconsequential for the larger storyworld).

NONLINEAR SERIALITY: THE MARVEL CINEMATIC UNIVERSE AS REMAKE

The transmedial and (multi-)linear modes of serialization are not the only ones active in recent Marvel Studios productions. Although the MCU relies on the kind of linear, expansive, and transmedial seriality discussed above in order to proliferate, we can consider the cluster as a whole an instantiation of a third mode of serialization—one that is traditionally associated with the cinematic forms of the remake, the reboot, or the adaptation. This kind of serialization also involves the "telling again [of] a previous successful story," but it does so without establishing a narrative continuity between installments (cf. Eco, "Innovation" 167). As a nonlinear, "compounding or cumulative" form of seriality, it restages, reinvents, or restarts known properties (like copyrighted characters) by transferring them into new medial contexts—from the pages of comic books into live-action feature films, for example (Denson 532, cf. 536–539). In this form of serialization, no diegetic links between the different incarnations of the characters exist, and each installment can similarly claim to constitute a "definitive" version of the property.[9]

As an example of this type of seriality, the MCU as a whole constitutes only the latest installment in a series of succeeding serial clusters. Each of these clusters has featured its own versions of the iconic superhero characters established in the comics, and each has come with its own narrative continuity or storyworld. Throughout their history, Marvel comics have produced a number of such clusters, usually to reboot and retool their famous characters in order to attract new audiences.[10] Each of these clusters relates to the others only indirectly and non-diegetically—by evoking the audience's preexisting memory of, knowledge about, and familiarity with the properties and figures that it adapts and reinterprets. Similarly, the adventures of the MCU's superheroes always unfold against the backdrop of earlier incarnations of Iron Man, Captain America, Thor, and other figures as they exist in the cultural memory, operating within a horizon of expectations that knowledgeable audiences might bring to the texts.

The films of the MCU acknowledge and thematize their location within this history of succeeding variations of the same source materials in a number of self-reflexive scenes that allude to earlier versions of their central characters, sometimes invoking earlier storylines and plot elements. The title sequence of Louis Leterrier's *The Incredible Hulk* perhaps demonstrates this self-reflexivity most obviously: After the iconic Marvel Studios logo fills the screen (it appears at the beginning of all of the company's productions), the film's opening credits begin. Along with the credits we see a hyper-kinetic, two-and-a-half-minute-long montage sequence that recaps the origin story of Bruce Banner's alter ego, Hulk—along with his relationships to the other central characters and his escape from the military types that pursue him. Aside from fulfilling the traditional functions of introducing the names of the creative and industrial actors participating in the production and setting a mood for the rest of the film, the opening titles very openly pay homage to the *Incredible Hulk* TV show of the 1970s: they mimic the opening sequence of the series in both form and function (the framed shots of Bruce Banner and the failed experiment that turns him into the green superhero are nearly identical in the TV show and the movie, and both sequences are interspersed with shots of technical equipment and X-ray images). In recalling the TV show, the film aligns itself with a particularly popular and widely circulated incarnation of the Hulk character while at the same time distancing itself from a cinematic version of the figure that had underperformed commercially just five years earlier (Ang Lee's *Hulk*).

Since the opening sequence doubles as a vehicle for recalling the basic premise of Hulk's story—Banner's unfortunate lab accident and his subsequent plight (of having to live with the fact that he transforms into the titular green monster whenever he's sufficiently agitated, as well as with his antagonistic relationship to General Ross and his tragic love affair with Ross's daughter)—it effectively restages basic plot elements of Lee's film, which focused on the character's origin story and fleshed it out in great detail. The film here performs a curious double movement: on the one hand, its recapitulation of the basic elements of the hero's origin story attempts to "overwrite" some of the creative additions of Lee's film (such as the oedipal conflict between Bruce and his father, David) by omitting them and recasting the principal characters with new actors. At the same time, even though Lee's *Hulk* is not part of the MCU, Leterrier's film cannot help but acknowledge its existence (if only implicitly), as it is only because of the short time that passed between both movies—and the fact that the earlier film is still very much available to contemporary audiences—that *The Incredible Hulk* can afford to relegate the character's origin story to the opening credits.

Similar remediations of earlier versions of the iconic characters are present in other films of the MCU as well. *Captain America: The First Avenger*, for
example, takes up the World War II origins of its protagonist by turning
Steve Rogers into a poster child for the US government's wartime propaganda efforts in the 1940s time frame of the film. In his role as USO performer "Captain America," Steve subsequently goes on to star in a stage
show designed to promote the sale of war bonds, leading to a scene that
has him punching an actor dressed as Hitler—which allows the film to
restage the iconic cover of the first issue of the historical *Captain America*
comic book series without surrendering the internal logics of its diegesis.
The same motif reappears shortly afterward, when the popularity of Steve
Roger's stage persona inspires the creation of an ongoing comic book series
about the character, which gives the film an opportunity to reproduce the
original Hitler-punching image as the cover of the fictional comic book's
first issue. In another gesture of reverence to the long history of Captain
America in other media, the film features a brief scene in which Rogers stars
in a fictional *Captain America* film serial, thereby evoking the real-world
1944 Republic serial that was the first cinematic adaptation of the property.
In *Captain America: The First Avenger*, the restaging of these historical wartime incarnations of the figure represents a self-aware acknowledgment of
Captain America's propagandistic origin. By depoliticizing this origin story
and fictionalizing it as a lighthearted part of the narrative, the film renders it
less ideologically suspect. On a more general level, however, such restagings
also represent examples of the MCU's tendency to self-reflexively locate
itself within a larger history of Marvel products by referencing iconic earlier
versions of its characters.[11] In addition, such restagings offer knowledgeable
viewers the added pleasures of recognition and distinction if they manage
to correctly identify these and similar references to the Marvel canon.

In other instances, MCU uses its location within a larger history of Marvel
productions to include more subtle references and allusions to the comic
book origins of the franchise. It usually requires a degree of preexisting
familiarity with the larger Marvel Universe to spot and understand these
references—as well as, in more oblique cases, a considerable amount of
time, dedication, and attention. A recurring reference of this sort is the nod
to the fictional Roxxon Corporation, whose logo—known from the comics—
appears on several occasions within the MCU (as a neon-lit advertisement
visible for a split second during *Iron Man*, as signage on gas stations in the
One-Shot *A Funny Thing Happened on the Way to Thor's Hammer* and the

Agents of S.H.I.E.L.D. episode "Repairs," and as labeling on a container ship in *Iron Man 3*, for example; cf. "Roxxon").

In a similar manner, Captain America is referenced multiple times before he makes his official entry into the MCU: his iconic shield turns up in Tony Stark's basement workshop in *Iron Man* and then again in *Iron Man 2* (each time visible only for a few seconds), for example, and General Ross obliquely refers to the super-soldier program that turned Steve Rogers into the star-spangled hero in *The Incredible Hulk*, without explicitly acknowl-edging the connection to the Marvel canon. In these moments, the MCU appeals very openly to viewers with more than just a passing familiarity with the franchise, inviting them to engage in what Jason Mittell has called, in reference to complex television series, "forensic" fan practices—that is, a hyper-attentive, cognitively challenging, and textually productive mode of reception that is aimed at the analysis, discussion, and interpretation of popular texts in online fan communities ("Forensic").

SERIALITY AND ACCESSIBILITY: THE MARVEL CINEMATIC UNIVERSE AND THE TECHNICAL INFRASTRUCTURE OF THE CONVERGENCE ERA

Viewed on its own terms, the MCU's combination of several modes of serial-ization with different serial trajectories (through films, television, and short films), along with the fast expansion of the franchise since its beginning in 2008, appears to threaten its accessibility to a broad audience. Taken together, the narratives of the feature films, television episodes, One-Shots, and other entries of the MCU line up to a complex, multidimensional narra-tive architecture that expands simultaneously in multiple directions—and that is not even taking into account the multiple references, allusions, and connections to other parts of the Marvel oeuvre. The complex relationships between the MCU's different subseries and less obvious continuities are hardly transparent to the average viewer; in fact, an uninformed audi-ence might not even recognize the franchise's serial context, and instead consume the individual installments as self-contained texts, or as separate superhero series.

The narrative complexities of the MCU thus raise a number of questions about the franchise's commercial success, especially if one recalls that superhero comics no longer have the mass appeal they once possessed. Nowadays, as Jared Gardner notes, "few titles sell more than a hundred thousand an issue. Unlike during the early 1940s, when sales of upward of one million copies were not unheard of, current comics sales provide nowhere near the number of readers needed to guarantee a successful return on even a small-budget motion picture" (183). The MCU is not only complex, but—because of the decline in comic book readership—it is also based on relatively obscure source materials that are probably unfamiliar to the majority of its audience.[12] How, then, do viewers who do not possess an in-depth foreknowledge about Marvel comics keep track of the multilinear unfolding of the franchise and its intricate relationships among texts? The answer, I think, lies in the digital media environment in which these texts operate, which provide possibilities for an engagement with audiovisual media content that reduces the threshold of accessibility.

Gardner suggests that the recent omnipresence and success of comic book adaptations in the cinema are related to the changes in reception practices brought about by the transformation of film from an analogue to a digital medium. The switch to digital video, he argues, has completed film's transition from an art form that could be consumed only occasionally, mono-directionally, and within a limited time-frame to one that can be watched repeatedly, and that can be "read" in a manner that resembles the way in which one navigates the panels on a comic book page—by moving back and forth between individual scenes, moments, and images (cf. 183; cf. also Harper 96–101). Gardner's comments point us to the digital infrastructure of the convergence era and its corresponding forms of engagement with media texts: no longer meant to be watched exclusively at the movie theater, the films of the MCU, along with the franchise's other entries, are media content whose reception takes place (perhaps even predominantly) in the home, where viewing a movie is accompanied by all kinds of attendant audience practices, most centrally surfing the Web.

The Internet provides an abundance of professional and fan-produced discourses about the latest Marvel Studios productions—ranging from news about upcoming franchise entries, on sites like the science-fiction blog io9, to film criticism and episodic recaps of *Agents of S.H.I.E.L.D.* on Wired, to blog posts charting the complex narrative architecture of the MCU (like the series of "Annotations" to Marvel films on Newsarama) and the content of participatory online fora dedicated to the discussion of the Marvel Universe (such as the Marvel Comics Database and the Marvel Cinematic Universe Wiki).[13] These online resources effectively function as what Jason Mittell has termed "orienting paratexts," that is, material supplementing the texts of the MCU to provide orientation with regard to the "basic storytelling facets" of the franchise and to open up the complex web of interconnected Marvel Studios releases to an interested audience ("Serial Orientations"). By relying on the availability of such online paratexts, the MCU can thus capitalize on what Janet Murray has termed the "encyclopedic capacity" of digital environments (84, cf. 83–90; cf. Jenkins, *Convergence* 116) as well as on the readiness of textually productive audiences to provide the content for fan-operated fan sites, wikis, and other viewer-produced online paratexts that chart the complex narrative architecture of the franchise. The multidimensional seriality of the MCU is arguably hard to master without knowledge about its logics, trajectories, and history, but in the age of widespread Internet access, this knowledge (along with the films and episodes) is readily available online.

CONCLUSION

With its transmedial spread and multilayered complexity, the MCU complicates attempts at classification in terms of established terminology. Jenkins's and Ryan's conceptions of transmedial storytelling, as we have seen, only inadequately account for the MCU's combination of different types of seriality and cannot explain the franchise's relationship to earlier incarnations of the Marvel Universe. Other perspectives seem to be problematic as well: the attempt to understand the franchise exclusively in terms of linear serialization practices (or "sequelization") has its limits when it comes to the interactions of the different media formats involved in the MCU. A restricted perspective on interactions between the MCU and earlier Marvel comics properties, from the perspective of adaptation studies, might also fail to account for the broader serial dynamics of the franchise. In terms of its formal complexity, richness of intertextual references, and reliance on the digital infrastructure of the convergence era, we could consider the MCU a contemporary example of what Graeme Harper, almost a decade ago, called the "cinema of complexity"—were it not for the fact that the franchise is not only cinematic, but also televisual, an exercise in the short film form, a series of comic books, and a string of digital games.

For the time being, it might be enough to point out that the MCU combines aspects of all of the above—and that it is not the only contemporary media franchise to do so, as other studios and production companies have started to adopt similar serialization practices. Fox's franchise of *X-Men* films, for example, now also exists as a multi-tiered operation, as it encompasses ongoing subseries of loosely connected *X-Men*, *Wolverine*, and *Deadpool* films. For several years now, the film and television production arms of the TimeWarner conglomerate have been busy building not one, but two different franchises of DC comic adaptations. One of these, the so-called "Arrowverse," encompasses the television shows *Arrow* (since 2012), *The Flash* (since 2014), and *Legends of Tomorrow* (since 2016), all airing on The CW, as well as the animated web series *Vixen* (since 2015). Characters from these series frequently turn up in each other's shows, just as characters do in the MCU. In addition, the Arrowverse has crossed over with NBC's short-lived *Constantine* (2015) and with CBS's *Supergirl* (since 2015), two other superhero shows produced by Warner Bros. Television. At the cinema, Warner's *Man of Steel* (2013), *Batman v. Superman: Dawn of Justice* (2016), *Suicide Squad* (2016), and *Wonder Woman* (2017) represent the first installments in a separate franchise of interconnected superhero films that, if successful, will continue with additional entries for years to come.

A similar trend toward "universe building" can also be observed beyond the superhero genre: since becoming a Disney property, the *Star Wars* franchise has been retooled into a multilinear series that includes a new trilogy of "proper" *Star Wars* films, an additional "anthology series" of films that tell other stories set within the same storyworld (starting with 2016's *Rogue One*), several animated television series, and numerous tie-in novels and comics. Following these examples, the rebooted *Star Trek* film series (since 2009) will debut a new spin-off television show in 2017. In the meantime, Universal will try its hand at a series of interconnected monster movies.

What sets the MCU apart from all of these franchises is its rapid expansion—by now, it has established a rhythm of two or three film releases as well as at least two new television series per year (cf. Keyes, "Studios," "Netflix"). In many ways, the MCU thus represents a radicalization of recent trends in transmedial and serial storytelling, and, as such, can be understood not only as a particularly successful media franchise, but as a model for a new type of multidimensional, complex seriality that will go on to characterize popular culture in the coming years.

....

NOTES

This article draws strongly on ideas developed in the context of the German Research Foundation's research unit on "Popular Seriality—Aesthetics and

Practice," headed by Frank Kelleter (John F. Kennedy Institute, Free University of Berlin), of which I am an associated member. For an overview of the work of the research unit so far, see Kelleter, *Populäre Serialität*.

1. At the time of writing, the MCU as a whole ranks first among the "highest-grossing franchises and film series" on Wikipedia; the next super-hero series on the list are the *Batman*, *Spider-Man*, and *X-Men* films, which rank eighth, sixth, and fourteenth, respectively (cf. "List"). The latter two franchises also adapt Marvel properties but are not produced in-house by Marvel Studios—instead, they are leftovers from the company's earlier policy of licensing its properties, which, as Derek Johnson points out, could not be sustained as a business model in the long run (cf. Johnson 10–11). Currently, the upcoming additions to the MCU are the feature films *Captain America: Civil War* and *Doctor Strange* (both slated for 2016 releases); *Guardians of the Galaxy Vol. 2*, a yet-untitled *Spider-Man* reboot, and *Thor: Ragnarok* (all three 2017); *Black Panther*, *Avengers: Infinity War—Part 1*, and *Ant-Man and the Wasp* (projected for 2018); and *Captain Marvel*, *Avengers: Infinity War—Part 2*, and *Inhumans* (projected for 2019), as well as the television series *Marvel's Damage Control* (ABC, in development), and *Luke Cage*, *Iron Fist*, and *The Defenders* (currently filming or in production for Netflix). For the sake of brevity, I have limited this discussion to a detailed examination of the existing film, television, and short film installments of the MCU and disregard the comic books that are also part of the franchise. For an overview of all the entries of the MCU, see "Earth-199999" as well as "Marvel Cinematic Universe."

2. For a discussion of the MCU's narrative strategies and its political signifi-cance from the perspective of political economy, see Brinker.

3. Other authors have used "serial" and "series" in a more specific manner—Raymond Williams, for example, uses "series" as a term for serial narratives with self-contained, episodic installments and "serial" to refer to narratives that develop ongoing plotlines across various episodes (cf. Kelleter, "Einführung" 25, as well as Williams). In the context of this chapter, both terms are used interchangeably to refer to serial narratives in general, which I understand, in Jennifer Hayward's terms, as "ongoing narrative[s] released in successive parts. . . . [S]erial narratives . . . include refusal of closure; intertwined subplots; large casts of characters (incorporating a diverse range of age, gender, class, and, increasingly, race presentation to attract a similarly diverse audience); interaction with current political, social, or cultural issues; dependence on profit; and acknowledgement of audience response" (Hayward 3).

4. Both conceptions of popular series—as "machinic constellations" (Mayer, following Deleuze and Guattari's terminology of the "machine" and the "machinic"; cf. Deleuze and Guattari 283–289; Raunig 18–34), and as actor-networks (Kelleter, *Serial Agencies* 3–4, as well as Kelleter and Stein; cf. Latour 46–86)—stem from the context of the research unit "Popular Seriality— Aesthetics and Practice," and they are similar insofar as they understand series as constellations of interaction in which agency is not limited to human subjects and dispersed within a network of different kinds of actors.

5. Depending on the specific historical and medial contexts, this basic principle of variation within repetition can manifest itself in various different forms of serial narrative, each with its own norms of closure, continuity, and coherence. Cf. Eco, "Innovation" 166–172, for a very schematic (and somewhat dated) overview of serial types.

6. I will return to the technological preconditions for the accessibility of transmedially unfolding series toward the end of this chapter.

7. While most of *Captain America: The First Avenger*'s narrative is set during World War II, the film is not, strictly speaking, an exception to the linear temporality of the MCU's cinematic arm, as its core events are presented as an extended analepsis by a handful of framing scenes set in the early twenty-first-century time frame of the other films.

8. The "Marvel One-Shots" so far encompass the shorts *The Consultant* (included on the *Thor* Blu-ray), *A Funny Thing Happened on the Way to Thor's Hammer* (included on the *Captain America: The First Avenger* release), *Item 47* (bonus content for Marvel's *The Avengers*), *Agent Carter* (*Iron Man 3*), and *All Hail the King* (*Thor: The Dark World*). Aside from expanding the storyworld, the One-Shots serve another important purpose for the MCU, as they function to test the waters for the potential success of future installments of the franchise. The positive reception of the *Item 47* and *Agent Carter* shorts, for example, played a key role in Marvel Studios' greenlighting of the ABC television shows *Agents of S.H.I.E.L.D.* and *Agent Carter*, respectively (cf. Breznican).

9. Denson argues that it is this "concrescent" form of seriality that ensures the cultural longevity of iconic serial figures like Batman, Spider-Man, Dracula, Frankenstein, or Sherlock Holmes—that is, figures that coexist in multiple versions in several media, but whose incarnations do not relate directly (diegetically) to each other (cf. 537, see below). As he and Ruth Mayer have argued, it is through periodic restagings for new medial contexts that such serial figures acquire their iconic features (and instant recognizability) in the first place (cf. Denson and Mayer, as well as Mayer 7–12). Denson notes that the combination of this nonlinear seriality with the more standard, linear form mentioned above is a defining feature of several popular comic book properties (cf. 536–537).

10. To differentiate and separate the multiple continuities that resulted from the tumultuous publication history of Marvel comics, the company at some point began the practice of naming and numbering these clusters—from "Earth-616," the mainstream continuity of the comics, for example, to Ultimate Marvel's "Earth-1610" and the "Earth-199999" of the MCU (as well as many more; cf. "Multiverse/Universe Listing"). However, not all of the existing "Earths" are actually separate clusters in the sense of series with a storyworld that is distinct and separate from others. In Marvel comics, the concept of parallel continuities (also known as the "multiverse") is a matter of theme and content as much as it is an industrial strategy of product diversification—and therefore, several of these "Earths" might be part of one and same diegesis or cluster.

11. In logical conclusion of this acknowledgment of the character's history, the sequel to the MCU's first Captain America film, 2014's *Captain America: The Winter Soldier,* uses an exhibition about the protagonist at the Smithsonian as a way to recapitulate parts of his origin story from the first film—and again historicizes the character as a product of World War II. A similar phenomenon to that of the restaging of iconic scenes and characters is the MCU's inclusion of cameos by actors and creatives with a connection to earlier incarnations of the source material. *The Incredible Hulk,* for example, features a cameo by Lou Ferrigno, who played the green superhero in the 1970s TV series; similarly, each of the MCU's feature films includes a short cameo by Marvel legend Stan Lee.

12. This effect is even more significant in international markets, where Marvel comics properties are less well established and have to compete against homegrown traditions of graphic literature.

13. Among other things, io9 features daily blog posts in the category "Morning Spoilers" that cover news about the latest Marvel Studios films and television episodes; *Wired* has featured recaps for the first few episodes of *Agents of S.H.I.E.L.D.* that centered on the multiple references to the movies and Marvel comic books present in the series (cf. Rogers). In addition to the sites listed above, Wikipedia also lists a number of detailed articles on the MCU as well as links to other online discourses about the show. For Newsarama's MCU annotations, cf. Kistler.

WORKS CITED

Agent Carter. Dir. Louis D'Esposito. Perf. Hayley Atwell, Dominic Cooper, Neal McDonough, Chris Evans, and Bradley Whitford. In *Iron Man 3.* 2013. Blu-ray.

All Hail the King. Dir. Drew Pearce. Perf. Ben Kingsley, Sam Rockwell, Lester Speight, and Scoot McNairy. In *Thor: The Dark World.* 2014. Blu-ray.

"All Time Worldwide Box Office Grosses." *Box Office Mojo,* n.d. Web.

Ant-Man. Dir. Peyton Reed. Perf. Paul Rudd, Evangeline Lilly, Corey Stoll, Michael Peña, and Michael Douglas. Marvel Studios, Walt Disney Studios Motion Pictures, 2015. Film.

Breznican, Anthony. "'Marvel One-Shot: Agent Carter'—FIRST LOOK at Poster and Three Photos from the New Short!" *Entertainment Weekly,* 11 July 2013. Web.

Brinker, Felix. "On the Political Economy of the Contemporary (Superhero) Blockbuster Series." In *Post-Cinema: Theorizing 21st Century Film.* Eds. Shane Denson and Julia Leyda. Sussex: Reframe Books, 2016. Print.

Captain America: The First Avenger. Dir. Joe Johnston. Perf. Chris Evans, Samuel L. Jackson, Hugo Weaving, Tommy Lee Jones, and Haylee Atwell. Marvel Studios, Paramount Pictures, 2011. Blu-ray.

Captain America: The Winter Soldier. Dir. Anthony Russo and Joe Russo. Perf. Chris Evans, Samuel L. Jackson, Scarlett Johanson, Anthony Mackie, and Robert Redford. Marvel Studios, Walt Disney Studios Motion Pictures, 2014. Film.

The Consultant. Dir. Leythum. Perf. Clark Gregg, Maximiliano Hernández, Robert Downey Jr., and William Hurt. In *Thor. 2011. Blu-ray.*

Deleuze, Gilles, and Félix Guattari. *Anti-Oedipus: Capitalism and Schizophrenia.* Minneapolis: University of Minnesota Press, 1983. Print.

Denson, Shane. "Marvel Comics' Frankenstein: A Case Study in the Media of Serial Figures." *Amerikastudien / American Studies* 56:4 (2011): 531–553. Print.

Denson, Shane, and Ruth Mayer. "Grenzgänger: Serielle Figuren im Medien-wechsel." In Kelleter, *Populäre Serialität.* 185–203. Print.

"Earth-199999." *Marvel Comics Database. Wikia, Inc.,* n.d. Web.

Eco, Umberto. "Innovation and Repetition: Between Modern and Post-Modern Aesthetics." *Deadalus* 114.4 (1985): 161–184. Print.

———. "*Casablanca*: Cult Movies and Intertextual Collage." *Substance* 14:2, no. 47: In Search of Eco's Roses (1985): 3–12. Print.

A *Funny Thing Happened on the Way to Thor's Hammer.* Dir. Leythum. Perf. Clark Gregg, Jessica Manuel, Jeff Prewett, and Zach Hudson. In *Captain America: The First Avenger.* 2011. Blu-ray.

"F.Z.Z.T." Dir. Vincent Misiano. *Marvel's Agents of S.H.I.E.L.D.* Perf. Clark Gregg, Ming-Na Wen, Brett Dalton, J. Chloe Bennet, and Titus Welliver. Disney-ABC Domestic Television, 5 November 2013. Television.

Gardner, Jared. *Projections. Comics and the History of Twenty-First-Century Storytelling.* Stanford, CA: Stanford University Press, 2012. Print.

Grainge, Paul. *Brand Hollywood: Selling Entertainment in a Global Media Age.* New York: Routledge, 2008. Print.

Guardians of the Galaxy. Dir. James Gunn. Perf. Chris Pratt, Zoe Saldana, Bradley Cooper, Vin Diesel, and Lee Pace. Marvel Studios, Walt Disney Studios Motion Pictures, 2014. Film.

Hagedorn, Roger. "Technology and Economic Exploitation: The Serial as a Form of Narrative Presentation." *Wide Angle* 10:4 (1988): 4–12. Print.

Harper, Graeme. "DVD and the New Cinema of Complexity." In *New Punk Cinema.* Ed. Nicholas Rombes. Edinburgh: Edinburgh University Press, 2005. 89–101. Print.

Hayward, Jennifer. *Consuming Pleasures: Active Audience and Serial Fictions from Dickens to Soap Opera.* Lexington: University Press of Kentucky, 1997. Print.

The Incredible Hulk. Dir. Louis Leterrier. Perf. Edward Norton, Liv Tyler, Tim Roth, William Hurt, and Robert Downey Jr. Marvel Studios, Universal, 2008. DVD.

Io9. *We Come from the Future,* n.d. Annalee Newitz, founding editor. Rob Bricken, editor in chief. Univision Communications, n.d. Web.

Iron Man. Dir. Jon Favreau. Perf. Robert Downey Jr., Jeff Bridges, Gwyneth Paltrow, Terrence Howard, and Shaun Toub. Marvel Studios, Paramount Pictures, 2008. iTunes digital video.

Iron Man 2. Dir. Jon Favreau. Perf. Robert Downey Jr., Don Cheadle, Scarlett Johansson, Sam Rockwell, and Mickey Rourke. Marvel Studios, Paramount Pictures, Concorde Video, 2010. Blu-ray.

Iron Man 3. Dir. Shane Black. Perf. Robert Downey Jr., Guy Pearce, Gwyneth Paltrow, Jon Favreau, and Don Cheadle. Walt Disney Video, 2013. Blu-ray.

Jahn-Sudmann, Andreas, and Frank Kelleter. "Die Dynamik serieller Überbietung: Amerikanische Fernsehserien und das Konzept des Quality TV." In Kelleter, *Populäre Serialität.* 205–224. Print.

Jenkins, Henry. *Convergence Culture: Where Old and New Media Collide.* New York: New York University Press, 2006. Print.

———. "Transmedia Storytelling 101." *Confessions of an Aca-Fan: The Official Weblog of Henry Jenkins,* 22 March 2007. Web.

Johnson, Derek. "Cinematic Destiny: Marvel Studios and the Trade Stories of Industrial Convergence." *Cinema Journal* 52:1 (2012): 1–24. Print.

Kelleter, Frank, ed. "Populäre Serialität: Eine Einführung." In Kelleter, *Populäre Serialität.* 12–46. Print.

———. *Populäre Serialität: Narration—Evolution—Distinktion. Zum seriellen Erzählen seit dem 19. Jahrhundert.* Bielefeld: Transcript, 2012. Print.

———. *Serial Agencies. The Wire and Its Readers*. Winchester, UK: Zero Books, 2014. Print.

Kelleter, Frank, and Daniel Stein. "Autorisierungspraktiken seriellen Erzählens: Zur Gattungsentwicklung von Superheldencomics." In Kelleter, *Populäre Serialität*. 259–290. Print.

Keyes, Rob. "Marvel & Netflix Confirm Deal for 4 TV Shows & 'Defenders' Miniseries." *Screen Rant*, n.d. Web.

———. "Marvel Studios Adds Third 2018 Release Date." *Screen Rant*, 24 July 2014. Web.

Kistler, Alan. "Marvel Studios Avengers Film Annotations." *AlanSizzlerKistler* (blog), n.d. Web.

Latour, Bruno. *Reassembling the Social: An Introduction to Actor-Network-Theory*. Oxford: Oxford University Press, 2005. Print.

"List of Highest-Grossing Films." *Wikipedia*, n.d. Web.

"Marvel Cinematic Universe." *Wikipedia*, n.d. Web.

Marvel Cinematic Universe Wiki. Wikia, Inc., n.d. Web.

Marvel's Agent Carter, Season 1. Perf. Hayley Atwell, James D'Arcy, Enver Gjokaj, Chad Michael Murray, Bridget Regan, and others. ABC Studios, Marvel Television, 2015. iTunes digital video.

Marvel's Agents of S.H.I.E.L.D., Season 1. Perf. Clark Gregg, Ming-Na Wen, Brett Dalton, J. Chloe Bennet, Iain De Caestecker, and others. ABC Studios, Marvel Television, 2013. iTunes digital video.

Marvel's Daredevil. Perf. Charlie Cox, Vincent D'Onofrio, Deborah Ann Woll, Elden Henson, Rosario Dawson, and others. ABC Studios, Marvel Entertainment, 2015. Netflix digital video.

Marvel's Jessica Jones. Perf. Krysten Ritter, Rachael Taylor, Eka Darville, David Tennant, Carrie-Anne Moss, and others. ABC Studios, Marvel Entertainment, 2015. Netflix digital video.

Marvel's The Avengers. Dir. Joss Whedon. Perf. Robert Downey Jr., Chris Evans, Chris Hemsworth, Scarlett Johansson, and Samuel L. Jackson. Marvel Studios, Walt Disney Studios Motion Pictures, 2012. Film.

Marvel's The Avengers 2: Age of Ultron. Dir. Joss Whedon. Perf. Robert Downey Jr., Chris Evans, Chris Hemsworth, Scarlett Johansson, and Samuel L. Jackson. Marvel Studios, Walt Disney Studios Motion Pictures, 2015. Film.

Mayer, Ruth. *Serial Fu Manchu: The Chinese Supervillian and the Spread of Yellow Peril Ideology*. Philadelphia: Temple University Press, 2014. Print.

Mittell, Jason. "Forensic Fandom and the Drillable Text Comments." In *Spreadable Media: Creating Value and Meaning in a Networked Culture*. Eds. Henry Jenkins, Sam Ford, and Joshua Green. New York: New York University Press, 2013. Print. *Spreadable Media*. Web.

———. "Narrative Complexity in Contemporary American Television." *Velvet Light Trap* 58 (Fall 2006): 29–40. Print.

———. "Serial Orientations." *JustTV: Random Thoughts by Media Scholar Jason Mittell*, 14 November 2011. Web.

"Multiverse/Universe Listing." *Marvel Comics Database*. Wikia, Inc., n.d. Web.

Murray, Janet Horowitz. *Hamlet on the Holodeck: The Future of Narrative in Cyberspace*. New York: Simon and Schuster, 1997. Print.

"Pilot." Dir. Joss Whedon. *Marvel's Agents of S.H.I.E.L.D.* Perf. Clark Gregg, Ming-Na Wen, Brett Dalton, J. August Richards, and Shannon Lucio. Disney-ABC Domestic Television, 24 September 2013. Television.

Raunig, Gerald. *A Thousand Machines: A Concise Philosophy of the Machine as Social Movement*. Los Angeles: Semiotext(e), 2010. Print.

Rogers, Adam. "Agents of S.H.I.E.L.D.'s Comic Book Easter Eggs: Episode 2." *Wired*, 10 October 2013. Web.

"Roxxon Corporation." *Marvel Cinematic Universe Wiki*, n.d. Web.

Ryan, Marie-Laure. "Story/Worlds/Media: Tuning the Instruments of a Media-Conscious Narratology." In *Storyworlds Across Media: Toward a Media-Conscious Narratology*. Eds. Marie-Laure Ryan and Jan-Noël Thon. Lincoln: University of Nebraska Press, 2014. Kindle version.

———. "Transmedial Storytelling and Transfictionality." *Poetics Today* 34:3 (Fall 2013): 361–388. Print.

Thor. Dir. Kenneth Branagh. Perf. Chris Hemsworth, Natalie Portman, Tom Hiddleston, Anthony Hopkins, and Samuel L. Jackson. Marvel Studios, Paramount Pictures, Concorde Video, 2011. Blu-ray.

Thor: The Dark World. Dir. Alan Taylor. Perf. Chris Hemsworth, Natalie Portman, Tom Hiddleston, Anthony Hopkins, and Idris Elba. Marvel Studios, Walt Disney Video, 2014. Blu-ray.

"Turn, Turn, Turn." Dir. Vincent Misiano. *Marvel's Agents of S.H.I.E.L.D.* Perf. Clark Gregg, Ming-Na Wen, Brett Dalton, Bill Paxton, and Saffron Burrows. Disney-ABC Domestic Television, 8 April 2013. Television.

"The Well." Dir. Johnathan Frakes. *Marvel's Agents of S.H.I.E.L.D.* Perf. Clark Gregg, Ming-Na Wen, Brett Dalton, Michael Graziadei, and Erin Way. Disney-ABC Domestic Television, 19 November 2013. Television.

Williams, Raymond. *Television: Technology and Cultural Form*. London: Fontana, 1974. Print.

The Marvel One-Shots and Transmedia Storytelling

MICHAEL GRAVES

" Y ou've become part of a bigger universe" (*Iron Man*). This declaration by Nick Fury, at the conclusion of *Iron Man* (Jon Favreau, 2008), alludes to Tony Stark's newfound involvement with the characters and institutions that make up the Marvel Cinematic Universe (MCU), a storyworld that expanded considerably over the course of Marvel Studios' following six feature film releases. The narrative universe established in these films broadened further with the Marvel One-Shots, a series of short films. Included in the special features of five Marvel home-video releases, these short films advanced self-contained stories tied to the characters and events established in previous Marvel movies. For example, *The Consultant*, the first entry in the Marvel One-Shots series, finds Agent Phillip Coulson using Tony Stark (Iron Man) to sabotage the release of Emil Blonsky (the Abomination) from prison, thereby linking the storylines of *Iron Man*, *The Incredible Hulk* (Louis Leterrier, 2008), and *Thor* (Kenneth Branagh, 2011) into a coherent narrative universe.

While such a strategy is part of a traditional business model in which value-added paratexts, such as filmmaker commentaries and deleted scenes, incentivize DVD and Blu-ray purchases, the Marvel One-Shots series is also emblematic of a shifting industrial logic. Transmedia storytelling—a narrative approach in which integral story elements are dispersed across multiple media platforms—increasingly provides a way for conglomerates to capitalize on successful intellectual properties by expanding revenue-generating content across their vast media holdings. For instance, the production of the ABC television series *Agents of S.H.I.E.L.D.* (2013–present) enabled The Walt Disney Company to synergistically extend the lucrative

MCU into a new market, as Disney owns both Marvel Studios and the ABC television network.

Despite the increasing prevalence of transmedia storytelling franchises, there is surprisingly little consensus regarding the qualities of a story that effectively spans media platforms. In 2006, leading transmedia scholar Henry Jenkins argued that "we do not yet have very good aesthetic criteria for evaluating works that play themselves out across multiple media" (*Convergence* 96). Three years later, however, Jenkins offered seven principles of transmedia storytelling: seriality; world-building; subjectivity; performance; continuity vs. multiplicity; spreadability vs. drillability; and immersion vs. extractability ("Revenge"). Yet little work has been dedicated to applying this framework to specific transmedia storytelling franchises. Through the application of Jenkins's model to the MCU—a franchise consisting of twelve feature films, three television series, and five Marvel One-Shots—this essay modifies the concept of extractability and adds the principle of unidirectional flow vs. omnidirectional flow to the framework, thereby providing a fuller picture of the unique ways in which transmedia storytelling franchises operate.

EIGHT PRINCIPLES OF TRANSMEDIA STORYTELLING

Because transmedia franchises are largely characterized by a serialized narrative approach, Jenkins's first principle is seriality. This privileging of serialization is part of a larger shift, within the television industry, toward increased serialized storytelling (Mittell, *Complex TV* 17). Transmedia storytelling franchises augment such serialization by expanding the narrative across multiple platforms, producing a robust mythology or complex serialized narrative.

The paratexts within a serialized transmedia storytelling franchise can serve an array of purposes: for example, they may depict previously unseen aspects of a narrative universe, fill in the narrative gaps in an existing storyline, or further develop characters. By creating a fictional universe that cannot be comprehended within a single text, transmedia franchises often facilitate a sense of world-building, Jenkins's second principle (*Convergence* 114). Furthermore, the presence of paratexts can increase the franchise's "subjectivity," the third principle of transmedia storytelling, enabling the audience to gain new insights through access to multiple points of view ("Revenge"). Instead of focusing on the franchise's central protagonists, transmedia extensions often depict secondary characters, giving the audience new insights into previously unseen aspects of the franchise's narrative universe, and thereby fostering what game designer Neil Young terms "additive comprehension" (qtd. in Jenkins, *Convergence* 123). In other words, by including revelatory details in each paratext, the franchise deepens the audience's perception of the narrative universe, providing for a fuller understanding of the characters, events, and storyworld.

Frequently, the additive comprehension fostered by paratextual expansion is encouraged, from producer to audience, through the use of invitations to explore other platforms. Performance, Jenkins's fourth principle of transmedia storytelling, details the ways in which transmedia producers promote such audience participation. In her discussion of the television industry's increasing use of the Internet, for instance, Sharon Marie Ross points to the ways in which television programs "rely on obscured invitations to move viewers to the Internet (and elsewhere) in pursuit of narrative enhancements" (173). The use of hidden cues within these television series is a savvy storytelling strategy, encouraging participation in transmedia storyworlds without potentially diminishing the experience of those who are interested only in the centralized text. Yet, as Louisa Stein points out, invitations to participate can also be overt (342). In this manner, transmedia storytelling franchises are sites for participation in which producers encourage audiences to take part in the telling of the story through multi-platform media use or a range of performative actions.

By distributing narrative elements across multiple platforms in a unified and coordinated manner, transmedia storytelling producers create a narrative comprising interlocking texts. Although such an approach privileges narrative continuity, it also makes possible the depiction of alternate versions of characters and narrative universes. Hence, for Jenkins, transmedia storytelling represents opportunities for both narrative continuity and multiplicity, the fifth principle of transmedia storytelling. With Sam Ford, Jenkins observes the ways in which comic book franchises negotiate decades-long narrative arcs with alternate and contradictory accounts of a character's storyline (Ford and Jenkins 307–308). For example, while Marvel's *The Amazing Spider-Man* comic franchise advances one continuous Spider-Man narrative, the *Ultimate Spider-Man*, *Spider-Man 2099*, and *Spider-Man: India* titles depict differing versions. Rather than competing with the stories contained in the mainstream Marvel Universe, these spin-off comics encourage readers to revel in alternate retellings in which Spider-Man leads parallel lives as Peter Parker, Miguel O'Hara, and Pavitr Prabhakar, respectively. As such, parallel and even contradictory representations of characters and events can function as narrative extensions that fuel an audience's interest in a franchise.

Spreadability vs. drillability, the sixth principle of transmedia storytelling, foregrounds two potentially contradictory trends within contemporary media industries. "Spreadability" refers to a media text's ability to encourage the sharing of text components between audience members and others; it is dependent upon a range of technological, economic, and cultural factors (Jenkins et al. 3). "Drillability," in contrast, refers to the ability of a media text (a complex television series, for example) to encourage audiences to probe the text deeply to discover new facets of the text (Mittell, "Forensic Fandom"). Although spreadability and drillability often work in opposing directions, with spreadable media generally reaching a larger, less engaged audience, and drillable media typically reaching a smaller, yet more engaged one, the possibility exists for a text to be simultaneously spreadable and drillable (Mittell, "Forensic Fandom"). The 24 (Fox 2001–2010, 2014) franchise, for example, which consists of a long-running television series, an array of novels and comic books, multiple webisode series, a "mobisode" series (accessible primarily on mobile devices), and several video games, is both spreadable and drillable. The franchise encourages the audience to analyze transmedia extensions in an effort to parse out the relationships between "interstitial microstories, parallel stories, and peripheral stories" (Scolari 598). Therefore, although Jenkins positions spreadablitity and drillability in opposition, transmedia franchises can demonstrate both logics.

The seventh of Jenkins's transmedia storytelling principles is immersion vs. extractability, notions describing the potential for audiences to enter fictional worlds (immersion) or to take aspects of the fictional world into their everyday experiences (extractability). The sprawling, boundary-blurring nature of transmedia stories fosters sustained engagement and immersion by granting the audience prolonged access to a narrative universe. In immersion, an individual enters an imaginary world. Extractability inverts that focus, with the individual bringing an artifact of the fictional world into everyday life. The presence of new story elements does not factor into Jenkins's concept of extractability in a way that aligns with simple merchandising. And yet we can modify Jenkins's concept of extractability to refer to tangible artifacts of a narrative universe—artifacts that either broaden that universe or advance the narrative in new ways. Such modification is pivotal to creating a more accurate picture of how transmedia storytelling franchises operate. This kind of extractability is evident in the franchises of *G.I. Joe*, *Masters of the Universe*, and *Transformers*, which consist of comics, animated television programs, films, and action figures (Bainbridge 838-839). Text introducing narrative information may be contained in (or on) the packaging for such artifacts, but beyond that, these franchises' action figures enable audiences to extract fictional characters and insert them into real-world spaces. Although Jenkins again situates the notions of immersion and extractability in opposition to each other, transmedia storytelling franchises, as these examples illustrate, can simultaneously encourage both principles.

Jenkins's principles demonstrate the unique characteristics of transmedia storytelling franchises. Yet this framework does not take into account the flow of story elements between the franchise's central, privileged text and the paratextual extensions. Hence, a new principle, unidirectional flow vs. omnidirectional flow, can be identified. This principle describes the two primary ways that narrative information can move within a transmedia franchise. It describes how story elements progress either outward, from the center of the franchise to the surrounding paratexts (unidirectional), or both outward and inward (omnidirectional). When transmedia franchises favor a unidirectional flow of story elements, it is usually to aid in comprehension among audience members. In other words, characters, institutions, and storylines spread outward from the central text or body of texts, such as a film franchise or a television series, to the supporting paratexts. Such unidirectional franchises position paratexts as ancillary to one's understanding of the franchise. When transmedia storytelling franchises exhibit an omnidirectional movement of narrative information, in which the revelations depicted in the franchise's paratexts are specifically referenced in the central text or body of texts, the story becomes more complex. Although the omnidirectional flow of story elements runs the risk of alienating those who are unfamiliar with a franchise's paratexts, it can also encourage greater audience investment by validating audience members' engagement with the narrative extensions. The paratexts are positioned as being integral to an understanding of the franchise. When coupled with Jenkins's existing framework, the principle of unidirectional flow vs. omnidirectional flow provides a fuller picture of transmedia storytelling.

THE MARVEL ONE-SHOTS

Beginning in 2011, Marvel Studios announced the production of a direct-to-video series of short films, the Marvel One-Shots, based on stories and characters already existing in the MCU. Given the MCU's comic book lineage, the name chosen for the series is fitting. In contrast to the long-term serial or limited series comic books, the term "one-shot" is used within the comic book industry to denote a self-contained, single-issue title (Serchay). Often one-shot issues contain noncanonical stories in which the events detailed are not considered official continuations of the character or of the established narrative universe. Marvel's *What If?* one-shot series, for example, depicted hypothetical scenarios, such as "What if Spider-Man joined the Fantastic Four?" One-shot issues are occasionally used to gauge audience interest in new characters or storylines. Marvel's *Franklin Richards: Son of a Genius*, which details the often humorous misadventures of the son of Reed Richards (Mister Fantastic) and Sue Richards (the Invisible Woman), began as a one-shot. As a result of this one-shot's favorable reception, Marvel began publishing the series on a quarterly basis ("Franklin Richards One-Shot Sells Out"). The Marvel One-Shots had a similar exploratory aim.

Featured on the Blu-ray release of *Thor* in 2011, *The Consultant* was the first in the Marvel One-Shots series. It begins with Agent Coulson, a character who had appeared in *Iron Man* (2008), *Iron Man 2* (Jon Favreau, 2010), and *Thor* (2011), discussing the World Security Council's desire to see Emil Blonsky released from prison so that Blonsky can join the Avengers Initiative. While a glimpse of Blonsky's destruction in Harlem, from *The Incredible Hulk* (2008), is briefly shown, Coulson notes that this devastation is being blamed on Bruce Banner (the Hulk). Deeming the request ill-advised, Agents Coulson and Jasper Sitwell conspire to send a liaison to sabotage the meeting with General Thaddeus Ross in which the prisoner release will be discussed. Coulson and Sitwell then enlist Tony Stark, a character also appearing in *The Incredible Hulk*, to convince General Ross not to exonerate Blonsky. After Stark meets General Ross in a bar, Coulson and Sitwell note that their plan to keep Blonsky incarcerated has been successful, and the approximately four-minute-long film concludes.

The second One-Shot, *A Funny Thing Happened on the Way to Thor's Hammer* (2011), was included on the Blu-ray release of *Captain America: The First Avenger* (Joe Johnston, 2011) and also features Agent Coulson. Set before the events of *Thor*, the four-minute short depicts Coulson traveling to New Mexico to retrieve Thor's hammer. On his way, Coulson stops at a gas station that is subsequently robbed by two armed perpetrators. After voluntarily disarming himself, Coulson subdues the robbers using an array of acrobatic maneuvers, and subsequently drives off into the night.

Accompanying the Blu-ray release of *The Avengers* (Joss Whedon, 2012), another One-Shot, *Item 47*, centers on an impoverished couple-turned-bank-robbers, who find an alien-created gun in the aftermath of the climactic Battle of New York depicted in *The Avengers*. In the roughly eleven-minute video, Agent Blake orders Sitwell to apprehend the suspects and retrieve the alien technology—the sole piece of alien technology still unaccounted for from the Battle of New York. Following a firefight involving the alien gun, Sitwell captures the bank robbers. Impressed by the technological prowess demonstrated by the couple, who were able to arm the weapon, Sitwell gives the man a job in S.H.I.E.L.D.'s research and development division. The film concludes with the woman becoming Agent Blake's protégée.

Agent Carter, the fourth in the Marvel One-Shots series, is featured on the Blu-ray release of *Iron Man 3* (Shane Black, 2013). It begins with a flashback to *Captain America: The First Avenger*, as Agent Peggy Carter and Steve Rogers (Captain America) say their goodbyes before Rogers selflessly crashes a Hydra aircraft carrying a payload of destructive weaponry. But the short takes place one year after the events of the first Captain America film, and Agent Carter is now toiling under the chauvinistic command of Agent Flynn. Believing Carter was unfairly granted her position in the Strategic Scientific Reserve because of her romantic relationship with Rogers, Flynn refuses to give her an assignment in the field. After Flynn and the rest of the male personnel go out drinking one night, Carter answers the office's secure line and accepts a mission to infiltrate a criminal hideout. Demonstrating her expertise in the field, she incapacitates numerous assailants and successfully completes the mission, resulting in Howard Stark, Tony Stark's father, offering her a position running S.H.I.E.L.D. At over fifteen minutes, *Agent Carter* is the longest of the One-Shot series.

The fifth One-Shot, *All Hail the King*, focuses on a journalist interviewing the imprisoned Trevor Slattery, the actor posing as the Mandarin in *Iron Man 3*. During the final day of Slattery's interview, the journalist reveals himself to be an associate of the real Mandarin, an individual greatly displeased by Slattery's co-opting of his persona. After providing background information about the Mandarin, including his involvement with a terrorist group known as the Ten Rings, the journalist kills Slattery's entourage and kidnaps Slattery, so that the real Mandarin may exact his revenge for Slattery's use of the "Mandarin" moniker. *All Hail the King* was included on the Blu-ray release of *Thor: The Dark World* (Alan Taylor, 2013) and is currently the final entry in the Marvel One-Shots series.

THE MARVEL ONE-SHOTS AS TRANSMEDIA STORIES

The Marvel Cinematic Universe franchise was first established in 2008 with *Iron Man*. The subsequent films—*The Incredible Hulk* (2008), *Iron Man 2* (2010), *Thor* (2011), *Captain America: The First Avenger* (2011), and *The Avengers* (2012)—constituted Phase One of Marvel Studios' coordinated efforts to bring the characters and events depicted in each film into a shared narrative universe. In contrast to Marvel's earlier films, such as *X-Men* (Bryan Singer, 2000), *Hulk* (Ang Lee, 2003), and *The Punisher* (Jonathan Hensleigh, 2004), which made no attempts to draw links between the depicted events, the MCU franchise "presented individual films as mere episodes in a larger, cohesive work" (Johnson 6). Rebecca Romijn's portrayal of two different roles in *X-Men* and *Punisher* is indicative of Marvel's approach to narrative continuity (or lack thereof) prior to the release of *Iron Man*.

Taking place between entries in the franchise, the Marvel One-Shots represent the studio's continued efforts to advance a serialized overarching narrative. The Marvel films from *Iron Man* to *Iron Man 3* (2013) and the Marvel One-Shots create an interlocking mosaic of narrative texts forming a continuous storyline. Furthermore, by releasing the feature films and One-Shots in a unified and coordinated manner, the MCU demonstrates the principles of seriality and narrative continuity. Such continuity is achieved through a focus on notable secondary characters, such as Agent Coulson, Agent Carter, and Trevor Slattery, in a way that provides new insights through access to multiple points of view. This subjectivity, a central principle of transmedia storytelling, is best evidenced in *The Consultant*, *All Hail the King*, and *Agent Carter*. In *The Consultant*, for example, the audience learns that the World Security Council, the group spearheading the Avenger Initiative, originally wanted Emil Blonsky to become a member of the Avengers. Moreover, although the Mandarin ostensibly appeared to be a fictional creation of scientist Aldrich Killian, who was portrayed by actor Trevor Slattery in *Iron Man 3*, *All Hail the King* reveals that the Mandarin is, in fact, a real individual. Finally, *Agent Carter* elaborates on the formation of S.H.I.E.L.D., with Howard Stark promoting Agent Carter from her position within the Strategic Scientific Reserve to become the co-head of the newly created S.H.I.E.L.D.

organization. This background information about a fictional institution that already exists in the MCU illustrates the strategy of world-building. The extension of the World Security Council, the Ten Rings, and S.H.I.E.L.D. across multiple platforms facilitates the creation of a narrative universe that has a clear history and operates according to an internally consistent logic. By advancing a continuous serialized narrative, featuring characters from previous Marvel films, the creators further bolster this logic. Hence, the Marvel One-Shots exhibit at least four principles of transmedia storytelling: seriality, continuity, subjectivity, and world-building.

The short film series less successfully embodies the principles of performance, spreadability vs. drillability, and immersion vs. extractability. Unlike more performative paratexts, such as *Agents of S.H.I.E.L.D.: Double Agent*, a Web series that provides extra-textual information about the television series production, the Marvel One-Shots require little participation from the audience to glean new insights. In addition, the Marvel films do not feature invitations for viewers to seek out and explore further transmedia content. And while the narrative of the Marvel Cinematic Universe is distributed across multiple platforms, the Marvel One-Shots are not spreadable. Small segments of the One-Shots are accessible on the Marvel Studios YouTube page as teasers of sorts, which can in turn be shared by viewers. However, the One-Shots lack a mechanism enabling individuals to circulate the full-length short films.

Furthermore, whereas the Marvel films encourage fans to "drill down" into the texts through the incorporation of visual references and verbal allusions to aspects of the greater Marvel mythos, the Marvel One-Shots do not foster prolonged scrutiny or drillability. This is not to suggest that the short films lack insights into the MCU; yet the One-Shots are not sufficiently complex or oblique to encourage long-term analysis. The short films of the series are neither numerous enough nor long enough to foster sustained immersion in the world of the MCU. Alternatively, although an array of licensed merchandise enables individuals to extract an artifact of the Marvel narrative universe into real-world spaces, these tangible artifacts do not effectively broaden the world or advance the narrative of the universe in new and revelatory ways.

Lastly, the MCU demonstrates a unidirectional flow of story elements: the additive comprehension enabled by the Marvel One-Shots has not, at least yet, factored into the narratives of the feature films. Neither Agent Coulson's effort to sabotage Emil Blonsky in *The Consultant* nor his handling of the two robbers in *A Funny Thing Happened on the Way to Thor's Hammer* has been mentioned in the Marvel films to appear since these One-Shots' were released. The bank-robbing couple depicted in *Item 47*, and the Ten Rings organization referenced in *All Hail the King*, also have not played a role in subsequent feature films. Marvel's television series represent a greater degree of omnidirectionality. Agent Blake, a character introduced in *Item 47*, appears in two episodes of *Agents of S.H.I.E.L.D.* The first episode of *Marvel's Agent Carter* (ABC, 2015-present) begins with a quick montage of images from *Captain America: The First Avenger* and the *Agent Carter* One-Shot. Although significant in this regard, *Marvel's Agent Carter* represents something of a narrative conundrum, as the One-Shot in which Agent Carter is featured concludes with the character being offered a position running S.H.I.E.L.D. Because Agent Carter continues to work for the Strategic Scientific Reserve—while suffering under the same sexist conditions that were seemingly ended by Howard Stark at the end of the *Agent Carter* One-Shot—*Marvel's Agent Carter* violates the narrative continuity established by *Captain America: The First Avenger* and the *Agent Carter* One-Shot.

While the additive comprehension surrounding Agent Blake and Agent Carter is rather inconsequential—and potentially contradictory—to one's understanding of the respective television series, *Agents of S.H.I.E.L.D.* does feature a notable instance of the omnidirectional flow of integral story elements. Coordinated with the April 4, 2014, theatrical release of *Captain America: The Winter Soldier* (directed by Anthony and Joe Russo), the Season 2 episode "Turn, Turn, Turn," which aired on April 8, 2014, began a season-long arc linking the narratives of the film and television series. *Captain America: The Winter Soldier* centers on S.H.I.E.L.D.'s downfall as a result of infiltration by Hydra, a group bent on global domination. The second season of *Agents of S.H.I.E.L.D.* continues this storyline, further depicting the ramifications of S.H.I.E.L.D.'s collapse as well as S.H.I.E.L.D. director Nick Fury's apparent death, an event also occurring in *Captain America: The Winter Soldier*. As such, the second season of the television series embodies the principles of subjectivity and unidirectionality. For instance, the episode "One Door Closes" flashes back to the *Captain America: The Winter Soldier*'s climax on a helicarrier and focuses on the actions of secondary characters Agents Morse and Mackenzie during the Hydra uprising. Further demonstrating the unidirectional flow of story elements, Season 2 of *Agents of S.H.I.E.L.D.* also features references to Ultron, the central antagonist in *The Avengers: Age of Ultron* (Joss Whedon, 2015). However, the Season 2 episode

"Scars" reverses this narrative directionality by referencing a secret society of individuals with unique abilities who are known as "the Inhumans." By establishing the presence of the characters appearing in Marvel's *Inhumans*, a film scheduled for release in 2019, *Agents of S.H.I.E.L.D.* represents a significant instance of omnidirectionality within the Marvel Cinematic Universe. For the first time, a central storyline in the MCU has begun in a paratextual extension of the franchise, and will subsequently flow to the franchise's center. Reflecting this innovative approach, Marvel Studios president Kevin Fiege noted that the treatment of the Inhumans storyline is "blazing new ground" within the franchise (qtd. in Faraci). Although it remains to be seen how the narratives of *Agents of S.H.I.E.L.D.* and the *Inhumans* will further intertwine, a press release for the television series' third season centered heavily on the Inhumans, suggesting that Marvel Studios' inventive transmedia storytelling efforts will continue (Abrams).

CONCLUSION

In addition to incentivizing home-video purchases, the Marvel One-Shots have represented Marvel Studios' attempt to maintain audience engagement by both expanding the franchise's narrative universe and advancing a serialized narrative centering on compelling secondary characters in a way that will provide the audience with a fuller understanding of the Marvel Cinematic Universe's mythos. Although the Marvel One-Shots fulfill the principles of seriality, narrative continuity, subjectivity, and world-building, the series does not effectively demonstrate the principles of performance, spreadability vs. drillability, and immersion vs. extractability. From the perspective of transmedia storytelling, therefore, the One-Shots suffer from numerous weaknesses.

Marvel Studios' future transmedia endeavors would benefit from the fostering of a more interactive and participatory engagement by encouraging the audience to actively seek out and combine spreadable story elements in order to uncover new, immersive aspects of the franchise's mythology. For example, as opposed to including narrative extensions on Marvel Studios' home-video releases, the incorporation of paratexts, such as alternate reality games or diegetic websites, containing hidden or oblique information pertaining to the mythos of the Marvel Cinematic Universe would encourage greater audience interactivity and participation than the One-Shots provide.

Moreover, although Marvel's current approach to transmedia storytelling favors narrative continuity, other possibilities exist. Given the films' and One-Shots' comic book origins—a storytelling form known for its use of multiple, parallel storylines within franchises—this would be possible, but it remains to be seen if Marvel Studios would be open eventually to supplementing the Marvel Cinematic Universe in this way. Marvel would have to embrace narrative multiplicity in subsequent phases of the franchise's development. Marvel's television series provides additional opportunities for the flow of narrative information to become more omnidirectional.

Captain America: The Winter Soldier was the first home-video release not to feature a One-Shot since the One-Shot series began. Moreover, no One-Shot was included in the following entry in the Marvel Cinematic Universe, *Guardians of the Galaxy* (James Gunn, 2014). Such a move was surprising, considering that the One-Shots had been growing in scale with each new entry. When asked about the short film series in May 2015, Feige said there were "no active plans for the One-Shots to return" (qtd. in White). Along with budgetary concerns, the One-Shots present logistical obstacles. Hiring cast and crew for a One-Shot requires the studio to sign stars and filmmakers long in advance of the respective films beginning production (Breznican). The One-Shots also require a considerable amount of coordination among numerous arms of the Marvel Entertainment and Walt Disney empires. As Marvel Studios co-president Louis D'Esposito observed in 2013, "I don't know if really we . . . [have] been thinking that far ahead. It's difficult enough to find something that's enjoyable, that we can tell with the budget limitations, and in the time we have. Introducing a lot of complicated variables might weaken that" (Breznican). Given the presence of such complicating factors, the eight principles of transmedia storytelling could provide an effective framework by which Marvel Studios might conceptualize and implement further transmedia extensions of the Marvel Cinematic Universe in ways that significantly contribute to the Marvel mythos.

WORKS CITED

Abrams, Natalie. "ABC Releases New *Agents of S.H.I.E.L.D.* Season 3 Details, Including Lash Casting." *Entertainment Weekly*, 26 August 2015. Web.

Bainbridge, Jason. "Fully Articulated: The Rise of the Action Figure and the

Changing Face of 'Children's' Entertainment." *Continuum: Journal of Media and Cultural Studies* 24.6 (2010): 829–842. Print.

Breznican, Anthony. "Marvel One-Shots: Might 'Agent Carter' Clear Way for Ms. Marvel, Loki, Young Nick Fury, or Black Panther?" *Entertainment Weekly*, 17 July 2013. Web.

Cheshire, Tom, and Charlie Burton. "Transmedia: Entertainment Reimagined." *Wired*, 8 July 2010. Web.

Faraci, Devin. "Don't Expect to See the Blue Area of the Moon on AGENTS OF SHIELD." *Birth Death Movies*, 14 April 2015. Web.

Ford, Sam, and Henry Jenkins. "Managing Multiplicity in Superhero Comics: An Interview with Henry Jenkins." In *Third Person: Authoring and Exploring Vast Narratives*. Eds. Pat Harrigan and Noah Wardrip-Fruin. Cambridge, MA: MIT Press, 2009. Print.

"Franklin Richards One-Shot Sells Out." *Marvel*, 7 October 2005. Web.

"Interview with Buffy Creator Joss Whedon." *Dark Horse Comics*, 26 March 2007. Web.

Iron Man. Dir. John Favreau. Marvel Studios, 2008. Film.

Jenkins, Henry. *Convergence Culture: Where Old and New Media Collide.* New York: New York University Press, 2006. Print.

———. "Revenge of the Origami Unicorn: The Remaining Four Principles of Transmedia Storytelling." *Confessions of an Aca-Fan: The Official Weblog of Henry Jenkins*, 12 December 2009. Web.

———. "The Revenge of the Origami Unicorn: Seven Principles of Transmedia Storytelling (Well, Two Actually. Five More on Friday)." *Confessions of an Aca-Fan: The Official Weblog of Henry Jenkins*, 12 December 2009. Web.

———. *Transmedia Storytelling: Moving Characters from Books to Films to Video Games Can Make Them Stronger and More Compelling. MIT Technology Review*, 15 January 2003. Web.

———. "Transmedia Storytelling 202: Further Reflections." *Confessions of an Aca-Fan: The Official Weblog of Henry Jenkins*, 1 August 2011. Web.

Jenkins, Henry, Sam Ford, and Joshua Green. *Spreadable Media: Creating Value and Meaning in a Networked Culture.* New York: New York University Press, 2013. Print.

Johnson, Derek. "Cinematic Destiny: Marvel Studios and the Trade Stories of Industrial Convergence." *Cinema Journal* 52.1 (2012): 1–24. Print.

Mittell, Jason. *Complex TV: The Poetics of Contemporary Television Storytelling.* New York: New York University Press, 2015. Print.

———. "Forensic Fandom and the Drillable Text." *Spreadable Media*, n.d. Web.

Ross, Sharon Marie. *Beyond the Box: Television and the Internet.* Malden, UK: Blackwell Publishing, 2008. Print.

Scolari, Carlos Alberto. "Transmedia Storytelling: Implicit Consumers, Narrative Worlds, and Branding in Contemporary Media Production." *International Journal of Communication* 3 (2009): 586–606. Print.

Serchay, David S. "Comic Book Collectors: The Serials Librarians of the Home." *Serials Review* 24.1 (1999): 57–70. Print.

Stein, Louisa. "*Gossip Girl*: Transmedia Technologies." In *How to Watch Television*. Eds. Ethan Thompson and Jason Mittell. New York: New York University Press, 2013. Print.

White, Brett. "Feige Talks Contracts, Death and If Marvel's Movies Will Take a 'Dark Turn.'" *Comic Book Resources*, 7 May 2015. Web.

Spinning Webs

CONSTRUCTING AUTHORS, GENRE, AND FANS
IN THE SPIDER-MAN FILM FRANCHISE

JAMES N. GILMORE

pider-Man has been one of twenty-first-century Hollywood's most financially successful franchises, to date straddling five movies across twelve years to consistently high box-office returns.[1] As such, the films themselves—*Spider-Man* (Sam Raimi, 2002), *Spider-Man 2* (Sam Raimi, 2004), *Spider-Man 3* (Sam Raimi, 2007), *The Amazing Spider-Man* (Marc Webb, 2012), and *The Amazing Spider-Man 2* (Marc Webb, 2014)—are useful texts for analyzing the superhero genre's forms, structures, and repetitions across a single brand. Academic and popular discourses surrounding these films to date have cohered around issues of genre, adaptation, and narrative analysis, offering rich assessments of how various spectator groups have constellated under the franchise and read its contributions to the genre, and particularly how they have read them in a plurality of ways.

Little has been made, however, of the franchise's "*paratexts*," a concept from Gerard Genette's work on the liminal devices relating the audience and the text. Paratexts constitute important means for developing interpretations and value. As Jonathan Gray has noted, "paratexts fill the space between" texts, audiences, and industries, "variously negotiating or determining interactions among the three" (23). Media paratexts consist of, but are by no means limited to, trailers, posters, DVD documentaries, and audio commentaries—existing outside the text, they nevertheless inform spectator interactions and interpretations. For Gray, paratexts condition "passages and trajectories that criss-cross the mediascape" (23), and so taking them as objects of analysis allows scholarship to "make sense of the wealth of other entities that saturate the media, and that construct film and television" (4). Paratexts have become increasingly important for Henry Jenkins's conception of "convergence culture," as the location and development of "meaning" for the text exists across an ever-expanding range of media experiences. Jenkins crucially observes that "the emerging convergence paradigm assumes that old and new media will interact in even more complex ways" (6), and so digital paratexts continually shift and amplify the sites of interpretation and interaction with any given media text.

In this chapter I argue that the special edition DVD is itself a site of converged materials that places the text in direct interaction with its paratexts. The special edition DVD constructs particular views of adaptation, genre, and authorship designed to appeal to an imagined fan community. More specifically, paratexts are key sites for considering how Marvel constructs its cinematic brand, and how it discursively imagines its fan audiences participating in and valuing that brand. DVD paratexts such as audio commentaries and making-of documentaries, by attempting to address—however broadly—the consumer through the producer, continue the Marvel Universe's tradition of authorial editorializing found in its comics, such as Stan Lee's "Soapbox" in the "Marvel Bullpen Bulletins" of the late 1960s. As such, I draw from Derek Johnson's notion of media franchises and popular culture as bound up in "multiplication and replication" (*Media Franchising* 2) to explore the repetitions of discursive branding across comics and film paratexts from the 1960s and 2000s, respectively.

My goal is not to argue that little has changed in how the company constructs its "Marvel Universe"; such a claim would mask the immense cultural and industrial changes that have taken place at Marvel over the course of its history. Rather, I wish to show that certain paratextual devices that were put in place in the late 1960s to construct authorship, value, and imagined fan groups have maintained their importance as Marvel has expanded its intermedial and transmedial universe. The *Spider-Man* film franchise demonstrates how genre and adaptation are important paratextual discourses for the superhero genre generally—and for Marvel in particular—because they allow the company to create intermedial continuity between the comic books and the film franchise. These paratexts utilize a plurality of fan-authors who reflexively consider the importance of adaptation and genre for the Marvel Universe.

I have focused on the *Spider-Man* franchise not only because of its ongoing success and production, but also because it falls outside of Marvel's "Cinematic Universe" project. Licensed under Sony and thus outside of the more integrated Marvel Studios projects, such as *The Avengers* (Joss

Whedon, 2012), the *Spider-Man* films provide a more isolated take on how the company discusses its cinematic properties. Derek Johnson ("Cinematic Destiny"), Matthias Stork ("Assembling the Avengers"), and others have engaged the discursive construction of the Cinematic Universe brand through the cross-property franchising of *The Avengers*, and so this analysis of *Spider-Man* adds to the growing discussion of Marvel's branding strategies for its film franchises. The special edition DVD is among the company's officially packaged branding efforts; as such, it is a potent site for analyzing who discusses the process of filmmaking, in what terms, and to what ends. The assembled paratextual features on these discs collectively construct certain kinds of fan-authors who embody the very ethos of *Spider-Man*—with great power (of production) comes great responsibility (to the fans).

In his study of contemporary Hollywood's "production cultures," John Thornton Caldwell suggested that "practitioners constantly dialogue and negotiate a series of questions that we traditionally value as part of film studies" (26). In this chapter I trace that dialogue and negotiation across the *Spider-Man* DVD paratexts. This focus differs somewhat from other academic analyses of *Spider-Man* to date. For example, Katherine A. Fowkes has provided a broad textual overview of the film's relationship to the fantasy genre; Wilson Koh has analyzed the film's modality of nostalgia to place it in conversation with Joseph Campbell's mythological theories; Lisa Gotto has considered the operation of digital technology in the film; and Richard L. Kaplan has analyzed its masculine representations in connection to Sigmund Freud. Although these examples do not represent an exhaustive list of the academic works on this film franchise, they underscore the fairly common methodology of bringing a theoretical model to bear on textual analysis. Whereas these scholars consider ways of reading the underlying structures, meanings, and aesthetics of the films as texts, I have used DVD paratexts to ask how industry practitioners themselves articulate academic concerns, and in turn place my findings into the broader discursive construction of the Marvel Universe brand.

Practitioners are ostensibly less concerned with questions of gender and psychology and more concerned with questions of adaptation and authorship, but they share with academics an interest in the underlying "meanings" of the superhero film and what superheroes "mean" to their fans. Industrial reflexivity has limits to what it discusses: practitioners *do* self-theorize on topics important to academics, but these topics—in the case of the superhero genre—typically fall into three areas: first, authorship, or who is responsible for creating the text; second, genre, which here constitutes definitions of the superhero's narrative and visual style; and third, adaptation, which here has much to do with intermediality, or the relationships between the comics and films.

Throughout paratextual interviews, practitioners maintain a strict focus on the industrial processes of adaptation in terms of genre and authorship, rarely, if ever, considering the social or cultural contexts of their work. For example, *Spider-Man* was the first superhero movie released after 9/11. Despite having been shot largely *before* 9/11, the film digitally "erases" the Twin Towers from all establishing shots. The DVD paratexts offer no comment on September 11, despite chunks of all five films being shot on location in New York City. The only remark that comes close is from Sam Raimi at the end of the "Making the Amazing" documentary on the *Spider-Man 2* DVD: "These are tough and scary times, and during these kinds of times we always look to stories of heroes to give us hope, and maybe that has something to do with why audiences look to Spider-Man." DVDs construct meaning both through inclusion and erasure; the importance of their paratexts can be deduced both from presences and absences. For example, the earliest *Spider-Man* preview involved Spider-Man trapping a helicopter of robbers between the Twin Towers with his web, emphasizing *Spider-Man's* relationship to the iconography of New York City. After September 11, this trailer was pulled; it was subsequently not included in the "Trailers" section of the DVD, but it still has an afterlife of its own, circulating through YouTube. This trailer indicates not only how DVDs consciously bind certain kinds of materials, but, more importantly, how spectral paratexts continue to spread beyond their officially sanctioned lives.

The *Spider-Man* paratexts establish creative personnel as hard laborers and creative thinkers, revealing not only the technical challenges of filmmaking but also crucial self-theorizing about genre, adaptation, and audience. Yet special edition DVDs also consciously *conceal*, constructing particular meanings by choosing to include certain paratexts over others. The digital circulations of video sites like YouTube become a paratextual graveyard, yet they also liberate these videos from the boundedness of the corporate-created DVD. Much as films now "grow old elsewhere," to borrow Charles R. Acland's phrase (65), this method of erasure removes social topicality to focus on industrial accomplishment. It emphasizes the brand's timelessness for fan assessment as the film ages in home entertainment, as opposed to the timeliness of its theatrical release.

LOCATING PARATEXTS

These DVD paratexts, by virtue of being attached to the "home video" release of the film, are often viewed in the home or in the consumer's personal space. As Caldwell explained, "the electronically mediated home now functions as the most economically strategic site for both television reception *and* film consumption" (9). This consumption, Caldwell points out, is not limited to the film itself. It is constantly extra-textual. Barbara Klinger has in part taken up similar concerns in her work on home theater technology, arguing that DVD paratexts "produce a sense of the film industry's magisterial control of appearances. . . . Viewers do not get the unvarnished truth about the production; they are instead presented with the 'promotable' facts, behind-the-scenes information that supports and enhances a sense of the 'movie magic' associated with Hollywood production" (73). In emphasizing audio commentaries and behind-the-scenes documentaries, DVDs employ top "creative personnel"—directors, producers, actors, and department heads—as the chief communicators of authorial vision. Many of these voices echo across multiple films, such as producers Avi Arad and Laura Ziskin and director Sam Raimi. The *Spider-Man* franchise cultivates an aura of respect by consciously imagining itself as a "fan's franchise" that caters to emotionally invested fans of many demographics and tastes throughout the production process. The *Spider-Man* films become, through these paratexts, acts *of* fan labor as much as films *for* fans.

Paratexts expand the boundaries of experience, and so the DVD allows the text to be *rewritten* as it ages beyond the initial cinematic experience. Paratextuality "feeds into, conditions, and becomes part of" the experience of a text, both before the first viewing (via promotional materials), and throughout subsequent viewings (via audio commentaries or behind-the-scenes documentaries) (Gray 38). In this sense, the text becomes *boundless*, in that DVDs permit limitless repetitious experience, even though the DVD is itself a *bounded* piece of technology. The DVD is material; it must be inserted into a drive and viewed through an adjoining screen. In special edition DVDs, many paratexts are contained on a second "bonus disc." As such, it is difficult to determine who watches these features, as buying the DVD does not require the consumer to view all or any of them. For the purposes of this analysis, I am interested less in the reception of these paratexts than in their discursive properties—who they imagine they are speaking to, and to what end. In most instances, the addressed viewer is imagined to be active, curious, and armed with an understanding of both the film text and the *Spider-Man* mythos. Much as Hollywood films use genres to facilitate "the integration of diverse factions into a single unified social fabric" (Altman 195), so, too, do paratexts integrate the diverse experiences of fans—both those who are well-versed in Marvel Comics lore as well as the less knowledgeable—under a singular mode of address.

The *Spider-Man* franchise DVDs are part of a rapidly changing home video market that spans everything from DVDs and Blu-rays to a number of video-on-demand streaming services. Indeed, they straddle a wide spectrum of ways for DVDs to utilize paratexts, from recycling HBO promotional specials (*Spider-Man*) to a plethora of documentaries on every aspect of the filmmaking process (*Spider-Man 2*). With *The Amazing Spider-Man*, the two-disc collection shrinks to one, and extras are largely exported to the more "premiere" Blu-ray disc. When purchasing *The Amazing Spider-Man 2* as a digital file through iTunes, the consumer receives "over 100 minutes of special features," including behind-the-scenes footage and deleted scenes. The paratext-heavy home video format still exists, but from 2002 to 2014 it expanded well beyond the materiality of the DVD disc. The increasing complexity of media circulation makes pinning down encounters with paratexts harder to do. Rental service Redbox, for example, often provides only a paratext-free "Rental Copy." Cloud services and digital downloads, such as Amazon Instant Video, often offer just the film. Furthermore, the location of many features—on a second disc—intrinsically separates them from the film, even if they are sold in the same plastic container. Much as spectral circulations pose a challenge to the negotiations of inclusion and erasure, so, too, do the flows of the home video marketplace pose a challenge for any perceived stability in analyzing interactions with paratextual material.

The continued decline in DVD revenue threatens the perpetuation of paratexts on many DVD releases. The *Los Angeles Times* estimated in March 2012 that "the number of movies rented or bought online . . . will grow 135% this year to 3.4 billion . . . [but] people will spend only $1.72 billion on digital movies, compared to $11.1 billion on DVDs and Blu-ray discs." Put another way, online services constitute 57 percent of consumption, but 12 percent of spending (Fritz). *Forbes* noted a year later that since 2004, "physical disc sales [had] fallen by about 30%," but "physical goods still [made] up about two-thirds of major studios' total home entertainment revenue" (Hayes). Digital technologies allow audiences to interface with films through a variety of industry-constructed paratexts, but a fundamental shift in film consumption *environments* is underway that is altering the culture of film collecting that Barbara Klinger elucidated in 2006, or the flows of global film culture that Charles R. Acland delineated in 2003.

To date, the discussion of DVD bonus features has centered on constructions of authorship. Scholars such as John Thornton Caldwell, Catherine Grant, Deborah Parker and Mark Parker, Pat Brereton, and Robert Alan Brookey and Robert Westerfelhaus have all considered ramifications for constructing authorship and meaning through DVDs. Caldwell's work on industrial reflexivity provides a crucial intersection for understanding how the *Spider-Man* DVDs promote genre and adaptation to a presumably active fan audience. Further, his "Taxonomy of DVD Bonus Track Strategies and Functions" imagines a variety of uses for paratexts transcending authorship (362–367). Regardless of what consumers *actually* use paratexts for, Marvel nevertheless imagines, addresses, and courts them in ways designed to create and sustain fandoms. In the following sections I will first consider authorship in the context of the above-mentioned writers to stress how the *Spider-Man* movies negotiate a push-and-pull between a sole creative vision and a community of workers; I then shift this analysis to consider how the texts' "authors" discuss genre and adaptation in addressing a consumer community.

My analysis pulls from Michel Foucault's notion of the author and Rick Altman's notion of genre, where both terms have discursive functions beyond means of classification. These paratexts construct genre alongside authorship, showing the latter intimately concerned with the former. For Foucault, "the function of an author is to characterize the existence, circulation, and operation of certain discourses within a society" (452). As Gray observed, the discourse stemming from the author function includes "notions of value, identity, coherence, skill, and unity" (109). The author function is ascertained through paratexts that are constructed through discourse. Similarly, genre builds itself out of discursive structures: "Pronounced *by* someone and addressed *to* someone, statements about genre are always informed by the identity of speaker and audience" (Altman 102). Borrowing from Altman, the dual analysis below asks: Who speaks this generic/authorial vocabulary? To whom? And for what purpose (108)? The goal of this paratextual analysis, then, is to chart how author and genre function as two key discourses for the construction of the intermedial Marvel Universe as a way to promote a unified identity of fan-centered production.

AUTHORSHIP: "HOW'S THAT FOR PRETENTIOUS?"

DVDs construct authorship in two ways: by assigning creative control to one or several individuals (usually the director and the producers), and by revealing the labor of select departments. As Brereton notes, production histories trace "major difficulties in bringing the final concepts to the screen, while also outlining the extensive use of creative labor involved in the process" (7). The first three *Spider-Man* DVDs explore this aim via two commentary tracks for each film. One usually has director Sam Raimi, a member of the cast, and several producers (the "creative" personnel); the other has visual effects supervisors, production designers, and other key department heads (the "technical" personnel). Much as commentaries construct intent, they also spread intent across multiple persons and segments, delegating aspects of creative labor to certain personnel.

Whereas Parker and Parker see intent utilized "self-conscious[ly]" (17) as a discursive method of understanding industrial practice, Grant sees DVD audio commentaries as "*Auteur* Machines." Grant notes that DVD features provide information "*alongside, over,* or even *during* the film," providing "a simultaneous and aural 're-writing' of the film, an optional, *documentary* voice-over, which cannot be accessed autonomously from the film, at least not in isolation from its visual track" (104). Commentaries "rewrite" films by providing guideposts—explaining certain shots or themes—such that the viewer becomes embedded in the perspective of the commentator, relating to him or her as an author of the film, and by extension, of its meaning. For example, Brookey and Westerfelhaus argue that *Fight Club*'s (David Fincher, 1999) DVD uses authorial voices to construct preferred interpretations by dismissing other, resistant interpretations throughout the commentaries. For *Spider-Man*, paratexts construct fan-authors, consciously weaving the look and history of the comics into the films. Sociocultural interpretations are not so much dismissed or "overpowered" (Gray 89) as they are absent, and their absence speaks to the perceived importance of constellating paratexts that address the desires of fan communities.

Director Sam Raimi is often idolized as a true creative author who has particular affinities with Spider-Man. The paratexts across *Spider-Man*, *Spider-Man* 2, and *Spider-Man* 3 position him as an accomplished filmmaker and a Hollywood outsider, primarily through his direction on the three *Evil Dead* films (1981, 1987, 1992). Most importantly, he represents a fan. As he says in "The Making of *Spider-Man*," "I'd been reading Spider-Man ever since

I was a little kid." In the same featurette, producer Avi Arad cites this fact as a reason for hiring Raimi: "I saw there was a goodness in his face. I trust this guy." Raimi is essentially equated with the titular character; he embodies Spider-Man in his biography and his creative ideology. Arad promotes him as a über-fan across other paratexts on the *Spider-Man* DVD. In a second "Making of *Spider-Man*" featurette, he says, "Sam [Raimi] grew up having Spider-Man painted on a wall in his room, which is the best kind of man to take the helm for a movie like that." Skill here is not conceived as Raimi's technical craftsmanship or his ability to marshal the many departments of a large-scale production. Rather, skill itself is defined by the director-author's foundational relationship to the character. In the DVD's "Director Profile," Raimi continues to affirm this characterization: "All I did was explain to the executives what my love for the character was . . . and the next day I got the call." The ultimate reason for hiring Raimi—in this narrative—is his *fandom*. The paratexts take pains to embed the very ethos of *Spider-Man*—with great power comes great responsibility—into the figure of Sam Raimi.

Although the personnel around Raimi bolster him as a creative author throughout the interviews and commentaries, Raimi himself often tapers this characterization. He notes in a *Spider-Man 2* making-of segment, "I want people that are working to be proud of their work on the screen, but mostly I do want the audience to have a good experience with the picture." Raimi "modestly" envisions himself as the head of a vast network rather than a sole creative visionary: "So many artistic contributors, from the actors, to the grips, to the electricians . . . the wardrobe, everybody. So the fact that [*Spider-Man*] did well made me feel great in the sense that all the people who had worked long and hard on the picture must have thought I had led them well." Actor Tobey Maguire, in particular, constantly praises Raimi's managerial skill throughout the *Spider-Man 2* commentary:

> **Maguire:** Movies are a collaborative process, and one of the things I've heard you [Raimi] talk about, you don't possess Spider-Man or the character of Spider-Man; it's all of our movie. We look at you as Captain of our ship, and as Captain you let us come to you with ideas. . . . [W]e all feel like we're filmmakers. . . . [E]veryone working on the movie feels free to tell you our opinion.
> **Raimi:** I definitely do that. . . . [I]t's my way to make the movie great. . . . I need it.

Although he notes the collaborative process, Maguire gives Raimi substantial clout by calling him a "Captain." Maguire also equates himself with a "filmmaker"—an author—while acknowledging Raimi's "higher" authorial status.

The Marvel Universe has traditionally relied on a plurality of authors corralled by one or several discursively marked "true creative authors." In the Silver Age of Marvel Comics, this discourse often coalesced around Stan Lee, who used the editorial pages of the "Marvel Bullpen Bulletin" to launch "Stan's Soapbox" in 1967. There, he injected vernacular musings on fan letters, Marvel's production, civil rights, and other issues. The "Bulletin" itself functions as a kind of ongoing paratext to let fans know which comics issues are available, create a place for fan letters, and give the Marvel "authors" a space to construct their identities. As such, the "Marvel Bullpen Bulletin" collapsed the distance—or at least presented the imagined possibility of a collapse—between producer and consumer, between "author" and fan. In the August 1967 "Bulletin," for instance, Lee thanks "the most wonderful fans" for their support, adding, "If Marvel is on top of the heap, it's your support that's put us there! If Marvel gives you the type of mags you want, it's your letters that have told us how!"

Like the DVD paratexts, "Marvel's Bullpen Bulletin" imagines an actively engaged fan, and "Stan's Soapbox" bolsters the credibility of the authors in the same way as the commentaries and DVD featurettes. The comics labor is largely focused onto Lee in these columns, and he uses the "Soapbox" to present himself as the model for all fan-authors permeating Marvel's intermedial universe. Just as Sam Raimi is in many senses equated with Spider-Man, so, too, does Lee proclaim that he and other unnamed Marvel workers "BELIEVE in our swingin' superheroes!" (Nov. 1967). This is not to say that the "Bulletins" as a whole avoid discussing the other artists, writers, and laborers—a news item in the October 1968 "Bulletin" introduces new writer Arnold Drake as "a lovable leprechaun who combines his own unique dramatic quality with a fabulous flair for biting satire and crafter characterization"—but they are largely separate from the clearly demarcated "Stan's Soapbox."

Less than a year after starting the "Soapbox," Lee declared it "the most widely-read paragraph in all of comicdom" (Jan. 1968). Regardless of the validity of Lee's claim, the "Soapbox" and the "Bulletins" represent how Marvel discursively constructs a paratextual experience of its universe and its brand. In this projection it is led by a small collection of authors with Stan Lee at the forefront. Marvel also caters to fans by, for example, responding to fan letters and offering exclusive news about changes in the comics or in the company's business practices. In one respect the "Soapbox" is markedly different from the DVD paratexts: how it engages cultural and political discourses. Whereas the DVDs erase or do not acknowledge important contexts such as 9/11, Lee does sometimes comment on current events in the "Soapbox." For example, in the April 1972 edition of the "Soapbox," Lee discusses the Attica State Prison riot, taking a typically neutral stance in order to wax philosophically about morality and social responsibility:

> I've no intention of imposing my own opinions upon you about which side, which party or parties might have been right or wrong. Instead, I'd like to discuss the theory of "right or wrong" itself. . . . I wonder what life would be like if we weren't so preoccupied with proving ourselves right and the other guy wrong. I wonder if we might not find the peace, the understanding we all seek by striving to relate to each other, to sympathize with each other's problems, to reach out to those who may differ from ourselves and to realize that they too may be "right" in their own way, from their own point of reference. I wonder—mightn't it be worth a try?

Lee's reference to a controversial current event in order to discursively engage his readers, rather than to articulate his own opinion on an issue, reflects his cautious attempts to keep the "Soapbox" entries topical, without alienating any of his readers. He takes this further when he emphasizes that such "Soapbox" musings are strictly his and do not necessarily reflect those of anyone else at Marvel, commenting in another "Soapbox" that "there ISN'T any unanimous 'Bullpen' opinion about anything, except possibly mother love and apple pie" (Oct. 1968). While "Stan's Soapbox" functions as a way to discursively mark Lee as a primary creative author of the Marvel Universe, he also disperses opinions on sensitive issues to the rest of the unnamed "Bullpen"—though he refuses to speak for them.

Whereas the DVD paratexts of the first three *Spider-Man* franchises constitute an intermedial continuation of Marvel's means of constructing authorship through its comics paratexts, the *Amazing Spider-Man* film reboot utilizes strategies of distinction and difference. The commentary on *The Amazing Spider-Man* features director Marc Webb, producer Mark Tolmach, and producer Avi Arad. In contrast to Raimi in his commentaries,

Webb spends most of his commentary time discussing his own ideas as if to validate himself as the true creative author. Of an early action scene, he says, "This was my homage to that old school [Charlie] Chaplin kind of scene. I hope you don't think I'm having delusions of grandeur. . . but this was at least my model." Webb shows off as a cultured artist with filmic (as opposed to comic) influences who is working hard to differentiate himself from Raimi. At the film's end, he says, "We do tell the same stories over and over again, and it's the inflection and the changes in themes that give it its specificity and power, but really at the end of the day, we're always exploring the same thing: 'Who am I?' How's that for pretentious? You like that?" Webb also comments on the franchise and genre, explaining the logic of creating a new *Spider-Man* franchise just ten years after the first film premiered. These notions of "inflection" and "change" work with his insistence throughout the commentary that he creates a different tone and look for the character.

In *The Amazing Spider-Man* commentary, Avi Arad shoulders most of the responsibility for discussing below-the-line labor. While Arad espouses something of a slack-jawed adoration for Raimi in many *Spider-Man* paratexts, here he tapers Webb's self-affirmed "delusions of grandeur" by describing production intricacies. He notes, for example, "There are more than 3,000 people who worked on this movie." Over the closing credits, he talks at length about labor: "It was a great privilege to be able to make this movie in Los Angeles, providing great employment to so many people in L.A. . . . It's so important for us, for the city, for the state. . . . It brings families; it gives them stability. That's it, that's my soap box." This is one of the few places in any *Spider-Man* paratext that explicitly addresses labor from an economic perspective. This plea for recognizing Hollywood as an industrial workforce is relegated to the credits, perhaps so we can see how many worked on this film via the scrolling of the names, but the credits also exist somewhat "outside" the narrative itself in a space where Webb—the author—largely has the proverbial floor to guide discussion.

More than any other DVD paratext, the full-length documentary "Making the Amazing" on the *Spider-Man 2* bonus disc explores the labor and authorship of the film from a variety of perspectives. The documentary is broken into featurettes examining the labor of different departments by interviewing department heads. Although the documentary gives ample space for personnel to self-theorize on their work, it is also *selective* regarding which personnel get interviews and, by extension, an "authorial" status. For example, no screenwriters speak in audio commentaries or in any behind-the-scenes documentaries. The franchise has attracted high levels of writing talent, including David Koepp, Alvin Sargent, and James Vanderbilt, but the only screenwriter whose voice is ever heard is Sam Raimi—who co-wrote *Spider-Man 3*. In the "Story and Character" segment of "Making the Amazing," Raimi speaks *for* the screenwriters: "We had a lot of great writers . . . a lot of different people brought things to the story, and it was really finding our way through these different ideas to the ones that reverberated."

With screenwriters ostensibly removed from the creative labor process explored on the DVDs, in their stead the focus shifts to the directors and producers who identify with and as fans, such that authorship becomes a kind of fan-adaptation. Importantly, the ostensible erasure of screenwriting contributions is transferred here not necessarily to Sam Raimi or Marc Webb, but to Stan Lee, who makes appearances in many of the paratexts discussing his original authorship of the character (with little mention of Steve Ditko). The authorship of Spider-Man becomes, in part, mythic: it springs forth from Lee's mind, and other writers, directors, and "authors" are responsible for carrying on his vision. From here, the constructs of authorship begin to inform the constructs of genre and adaptation as the prime sites for imagining the address to fan-consumers.

GENRE AND ADAPTATION: "RESPECT THE ICON"

Authorship is perhaps a far easier concept to investigate through para-texts than genre, given the omnipresence of talking-head interviews and audio commentaries, whose very form ascribes an authorial voice. The extensive use of interviews and on-set footage organizes the voices in a way that constructs a clear hierarchy of creative labor. Although authors are discursively established, they are nevertheless also at the service of forces beyond their creative visions, especially in a Marvel Universe striving to develop coherency across media. Marvel's Hollywood productions aim to satisfy expectations of story, tone, and aesthetic from its comics; the semantics and syntax of the genre became a way to mark successful intermedial adaptation. Genre, like authorship, is in part a classificatory mechanism negotiated through intertextuality and paratextuality; in addition, it offers a guidepost for formulating expectations of a given text or set of texts. Adaptation relies on what Robert Stam calls the "ongoing whirl of intertextual references and transformation" (66). These transformations resonate between a text's relationships to others bearing similar features, and so beyond adapting the style of Spider-Man, the films needed to import the ways in which the comics had defined the genre and the character. The *Spider-Man* franchise dialogues with other filmic iterations of its genre as well as the predecessor comic images. Comics in this model are like Ur-texts, scriptures to be followed that will lead faithful fans to new iterations if transformed appropriately.

In superhero films, meeting the perceived expectations of the *genre* is just as important as meeting the perceived expectations of the *adaptation*. The superhero film emerges from a wealth of comics texts generated across decades in addition to television shows, video games, and other forms of media, and all of these prior iterations come into play as fans assess the merits of film adaptations. As producer Ian Bryce suggests in "Making the Amazing," "There's always the need of finding the right blend of maintaining that history [of the comics] and yet making it contemporary enough that the audience is going to accept it being new." Film production is thus a process of constant adaptation that makes sure the hero and the genre are adequately translated. Marc Webb, in his commentary, also separates himself from Raimi and his trilogy on these grounds: "I wanted to stay away from stylizing the universe. I didn't want to feel like we were re-creating panels from the comic books." Raimi et al.'s commentary on *Spider-Man 2*, by contrast, discusses explicit instances of re-creating specific comics panels for the fans' pleasure.

Raimi discusses multiple instances where he attempts to mimic comic book imagery and even specific panels in order to create resonance between the mediums. These re-creations operate as hidden bonuses for the devoted fan who wants the comics mythology to be honored cinematically. At one point, producer Laura Ziskin asserts that Raimi "is the audience," because his fandom gives him an innate idea of what will make "the fans" happy. Although he occasionally embodies the ethos of Spider-Man, in these conversations he also embodies the desired practices and ideals of Marvel fans. On a *Spider-Man 3* commentary, actor Topher Grace vocalizes "a lot of fear, because I love the character . . . and I want to, y'know, please the fan in myself." Even though some members of the creative personnel distance themselves from the comic books—Kirsten Dunst remarks in a *Spider-Man* making-of featurette, "Look at me! You think I was gonna read *Spider-Man* when I was a little girl? No!"—paratexts stress that the personnel assembled on the film share an affinity with the character and the history of the comics. Producer Grant Curtis thus stresses a commitment to fidelity in a *Spider-Man* 2 commentary: "One of the things I did early on . . . was to come up with a pose book for Sam and everyone to reference." Comments like Grace's and Curtis's create a self-knowing sense of interrelating *adaptation* and *genre*—for Raimi's films, the discourse emerges from one of "proper" (read: faithful) adaptation of the comics that *always* considers the fans' reaction.

Genre functions as a chief site through which Caldwell's notion of "industrial reflexivity" manifests. Both above- and (though far less frequently) below-the-line workers self-consciously reflect and promote certain ideologies about their work; in the case of the *Spider-Man* franchises, these moments of opening up the logics of production often have to do with ideas of genre. "Such reflexivity," Caldwell observes, "brings with it a plurality of meanings" (16). As such, focusing on different areas of labor throughout "Making the Amazing" demonstrates "how self-theorizing is being used to make creative and technical decisions on the set and within production organizations" (15). Genre and adaptation are valued both academically and as part of industrial reflexivity. Thus, Caldwell notes two types of knowledge found in paratextual reflexivity: "functional" knowledge, or practical applications of labor and technology; and "self-theorizing" knowledge, rationalizations for choices on a conceptual level (26). The negotiation between these two realms plays out in the "Costume Design" chapter of "Making the Amazing." Assistant costume designer Paul Spadone walks viewers through "commonsensical" costume design, detailing the technical process of creating Spider-Man's suit and discussing "a lot of work with the color with the suit and the print process." He is more interested in sharing the physical creation process and the practical elements of the design than in theorizing. Conversely, costume designer James Acheson says, "over a six-month period we came back to believing we sort of had to respect the icon. The closer and more truthful we were to the image of Spidey . . . then that was the way to go." Acheson talks from a more theoretical perspective, one that considers the importance of adaptation, of preserving the comic iconography of Spider-Man.

This chapter has paid much attention to interviews with key personnel. However, *Spider-Man* and *Spider-Man* 2 also include a "Spidey Sense" feature that allows one to watch the film with both the image and the audio intact (whereas audio is often lowered or muted during commentaries) while seeing small subtitles of information overlaid across the screen. This form of intermediality draws on the tradition of narration boxes in comics. "Spidey Sense" attempts to account for *all* the trends discussed in this chapter. Some subtitles detail how shots were performed, how sets were built, or where scenes were shot. Others provide biographical information for key crew and cast members. One box during *Spider-Man* reveals, for example, "Sam Raimi asked the stunt doubles to look at the comics of 'Spider-Man' and learn all of his classic poses." Here, the subtitled text reveals both Raimi's creative process and the project's investment in faithful adaptation, extending processes of adaptation to the kind of work that the stuntmen—the below-the-line workers—performed. Most importantly, however, this fundamentally intermedial construction of an editorial voice draws on a comics aesthetic and imports it into cinematic paratexts, creating continuity for a fan's transmedial journey through the Marvel Universe.

The "Spidey-Sense" special feature also provides aesthetic links to comics paratexts such as the "Marvel Bullpen Bulletins." "Spidey-Sense" cultivates a knowledge about the films that in many ways shows the intermedial continuum between film and comic; the "Marvel Bullpen Bulletins" cater to the same kind of knowing, active fan through nods to the vastness of the Marvel Universe. For instance, a January 1968 "Bulletin" item reminded readers of the "whole caboodle of Marvel toys, games, and novelties on sale at a store near you right now." Each month, the "Bulletins" included "The Mighty Marvel Checklist" of "Marvel-ous Mags on Sale Right Now," a list of magazines on the shelves along with a brief summary, so that fans would know what they needed to buy each month to stay on top of their favorite stories. The "Bulletins" also provide information about the development and broadcasting of the *Fantastic Four* and *Spider-Man* television programs, again pushing out to other trans- and intermedial constructions of the Marvel Universe.

Paratexts guide an audience's conception of genre by singling out authors who can articulate the terms of a film's relationship to its source material and the rest of its genre. To understand how Marvel articulates its brand to fan-consumers, one must understand both its address to fan-consumers in the paratextual material and its repeated insistence that the "authors" themselves are fans who "respect the icon." Constructions of authorship are performed in similar discursive ways in both the paratextual features of the films and the paratextual "Bullpen Bulletins" of the Marvel Comics Silver Age; the films' paratexts, however, place more importance on issues of genre and adaptation, directly considering the textual pleasures and aesthetics of the comics as foundational to the films' aesthetic. The imagined fan is always at the heart of this discourse—in everything from the mention of specific names of Merry Marvel Marching Society fan club members at the bottom of each month's "Bulletin" to the way film practitioners discuss the need to please fans who have particular expectations. As such, the construction of the Marvel Universe is constantly presented as the construction of the fans' ideal representations.

CONCLUSION: THE CONTINUITIES OF THE INTERMEDIAL MARVEL UNIVERSE

In this chapter I have paid attention to the discursive constructs of authorship, genre, and adaptation in the *Spider-Man* DVD paratexts in order to demonstrate how they in part address an imagined community of devoted comics fans. The *Spider-Man* franchise replicates and extends many of the established patterns from the comics into the film texts and paratexts because the cinematic franchise has a vested interest in preserving the integrity of the Spider-Man icon. In part this goal is accomplished through the construction of an editorial voice, whether that is through Stan Lee or through one of the many other authors who have been associated with the Marvel Universe, including directors such as Sam Raimi and producers such as Avi Arad. The paratextual history of the Marvel Universe—from the editorial pages of the "Bullpen Bulletin" to the multiple DVD audio commentaries—is a history of repetition, multiplication, and continuity, one that takes a strategy and transforms it across media to maintain familiarity and authenticity among discerning fans while at the same time cultivating new fans. The result is the construction of *Spider-Man* as a quality, creatively driven brand.

Imagining fans as active, loyal, and knowledgeable consumers throughout the paratexts serves two functions: first, it allows the DVDs to respectfully address those fans who *do* demand continuity between comics and films. Second, it promotes the adoption of such behavior throughout fandoms. The vast amount of work that goes into maintaining a Marvel brand—a brand that cares immensely about who "authors" its films and how those films will cater to fans—asks, however implicitly, for fans to support the films as sanctioned adaptations. Paratextual studies open up possibilities for probing how different media construct different kinds of value as well as how the paratexts themselves, by strategically employing particular forms and functions, construct a coherent, branded Universe of production.

Although *genre* and *author* are broad terms that speak to a number of different consumer groups for a number of different reasons, the *Spider-Man* franchise's DVD paratexts use these concepts for specific ends: to bolster the connection fans might feel to the creative personnel, to demonstrate the processes of labor on technical and theoretical levels, and to actively link the films to *Spider-Man* comics. Ultimately, the franchise's attempts to build cultural capital become a series of accumulating, intersecting, and contrasting visions seemingly united under similar generic and adaptation-based goals. These goals all direct us back to a discursively coherent Marvel Universe banner (and, perhaps secondarily, to Stan Lee as the assumed author of *Spider-Man*). The resulting discursive coherence presents Marvel as a studio devoted to satisfying its fan-consumers.

Finally, if paratextual material is key for the intermedial constitution of the Marvel Universe, it also helps to "make" the transmedial story and experience of the Marvel Universe. Certainly, this is not transmedia storytelling in Jenkins's sense of the term, where paratexts across media must be consumed in order for a reader/viewer to grasp the entirety of the story (93–130). Rather, it points to how similar modes of engagement are deployed across media to give fan-consumers the textual production's "whole story" in remarkably similar terms. Gray suggests that paratexts fill in gaps between texts and audiences, but we can also see paratexts as filling in gaps between media forms and repeating modes of address across decades of production. They discursively construct and, ultimately, unite the key values and voices for the characters, franchises, and texts that populate Marvel's vast media landscape.

....

NOTES

I would like to thank John T. Caldwell and Matthias Stork for their immensely helpful comments on earlier versions of this chapter.

1. The domestic grosses for the five films, respectively, are $403,706,375; $373,585,625; $336,530,303; $262,030663; and $202,644,001. All figures are from the Internet Movie Database, www.imdb.com.

WORKS CITED

Acland, Charles R. *Screen Traffic: Movies, Multiplexes, and Global Culture.* Durham, NC: Duke University Press, 2003. Print.

Altman, Rick. *Film/Genre.* London: BFI, 2000. Print.

The Amazing Spider-Man. Dir. Marc Webb. Perf. Andrew Garfield, Emma Stone, and Rhys Ifans. Sony/Columbia Pictures, 2012. DVD.

The Amazing Spider-Man 2. Dir. Marc Webb. Perf. Andrew Garfield, Emma Stone, and Jamie Foxx. Sony/Columbia Pictures, 2014. Blu-ray.

Brereton, Pat. *Smart Cinema, DVD Add-ons, and New Audience Pleasures.* Houndsmills, UK: Palgrave Macmillan, 2012. Print.

Brookey, Robert Alan, and Robert Westerfelhaus. "Hiding Homoeroticism in Plain View: The *Fight Club* DVD as Digital Closet." *Critical Studies in Media Communication* 19:1 (2002): 21–43. Print.

Caldwell, John Thornton. *Production Cultures: Industrial Reflexivity and Critical Practice in Film and Television.* Durham, NC: Duke University Press, 2008. Print.

Foucault, Michel. "What Is an Author?" In *Rethinking Popular Culture: Contemporary Perspective in Cultural Studies.* Eds. Chandra Mukerji and Michael Schudson. Berkeley: University of California Press, 1991. 446–464. Print.

Fowkes, Katherine A. *The Fantasy Film.* Malden, MA: Blackwell, 2010. Print.

Fritz, Ben. "Internet to Surpass DVD in Movie Consumption, Not Revenue." *Los Angeles Times*, 23 March 2012. Web. http://latimesblogs.latimes.com /entertainmentnewsbuzz/2012/03/internet-to-surpass-dvd-in-movie -consumption-not-revenue.html.

Genette, Gerard. *Paratexts: Thresholds of Interpretation.* Trans. Jane E. Lewin. New York: Cambridge University Press, 1987. Print.

Gotto, Lisa. "Fantastic Views: Superheroes, Visual Perception and Digital Perspective." In *Superhero Synergies: Comic Book Characters Go Digital.* Eds. James N. Gilmore and Matthias Stork. Lanham, MD: Rowman and Littlefield, 2014. 41–56. Print.

Grant, Catherine. "Auteur Machines? Auteurism and the DVD." In *Film and Television After DVD.* Eds. James Bennett and Tom Brown. New York: Routledge, 2008. 101–115. Print.

Gray, Jonathan. *Show Sold Separately: Promos, Spoilers, and Other Media Paratexts.* New York: New York University Press, 2010. Print.

Hayes, Dade. "Six Reasons Why DVDs Still Make Money—And Won't Die Anytime Soon." *Forbes*, 8 July 2013. Web. www.forbes.com/sites/dadehayes /2013/07/08/six-reasons-why-dvds-still-make-money-and-wont-die -anytime-soon.

Jenkins, Henry. *Convergence Culture: Where Old and New Media Collide.* New York: New York University Press, 2006. Print.

Johnson, Derek. "Cinematic Destiny: Marvel Studios and the Trade Stories of Industrial Convergence." *Cinema Journal* 52:1 (2012): 1–26. Print.

———. *Media Franchising: Creative License and Collaboration in the Culture Industries.* New York: New York University Press, 2013. Print.

Kaplan, Richard L. "Spider-Man in Love: A Psychoanalytic Interpretation." *Journal of Popular Culture* 44:2 (2011): 291–313. Print.

Klinger, Barbara. *Beyond the Multiplex: Cinema, New Technologies, and the Home.* Berkeley: University of California Press, 2006. Print.

Koh, Wilson. "Everything Old Is Good Again: Myth and Nostalgia in *Spider-Man.*" *Continuum: Journal of Media & Cultural Studies* 23:5 (2009): 735–747. Print.

"Marvel Bullpen Bulletin." August 1967. Web. http://web.archive.org/web /20100507075602/http://costa.lunarpages.com/bp/bp6708.html.

———. November 1967. Web. http://web.archive.org/web/20100507073815 /http://costa.lunarpages.com/bp/bp6711.html.

———. January 1968. Web. http://web.archive.org/web/20100506015815/http:// costa.lunarpages.com/bp/bp6801.html.

———. October 1968. Web. http://web.archive.org/web/20100506015845/http:// costa.lunarpages.com/bp/bp6810.html.

Parker, Deborah, and Mark Parker. "Directors and DVD Commentary: The Specifics of Intention." *Journal of Aesthetics and Art Criticism* 62:1 (2004): 13–22. Print.

Spider-Man. Dir. Sam Raimi. Perf. Tobey Maguire, Kirsten Dunst, and Willem Dafoe. Columbia Pictures, 2002. DVD.

Spider-Man 2. Dir. Sam Raimi. Perf. Tobey Maguire, Kirsten Dunst, and Alfred Molina. Columbia Pictures, 2004. DVD.

Spider-Man 3. Dir. Sam Raimi. Perf. Tobey Maguire, Kirsten Dunst, and James Franco. Columbia Pictures, 2007. DVD.

Stam, Robert. "The Dialogics of Adaptation." In *Film Adaptation.* Ed. James Naremore. New Brunswick, NJ: Rutgers University Press, 2000. 54–76. Print.

Stork, Matthias. "Assembling the Avengers: Reframing the Superhero Movie Through Marvel's *Cinematic Universe.*" In *Superhero Synergies: Comic Book Characters Go Digital.* Eds. James N. Gilmore and Matthias Stork. Lanham, MD: Rowman and Littlefield, 2014. Print.

Playing Peter Parker

SPIDER-MAN AND SUPERHERO FILM PERFORMANCE

AARON TAYLOR

P eter Parker is not just the defender of your friendly neighborhood, he's the nerd whose labor supports an age of marvels. And why shouldn't the exploits of this nebbish teen from Queens inspire delight, play, creativity, and even lunchboxes? Like Billy Batson and Steve Rogers before him, he is the ninety-eight pounder's revenge, the secret hope of every locker-stuffed milquetoast, the ugly duckling's swan song. He heralds a Silver Age because he embodies a simple narrative truth: power fantasies are not universally palatable visions of infantile wish fulfillment; rather, they are illusions that render the helplessness of one's everyday circumstances more salient. Simply put: superpowers wouldn't make things better; they'd only limn the ordinary pain we struggle to overcome. Stan Lee and Steve Ditko's profound revision of a basic superheroic trope is arguably the conceptual cornerstone upon which Marvel was built, and it is certainly no accident that the child of their insight—Spider-Man—is the company's most public face.

Marvel Entertainment (ME) became a limited liability company in 1998. Since then, the company has primarily been in the business of generating and exploiting creative intellectual property (IP) (Johnson 64–67). Specifically, this IP takes the form of superheroic characters—*range brands* that originate within the comics produced by their publishing subsidiary, Marvel Worldwide (MW), but can extend as an elastic range of *sub-brands* across media (Aaker 68–69). These sub-brands include the various MW publications, cinematic and televisual adaptations (whether licensed by other studios or produced in-house by Marvel Studios [MS] or Marvel Television [MTV]), cartoons (licensed or in-house productions by Marvel Animation

[MA]), and electronic games. The relationship between these range brands and sub-brands can also be parsed in narratological terms: the former serve as *hypotextual* commodities with considerable adaptogenic fertility—that is, they spawn any number of transformed *hypertextual* narrative instantiations (Genette 5). With a production history that dates back to 1962, Spider-Man is arguably Marvel's most fertile flagship brand (or hypotext). At the time of this writing, the range brand has spawned eight cartoons, a newspaper strip, two television series, numerous paperback novels and children's books, over thirty video-game iterations, a BBC radio series, four stage productions, and eight feature-length films (two of which are unauthorized by Marvel).

Like other iconic range brands in the Marvel Universe, Spider-Man's pop cultural saturation makes him an ideal case study to help us understand ME's contemporary approach to intellectual property. Specifically, we are interested in *performance*—the relationship between the dramatic performance of an actor in a filmic sub-brand of a Marvel property and the ensuing economic and cultural performance of the broader range brand itself. Increasingly, screen performers are playing a key role within the complexly intertwined factors that enable Marvel to function as a twenty-first-century transmedia conglomerate. Their situation within Marvel's corporate aesthetics and business practices warrants substantial consideration. Therefore, I will show how an actor's embodiment of an iconic superheroic property makes manifest the interplay of broader economic, technological, and discursive forces.

As high-profile commercial enterprises, superhero film franchises are predicated upon their anticipated fulfillment of several industrial objectives. First and foremost is their central role as economic linchpins in the output of many twenty-first-century studios, to say nothing of the synergistically integrated ancillary enterprises undertaken by the studio's parent company. Within a creative production culture, the superhero film has also become a privileged vehicle for the cultivation of new technological conventions, particularly the showcasing of bleeding-edge digital craftsmanship. Finally, at the level of reception, the superhero film is a transmedia object par excellence insofar as it is required to serve as the hub of networked fannish activity. Discursively speaking, to produce a superhero film is to deliberately engage in cage rattling: it is an enterprise predicated upon proffering an as-yet-unsanctified object for cultic scrutiny and potential canonization by a community of exacting subcultural gatekeepers.

The three industrial objectives outlined above create distinct challenges for the twenty-first-century actor appearing in a Marvel film, particularly those privileged laborers and spectacular bodies known as stars. I will provide a description of the complex system in which the various actors who have played the arachnoid hero operate. In being tasked with the responsibility of physically embodying an iconic transmedia property, these actors are confronted with obligations and expectations that are atypical of performative instantiation. My aim is to demonstrate how a superheroic performance might be circumscribed by a particularized interweaving of economic, technological, and discursive preconditions. Furthermore, this circumscription—a veritable web of industrial complexities—will be shown as a set of parameters unique to the production of transmedia superhero franchises.

A caveat is necessary here. In this chapter I will restrict the discussion to the analysis of performances by Tobey Maguire and Andrew Garfield in Columbia's five feature-length Spider-Man films: Sam Raimi's *Spider-Man* trilogy (2002–2007) and Marc Webb's subsequent reboot, *The Amazing Spider-Man* (2012), and its sequel (2014). Of course, there have been other Spider-Men: Danny Seagren in *The Electric Company*'s recurring "Spidey Super Stories" skit (1974–1977); Nicholas Hammond in CBS's live-action *Amazing Spider-Man* TV series (1978–1979); Yamashiro Takuya in Toei's *tokusatsu* series (1978–1979); and Reeve Carney in the Broadway show *Spider-Man: Turn Off the Dark* (2011–2014). Numerous actors have also lent their talents to voicing the character in his numerous cartoon and video-game incarnations. However, the specificities of these other media, as well as the socio-historical particularities of their production contexts, have their own requirements for performers that are beyond the scope of the chapter. Moreover, the economic and cultural prominence of these films—Raimi's *Spider-Man* was the first movie "to cross the $100 million mark in its first three days"—means that the cinematic adaptations reciprocally affect the overall Spider-Man range brand to a much greater extent than these other sub-brands do (Robson 50). Finally, in the period between the writing of this chapter and its publication, a third film actor will have assumed the wall-crawler's mantle: Tom Holland. However, this volume will go to press before the release of Holland's heroic debut in *Captain America: Civil War* (2016), which obviously means his work will not be considered here. For these reasons, the discussion is limited to the dramatic work of Maguire and Garfield, who are arguably the most historically visible of web-heads.

SPIDEY AS CELEBRITY: STAR SUPERHEROES

Does a famous property necessitate representation by an equally famous actor? For some industry analysts, the question is debatable. The diminishing box-office returns of aging male stars since 2010 (typically Tom Cruise, Brad Pitt, and Will Smith) and their lack of economically consistent heirs are often offered as proof positive of a new "New Hollywood" in which content is king (Aftab). Film journalists increasingly posit that blockbuster properties can no longer be presold on the basis of their star performers (Bart). Following the publication of its "100 Most Valuable Stars of 2013" survey, for example, *Vulture* reported that most of the actors appearing in high-grossing superhero films accrued the survey's lowest public awareness scores (Buchanan). As one jeremiad for movie stars opines flatly, "currently, the over-saturation of the market by . . . franchises has relegated actors as a complement in a movie rather than its star. . . . The continuations of these types of films show that an actor's name no longer makes the franchise; instead, the franchise makes the actor" (Insignares).

Given the prevalence of these kinds of claims, and the frequency with which up-and-coming (rather than top) stars are cast in superhero franchises, are we to minimize Maguire and Garfield (both rising stars when cast in the first Spider-Man films) as mere cogs in a machine? This view would be shortsighted. Instead, it is necessary to consider how their situation as stars might be sublimated within the commercial logic of ME's transmedia productions. The position and meaningfulness of celebrity actors within Marvel's feature films are of a different nature than similar attributes in (relatively) unknown performers. Specifically, the integration of the star actor's body and the body of the character s/he portrays needs theorization, as it presents a unique challenge for the performer. Concomitantly, a pressing concern for media producers at ME is how to contend with the specificity of a star's body in the production of ancillary products—including MW's own ongoing titles and subsequent comic spinoffs.

It is useful to place our considerations here within ongoing theoretical distinctions between star vs. "ordinary" acting. The actor has (at least) two bodies with which to contend during a performance: her/his own actual corporeality and the fictional physicality of the character s/he portrays. An anonymous actor might readily achieve an "integrated performance," as her/his publicly unknown figure helps to minimize the distance between actor (actual body) and role (possible person) (Maltby 399). By contrast, the dramatic problem for the star actor is the substantial visibility of her/his individualized and publicly familiar body. It never quite becomes integrated within the fictional reality of the film, but instead remains diegetically "semi-autonomous" (Maltby 389). The star's body is "hypersemioticised": it bears an accrual of associative significations amassed from its mediated appearances over the course of the star's career (King 142). These signs have always already come into semiotic play as the star begins to represent a character. In this way, the star's body becomes "ostensive": presentational and visible within a dramatic performance frame in which (character) representation and (technical) invisibility have aesthetic primacy (Naremore 80). We are always required to look both at and through a star.

With superhero adaptations, highly visible celebrity actors are further required to integrate their bodies within equally recognizable corporate matrices. The superhero is a locus of multiple discourses—creative/authorial, economic/legal, receptive/cultic—that collectively define the character as an iconic body. "Spider-Man" is not just a second physicality with which an actor must align his specific body; he is a pluralistic figuration within a public's collective or intersubjective memory. As such, he represents a unique challenge to the celebrity actor whose own ostensive image competes with the notoriety of the superhero's iconic image. This discursively resonant image is the third body with which an actor must productively contend.

In order to better appreciate this iconic, third body, we might compare it to Jean-Louis Comolli's description of a star's appearance in a biopic as "a body too much." For Comolli, the dramatic problem for historical fiction is that the material referentiality of a historical body (i.e., the famous individual in question) is at odds with the "empty mask" of the actor's body (50). As such, these odds produce discomfort in spectators who are familiar with the actual appearance of the historical personage. They never become fully committed to the film's simulation of historical reality, and wish for the actor's diegetically semi-autonomous body to "disappear" (ibid.). Therefore, the body-too-much of the historical character produces a "double inscription": a ghosting effect whereby historically knowledgeable viewers become hyperaware of the absent individual's spectral superimposition upon the actor (ibid.). The actor's body, in turn, is regarded as a denegation—a refusal to adequately comply ontologically with the world perceived.

So, analogously, the iconic cinematic superhero is also a body-too-much. However, the double inscription it may produce is much more complex than that of the biopic performer. For it is not the material specificity of an actual historical body that is the problem; instead, it is the iconicity and intense plurality of the adaptogenic superhero's body. Meryl Streep, for example, might labor to affect precisely the fluty cadences of Margaret Thatcher's voice, and makeup artists might prosthetically alter her features to affect a closer approximation to the former prime minister. But Streep's "disappearance" in *The Iron Lady* (2011) is comparably easier to achieve than the analogous integrations of Maguire or Garfield. Streep has but one referent with which to contend mimetically: the physical referent of Thatcher. Maguire's and Garfield's respective vanishing acts are trumped by the fluid and composite nature of Spider-Man's own body-too-much. And thus, these stars find that their attempts at dramatic integration must satisfy a bewildering array of creative, receptive, and legal authorities.

With great talent comes great responsibility, certainly. But responsibility to whom? Just whose Spider-Man is an actor to instantiate? The one that best embodies an acclaimed writer-artist team's vision? The one that is authenticated by fan consensus for its perceived adherence to the character's "essence"? Or the one approved by executives for its downstream market profitability? Any actor appearing within an adaptation faces the various challenges presented by expectations of fidelity. But Maguire's body must cohere with an arguably less specific emblematic referent when he plays Nick Carraway in *The Great Gatsby* (Baz Lurmann, 2013) than when he plays Spider-Man, and Garfield is also afforded a proportionately greater distance from his clone, Tommy, in *Never Let Me Go* (Mark Romanek, 2010). Actors are typically granted considerable latitude to make noteworthy authorial contributions to a film. But the performance choices of the superheroic actor are always circumscribed by authorities with whom actors in other types of films need not contend.

Let us consider, for example, the collaborative model of serialized comic production, with its multiple author-figures contributing to a single range brand. Dozens of writer-artist teams have developed the range brand since Ditko's departure from *The Amazing Spider-Man* (TASM) in 1966 and the end of Lee's tenure in 1973. Other fan-favorite pairings with influential runs on Spider-Man titles include Lee and John Romita Sr., Roger Stern and John Romita Jr., J. M. DeMatteis and Sal Buscema, David Micheline and Todd McFarlane, and Brian Michael Bendis and Mark Bagley. In what sense, then, might an actor incorporate the intentions of these different creators through his gestural references, or by virtue of his own integrated persona?

A profitable suggestion is to consider the graphical resemblance between performance and comic text. The competing ontologies of drawing and photography in a comic book adaptation allow us to note the overlaps and discrepancies between actor and illustration. If "every drawing is by its style a visual interpretation of the world, in that it foregrounds the presence of an enunciator," then Maguire and Garfield enact their own performative enunciations (Lefèvre 8). These two actors vie for their own place within Spider-Man's ever-expanding portrait gallery, just as Paul Giamatti—in a different medium—is yet another graphic instantiation of Harvey Pekar in *American Splendor* (Shari Springer Berman and Robert Pulcini, 2003). And for fans, the cultic appeal of the actors' enunciations lies in the feedback loops they generate with regard to earlier comic hypotexts.

The casting of Maguire and Garfield follows the comics' graphic remodeling of Peter Parker from nerd to heartthrob. Ditko envisioned Peter as a rail-thin, gangly teen with owlish glasses and bad posture. Other more recent artists, such as Neil Edwards, Tony Harris, and Ramón Perez, echo this canonical treatment in their respective revisitations of the character's origins in *Spider-Man: Season One* (2012), *Spider-Man: With Great Power* (2008), and *TASM* vol. 3, no. 1.1 (2014), respectively. By contrast, Ditko's successor, Romita Sr., reengineered Peter as a more conventionally handsome and husky young man beginning in *TASM* no. 39 (1966). Romita Sr.'s interpretation of the character would become the dominant one within the comics for over two decades, and his Peter is probably the Peter with whom a general audience is most familiar. Some later hybrids of Ditko's and Romita Sr.'s respective approaches are also evident. For example, the co-creator of the alternate-continuity title *Ultimate Spider-Man* (USM), Mark Bagley, envisioned a smoldering Peter in the 118 issues he drew for the series (2000–2007), but he retained Ditko's emphasis on the character's diminutive physique and boyish features.

Tobey Maguire's Parker, then, can be said to evoke Ditko's early, more esoteric representation (fig. 10.1). Maguire is among the more neotenic of young stars, which makes him a logical heir to Ditko's milk-fed Parker. He also retains the spectacles and defeated physiognomy. "You're taller than you look," Mary Jane [Kirsten Dunst] tells him in *Spider-Man*, chiding his penchant to slouch. His overnight transformation to buffed-out hunkiness is treated with a comic wink ("Whoa," he gawps at the newly muscled reflection in his bedroom mirror). One can easily imagine Ditko's Parker yawping with Maguire's endearingly pubescent squeak. Arguably, his most interesting quality as a performer is his tendency to make idiosyncratic

10.1. Tobey Maguire vs. Steve Ditko's Peter Parker.

10.2. Emo Peter Parker: Maguire as meme fodder.

facial expressions at moments of extreme emotional or physical duress. Abruptly, his baby-faced features might contort into a strangely sharpened or flattened nose, a doubled chin, a saucer-eyed goggle, a weirdly cavernous philtrum. These expressive extremities receive their fullest workout during his expressivist turn as a Spidey-gone-bad in *Spider-Man 3* (the so-called "Emo Peter Parker" sequences), and several of Maguire's gonzo faces have become fodder for popular memes (fig. 10.2). Suffice it to say, Maguire's surprisingly pliable face is well-suited to Ditko's signature tendency toward caricature and exaggeration.

By contrast, the casting of Andrew Garfield for Webb's films evokes Romita Sr.'s take on Peter Parker, and even more specifically, Bagley's version for *USM*. Webb himself testified that his films are "less based in Steve Ditko's world and probably closer visually . . . [to] *Ultimate Spider-Man*" (Boucher, "'Spider-Man' Director"). Garfield is slighter than Maguire, and his physique—with his lanky build and gangling neck—has some similarities to Bagley's pipsqueak Parker. His carelessly tousled hair also leans toward Bagley's interpretation and away from Romita's widow-peaked Peter. Blessed with strikingly expressive eyebrows, however, Garfield recalls Romita's revision of Peter as a matinee idol (fig. 10.3). Romita had Peter shed his specs for good, and in *The Amazing Spider-Man*, Garfield also typically goes without glasses, preferring contact lenses instead. Above all, Garfield comports himself with a palpable aloofness, as if channeling Robert Pattinson's ageless sense of superiority in *Twilight*'s (Catherine Hardwicke, 2008) high school scenes. Whereas Maguire was a Ditkoesque victim and pariah, Garfield drifts through Midtown High as if carried on the breeze of

10.3. Andrew Garfield and Emma Stone vs. John Romita Sr.'s and Ron Frenz's Peter and Gwen.

10.4. Andrew Garfield vs. Stefano Caselli's Peter Parker.

a secreted self-regard: less charismatic nerds are left to Flash Thompson's tender mercies in his stead. In *TASM*, this "Superior Spider-Man" intercedes on behalf of more hapless geeks, hefts his skateboard through the halls like a Roman standard-bearer, grinningly eavesdrops on a pair of dorks debating the physics of his web-slinging, and, in *TASM 2*, even high-fives his principal on graduation day. Garfield enacts these moments with nary a suggestion of the character's trepidation in early issues of *TASM*.

It should not be assumed, however, that Maguire's and Garfield's enunciations are authenticated simply because they are backward-compatible with MW's comic hypertexts. Otherwise, the comics take on a privileged and falsely generative hypotextual status. Garfield, for example, has declared that he fervently respected the comics that "saved [his] life" as a child, but he was equally inspired by his predecessor, Maguire, and "practiced [his] last line in the mirror" as an adolescent (Kit; David). Again, because Garfield's referent is a palimpsest, Maguire's model is as credible as the Spider-Man produced by Romita Sr. or Bagley. Just as noteworthy is the way in which Garfield's Parker serves as its own privileged feedback loop within MW's Spider-Man titles. Parker's graphical appearance can be said to increasingly resemble Garfield, particularly in the tousle-haired takes on the character by Stefano Caselli for *TASM* (fig. 10.4) and by Marco Checchetto for *Superior Spider-Man Team-Up*.

Given that the filmic sub-brands are now the more publicly visible manifestations of ME's range brands, such semblance has an undeniable corporate logic. Bryan Hitch's revision of the timeworn character of Nick Fury in *Ultimates* no. 1 (2002) to adhere to Samuel L. Jackson's physical and racial identity is a well-known example—a reimagining that later prompted MS to offer the star a multi-picture deal. Derek Johnson has also noted ME's efforts to ensure that MW's version of Wolverine would have a closer physical resemblance to the character's onscreen instantiation by Hugh Jackman. And, as Johnson correctly pointed out, these instances of graphic coherence are all prompted by ME's interest in aligning the various offerings in its most lucrative range brands (77–84).

So, while a superheroic star actor's work might gain authorial credence by graphically referencing the work of star creators, the actors' labor is also subject to executive authority. From a fiscal perspective, it must be understood that media producers are tasked with aligning a star's individually owned and managed persona (a commodified and monopolized personal brand) with the sub-brand that the star is cast to instantiate on screen. For example, Raimi allegedly petitioned Columbia to cast Maguire as the studio's first Peter Parker because of Maguire's emerging star image as a likeable but sensitive adolescent. The actor's associations with young men who must struggle with prematurely adult responsibilities thus squared with publicly recognized and corporately sanctioned conceptions of the character he was chosen to represent. In turn, and from a labor perspective, a star negotiates a fiduciary relationship with a studio that reinforces the monetary and cultural currency of her/his personal brand. Maguire, for example, was offered $4 million, $17.5 million, backend deals, and $50 million for his *Spider-Man* roles (Outlaw). He subsequently attained starring roles in such high-profile middlebrow fare as *Seabiscuit* (Gary Ross, 2003), *Brothers* (Jim Sheridan, 2009), and *The Great Gatsby*. His position as a Hollywood power-broker was also enhanced, as he has accrued twelve producer credits since 2002.

In light of stars' declining fortunes in a Hollywood preoccupied by franchises, however, many have argued that they are no longer an inherent strategic asset to a film's profitability. MS has played a significant role in redefining executive-labor relations in this new corporate climate. Several stars contracted to MS have signed on for an unprecedented nine productions (e.g., Chris Evans, Samuel L. Jackson, and Sebastian Stan). While these multi-picture contracts are a far cry from the seven-year exclusive contracts of the studio era, their value to contemporary stars is hardly straightforward. The contracts' rewards are often indirectly careerist rather than fiscal, and MS uses the perceived boost to a star's exposure as leverage during contract negotiations. Chris Hemsworth, for example, was offered a low upfront fee of $150,000 to appear in *Thor* (2011), and the studio typically attempts to withhold backend compensation or breakeven points (Fernandez and Kit; Graser). MS also allegedly offered contracted stars a mere $500,000 raise to appear in Marvel's "Phase Two" features, with only another $500,000 proposed as a bonus if the films cleared $500 million at the box office (Finke). Only after Robert Downey Jr. renegotiated his fee for *The Avengers*—at least $50 million—were other contracted stars able to secure fees closer to their preferred asking price from the tightfisted studio (Eisenberg).

However, the extensive publicity demands, intensive physical workout regimes, salary disparities, hardball negotiations, and multiyear agreements have prompted grumblings from many contracted MS stars. Scarlet Johansson, for example, has described her employment by Marvel as "a gilded cage" (Barker-Whitelaw). Her co-star, Chris Evans, has announced plans to retire from acting altogether following the fulfillment of his contract. The parsimonious executive-labor relations at MS are certainly not the only example of studio frugality in the production of ME's film brands. Sony contracted Garfield for $500,000, with an escalating raise of $1 million per sequel—a stark about-face from the studio's star-struck attitudes of the early 2000s (Outlaw). With the 2015 casting of Tom Holland, another young actor (with only three previous features to his credit) has been entrusted to lead Sony's latest reboot of a filmic sub-brand—this time co-produced with MS as part of Marvel's own branded "Cinematic Universe." But such a decision is in keeping with the latter's parsimonious reputation as a studio with "constricting" contractual terms for aspirant stars with their sights on Hollywood's A-list (Masters). So, the studio's penchant for casting lesser-known actors is a key strategy that serves "the management of paratextual star narratives and trajectories, . . . the verisimilitude of the onscreen fantasy, and . . . the studio's present and future bargaining leverage" (Koh 488).

These examples demonstrate that the value of star labor and its affiliation with the corporate properties it helps to create are being redefined. MS has played a pivotal role in the declining proportional weighting of a star's symbolic value, which has arguably diminished in relation to the value of the product itself. The actor—the bearer of that value—now finds her/

himself in a contingent (rather than authorial) relation to the work. Her/his professional fortunes and cultural capital are now driven by product—rather than dramatic—performance. In short, the star no longer transcends the role; the role, or rather the product, subsumes the performer.

CREATING SHOW: SUPERHEROIC PERFORMANCE AS SPECTACLE

In speaking of stars' ostensive bodies and the body-too-much of the iconic superhero, we should remember that a star is never completely diegetically integrated. S/he never quite disappears; nor, it should be argued, should we be desirous of this vanishing. Maguire and Garfield are physical attractions in Columbia's *Spider-Man* adaptations, and not just as exemplars of male beauty. Like any superhero blockbuster, these adaptations serve as conventional occasions for the demonstration of the latest innovations in special-effects-driven spectacle. As a consequence, Maguire and Garfield must subject their actorly craft to the technological craft of digitally enabled filmmaking. However, this subjection does not represent the diminishment of contemporary acting; the crafting of so-called synthespians does not "replace" the performance craft developed in old media forms. Rather, new conceptual vocabulary is necessary to evaluate the achievements of digitally enabled performances.

As Paul McDonald reminds us, the star's body is itself used to "create show" as a site of spectacle—it is a humanized special effect, so to speak (62). The ostensiveness of stars' bodies has ensured that the diegetic absorption of so-called classical cinema has never been as totalizing as some have assumed. Rather, the delight of Hollywood cinema lies in acknowledging the achievements of a familiar personage who creatively instantiates an unfamiliar possible person. And thus our sympathetic allegiance with a character is always imbricated by our appreciation for the manner in which the character is enacted by a performer. The pleasures involved in looking both through and at Maguire or Garfield as he enacts his respective Spider-Man, then, can be connected to Marvel's considerable contribution to emerging forms of performance-based spectacle.

The unprecedented box-office opening of *Spider-Man*—with its extended sequences of a completely computer-rendered web-head—ensured that future onscreen heroes would be at least partial products of computer-generated imagery (CGI). Since 2002, then, the onscreen superhero body has been hybridized, becoming a synthesis of a star's corporeality, the physical work of stunt actors and stand-ins, digital animation, and/or motion-captured action. Consequently, our apprehension of and appreciation for performance in the Spider-Man films is not limited to attending to the dramatic, representational work of Maguire and Garfield as they instantiate Peter Parker; we note the particularities of CGI characterization in the first trilogy, adjust phenomenologically to TASM's first-person 3D sequences, admire the integration of Garfield's movement into TASM 2's animation, and marvel at the dangerous gymnastics of stunt work throughout the series.

These various responses show that the spectacle of the star superhero's body is always doubled: it is both performatively and technologically ostensive. Consequently, we oscillate between sympathetic engagement with a costumed Peter careening delightedly through the canyons of Manhattan (for example, in the extraordinary long take at the end of Spider-Man) and knowing admiration of the laborious craft that produces Maguire's digital double in the same takes. In Dan North's words, our appreciation for Peter's dramatic struggles "is complemented by the image of computer technologies facing similar challenges in their task of representing near-impossible heroic deeds in a perceptually realistic manner" (168). Moreover, we recognize the "creative partnership that exists between animator, director and performer" as they collectively labor to produce this mediated action (Pallant 48). Our attention is dispersed: we thrill at the represented action but recognize that it is crafted by multiple authorial sources above and beyond the actor.

Our oscillating engagement between absorption and evaluation means that we might not "identify" with Peter in a traditional sense. Rather, this digitally enabled performance "puts us less in the position of Spider-Man/Peter and more in the position of a dance partner, in a kind of superhero pas de deux" (Richmond 130). Such a partnership necessitates a recasting of more familiar ways of evaluating actorly achievement. We can advance a few criteria here for the appreciation of the spectacular superheroic performance: the circumvention of *expressive restriction*; the achievement of *gravity*; and the adjustment to *digital mediation*.

Like his equally faceless or disfigured contemporaries Iron Man, the Thing, and Ghost Rider, a cinematic Spider-Man suffers from a featureless anonymity due to a mask that completely obscures his face. Various comic artists (e.g., Erik Larsen) and animators (e.g., the USM cartoonists) occasionally compensate for this restriction by allowing the mask's iconic eye lenses to change shape—narrowing or widening—when the costumed hero is angry or shocked. But when Maguire and Garfield are featured in full costume, they are deprived of the ability to facially convey characterization and emotion, and encased in a costume that arguably appears more comical than imposing onscreen. Like all similarly outfitted actors, then, they adopt compensatory performance choices that offset these expressive restrictions. These techniques not only advance character but also serve as pleasurable signs of the actor's artistic ingenuity.

The most literal of strategies is simply to remove the mask. Without the encumbrance of an all-concealing disguise, the iconicity of the range brand gives way to the iconicity of the star. Or, we might also say that the iconicity of both figures is momentarily fused. As a clichéd bit of publicity might trumpet: "Tobey Maguire IS Spider-Man!" Both Raimi's and Webb's series feature a Peter who goes unmasked in public, or reveals his alter ego to various supporting characters. However, these unmaskings are often utilized at climactic moments that call for maximal expressive impact: the revelation of his identity to Mary Jane in *Spider-Man* 2, the confrontation with Captain Stacy in *TASM*, the death of Gwen Stacy in *TASM* 2. But beyond the practical necessity of allowing Maguire and Garfield to achieve their very moving reactions to such dramatic action, unmaskings in the films also reinforce Peter's youthful ordinariness—the very quality that makes the character such a remarkable addition to the superhero canon.

Spider-Man 2 and *TASM*, for example, implicitly meditate on the superhero's public revelation of ordinariness. "He's just a kid. No older than my son," exclaims one gobsmacked bystander at Maguire's exposed face as he lies unconscious in a subway car. Upon awakening, he meets the passengers' stares and anxiously touches his revealed face. "We won't tell nobody," one boy promises as he returns Peter's mask. This gesture of reciprocity both restores Peter's superheroic secrecy and marks his communal belongingness: he's a friendly, neighborhood New Yorker—just like anyone else on the train. In *TASM*, Garfield removes his mask in order to console a terrified boy he is rescuing from a car dangling precariously from the Williamsburg Bridge. "I'm just a normal guy, all right?" he assures him. Passing the mask to the boy, Peter urges him to put it on, so that it will give the boy the courage to climb from the burning vehicle. "It'll make you strong," Peter promises. Alone in his bedroom afterward, Peter gazes somberly down at his mask, as if committing himself to the truth of this promise, and again we are witness to the assurance of valor's commonplace attainability. The final narrated caption of *TASM* no. 9 famously proclaims Spider-Man as "the superhero who could be—YOU!" Both of these unmasking scenes, then, preserve Stan Lee's accomplished insight.

While Maguire's and Garfield's revealed expressions are effective here, the two are also both accomplished at imbuing the faceless hero with a considerable degree of physical humor. Witness Maguire's embarrassed avoidance of a fellow elevator passenger's gaze in *Spider-Man 2* after he has shared too much information about the pelvic discomfiture of his costume. Comparably, in the course of humiliating *TASM*'s would-be car thief, Garfield orchestrates an evolving slapstick routine involving mock-groveling, webbing sneezes, and pseudo-kung fu. Well-timed gestures and comically graceful body language carries the day in both of these cases. Garfield asserts that he incorporated his studies of spider movement into his performance, in both action and interpersonal scenes. In one interview, he describes his technique: "Imagine all of your skin was as sensitive as a spider, the slightest gust of wind would feel like a tornado going by. You'd always be rushing. . . . And I looked at the idea of having more legs, more arms, and the spatial awareness. A spider moves up, down, side-to-side, all around. He's not linear. . . . [H]e can be here and then over there incredibly fast" (Boucher). The spidery skittishness is discernible in *TASM* as Peter evades Gwen's questions about his bruised face, and lies about his familiarity with branzino. Garfield hurtles from his locker, bobs and weaves around Emma Stone's scrutinizing looks, and jitters from a panicked lack of awareness about European sea bass to overly vigorous nodding ("No, no, I know . . .").

All of these examples amount to an actor's accomplished circumvention of expressive restriction in superhero films. Why, then, should "gravity" be considered another important criterion for a proficient superheroic performance? This quality has two senses. Metaphorically, it refers to the actor's traditional responsibility to bring dramatic gravitas to the scenario s/he inhabits. Such performative sobriety can take the form of moral seriousness—for example, Maguire demonstrating Peter's commitment to Uncle Ben's maxim of great power necessitating great responsibility, or Garfield contending with the consequences of vacillating from his promise to a dying Captain Stacy. Actors also might help a film achieve weightiness through the intensity of their emotional investment—for example, Maguire's abrupt, volcanic scream as a ceiling begins to collapse upon Mary Jane in *Spider-Man 2* (fig. 10.5), or Garfield's shudders as he strokes the hair of a lifeless Gwen in *TASM 2*. Such commitment is necessitated by the superhero

10.5. Tobey Maguire's scream in *Spider-Man 2*.

genre's imbrication within the tradition of melodrama, but it is also culturally warranted in order to stave off comics' historical associations with bathos and emotional immaturity. Certainly such moments are perceived by fans as affective testaments to *TASM*'s historical import as a superhero comic of surprising emotional sophistication. Indeed, Gwen's murder in *TASM* no. 121 is regarded as a subcultural watershed: the abrupt death of a recurring and much-loved comic book character is cited as effectively ending the lightheartedness of the Silver Age and ushering in a new era of seriousness and self-awareness within the genre (Blumberg).

The achievement of gravity also has technological connotations. Positing weightiness as a new evaluative measurement of superheroic performance counters frequent complaints about the "weightlessness" of digitally enabled performance. Describing the initial battle between Doctor Octopus and Spidey in *Spider-Man 2*, Scott Bukatman complains that "the net effect is of some vaguely rubberoid action figures harmlessly bouncing each other around the space" (120). If "the pleasures of the digital are about transcending gravity, about bodies exceeding their limits," clearly not everyone feels that anything goes (Landay 134). Consequently, twenty-first-century filmmakers take extraordinary measures to ensure that even the most outlandishly dynamic physical movement is in accordance with the tenets of perceptual realism. *TASM 2*'s animators crafted plausible movement by ensuring accurate weight shifting, anatomically precise bodily compressions, responsive muscle jiggle, and detailed fabric wrinkling. The Spider-Man franchises, then, are instrumental in establishing a new representational mode in which gravity has become a preeminent aesthetic and critical concern.

This new mode necessitates the actor's adaptation to the unique production demands of digital mediation. Just as we might appreciate a superheroic actor's circumvention of physical expressive restrictions, so, too, might we accredit her/his engagement with the affordances made possible by new media—particularly digital animation and performance-capture systems. Just as animators manipulate in various ways the data produced by actors, the actor must adjust to the alienating emptiness of a motion-capture volume or facial scan system, and learn how to move her/his body in a way that allows a capture program to "read" it in the desired fashion (Allison 329). Accordingly, it is critical to recognize how such systems can actually showcase the fruits of the actor's labor. In *Spider-Man 3*, the piteous qualities of Flint Marko's horrified expression as his body devolves into a living mound of sand are produced by an amalgamation of two wire frames constructed from scans of Thomas Haden Church's face (fig. 10.6), realistic

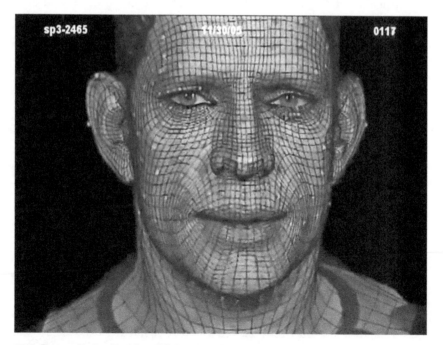

10.6. Thomas Haden Church and *Spider-Man 3*'s facial capture process.

facial data captured by the strobing cameras of Imagework's Lightstage, and a performance-capture system's translation of Church's own facial emoting (Curtis 130). The end result is that the authenticity of the actor's emotionally informed movement is foregrounded even "while the world around them vibrates with detail actualized from the imagination" (Landay 134).

It is equally important to recognize that the actor is not inherently supplanted by her/his animated analogues. Computer-generated stunt doubles have been employed since 1995, but Raimi's films established the precedent for extended sequences of character animation. Unfortunately, his substitution of Maguire for a completely animated double led many critics to decry the loss of Spider-Man's indexicality. Bukatman, for example, asserted that the substitution of live action for animation "has the unfortunate effect of severing the connection between the inexpressive body and the liberated, expressive one" (121). As if to rectify these grievances, Webb's later films are noteworthy for their reintegration of the actors' alienated labor within the animation process. Rather than relying exclusively on data acquired from performance-capture systems, animators working on the TASM films took their cues from the motion studies of preproduction stunt doubles, or Garfield himself. During the course of these motion studies, and even during principal photography, the actors or stuntpersons made performance choices—gestures, movements, postures—which were then often used as reference points, or virtual keyframes, to guide the subsequent animation process.

Interestingly, Randall William Cook, TASM's animation supervisor, bequeaths authorial status to Garfield as the originator of the process, and not just a source of inputted data. "Andrew created a unique pattern of movement and body language that helped define the character," he asserted, "and we could emulate it wherever appropriate" (Robertson 28). Jerome Chen, TASM's visual effects supervisor, offered specific details of Garfield's contributions: "He was specific about the poses Spider-Man would hit. If he attached to a wall or crawled on the ground, he extended his fingers. His palms didn't hit the ground. He did specific things with his elbows, knees, how his back arched when he was in the suit that our animators had to pick up on. Our CG Spider-Man was an enhanced version of what Andrew could do, but with the same poses and feeling" (ibid.). Not only are the actor's contributions given pride of place in the animation process, but his performance choices are retranslated as iconic markers—keyframes—that guide the process of graphic inscription. Gesture and posture—two basic, physical components of any traditional performance—are bequeathed a new importance as beginning and end points in a digitally crafted trajectory of dramatic movement co-crafted by actor and animator.

Equally impressive, though, is the actors' integration of comic book hypotexts through inspired performance choices. In particular, Garfield's gestures and poses are themselves performative quotations of graphic representations of Spider-Man comics. His precisely executed contortions intentionally reference the penchant for post-McFarlane artists to render impossibly exaggerated full-bodied acrobatics (Robertson 28). Moreover, the animation team—attuned to Garfield's embodied quotations—systematically enhanced the iconicity of his poses. *TASM*'s animation supervisor, David Schaub, explained further: "The way we choreographed the character in and out of the poses makes the comic book [poses] seem like snapshots taken of those performances. In many of the action sequences, we'd ramp down to slow motion so that the iconic poses really paid off" (Robertson 30). Through such techniques, performance and animation establish a technologically complex intertextual relationship to a comic hypotext. Webb's films provide another instance of three distinct ontologies overlapping to produce a new, digitally enabled performance technique that binds together the heretofore distinct work of comic artist, digital animator, and screen actor.

"BEST . . . SPIDER-MAN . . . EVER!": SUPERHEROIC PERFORMANCE AND FANDOM

In the age of social media, superhero films require the careful management of fandom, which is now replete with online petitions, casting scandals, viral campaigning, and the like. Actors who are hired to appear within a Marvel adaptation are therefore necessarily subject to an atypically loaded set of creative conditions. These performers must contend with the particularly dense prehistory of their project: its seriality, its multiple authors, and the intimidating "collective intelligence" of an "always-already" mobilized fan base (Jenkins 136). Each Spider-Man adaptation merely represents a potential contribution to what Thomas Leitch calls a larger "macrotext": that is, ME's canonical and continuity-based franchise (216). Of course, each new addition to this macrotext is subject to the exacting authority of fan experts who might be ready to cry foul at the prospect of, say, organic web-shooters. Therefore, each actor who is hired to make a creative contribution to the franchise faces a number of unique questions: How will s/he make performance choices that encapsulate an ever-evolving, fifty-year-old serialized character? Why might the performative differences of a newly minted wallcrawler stretch the limits of fan tolerance? What encoded gestures might be included to signal a deference to fans' communal knowledge, expertise, and commitment—which always exceeds that of the individual performer?

Fandom derives a sense of empowerment from its certainty that it knows Peter Parker better than Hollywood dilettantes—or even MW itself—and filmmakers and actors are increasingly finding canny ways to both flatter and exploit this collective intelligence. Predictable bouts of fan outrage typically follow press releases announcing the casting of an actor considered to be "inappropriate" for a superheroic role. For example, there were 68,222 negative Tweets in the first hour that followed the August 2013 announcement that Ben Affleck would play the Caped Crusader in the forthcoming *Batman v Superman* (2016) (Breznican 14). And yet, although the film industry is becoming increasingly canny at cultic management, there may be no such thing as bad press; everything—even fan outrage—becomes free publicity. Therefore, when Michael Cera's name circulated in January 2010 as a *TASM* hopeful, Columbia stood to profit from the uncorroborated rumor. On the one hand, the film's producers would certainly not deliberately engage in fan-baiting by issuing press releases about potential talks with an actor as "unsuitable" as Cera. On the other, they stood to gain much subcultural capital by "listening to fans" and eventually casting a "respected" actor, Garfield, instead. And with the 2015 casting of Tom Holland as the next incarnation of the character, Sony was able to wrest its own share of nerd points from MS (and their favored candidate, Charlie Plummer). Holland mounted his own (unofficial) personal campaign for the role via Instagram videos of the impressive gymnastic stunts he performed in his backyard—a savvy (read: strategically "cool") use of social media that in turn enabled Sony to position itself as a forward-thinking company.

These casting controversies are frequently embroiled within both cultural and identity politics. Famously, Donald Glover jokingly petitioned on his Twitter feed for the part of Peter Parker in 2010 after being inspired by an *io9* editorial about the importance of opening the role to non-white actors (McWilliams). But after Glover appeared in his recurring role on *Community* wearing Spider-Man PJs, extremist fans—and even the occasional retailer—countered the lighthearted campaign online in a racist backlash.

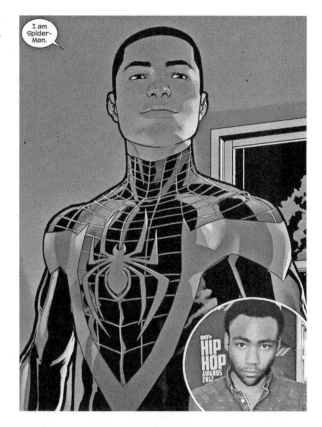

10.7. Miles Morales and Donald Glover, *Ultimate Comics: Spider-Man* no. 28. Donald Glover at the 2012 BET Hip Hop Awards.

Such comments were often explicitly prefaced as being driven by a respect for hypotextual fidelity rather than as part of an outright xenophobic agenda (Cunningham 25). And yet Glover's critics were usually unable to articulate why such filmic conformity ought always to trump unconventional acts of remediation, or to demonstrate a sensitivity to the interests of a multiracial demographic.

Fascinatingly, the Glover campaign prompted writer Brian Michael Bendis to usher in a new black Hispanic Spidey, Miles Morales, outside of regular continuity in *USM* (fig. 10.7). Glover showed up in *TASM* as a subliminal Easter egg: a poster of his *Community* character, Troy Barnes, hangs in Peter's bedroom. And in another reciprocal instance of fan-driven, transmedia cross-pollination, Glover provides the voice of the animated version of Miles Morales in episode 63 of *Ultimate Spider-Man: Web Warriors*. However, and sadly, racist fans' animus at the prospect of a non-white Spider-Man corresponds with a more benign version of mandated racial "policing":

the licensing agreement between Sony and ME involving future filmic sub-brands. The 2011 contract mandates that a filmic Peter Parker must be Caucasian, as well as heterosexual (McNary). Thus, Sony and ME not only set legal parameters restricting opportunities for actors of color to appear in their high-profile transmedia franchises, but make visible and explicit the usually invisible and tacit racial dimensions of corporate branding.

Just as unruly fan tactics can prompt both responsive and contrarian strategies from media producers, fandom's daunting collective intelligence may react in both positive and negative ways to the superheroic actor and her/his singular, subjective representations. For example, Maguire achieves fannish accreditation for emphasizing Peter's jejune decency: he is predictably "sweet, naïve and gentle" (Morton). By contrast, Garfield's amplification of Peter as "a kewl badass" in *TASM 2* is perceived by other fans as a betrayal of the character's essence (Film Crit Hulk). How, then, does an actor—even a self-professed Spider-fan like Garfield—navigate myriad interpretations and conflicting expectations? Even the ongoing production of the venerated comic book hypotext is subject to authorial schism and fan resistance. An editorial team (headed by Nick Lowe as of February 2014) oversees all of MW's Spider-Man output, with crucial plot points affecting story continuity being decided at annual creative summits. This team exercises editorial fiat over all decisions undertaken by the creative teams working on the books and ensures that broader corporate mandates are upheld within published titles. But this team-based brand management often faces both internal friction and opposition by fandom, with notable consequences for the actors who are chosen to embody ME's cinematic sub-brand.

The storyline of "One More Day" (2007) and its relationship to the production of the rebooted film franchise offers a compelling example of the creative synthesis between fan desire and responsive corporate strategy.[1] The controversial crossover story saw MW editor in chief Joe Quesada mandating the dissolution of Peter and Mary Jane Watson's long-running marriage. The MJ/Peter pairing is one of the most familiar romantic partnerships in comics outside of Lois and Clark, and it represents a core structural element in Spider-Man's association with the romance genre. The problems that Peter's superheroic career poses for his love life are a recurring source of drama in many iterations of the brand—both comic and filmic. Notably, *TASM*'s writer, J. Michael Straczynski, publicly aired his grievances over Quesada's editorial decision, and he considered removing his name from the final two issues of the storyline (Straczynski). "One More Day" also resulted in vitriolic criticism from fan communities, largely on account of the editorial team's perceived disrespect for the relationship.

Following the "One More Day" debacle, then, Webb's *Amazing Spider-Man* reboot acquired subcultural capital within fan communities by reintroducing the centrality of romance within the Spider-Man brand. Webb's films execute a romantic retcon by resituating Gwen Stacy as Peter's first girlfriend and quasi-partner in his early crime-fighting career. But his revision is not without precedent; in the alternate-continuity *USM* series, Mary Jane is Peter's girlfriend and confidante from the very outset, and Raimi's trilogy follows suit. Indeed, as Peter tells us in the opening voiceover of Raimi's first film, "this story, like any story worth telling, is all about a girl." This voiceover immediately cuts to a close-up of MJ—"the Girl Next Door," and the very first character seen in the film. By playing up *TASM* as a screwball romantic comedy of sorts, then, Webb takes his cue from Raimi's generic hybridity of action and romance. More importantly, the primacy granted to Gwen simultaneously undoes the perceived disrespect for female characters in "One More Day," helping to smooth over fans' ruffled feathers. Webb's film also reintroduces the lesser-known character of Gwen to a wider public (she is accorded a minor role only in *Spider-Man 3*) and maintains a thematic consistency with the broader world of ME and its insistence on Spider-Man's unmarried status.

The furor over Spider-Man's nuptials is not simply a subcultural tempest in a teacup; it exemplifies the complex interplay between ME's various Spider-Man sub-brands. We recall that the basic purpose of ME's brand system "is to clarify a range of product offerings," and that ME strives to "eliminate the inconsistencies and contradictions between incarnations of its characters" (Johnson 77). A vital dimension of the Spider-Man range brand—the character's romantic status—is revealed as a tumultuous site of contestation between creators, managers, and audiences. Concretely, then, *USM*, the "One More Day" arc, Raimi's trilogy, and Webb's films are entwined in a complex palimpsest of textual reciprocity spanning more than a decade.

This managerial process of clarification extends to the performative instantiations of the filmic sub-brands. We have seen how hopefuls for the cinematic Spider-Men were auditioned for their proximal adherence to audience expectations of a romantic male lead. Most importantly—in terms of *TASM*'s subcultural credentials—Garfield's casting helped to revivify the brand's generic associations with romance, which the "One More Day" storyline had undermined. Webb has remarked that it was largely Garfield's chemistry with Emma Stone that won him the role over other shortlisted actors, including Jamie Bell and Josh Hutcherson. Of particular note was Garfield's use of expressive objects to bring out a scene's amorous undertones: "We were doing a scene that's not in the movie, where he was eating a cheeseburger and . . . trying to put [Gwen] at ease, while he is eating food. And the way he ate this food . . . I felt like there's something in the way he embodied and committed to that really tiny minutia—I just hadn't seen before" (McDaniel).

This minutiae is evident in the evasive shyness Garfield employs when Peter is confronted head-on with significant decisions involving Gwen. In *TASM*, he and Stone tentatively encircle each other—abruptly pivoting, nervously twirling—as they fumble toward committing to a first date. Such rebounding and encircling movements have action-based correlatives. When Garfield gets his first costumed workout, his web-slinging—careening, spinning, free-falling, fumbling—is both nervously and joyously reckless, not unlike working oneself up to asking out the girl of one's dreams. And in *TASM 2*, Garfield weaves and ducks his face behind a tree as Gwen confronts him about their foundering relationship (fig. 10.8). In a story deeply involved in the difficulties of facing up to moral and romantic responsibility, Garfield's graceful evasiveness reveals his impressive attunement with the character he embodies.

10.8. Andrew Garfield and Emma Stone talk it out in *The Amazing Spider-Man 2*.

Both Maguire's and Garfield's actorly interpretations of Peter Parker are instantiations within a larger continuum of intertwining texts. Accordingly, they make performance choices that honor fandom's collective intelligence. The actors make reference to previous incarnations of the character across media, include encoded gestures to be recognized by attentive fans, and allow opportunities for knowledgeable interpretations to be made about the personality traits they choose to highlight. At *Spider-Man 2*'s dramatic turning point, Raimi, in an act of fan deference, visually quotes Romita Sr.'s famous "Spider-Man No More" panel composition in *TASM* no. 50, in which a rain-drenched Peter turns his back on the costume he has left in an alley garbage can. The two talented actors who have memorably embodied one of ME's most enduring range brands emulate such moments in ingenious ways. These cinematic Spider-Men are remarkable symptoms of changing star labor, evolving technological norms, and mercurial subcultural desires. Their accomplishments make salient new performative developments that we are only beginning to understand, and they signal delights available especially to the most devoted of True Believers.

....

NOTES

1. I also address the relation of "Brand New Day" to *TASM* elsewhere. See Taylor in "Works Cited."

WORKS CITED

Aaker, David. *Building Strong Brands*. New York: Free Press, 1996. Print.

Aftab, Kaleem. "The Last Action Heroes: Have Tom Cruise, Will Smith and Brad Pitt Lost Their Mojo?" *The Independent*, 28 June 2013. Web.

Allison, Tanine. "More Than a Man in a Monkey Suit: Andy Serkis, Motion Capture, and Digital Realism." *Quarterly Review in Film and Video* 28.4 (2011): 325–341. Print.

The Amazing Spider-Man. Dir. Marc Webb. Columbia Pictures, 2012. Film.

The Amazing Spider-Man 2. Dir. Marc Webb. Columbia Pictures, 2014. Film.

Barker-Whitelaw, Gavia. "Being a Superhero Isn't Very Super for Marvel's 'Avengers' Actors." *Daily Dot*, 28 March 2014. Web.

Bart, Peter. "Movie Stars Have Become an Endangered Species." *Variety*, 12 June 2014. Web.

Blumberg, Arnold T. "'The Night Gwen Stacy Died': The End of Innocence and the Birth of the Bronze Age." *Reconstruction* 3.4 (2003): n. pag. Web.

Boucher, Geoff. "'Spider-Man' Director Marc Webb Feels a 'Responsibility to Reinvent' the Hero." *Los Angeles Times*, 18 July 2011. Web.

———. "'Spider-Man' Star Andrew Garfield on Fame: 'It Terrifies Me.'" *Los Angeles Times*, 26 August 2011. Web.

Breznican, Anthony. "Holy Backlash, Batman!" *Entertainment Weekly*, 6 September 2013, 14. Print.

Buchanan, Kyle. "Why the Newest Superhero Movies Can't Seem to Make Their Actors into Superstars." *Vulture*, 8 November 2013. Web.

Bukatman, Scott. "Why I Hate Superhero Movies." *Cinema Journal* 50.3 (2011): 118–122. Print.

Comolli, Jean-Louis. "Historical Fiction: A Body Too Much." Trans. Ben Brewster. *Screen* 19.2 (1978): 41–54. Print.

Cunningham, Phillip Lamar. "Donald Glover for Spider-Man." In *Web-Spinning Heroics: Critical Essays on the History and Meaning of Spider-Man*. Eds. Robert Moses Peaslee and Robert G. Weiner. Jefferson, NC: McFarland, 2012. 22–28. Print.

Curtis, Grant. *The Spider-Man Chronicles: The Art and Making of Spider-Man 3*. San Francisco: Chronicle Books, 2007. Print.

David, Elliott. "The Amazing Andrew Garfield." *V Man* 26 (Summer 2012): 54-61. Print.

Eisenberg, Eric. "Robert Downey Jr. Playing Hardball During *Avengers 2* Contract Negotiations." *Cinema Blend*, 7 May 2013. Web.

Fernandez, Jay A., and Borys Kit. "How Marvel Went from Near-Bankruptcy to Powerhouse Game-Changer for the Entire Movie Industry." *Hollywood Reporter*, 2 November 2010. Web.

Film Crit Hulk. "Hulk's 237 Burning Questions for *The Amazing Spider-Man 2*." *Badass Digest*, 6 May 2014. Web.

Finke, Nikki. "*Avengers* Cast and Stingy Marvel Ready to Rumble over Sequel Cash & Strong Arming." *Deadline*, 7 May 2013. Web.

Genette, Gérard. *Palimpsests: Literature in the Second Degree*. 1982. Trans. Channa Newman and Claude Doubinsky. Lincoln: University of Nebraska Press, 1997. Print.

Graser, Marc. "Marvel Offers Stars Franchise Potential." *Variety*, 26 March 2010. Web.

Hewitt, Chris, and Simon Braund. "*Spider-Man*." *Empire*, July 2002, 58–62. Print.

Insignares, Giovanni. "Tom Cruise and the Dying Nature of Movie Stars." *The Artifice*, 26 June 2014. Web.

Jenkins, Henry. "Interactive Audiences? The 'Collective Intelligence' of Media Fans." 2002. In *Fans, Bloggers, and Gamers: Exploring Participatory Culture.* Ed. Henry Jenkins. New York: New York University Press, 2006. 134–151. Print.

Johnson, Derek. "Will the Real Wolverine Please Stand Up? Marvel's Mutation from Monthlies to Movies." In *Film and Comic Books.* Eds. Ian Gordon, Mark Jancovich, and Matthew P. McAllister. Jackson: University Press of Mississippi, 2007. 64–85. Print.

King, Barry. "Articulating Stardom." In *Star Texts.* 1985. Ed. Jeremy G. Butler. Detroit: Wayne State University Press, 1991. 125–154. Print.

Kit, Borys. "Andrew Garfield's Comic-Con Speech: 'Spider-Man Saved My Life.'" *The Hollywood Reporter,* 25 July 2011. Web.

Koh, Wilson. "'I Am Iron Man': The Marvel Cinematic Universe and Celeactor Labor." *Celebrity Studies* 5.4 (2014): 484–500. Print.

Landay, Lori. "The Mirror of Performance: Kinaesthetics, Subjectivity, and the Body in Film, Television, and Virtual Worlds." *Cinema Journal* 51.3 (2012): 129–136. Print.

Lee, Stan, et al. *Essential Amazing Spider-Man, Vol. 1.* 1963–1965. New York: Marvel, 2006. Print.

Lefèvre, Pascal. "Incompatible Visual Ontologies? The Problematic Adaptation of Drawn Images." In *Film and Comic Books.* Eds. Ian Gordon, Mark Jancovich, and Matthew P. McAllister. Jackson: University Press of Mississippi, 2007. 1–12. Print.

Leitch, Thomas. *Film Adaptation and Its Discontents.* Baltimore: Johns Hopkins University Press, 2007. Print.

Maltby, Richard. *Hollywood Cinema,* 2nd ed. Malden: Blackwell, 2003. Print.

Masters, Kim. "How Marvel Became the Envy (and Scourge) of Hollywood." *The Hollywood Reporter,* 1 August 2014. Web.

McDaniel, Matt. "'The Amazing Spider-Man' Director Marc Webb Reveals How Andrew Garfield Won the Role." *Yahoo! Movies,* 16 April 2012. Web.

McDonald, Paul. "Spectacular Acting: On the Exhibitionist Dynamics of Film Star Performance." In *Acting and Performance in Moving Image Culture.* Eds. Jörg Sternagel, Deborah Levitt, and Dieter Mersh. Bielefeld, Germany: Transcript Verlag, 2012. 61–70. Print.

McNary, Dave. "Spider-Man Needs to Be White and Straight, Say Leaked Sony Emails." *Variety,* 19 June 2015. Web.

McWilliams, Ora C. "Who Is Afraid of a Black Spider(-Man)?" *Transformative Works and Cultures* 13 (2013): n. pag. Web.

Mendelson, Scott. "Can Diversified Superhero Films Save Mainstream Genre Movies?" *Forbes,* 10 April 2014. Web.

Morton, Paul. "A Beautiful Man: On Peter Parker and the Amazing Spider-Man." *The Millions*, 2 May 2014. Web.

Naremore, James. *Acting in the Cinema*. Berkeley: University of California Press, 1988. Print.

North, Dan. *Performing Illusions*. London: Wallflower, 2008. Print.

Outlaw, Kofi. "Sony Can't Low-Ball Their New Spider-Man Forever." *Screen Rant*, 15 February 2014. Web.

Pallant, Chris. "Digital Dimensions in Actorly Performance: The Aesthetic Potential of Performance Capture." *Film International* 10.3 (2012): 37–49. Print.

Richmond, Scott C. "The Exorbitant Lightness of Bodies, or How to Look at Superheroes: Ilinx, Identification, and *Spider-Man*." *Discourse* 34.1 (2012): 113–144. Print.

Robertson, Barbara. "Channeling Spider-Man." *Computer Graphics World* 35.4 (2012): 26–31. Print.

Robson, Daniel. "Ultimate Spin: *Spider-Man*." *Film Matters* 3.4 (2012): 50–54. Print.

Spider-Man. Dir. Sam Raimi. Columbia Pictures, 2002. Film.

Spider-Man 2. Dir. Sam Raimi. Columbia Pictures, 2004. Film.

Spider-Man 3. Dir. Sam Raimi. Columbia Pictures, 2007. Film.

Straczynski, J. Michael. "Re: OMD Irony." *JMS News*, 4 December 2007. Web.

Taylor, Aaron. "Avengers Dissemble! Transmedia Superhero Franchises and Cultic Management." *Journal of Adaptation in Film and Performance* 7.2 (2014): 181–194. Print.

Spotting Stan

THE FUN AND FUNCTION OF STAN LEE'S
CAMEOS IN THE MARVEL UNIVERSE(S)

DRU JEFFRIES

O n July 29, 2014, Marvel Studios' *Guardians of the Galaxy* (James Gunn, 2014) screened at the Fantasia International Film Festival, three days in advance of its wide theatrical release. The savvy festival audience demonstrated its familiarity with some of Marvel's well-established conventions in a variety of ways throughout the screening—for instance, by staying through to the end of the credits for an additional scene,[1] and by cheering at the brief cameo appearance of the comics company's former writer and editor in chief, Stan Lee. Though Lee had professed in interviews prior to the film's release that he would not appear in *Guardians*,[2] his presence on the screen was clearly anticipated by many in attendance. Indeed, Lee's cameos in Marvel-branded films—not only those made by Marvel Studios, but any film featuring Marvel's expansive stable of characters— are now an expected part of the film experience. The playful background appearances by Alfred Hitchcock in the vast majority of his own directorial efforts, which his audiences came to expect and search for, is perhaps the closest comparison to this phenomenon; for the first time since Hitchcock's oeuvre, movies cohering as a body of cinematic work were being tied together in part by the repeated on-screen appearance of a single person: in this case, Stan Lee.

Following Ernest Mathijs's consolidation of director David Cronenberg's cameo appearances into a single and unified *supertext*, I would suggest that treating Lee's Marvel cameos in a similar way—that is, as a coherent body of work rather than a series of discrete performances in separate films—puts their recurring concerns and intertextual resonances in sharper focus. In this way, we can better appreciate how the Marvel Cinematic Universe (MCU) and its offshoots at other studios position and imagine Stan Lee—the living embodiment of Marvel Comics' past—within the company's contemporary context. I argue that the cameos perform a number of functions simultaneously: (1) they unify films featuring Marvel-branded characters, regardless of the individual film's corporate authorship (e.g., Marvel Studios, 20th Century Fox, Sony Pictures, etc.); (2) they encourage a playful mode of spectatorship modeled after a game of hide-and-seek (Hitchcock's "find the director" game is transformed into "spot Stan"); (3) they create intertextual and intermedial connections between comic book and cinematic diegeses; and, most crucially, (4) they provide a commentary on Lee's role—as well as the role of comics and their authors more generally—with regard to the contemporary cinematic manifestations of the fictional universe he helped to create in comics. While all four of these elements are significant, the fourth point is the primary focus of this chapter.

Stan Lee's cameos and Hitchcock's have some commonalities, and yet Lee's appearances complicate the tradition, given that his implicit authorial designation produced by these cameos collides with fan discourse about the validity and limits of that authorship. Maurice Yacowar points out that most of Hitchcock's cameos fit into one of two categories: the director tends to position himself within the diegesis as either an embodiment of the film's themes ("the emblematic") or as a director surrogate ("the maker") (218–225). Lee's cameos position him in recurring ways as well: as anonymous (when he plays himself, he is consistently mistaken for somebody else), as a blue-collar worker, as somewhat clueless, and as oblivious to or even a victim of superheroes' existence. While Lee's cameos are usually deployed to produce a fleeting comedic effect of recognition, the cumulative meaning of the cameos is undoubtedly more complex than it may at first appear, and even at times contradictory. Moreover, his status as *an* authorial figure, though not *the* author of the films in question (as Hitchcock was), further complicates his representation, suggesting that his appearances may be collectively read as a commentary on his contemporary authorial status in the MCU, rather than in the comics he wrote decades ago. Viewed collectively, these cameos reveal consistencies and recurring concerns that form a fairly coherent portrait of Lee as a discursive construct: "Stan Lee" (not to be confused with Stan Lee) is depicted as a laborer without the rights to his own work; as a bystander, victimized and discarded by his own creations; as an author without agency. In some ways, this is a deeply ironic characterization of Lee, but in order to understand why, we first need to understand his history with the company.

Stan Lee—née Stanley Martin Lieber—has held a variety of positions at Marvel Comics since his nepotistic hiring in 1940. Beginning as an office gofer, Lee was soon given the opportunity to write a short prose narrative for an issue of *Captain America*; it was not long before he was the editor of the company (at nineteen years of age) and also writing the majority of the comics.[3] In the early 1960s, he created the characters for which he has become best known: the Fantastic Four (co-created with Jack Kirby), Spider-Man (co-created with Steve Ditko), the X-Men (co-created with Kirby), and so on. The success of series like *The Amazing Spider-Man*, *The Uncanny X-Men*, *The Fantastic Four*, and the superhero team book *The Avengers* collectively reinvigorated the superhero genre, launching the so-called Silver Age and positioning Marvel as the most vibrant voice in the industry. That voice, specifically, was Lee's: the distinctive style of Marvel Comics—including nicknames for all credited personnel ("Smilin' Stan Lee," "Jolly Jack Kirby," etc.), informal narration ("See last ish" [for "issue"]), and various self-reflexive touches—was part of a larger effort to endear readers not only to the fictional characters in the comics but also to the characters who were creating them. Lee made himself and the rest of the Marvel "Bullpen" a crucial part of the proceedings: his editorials ("Stan's Soapbox," part of the "Bullpen Bulletin" page) may have begun as a means of including the text-only pages necessary to qualify for "magazine" status (and cheaper mailing costs) with the US Post Office, but they also fostered a personal connection between readers and Lee, giving the audience non-diegetic access to his persona and voice. In at least one case, this access was literal: in the mid-1960s, members of the Marvel fan club—the Merry Marvel Marching Society—received a vinyl record featuring five minutes of playful (and obviously scripted) banter between Lee and other Marvel staffers.

All of this contributed to the mythologizing of Marvel as a collegial, high-spirited workplace, if not necessarily an egalitarian one, given Lee's discursive dominance. The writer also became an in-demand speaker on college campuses, where he publicized Marvel to audiences old and new while further reinforcing the connection between his persona and the brand. Although he has written for Marvel only sporadically since the 1980s, Lee remains the public face of the company to this day (largely through promotional appearances connected to upcoming Marvel films and the cameo appearances therein), and he bears the official honorific "Chairman Emeritus."

Lee's legacy consists of roughly equal parts visionary, creative genius, and exploitative, opportunistic, self-aggrandizing company man. The "Marvel Method" of comics writing, in many, if not most, cases, puts the primary creative burden on the artist to outline, pace, and narrate the story based on as much as a fairly detailed summary of the story or as little as a short conversation with the writer, who fills in captions and speech balloons on the completed pages, by which point the narrative is more or less established. Many argue—particularly fans of Jack Kirby, who feel that the artist was given a raw deal by Marvel and that Lee took an undue amount of credit for their collaborative work—that Lee's role in making Marvel into a cultural force has less to do with his skill at crafting characters and narratives than with his tireless promotion of the brand (and, simultaneously, of himself). Unlike most Marvel employees, Lee managed to transcend the drudgery and insecurity of freelance work, and his promotion arguably came at the expense of his collaborators/subordinates; as Charles Hatfield suggests in his monograph on Kirby, "the question of Marvel's authorship is entangled in the question of what Lee—who was, after all, never Marvel's owner—did to shore up his own status at the company. Presumably the owners at Marvel understood what 'writer' meant, but did not understand the centrality of narrative drawing. Kirby thus languished while Lee throve" (89). Hatfield also notes that Lee's creative output diminished—forcing artists like Kirby to shoulder even more of the creative burden—"as his public role grew more prominent and his stumping for Marvel more constant" (85).

Although Lee wore many hats at Marvel, he is thus perhaps most accurately located in his managerial role at the company, which makes the "Stan Lee" depicted by the cameos an ironic doppelgänger of the real Lee. In short, the cameos present a revisionist version of his history with Marvel, disassociating him from his managerial role and relocating him in the trenches with the rest of the Marvel creative team: the freelancers, like Kirby, who were paid by the page and saw no additional income based on the afterlife of their creative work (e.g., reprints, licensing agreements for toys, films, etc.). The very presence of Lee in these films, and the marked absence of other seminal creative forces like Kirby and Ditko, confirms his special status with the company and his ongoing affiliation with it—he did, after all, coin the phrase "Make mine Marvel"—not to mention his continued interest in self-mythologizing via Marvel's creative output.

Among Lee's innovations as Marvel's editor in chief was his insistence on crediting each contributor by name in every issue, thereby creating something of a star system akin to that of Hollywood (Ro 88). Naturally,

11.1. Lee and Kirby write and draw themselves into the text and out of a narrative quandary. *Fantastic Four* no. 10 (Jan. 1963).

Lee himself was the biggest star of all, with the most well-defined persona and the greatest opportunity to express it.[4] In *Fantastic Four* no. 10 (Jan. 1963), however, Lee took the integration of his persona to new heights by writing himself and Kirby into the story, blurring the boundaries between the diegetic and non-diegetic worlds[5] and setting an early precedent for his cameos in Marvel films decades later. In this issue, Dr. Doom appears in the Marvel offices before Lee and Kirby as they brainstorm new villain ideas for the Fantastic Four; Doom uses the writer and the artist to lure Mr. Fantastic into a trap (fig. 11.1).[6] This self-reflexive, even postmodern conceit was not just a means of reinforcing the Bullpen myth, or for Lee to write himself out of a corner—he had killed off Doom, who would go on to become the Fantastic Four's most iconic nemesis, in a previous issue. It also strengthened the association between Lee and the Marvel brand by making him a player (albeit a peripheral one) in the narrative universe as well as its ostensible creator.

A similar strategy has been adopted by much postmodern fiction, especially literary fiction in which the reader's desire to locate the author's biography in the text may be teased or thwarted by the appearance of characters acting as author surrogates: indeed, the author has been called *the* stock character of postmodernism (Fokkema 39). As Robert McGill writes in *The Treacherous Imagination*, "instead of being encouraged to chase after the author directly, audiences are invited to occupy the same estranged, exploratory perspective on the fiction's characters that the author has assumed in creating them" (72). Such author surrogates—for instance, Nathan Zuckerman in many of Philip Roth's novels, or Lee's avatar in *The Fantastic Four* no. 10—are self-reflexive insofar as they mirror certain aspects of the author's biography; but they also deliberately blur the line between fiction and reality in playful ways. Lee's appearance in the Marvel Comics diegesis increases interest in the fiction by making it more closely resemble our own world, distorting its facts and stretching its boundaries in deliberately undefined ways. It thus becomes a "play-space of indeterminate referentiality," as McGill puts it (76): we are meant to be unsure where the fictional world ends and ours begins.

In future appearances, Lee would be less essential to the story, often appearing only for brief self-reflexive moments of comedy. For instance, in *Fantastic Four Annual* no. 3 (Oct. 1965), Lee and Kirby are shown walking away from the wedding of Mr. Fantastic and the Invisible Girl, having been denied entrance to the ceremony; in *X-Men* no. 98 (April 1976), written by Chris Claremont and drawn by Dave Cockrum, Lee and Kirby oversee Jean Grey and Cyclops kissing on the street, and Kirby remarks, "I tell ya, they never used to do *that* when *we* had the book." Lee responds, likely referring to Claremont and Cockrum as much as to Jean and Cyclops, "Ah, Jack. You

11.2. A reflexive nod to Marvel's past and present personalizes the company's self-mythology. *X-Men* no. 98 (April 1976).

know these *young kids*—they got no *respect*." This last example introduces Lee as the *former* author of *X-Men*, and is therefore distinct from the others (fig. 11.2).[7] Just as numerous film directors would later do, Claremont here deploys Lee's image and star persona to produce a bit of metatextual commentary, in this case regarding the difference between their creative approaches to authoring the mutant superteam. In comparison to the more emotionally expressive (perhaps even soap operatic) characters of Claremont's run, Lee's books seem quaint and sexless: in short, passé. To readers of the Claremont *X-Men*, having "no respect" for what has come before may seem like an appealing antiauthoritarian gesture, and one very much in line with the rebellious spirit of the X-Men characters.

Lee's film cameos are much more similar to these later appearances than to the earlier ones insofar as they tend to be brief, comedic in tone, and mostly inessential to the narrative as such. As with his appearance in *X-Men* no. 98, Lee in the films is expressly *not* the author of his own cinematic image. Although the source of the cameo is always important to consider—and the authorship of these cameos is an issue to be discussed later in this essay—Lee's film appearances can still be productively compared with those of Alfred Hitchcock, which have been discussed in some detail by both Yacomar in *Hitchcock's British Films* and Thomas M. Leitch in *Find the Director and Other Hitchcock Games*. Leitch, in particular, emphasizes the pleasurable and playful aspect of these cameos, arguing that they contribute to Hitchcock's "ludic approach to storytelling" (10).

Marvel Comics' house style is itself rather ludic, in that it is largely characterized by a friendly rapport between author and reader (e.g., nicknames, use of slang and abbreviations, inside jokes, etc.); films based on Marvel properties (and especially those made by Marvel Studios themselves) carry on this tradition by including a preponderance of "Easter eggs" (background details that contain references to Marvel lore and hints of what may come in future films), additional scenes hidden after the closing credits, and other intertextual references. All of these properties, as well as Lee's cameos, give the films a "scavenger hunt" quality, entreating viewers to collect knowledge from various sources in order to understand everything onscreen. Spotting and recognizing these details becomes an additional source of cinematic pleasure over and above that generated by the narrative and cinematographic elements. And as was the case with Lee's cameos in comics, to recognize them is to reinforce a certain myth about Marvel as a corporate entity and Lee's central status therein.

One of Lee's most influential creative decisions while writing at Marvel was to create a single diegesis that encompassed all of the company's characters, enabling them to cross paths and team up as stories (and sales) demanded. While Marvel Studios has had some success in replicating this model on a smaller scale, the film rights to many of Marvel's most popular characters—including Spider-Man, the X-Men, and the Fantastic Four—remain at other studios; consequently, Fox's Fantastic Four do not live in the same New York as Marvel Studio's Avengers. The appearance of Lee in all of these disconnected universes provides them with a trace of the kind of continuity that the comics enjoy and suggests the potential for an MCU as unified as its comics counterpart. Lee's close association with the comic book medium, however, may equally suggest that this kind of unification is only possible in comics. Moreover, Lee's multiplicity—he rarely plays the same character, even within the same franchise[8]—seems to thwart the possibility of an inter-studio world-building project.

Hitchcock's multiple appearances throughout his filmography were never problematic in this way, as his films were not presented as sequential entries in a single diegesis. If Hitchcock's cameos disrupt the narrative, it is because a non-diegetic figure—the director—is intruding into the diegetic space of the film. As Yacowar writes, "the Hitchcock appearances cause a ripple in the narrative flow, a disturbance in the film's surface. The other people in the film are actors playing roles. Hitchcock is himself, not to be identified by his character within this film but known from his association in other films and (later) from the impudent persona of his television series. The intrusion of this real person into the fictional setting heightens the tensions between *our* reality and the reality presumed by the fiction" (217). Lee's cameos are potentially disruptive for the same reason; even when he plays a character, the ostensibly ideal response to his appearance is "There's Stan Lee!" As a result, Lee's multiple appearances—in World War II and present day, on Earth and on the planet Xandar—do not necessarily undermine film-to-film continuity. Leitch argues that cameos are not "constrained in at all the same ways by the requirements of their dieseges" (5), and as such, that viewers are encouraged to take them at face value, in an autotelic manner rather than as a narrative linchpin. All in all, they contribute to the larger world-building project at work in these films insofar as they present a recurring figure across multiple films (he remains "Stan Lee," regardless of his "character" in a given film) while drawing attention to a shared awareness of his comics work and acknowledging the debt owed to him. The narrative value of the cameos, however, is about nil.

In an essay about Robert Altman's *The Player* (1992) as parody, Cynthia Baron argues that star cameos "draw attention *away from* the narrative," and that in doing so, they "disrupt conventional modes of identification [with] an alienating effect" (24). This kind of generalization, however, does not apply to all cameos, or at least fails to do justice to how spectators react to such moments. The disrupting effect that Baron associates with cameos presumably results from the intrusion of this alien figure—a star, often appearing as him or herself rather than as a fictional character—into the diegesis. Indeed, even if the cameo actor is ostensibly playing a character, he or she is also appearing as him or herself: cameo actors are "defined by their trans-textual star images," and these images lend them a "different ontological status" compared to "the fictional characters bound to the diegesis" (ibid.). This effect is similar to that of the aforementioned (surrogate) author character appearing so often in postmodern literature, an "ontologically ambiguous" figure compared to the actual author and to the other (presumably entirely fictional) characters (McGill 72).

In these works of semiautobiographical (or ambiguously autobiographical) fiction, McGill claims, the relationship between the text "and its readers is characterized by a dynamic tension between instrumental knowledge-acquisition and autotelic play. Readers can take on a flirtatiously noncommittal hermeneutics that alternates between the two approaches in the course of reading a single text" (76). Leitch characterizes the spectatorial practices of Hitchcock's cameo-spotters in a similar way: "Audiences who recognize Hitchcock at all are not really distracted, even pleasurably, from the story because their experience of the film as story and discourse is not nearly so sharply split; in watching a Hitchcock film, they do not shuttle neatly back and forth between two kinds of awareness" (6). In both cases, the reader or viewer is nimble enough to account for the brief appearance of this ontological other without becoming unmoored from the diegesis. Especially in Hitchcock or Marvel films, both of which address their audiences in a playful manner, the cameos are fairly consistent with the discursive strategies employed throughout. Although cameos always include the potential for disruption—as Leitch puts it, "to recognize the cameo is automatically to note its potentially disruptive force" (5)—here they seem a natural part of the films' ludic mode of narration rather than an unnatural or distracting addition. But whereas Hitchcock's cameos "remind us that we are watching a film" (Yacowar 217) crafted by Hitchcock, Lee's appearances remind us that we are watching a film based on a Marvel comic.

The main difference between Hitchcock and Lee in terms of their cameos is that the former, as the ostensible author of his films, uses them as a means of exerting control and expressing or shaping meaning, whereas the latter, as a former writer, former editor in chief, and current public face of Marvel, is treated more as a puppet of the individual filmmakers and the company in general. As he puts it in an interview with *Playboy*: "Mostly I'm just a pretty face they keep for the public. My entire career, I treated Marvel like one big ad campaign, with slogans like 'Make mine Marvel,' 'Welcome to the Marvel age of comics' and so forth. After a while, I became Marvel's ambassador to the world. . . . I have no standing at Marvel where I decide what projects get made or who gets hired, and certainly none at Disney, which now owns Marvel" (Hochman).

As the author of the films in which he appears, Hitchcock is able to control his cameos such that they "often [provide] a crucial approach to the meaning of the film" (Yacowar 217), especially when combined with this extra-textual knowledge of his persona. Unlike Hitchcock, Lee is never a creative agent, and he has little (if any) control over how and where he appears in these films. As such, Lee does not exert control, but rather *is controlled*; he does not express meaning, but rather *is used* to express or shape meaning.

Leitch makes an excellent case for how Hitchcock's cameos fit into the director's broader interest in games (and filmmaking-as-game), but it is Yacowar who provides the most comprehensive account of how each cameo functions within each film as well as part of a broader discursive strategy that creates meaning by connecting the director's public persona to his cinematic appearances. Ernest Mathijs, in an analysis of Canadian director David Cronenberg's cameos, refers to this amalgam as a "supertext," which he defines as "a string of moments stretched across films that, together with the films themselves (both his own and others) and the ancillary materials that circulate around those films, offer a compelling way of understanding his oeuvre's comments on the world" (144). In the discussion to follow, I will adopt a similar approach to reading Lee's cameos, albeit with the necessary caveat that he is not a creative agent in these films. Indeed, that fact is a key part of the significance of his appearances. In the remainder of this chapter I will be concerned with precisely what kinds of meanings are produced through his cameos in Marvel films.

——

As of 2014, Lee has appeared in twenty-one live-action film versions of Marvel properties, plus a guest appearance on *Marvel's Agents of S.H.I.E.L.D.* (ABC, 2013–) and a cameo in *The Trial of the Incredible Hulk* TV movie (Bill Bixby, 1989). Just as Hitchcock's cameos can be divided into two distinct tendencies (Yacowar), Lee's appearances in Marvel films can be usefully segregated into different categories, some of which overlap. Categorizing them in this way, in fact, helps to reveal their significance. Overall, Lee's cameos can be read as an extended commentary on his lack of creative autonomy in the contemporary MCU as well as on the role of comics personnel in general in a world where film revenues far surpass those of comics.[9] In Lee's case, the most salient recurring categories are the bystander, the victim, the blue-collar, and the oblivious.

Yet another category, however, should be discussed first, as it emphasizes the cameos' most immediate effect, which is humor. This category, the lecher, refers to cameos that play on the visual juxtaposition of Lee, who is now an extremely old man (ninety-three years old at the time of this writing), surrounded by or leering at beautiful young women. The viewer need not even recognize Lee in order to chuckle at these moments, though the savvy viewer is able to read the lecherous old man as comic book legend Stan Lee rather than merely an anonymous elderly extra: there is a joke as well as an in-joke, a feature that characterizes Lee's cameos in general. Moreover, the combination of recognition and humor—the two responses are intertwined and reinforce each other—functions as an expression of viewer mastery over the text, allowing audiences (such as the one that attended the aforementioned Fantasia screening of *Guardians of the Galaxy* and stayed hoping for an additional scene after the credits) the pleasure of having their extra-textual investment in the Marvel brand rewarded.[10]

The first appearance of the lecher is in *Iron Man* (Jon Favreau, 2008). Lee is seen outside of an elaborate black-tie event attended by Tony Stark, Pepper Potts, and the villainous Obadiah Stane. As Stark makes his entrance, paparazzi bulbs flashing, he pats Lee on the shoulder; misrecognizing him as *Playboy* founder Hugh Hefner, Stark says, "Looking good, Hef." The mistake is understandable, given Lee's dress and accompaniment: he is wearing a silk bathrobe, smoking a pipe, and has a young blonde woman on each arm. (The only clue that Lee is playing himself and not Hefner is in the closing credits.) The comparison that the film suggests between Lee and Hefner is a valid one: both revolutionized their respective industries and were arguably at the peak of their cultural influence in the 1960s. Today, both remain in the public eye but only as figureheads; neither is actively involved in the day-to-day operations of their respective firms, Marvel Comics and *Playboy* magazine.[11] Hefner, more so than Lee, has become something of a pop culture punchline, with his revolving door of ever-younger girlfriends and wives and his ever-present bathrobe and pipe ensemble; the fact that Lee is mistaken for Hefner, however, suggests that in this context the joke comes at his expense.

In *Iron Man 3* (Shane Black, 2013) and *Guardians of the Galaxy*, Lee reprises his role as a lecher. In the former, he appears as an overly enthusiastic judge at a televised beauty pageant; in the latter, Rocket Raccoon spies him flirting with a much younger woman on the planet Xandar (he is credited as "Xandarian Ladies' Man"). These seem to be much more straightforward examples of a cameo-as-joke: as Yacowar writes with regard to Hitchcock's cameos, "their first effect is comedy, our chuckle of recognition as we spot the chubby elf and [our] pride that we caught the in-joke" (217). The viewer's insider knowledge of Lee's extra-textual significance is rewarded and ironized by the additional "horny old man" gag. The combination of these two levels of meaning emphasizes the cameo as a moment of levity in the film. His appearance in *Iron Man 2* (Favreau, 2010) is arguably even more straightforward a joke: as in *Iron Man*, Stark mistakes Lee for a famous old man, but this time it is Larry King. The fact that the audience recognizes Lee, but Stark misrecognizes him as King, becomes the source of the humor.

Fantastic Four: Rise of the Silver Surfer (Tim Story, 2007), a direct homage to *Fantastic Four Annual* no. 3—the issue in which Lee and Kirby are turned away from the wedding of Mr. Fantastic and the Invisible Woman—features an inversion of the misrecognition depicted in the aforementioned cameos. In the comic, Lee and Kirby are refused entry to the ceremony; as they walk away, they threaten to use their creative authority over the superhero family to write them into more dangerous situations as retribution: "We'll show 'em, Jack! Let's get back to the bullpen and start writing the next ish!" (fig. 11.3). The filmic Lee, by comparison, has only his reputation to rely on: "Really, I'm Stan Lee!" he protests as a security guard escorts him away. He is not seen or heard from again in the film; no longer a creative agent, he has no leverage with which to threaten the superhero family. This is the fundamental difference between Marvel Comics' "Stan Lee" and the figure presented in the MCU.

The next substantial category to emerge in Lee's cavalcade of cameos is the bystander. Lee's bystander bears witness to, but does not interact

11.3. A self-deprecating cameo. Lee and Kirby are turned away from Reed Richards and Sue Storm's wedding. *Fantastic Four Annual* no. 3 (Oct. 1965).

with, superheroes (or other super-powered beings) and their superpowers. The first instance of this type of role can be seen in *Trial of the Incredible Hulk*, where he can briefly be seen in the jury box after David Banner has transformed into the Hulk. As a juror, Lee seems to wield control over the Hulk's destiny by partly determining the outcome of the trial. The scene, however, is merely a dream; in the reality of the film, Lee has no presence and therefore no authority over the Hulk's destiny or narrative. As with his contemporary role as the "public face" of Marvel, Lee only *appears* to be involved. Likewise, in *X-Men: The Last Stand* (Brett Ratner, 2006), Lee is seen watering his lawn with a hose when Jean Grey's telekinetic powers cause the water to float upward, to his astonishment. This scene is a flashback that occurs early in the film, and is thereby temporally separated from the rest of the narrative. Lee's presence is associated not with the present tense but with the past, echoing the disparity between Lee's strictly honorary role in 2006 and his creative centrality in the 1960s as the co-creator and writer of the X-Men.

The existence of superheroes in the Marvel Universe often puts bystanders in danger, and the recurring theme of Lee-as-victim springs from that theme. In both *Spider-Man* (Sam Raimi, 2002) and *Spider-Man 2* (Sam Raimi, 2004), Lee appears as an extra during large public altercations between Spider-Man and his enemies (the Green Goblin and Dr. Octopus). In both cases, he protects another bystander from coming to harm as a result of the chaos. In *Daredevil* (Mark Steven Johnson, 2003), it is young (and recently blinded) Matt Murdock who prevents Lee from coming to harm when he almost walks into oncoming traffic. A humorous twist on this motif is presented in *The Amazing Spider-Man* (Marc Webb, 2012), wherein Lee plays a librarian at Peter Parker's high school. A brawl between Spider-Man and the Lizard plays out on campus and eventually makes its way into the library, where Lee—immersed in the classical music playing on his headphones—casually goes about his work, blissfully unaware of the imminent danger.

It is *The Incredible Hulk* (Louis Leterrier, 2008), however, that takes the victimization of Lee to its logical conclusion. In an early chase scene, Bruce Banner is injured in a soda bottling plant in Brazil; some of his gamma-irradiated blood spills onto the conveyor belt and into one of the open bottles, contaminating it. That bottle is imported to America and consumed by Lee, who is poisoned by it. This is the clearest case in which he is not only put in danger by his characters but actively harmed by them (if only inadvertently). His own creation not only no longer needs him; it has symbolically turned against him. Given Lee's function in these cameos as a stand-in for the history of Marvel, this violence against him is a complicated moment: his very presence affirms his symbolic importance to the company as creator, but his possible death-by-poisoning simultaneously suggests his obsolescence; it represents a subtle renunciation not only of his creative role in the future of the Hulk but also, by extension, of the character's comics origins. In short, it implicitly signals the transformation of Marvel Comics into Marvel Studios.

Overwhelmingly, Lee is represented in his cameos as a blue-collar or working-class individual, a role providing an implicit commentary on the status of comic book writers and artists. As Richard Polsky puts it, "illustrators and storytellers were treated [by the comic book industry] as blue-collar workers and paid by the page rather than given a salary. It was all about productivity, not the quality of your effort" (33). As editor and later publisher of Marvel Comics, Lee was definitively *not* a blue-collar worker, which makes this tendency in the cameos deeply ironic. In contrast to freelance artists like Kirby, who toiled for decades without job security or adequate credit, Lee was (as one of his nicknames suggests) "The Man," a high-ranking employee who ensured that he was seen "as indispensable to the company's identity, no matter its owners" (Hatfield 89). In interviews, he tends to defend the company's rights over those of the artists in their employ; he seems to think like a businessman,[12] and yet he prefers to align himself with artists rather than management.[13]

It is this vision of "Stan Lee" that appears in films like *X-Men* (Bryan Singer, 2000). In one of his earliest cameos, Lee is seen as a hot-dog vendor on the beach where a mutated US senator washes ashore. Here the bystander is given a working-class twist, and hot dogs substitute for comics as the product that Lee, a salesman rather than an artist, is selling. In *Hulk* (Ang Lee, 2003), Lee appears as a security guard at the research facility that employs Bruce Banner. Another guard—played by television's Hulk, Lou Ferrigno, in another cameo appearance—accompanies him; together they represent the history of the character. Notably, they are exiting the building as Eric Bana's Bruce—the present of the character—enters it. Although this incident is not as violent as the one in *The Incredible Hulk* dispatching Lee by poisoning, the implication is the same: out with the old, in with the new.

In *Fantastic Four*, Lee's cameo is unusual in that he plays an actual character from the comics: Willie Lumpkin, the mailman servicing the superhero team's headquarters at the Baxter Building. In this scene, he welcomes Reed Richards / Mr. Fantastic back to the Baxter, and then delivers a large bundle of past-due bill notices: "I've got the usual for you," he says as he hands over the delivery. Though genial, Lumpkin is nevertheless the bearer of bad news, and his appearance is not necessarily one that is welcomed, diegetically speaking. In terms of audience enjoyment, however, the combination of the extra-diegetic Lee and the comics character Willie more than offsets the ostensibly negative implications of his delivery.

In *Captain America: The Winter Soldier* (Anthony and Joe Russo, 2014), Lee's cameo combines the blue-collar and victim types. Reprising his role as a security guard, this time at the Smithsonian Institution, he plays the scene tongue-in-cheek. His character, noticing during his nightly rounds that the historical Captain America costume has been stolen, fears that he will be blamed for the theft and lose his job. As in other examples of this type noted above, the role paints Lee as a blue-collar laborer rather than a creative/artistic type, which stands in stark contrast to many of Hitchcock's self-representations—for instance, as a photographer and possible director surrogate (*Young and Innocent*; Afred Hitchcock, 1937). These examples present ironic inversions of Lee's status as creative genius (in the eyes of some viewers), or, at the very least, implicit affirmations that his creative days are behind him.

The final recurring character trait that I want to discuss in Lee's cameos is obliviousness—an attribute not unlike the lack of awareness that Lee's librarian character exhibits in *The Amazing Spider-Man*. In the three cases to which we now turn our attention, Lee's lack of knowledge manifests itself, when combined with extra-textual knowledge of his persona, in another kind of irony.

In *Captain America: The First Avenger* (Joe Johnston, 2011), Lee appears as a high-ranking military officer in attendance at a ceremony in Captain America's honor; when the superhero fails to appear on stage, a man in a suit comes out to explain his absence. Lee, mistaking this anonymous officer for Captain America, says, "I thought he'd be taller." There are two sources of humor: first, we would expect a high-ranking military official to be able to identify his country's most famous and celebrated soldier; second, we would certainly expect Lee—who did not create Captain America but did reintroduce him to comics in the 1960s as a member of the Avengers—to recognize him.

Lee's role in *The Amazing Spider-Man 2* (Webb, 2014) is similar: at Peter Parker's graduation ceremony, Lee remarks that he thinks he recognizes him. As the co-creator of the character, viewers would expect at least this much, though his lack of certainty might also signify a variety of things in addition to the dramatic irony. The line calls attention to the startling difference between the skateboarding Peter as played by Andrew Garfield compared to the meek, nebbishy Peter originally portrayed in Lee's comics; as such, the cameo may function similarly to the *X-Men* no. 98 example discussed earlier, in which Lee remarked on the difference between the behavior of his X-Men compared to Chris Claremont's. Most simply, the line may be a cheap joke at Lee's expense: at his advanced age, his memory may not be what it once was. The humor of these cameos also hinges on the tension between the two prevalent understandings of Lee discussed earlier in this essay: as the author/creator of these characters and as the company man more concerned with promoting the books than writing them.[14]

As mentioned above, one of Lee's most ambitious creative decisions while co-creating the Marvel Universe was to locate his narratives in real-world locations—rather than the fictional cities of DC Comics (e.g., Metropolis, Gotham City, Coast City, etc.)—and in New York City, in particular. This choice facilitated the crossovers and diegetic coherence that defined the universe of Marvel's comics and, later, the MCU. In *The Avengers* (Joss Whedon, 2012), Lee appears on a television during a montage of man-on-the-street reactions in the wake of the film's climactic battle for New York. His response is disgruntled and disbelieving: "Superheroes in New York?

Gimme a break!" As the creative agent that placed superheroes in New York in the first place, his line here is particularly ironic.

In the two *Thor* films, Lee's obliviousness takes on particular significance. In the first film (Kenneth Branagh, 2011), Lee can be seen at the site of Mjolnir's desert landing in New Mexico. Various citizens are attempting to pick up Thor's hammer, but as in the legend of the sword in the stone, none are worthy, and therefore no one can move it. Lee's attempt is particularly laughable: he hitches Mjolnir to his pickup truck and accelerates. The bumper of his truck detaches before the mythical hammer budges even slightly. Oblivious to this fact, he asks, "Did it work?" This scene speaks implicitly to the comic book industry and to the status of creative personnel within it: in short, attempts to profit from your work creating or writing for characters like Thor are as fruitless and futile as attempts to move Mjolnir. Again, such employees are blue-collar in the sense that they are hired and paid for a particular task: royalties based on the success of that work are not part of the deal. As Lee put it in a recent interview: "I was always a Marvel employee, a writer for hire and, later, part of management.... Marvel always owned the rights to these characters. If I owned them, I probably wouldn't be talking to you now" (Hochman). His cameo in *Thor* dramatizes this situation, and even laughs at his supposed misfortune. In the film, Lee seems like a fool for trying to profit from this mythical found object; in reality, this is the stuff of countless protracted lawsuits: even Lee himself has sued Marvel for a larger share of movie profits in the wake of the first *Spider-Man* film's runaway success (Kaplan 72). Nevertheless, we must also acknowledge the disparity between Lee's contemporary status as a powerless figurehead and his implicit alignment with freelancers: Lee's self-representation (as in the interview quoted above) and his cameo in *Thor* are in sync insofar as they present a revisionist history in which Lee has always been at the mercy of his corporate overlords. Like his other cameos, his role in *Thor* must be read ironically: the very fact that he appears onscreen at all suggests a continued degree of influence, if not creative agency; as a credited executive producer on this and all other Marvel films, there is no doubt that Lee continues to profit from his decades-old comics work—unlike his former collaborators.

In *Thor: The Dark World* (Alan Taylor, 2013), Lee is depicted as a patient at a psychiatric hospital. While his exact condition is not made clear in his short scene, it can be safely assumed that his experience includes constant supervision, a strictly regimented schedule, mandatory medications, and so on; he may have been admitted against his will and is unable to leave. In short, he has personal autonomy only in a very restricted sense. Additionally, his personal property—in this case, a shoe—has been taken by a fellow patient for the purpose of illustrating a scientific theory. (The punchline of the scene: "Can I have my shoe back?") This cameo most clearly articulates Lee's position within the MCU in which he so often appears: he has no autonomy, and his work is taken from him and used without his creative participation. Requests to return this property are played as jokes. Both *Thor* films thus place Lee in situations where he tries and fails to claim or reclaim property, an almost perfect appropriation of Jack Kirby's legal struggle to retain his original artwork—which *was* his legal property—from Marvel.[15] Whereas *The Incredible Hulk* dramatized Lee's lack of necessity in the MCU, *Thor* and its sequel mock the possibility of the former Marvel editor wanting or having some claim over the intellectual properties he helped to create. In so doing, however, they dramatize a situation more similar to the one faced by freelance artists than to the one faced by Lee, who is seen by many fans not just as the mouthpiece of the company but also as the enforcer of its exploitative policies vis-à-vis artists.

The final remaining cameo is perhaps the one that most resoundingly echoes Lee's appearances in the comic books that he wrote himself. In *Spider-Man 3* (Raimi, 2007), his persona as it comes across in comics columns like "Stan's Soapbox" reemerges. Stan and Peter Parker stand next to each other in Times Square, facing an LED ticker announcing a celebration of Spider-Man scheduled for that day. Lee turns to Peter and tells him that one man can make a difference after all; he even ends his appearance with one of his signature sign-offs—"'Nuff said!"—before walking away. (I suppose "Excelsior!" would have been too much.) Like many of the other cameos, this one can be taken two ways: within the diegesis, Lee's character admires Spider-Man and his positive contributions to the community; outside of it, he is congratulating himself for what a difference *he* has made in creating these long-lasting and influential characters. It's an almost complete inversion of Lee's oblivious appearances in *Captain America*, *The Amazing Spider-Man 2*, and *The Avengers*. Here, he seems to know more than he lets on, maintaining his extra-diegetic knowledge and persona and expressing, rather than suppressing or ironically inverting, his personality. In *The Avengers*, he ironizes and dismisses his contributions to culture; in *Spider-Man 3*, he is for once allowed to celebrate both them and himself. In so doing, he takes the appropriation of Kirby et al.'s exploitation to its logical conclusion:

he erases his collaborators from history entirely, placing total responsibility on the shoulders of "one person": himself.

Stan Lee's cameos are clearly more complex and loaded than one might expect, given their treatment in these films as throwaway jokes. As others have noted in various contexts, cameo actors are ontologically distinct from other characters in the films in which they appear. Indeed, they might be considered ontologically *unstable*, insofar as their reception is based more on extra-textual knowledge that will vary from viewer to viewer: "Stan Lee" to one viewer may be "elderly extra" to another, and we cannot disregard the notion that Lee's persona is just as much a construction as the personas of the superheroes he co-created are. Moreover, some of the viewers who recognize Lee may worship his contributions to popular culture unconditionally, while others may resent his tireless self-promotion, especially at the expense of his under-recognized (both culturally and financially) collaborators.

Lee's history with Marvel is full of contradictions and disputing narratives: the supertext of his collective Marvel film cameos provides yet another competing understanding that presents ironic variations on his public persona, portraying him as a blue-collar laborer, as a bystander on the periphery of the action, and as a victim of his own creations; most importantly, these cameos comment on Lee's creative obsolescence with regard to the contemporary film versions of the characters. And yet another contradiction emerges here: if Lee were truly and totally obsolete to the Marvel of today, would he appear in these films at all? Ultimately, his presence in twenty-one Marvel films between 1989 and 2014 confirms that the "real" Stan Lee is not the writer, the co-creator, the editor, or the publisher of Marvel Comics, but the huckster—not only of Marvel, but of himself.

....

NOTES

1. To avoid these scenes leaking online early, Marvel does not attach its post-credits tags to its films until release day. This being an advance screening, the additional scene was not present, which prompted this particular audience to boo loudly.

2. Lee did not think he would appear because he did not create the central characters in *Guardians of the Galaxy* (Looker). There is some precedent for him appearing in such cameos, however: Lee did not create Captain America,

either, but he did cameos in both Marvel Studios–produced *Captain America* films.

3. The story of Lee's ascendency within the company is more fully fleshed out in a variety of books (see Raphael and Spurgeon; Ro; and Howe). Lee has also co-written an autobiography (Lee and Mair).

4. As suggested by the Hatfield quotation above, the credits themselves were at least somewhat misleading insofar as artists had at least as much of a hand in narrating (and therefore writing, in a manner of speaking) the stories as the credited writer did. The situation was eventually redressed with amended "co-plotter" and "co-creator" credits for Ditko and Kirby, respectively (Raphael 214–215; Hatfield 91).

5. It is first established in this issue that a version of Marvel Comics exists within the fictional universe in which these stories take place; Lee and Kirby's stories are based on the real adventures of the superheroes in that world, and are written in consultation with the characters themselves!

6. Although it's impossible to determine the nature of Lee and Kirby's collaboration on this particular issue without primary documents (one page of Kirby's pencils appears in Mark Evanier's *Kirby: King of Comics* on p. 120), it seems very much in character for Lee to write himself into a story and for Kirby to execute the cameos without ever showing their faces.

7. Lee was, however, the editor of Marvel and thereby exercised control over the book's content in that capacity.

8. For instance, in *Fantastic Four* (Tim Story, 2005), Lee appears as Willie Lumpkin, the Baxter Building's doorman; in the film's sequel (Tim Story, 2007), he plays himself.

9. Derek Johnson notes that "by 2004, 83 percent of Marvel's total revenues (inclusive of publishing)" were from licensing its characters to film studios (9). Comics sales presumably make up an undisclosed fraction of the remaining 17 percent.

10. Stay after the post-credits scene in any Marvel movie and listen to the conversations happening around you: you are sure to hear Marvel experts holding court in the theater, explaining who the purple man was at the end of *The Avengers* (Joss Whedon, 2012), or what the chanting meant at the end of *X-Men: Days of Future Past* (Bryan Singer, 2014).

11. An additional (perhaps even "No-Prize" worthy) commonality: both worked with Pamela Anderson (Hefner in *Playboy* and Lee in the short-lived animated television series *Stripperella* [MTV, 2003–2004]).

12. "If the books didn't sell, the publisher went broke—and a lot of publishers did go broke. Marvel took a gamble doing what it did" (Hochman).

13. "They [Kirby and Ditko] were hired as freelance artists, and they worked as freelance artists. At some point they apparently felt they should be getting more money. Fine, it was up to them to talk to the publisher. It had nothing to do with me. I would have liked to have gotten more money too" (Hochman).

14. To this point, Lee has gone on the record saying that he's never heard of Ultron, the titular villain of *Avengers: Age of Ultron* (Whedon, 2015) (Hochman); Ultron was introduced in *Avengers* no. 55 (Aug. 1968), on which Lee is the credited editor.

15. On this lawsuit, see Evanier 200–205.

WORKS CITED

Baron, Cynthia. "*The Player*'s Parody of Hollywood: A Different Kind of Suture." In *Postmodernism in the Cinema*. Ed. Cristina Degli-Esposti. New York: Berghahn Books, 1998. 21–43. Print.

Evanier, Mark. *Kirby: King of Comics*. New York: Abrams, 2008. Print.

Fokkema, Aleid. "The Author: Postmodernism's Stock Character." In *The Author as Character: Representing Historical Writers in Western Literature*. Eds. Paul Franssen and A. J. Hoenselaars. Cranbury, NJ: Associated University Presses, 1999. 39–51. Print.

Hatfield, Charles. *Hand of Fire: The Comics Art of Jack Kirby*. Jackson: University Press of Mississippi, 2012. Print.

Hochman, David. "The Playboy Interview: Stan Lee on Superheroes, Marvel and Being Just Another Pretty Face." *Playboy*, 31 March 2014. Web. http://playboysfw.kinja.com/the-playboy-interview-stan-lee-on-superheroes-marvel-1554168459.

Howe, Sean. *Marvel Comics: The Untold Story*. Toronto: HarperCollins Canada, 2012. Print.

Johnson, Derek. "Cinematic Destiny: Marvel Studios and the Trade Stories of Industrial Convergence." *Cinema Journal* 52.1 (Fall 2012): 1–24. Print.

Kaplan, Arie. *Masters of the Comic Book Universe Revealed! Will Eisner, Stan Lee, Neil Gaiman, and More*. Chicago: Chicago Review Press, 2006. Print.

Lee, Stan, and George Mair. *Excelsior! The Amazing Life of Stan Lee*. New York: Boxtree, 2002. Print.

Leitch, Thomas M. *Find the Director and Other Hitchcock Games*. Athens: University of Georgia Press, 1991. Print.

Looker, Matt. "Stan Lee Won't Cameo in Guardians of the Galaxy." *Total Film*, 23 January 2014. Web. www.totalfilm.com/news/stan-lee-won-t-cameo-in-guardians-of-the-galaxy.

Mathijs, Ernest. "Cronenberg Connected: Cameo Acting, Cult Stardom and

Supertexts." In *Cult Film Stardom*. Eds. Kate Egan and Sarah Thomas. New York: Palgrave Macmillan, 2013. 144–162. Print.

McGill, Robert. *The Treacherous Imagination: Intimacy, Ethics, and Autobiographical Fiction*. Columbus: Ohio State University Press, 2013. Print.

Polsky, Richard. *The Art Prophets: The Artists, Dealers, and Tastemakers Who Shook the Art World*. New York: Other Press, 2011. Print.

Raphael, Jordan, and Tom Spurgeon. *Stan Lee and the Rise and Fall of the American Comic Book*. Chicago: Chicago Review Press, 2003. Print.

Ro, Ronin. *Tales to Astonish: Jack Kirby, Stan Lee and the American Comic Book Revolution*. New York: Bloomsbury, 2004. Print.

Yacowar, Maurice. *Hitchcock's British Films*, 2nd ed. Detroit: Wayne State University Press, 2010. Print.

Schrödinger's Cape

THE QUANTUM SERIALITY
OF THE MARVEL MULTIVERSE

WILLIAM PROCTOR

O n the surface, quantum physics and narrative theory are not easy bedfellows. In fact, some may argue that the two fields are incommensurable paradigms and that any attempt to prove otherwise would be a foolhardy endeavor, more akin to intellectual trickery and sleight-of-hand than a prism with which to view narrative systems. Yet I find myself repeatedly confronted by these two ostensibly incompatible theories converging as I explore the vast narrative networks associated with fictional world-building—most notably those belonging to the comic book multiverses of Marvel and DC Comics, which, as Nick Lowe argues, "are the largest narrative constructions in human history (exceeding, for example, the vast body of myth, legend and story that underlies Greek and Latin literature)" (Kaveney 25).

Contemporary quantum theory postulates that the universe is not a singular body progressing linearly along a unidirectional spatiotemporal pathway—as exponents of the Newtonian classic physics model believe—but, rather, a multiverse comprising alternate worlds, parallel dimensions, and multiple timelines. Both Marvel and *bête noire* DC Comics embrace the multiverse concept that allows multiple iterations, versions, and reinterpretations of their character populations to coexist within a spatiotemporal framing principle that shares remarkable commonalities with the quantum model. Where Marvel and DC deviate from one another, however, is that the latter utilizes the conceit as an intra-medial model for its panoply of comic books, whereas the Marvel multiverse functions as a transmedia firmament encapsulating an entire catalog within its narrative rubric, a strategy that is analogous with the quantum paradigm.

To offer a brief example, one to which I shall later return, part of the great pleasure for readers of vast narrative networks, especially comics, is the principle of continuity, which works both serially and sequentially to construct a storyworld of fragmented episodes, or "micro-narratives," into a unified "macro-structure" (Ryan 373). For DC Comics, films such as *Batman Begins* (Christopher Nolan, 2005) or *The Man of Steel* (Zack Snyder, 2013) do not belong to an overarching multiverse but instead operate outside of official narrative parameters. This positioning raises significant questions about legitimacy and canon, questions that matter a great deal to ardent fans and explorers of the kinds of vast narratives comics explore. The Marvel multiverse takes a different approach: it is an exemplar of what I describe as "quantum seriality"—that is, a labyrinthine narrative network that incorporates a wide array of transmedia expressions into an ontological order that rationalizes divergent textualities as part and parcel of the same story-system that canonizes *all* Marvel creations—whether in film, TV, or, indeed, comics—as official and legitimate. Unlike in DC, "in the Marvel universe, everything has happened" (Weaver 170).

A BRIEF HISTORY OF THE MULTIVERSE

In 1957, Hugh Everett III's "many-world interpretation" (MWI) challenged the classical physics model by hypothesizing that the universe is a many splintered organism of parallel branches perpetually reproducing and expanding. Thus, instead of one universe, we have a multiverse comprising an immeasurable array of alternative realities and parallel worlds. Everett developed his thesis as a way to solve the Schrödinger's Cat conundrum, which had its beginnings as a jocular thought experiment but became one of the principal cornerstones of the field. Angered by a subset of quantum theorists who he believed had misinterpreted his work, Erwin Schrödinger crafted his thought experiment to ridicule the Copenhagen interpretation of quantum physics, which claimed that observation or measurement was the key catalyst in the performance of atoms and electrons. If an experiment remains unobserved, then the outcome remains unknowable and exists in a superposition between two states, thus presenting a quantum aporia. Schrödinger's thought puzzle features a cat, a Geiger counter, a vial of acid, and a radioactive substance inside a steel chamber. The radioactive substance may decay—but there is an equal probability that it will not. If it decays, the acid will be released and the cat will die; if it does not, the cat will live. The paradox presented by Schrödinger, however, posits that until the steel chamber is opened and observed, then the cat exists in what is called a "superposition of states," that is, both alive and dead at the same time. The act of observation causes the superposition—or, alternatively, the wave function—to collapse, and the result is that the cat is definitively either alive or dead.

For Everett, however, the act of observation does not collapse the wave function or solve the superposition but creates "a bifurcation at the moment in time where the measurement or observation is made" (Gribbin 26). Thus, the superposition does not collapse into one state, "but the entire universe splits" into "two equally real worlds, superimposed on one another, but never able to influence one another—a universe with a dead cat and a universe with a live cat" (30). This quantum event, therefore, creates an alternative timeline or world that continues along its own pathway through time and space, completely cut off from the parallel line. Further bifurcations or forks in the road splinter into divergent pathways, rather like a branching tree that continues to grow new limbs ad infinitum (although, unlike a tree, the multiverse has no main trunk, and thus no hierarchical arrangement).

Schrödinger's Cat, however, does not do sufficient justice to the complexity of the quantum world, its growth spurts, and its perpetual reproductions. The thought experiment contains only two possible outcomes (or two "eigenvalues," in quantum language)—a cat that is alive or a cat that is dead. Chance and choice are also quantum events, so that every decision that we, as individuals, make also generates splinters in the space-time continuum. I might have made a different choice somewhere in the past that created an alternative pathway where I am not sitting here writing this chapter, but relishing the comfort and ostentation of a royal palace as I while away my days as king. In fact, quantum theory insists that my alternative life as king and defender of the faith is a reality somewhere across the multiverse, although I cannot possess the necessary cosmic skills to visit for tea and scones. As science writer John Gribbin states, "an infinite number of worlds allows for an infinite number of variations and, indeed, an infinite number of identical copies. In that sense, in an infinite Universe, anything is possible, including an infinite number of other Earths, where there are people identical to you and me going about their lives exactly as we do; and an infinite number of other Earths where you are Prime Minister and I am King. And so on" (8).

To complicate matters even further, imagine throwing a die. Rather than a bifurcation, we have multiple "eigenvalues" that split reality into six alternative universes. Some of these may continue unaffected, as identical copies of the pre-roll universe, and others may involve profound shifts. For a lot of people, this is nothing more than an intellectual parlor-game, one fit for *Star Trek* and other science fictions. In 1957, Everett's theorem, retroactively christened the "many-worlds interpretation," gained little credence and was considered highly speculative, yet these radical and contentious ideas have since become common parlance in contemporary science and culture (with the understanding that the existence of a multiverse remains a matter of intense debate, with many detractors continuing to repudiate the paradigm as science fiction).

What is also confounding is that scientists in the field of quantum theory cannot yet adequately explain why the quantum world behaves as it does, although, even more remarkably, quantum physics is essential for "the design of computer chips, which are in everything from your mobile phone to the supercomputers used in weather forecasting"; indeed, quantum physics explains "how large molecules like DNA and RNA, the molecules of life, work" (14–15). The impact of quantum physics has made a substantial mark in media cultures, too, such as film, TV, literature, and, of course, comic books. The concept of parallel worlds, alternate dimensions, and temporal paradoxes is a well-established convention of the science-fiction and fantasy genres in multiple media platforms, including television (*Fringe, Star Trek, Sliders*), film (*Source Code, Mr. Nobody, Sliding Doors*), and literature (Stephen King, Michael Moorcock, Thomas Pynchon).

What we can see here is the impact of quantum physics on popular culture texts, one which implies a discursive relay between the two fields. In *Fiction in the Quantum Universe*, Susan Strehle adroitly demonstrates the influence of the "new physics" on literary composition that resulted in a new kind of literature she labels "actualism," which she describes as "a literary version of the reality constituted by fundamentally new physical theories in the first half of the twentieth century." For Strehle, "changes in physical theories inspire changes in a culture's general attitudes, and art both responds to and shapes these assumptions. Physics and fiction inhabit the same planet, however divergent their discourses about it may be . . . [and] the new physics [has] exerted a profound influence on contemporary culture" (8–9).

Yet it would be rather myopic to establish a historical connection between Everett's many-worlds interpretation as a template for the hyperdiegetic principle at work within vast narratives such as *Star Trek*, *Fringe*, or the novels of King and Moorcock. In "Parallel Worlds," Andrew Crumey demonstrates that the multiverse has considerable vintage that predates the quantum paradigm, "cropping up in philosophy and literature since ancient times." Over two millennia ago, Democritus (c. 460–370 BC) thought "the universe to be made of atoms moving in an infinite void" that would "combine and recombine in every possible way: the world we see around us is just one arrangement among many that are all certain to appear" (Crumey, "Parallel Worlds"). Likewise, the ancient Greek philosopher Epicurus (341–270 BC) believed the future to be a multiple series of paths rather than strictly causal; Cicero celebrated this aspect of Epicureanism in a passage of his *Academia*: "Would you believe that there exist innumerable worlds . . . so there are countless persons in exactly similar spots with our names, our honours, our achievements, our minds, our shapes, our ages, discussing the very same subject?" (ibid). In an essay entitled "Of a History of Events Which Have Not Happened," Isaac D'Israeli, father of the future prime minister of Britain, Benjamin Disraeli, wrote of a series of "what ifs" where he imagined Cromwell and Spain united in alliance, or a Muslim Britain where "we should have worn turbans [and] combed our beards instead of shaving them" (ibid). "What If?" narratives feature prominently in the Marvel multiverse as counterfactual variations of canonical stories (a notion to be discussed further below). Readers of Philip K. Dick, Harry Turtledove, and countless others would no doubt recognize this concept as the basis of the "alternate history," an established convention of contemporary science fiction.

Even the term "multiverse" has a historic lineage: in 1895, William James referred to a "multiverse of experience." And four years later, poet Frederick Orde Ward wrote: "within, without, / nowhere and everywhere; / Now bedrock of the mighty Multiverse." But the usage of the word as a way to describe the cosmological system of parallel worlds comes from a different source: the popular novelist Michael Moorcock:

> I came up with the term itself in a story called *The Sundered Worlds* published in *Science Fiction Adventures* in 1962. The idea of a "quasi-infinite" series of interlocking worlds, each a fraction different from the next, where millions of versions of our realities are played out, fascinated me from the age of seventeen, when I had drafted the first version of what was to become *The Eternal Champion*. By 1965, when I was writing the

Jerry Cornelius stories, I put the notion to more obvious literary and satirical uses, but for me by then the Multiverse had already assumed physical reality. (32)

Consider, also, Jorge Luis Borges's celebrated short story "The Garden of Forking Paths," first published in 1941, almost two decades prior to Everett's postulations. In the story, it is revealed that the grandfather of one of the characters (Ts'ui Pên, grandfather of Dr. Yu Tsun) has succeeded in constructing a vast fictional narrative that is essentially a spatiotemporal labyrinth comprising "an infinite series of times, in a growing, dizzying network of divergent, convergent and parallel times. This network of times which approached one another, forked, broke off, or were unaware of one another for centuries, embraces all possibilities of time. We do not exist in the majority of these times; in some you exist, and not I; in others I, and not you; in others, both of us. . . . Time forks perpetually towards innumerable futures" (53).

It is remarkable that Borges's story predates and prophesizes the coming of Everett's many-worlds theorem and has so many astounding commonalities with contemporary scientific explanations of the mechanics of multiversal design. In *Programming the Universe*, physicist Seth Lloyd details a conversation he had with Borges in 1983 where he asked if he was aware of the similarities between his short story and quantum theory. Borges stated that he did not intentionally use Everett's theory—indeed, how could he, given the temporal distance between the two works: "Borges had not been influenced by work on quantum mechanics, [yet] he was not surprised that the laws of physics mirrored ideas from literature. After all, physicists were readers, too" (101). As Crumey stated, "physicists are not only readers, but part of history, and the multiverse . . . has a history far older than that of quantum theory." From this perspective, the quantum model predates Everett's theories and the quantum physicists themselves by a significant temporal distance, and cultural and scientific processes are rightly viewed as being entwined in discourse rather than as part of a one-way linear stream between source and influence.

THE MARVEL MULTIVERSE: QUANTUM SERIALITY

In "Film Futures," David Bordwell argues that both Borges's forking paths and quantum theory were inadequate framing principles for the analysis of narrative systems. Bordwell deconstructs a number of films[1] that present "forking-path" narratives as limited and ultimately linear, none of which "hints at the radical possibilities opened up by Borges or the physicists" (89). "None of these plots confronts the ultimate Borgesian demands," continues Bordwell. Instead, "we have something far simpler, corresponding to a more cognitively manageable conception of what forking paths would be like in our own lives" (90). By analyzing a set of forking-path narratives, Bordwell astutely demonstrates the limits of these narratives as linear, and essentially as being contained within traditional narrative schema; they certainly were not emblematic of Borges's limitless sprawl. "So instead of the infinite, radically diverse set of alternatives evoked by the parallel-universes conception, we have a set narrow both in number and in core conditions," he concludes. "In fiction, alternative futures seem pretty limited affairs" (90).[2]

It is not Bordwell's analysis that I wish to challenge here—as usual, he performs his examinations with a verve and dexterity that shines a discerning light on the mechanics of narrative. The limitations of his study are not in the realm of scholarly performance, however, but instead in his choice of texts, which excludes vast narrative story-systems that operate multiversally. Instead of Bordwell's narrow set of temporal parameters and core conditions, the Marvel multiverse is a sprawling metropolis comprising alternative realities and parallel narrative systems that comingle within a transmedia nebula. As Bordwell "zooms in" to single units of film, it behooves us to "zoom out" to take in the intricate vista of the vast narrative that the house of Marvel built.

The size and scope of the Marvel storyworld cannot be underestimated; an exhaustible catalog would be an impossible feat, especially when one takes into account the fact that new scaffolding is regularly being welded to the narrative architecture on a weekly basis. Even the latest edition of *The Marvel Encyclopedia* is out of date; indeed, it will always be out of date as soon as new editions are released. Thus, Marvel is not only a vast narrative, but an "unfolding text," which Lance Parkin describes as "fiction based around a common character, a set of characters, or location that has had some form of serial publication" ("Truths" 13). As Parkin goes on to explain, "the works that make up an unfolding text can have a single author, particularly in their early stages, but are typically written by many. An unfolding text is often not a single series; most contain a number of distinct series, in different media, usually with different creators and even intended audiences" (ibid.). What I would like to do here, then, rather than producing an exhaustive catalog of Marvel's multiversal design (an impossible endeavor even for a book-length study or a PhD thesis), is to illustrate how the vast narrative network of Marvel works as an exemplar of quantum seriality.

For regular readers of Marvel Comics, and, by extension, other sequential story-systems, the principle of continuity is an important affective site that provides a great deal of pleasure (Duncan and Smith 190; Reynolds 38; Dittmer 182; Geraghty 16). In *Building Imaginary Worlds*, Mark J. P. Wolf drafts an architectural blueprint for world-building and highlights the necessity of an "ontological realm"—that is, one with causal, spatial, and temporal interconnectivities—as a fundamental enhancement that allows successful world-building to take place. Consistency within the narrative fabric is an important characteristic of sequential storytelling and can be described as "the degree to which world details are plausible, feasible, and without contradiction" (Wolf 43). Wolf observes that "this requires a careful integration of details and attention to the way everything is connected together. Lacking consistency, a world may begin to appear sloppily constructed, or even random and disconnected" (ibid.).

As Parkin argues, "the natural instinct for the audience of any serial drama or other long-running series is to think that the fictional world is consistent" ("Canonicity" 253). One of the methods creators use to render a consistent serial system is an adherence to continuity, or the narrative history of a storyworld across a multiplicity of textual locations. Individual micro-narratives should "remember" other elements in the continuity network (Harvey 1). "Readers," claims Umberto Eco, "are supposed to interpret [the storyworld] as referring to a possible state of affairs" (64). For Eco, the storyworld is a "doxastic," or believable construct, a notion that dovetails with Matt Hills's concept of "hyperdiegesis"—that is, an interconnected, cohesive system that operates "according to principles of logic and extension" (137). One factor that all these conceptual designations share as a common principle is cohesion and consistency: whether it is in Wolf's secondary world, Eco's doxastic realm, Hills's hyperdiegesis, or Otsaku Eiji's "world-program," the obedience to a cohesive diegetic history is a prevalent feature of serial world-building.

At its most basic level, continuity can be described as the linkages between episodic sequences that connect "small narratives" into a rational and coherent "grand narrative" of metatextuality (Eiji 109). Richard Reynolds describes a serial metatext as the "summation of all existing texts" in the story system that function according to relations of chronology and causation (43). In short, a storyworld is a fictional history endowed with memory. Continuity consists of all previous stories within the narrative continuum, in some cases involving decades of material, "which the story-line must take into consideration in order to preserve coherence and consistency within the narrative" (Miettinen 6). It is possible, therefore, for readers of the serial macro-structure to cement individual micro-narratives into a chronological sequence, which should correspond with unidirectional models of time—even if sequences are produced and presented out of linear alignment.

At the time of writing, Marvel publishes in excess of fifty monthly and bimonthly comic book series, many of which feature characters that have been principal players for over seventy years, such as Captain America, Sub-Mariner, and the original Human Torch, Jim Hammond. During its resurgence in the early 1960s, Marvel introduced characters that have since become household names, such as Spider-Man, Hulk, Thor, Iron Man, and Daredevil, alongside superhero ensemble "team-ups" such as the Avengers and the X-Men. All of these characters feature in monthly comic book series, often in multiple titles, that have been a ubiquitous feature of the comics landscape for over half a century. Continuity works to cohere all of these texts within a hyperdiegetic framing principle of sequentiality. Characters regularly appear in other titles, and storylines often cross over into multiple books, especially in the perennial annual events that pull whole swaths of character populations into one, overarching narrative. (Recent examples include *Fear Itself* [2011], *Avengers vs. X-Men* [2012], *Infinity* [2013], and *Secret Wars* [2015].) These crossover events are often massive constructions comprising multiple titles with an in-built commodity logic that invites ardent fans to purchase books they may not usually buy (although, in recent years, discerning readers have become au fait with this technique, and sales figures indicate a growing "event-fatigue"). Storylines can begin in one book and cross over into another such that the narrative tapestry expands inexorably beyond the confines of a single title. In the *Infinity* miniseries, for instance, readers wanting to follow the entire canvas would need to purchase, or at least read, *The Avengers, The New Avengers, The Mighty Avengers, Avengers Assemble, Guardians of the Galaxy, The Fearless Defenders*, and an array of other tie-in episodes. Compared with other events, however, *Infinity* is a rather small-scale affair.

The Marvel multiverse structure allows multiplicity to cohere within an ontological order that subsumes a pantheon of characters within a singular hyperdiegesis representing the largest world-building exercise in any media. As Reynolds points out, even television's propensity for long-form narratives pales in comparison, even in series with decades of material, such as *Star Trek* and *Doctor Who*. But what complicates matters even further, and thus dovetails with the quantum model, is that multiple worlds coexist within this ambit. What I have been discussing thus far is what is known as the Earth-616 universe—that is, the main branch of the Marvel multiverse, which is the central spine and point of origin for many readers, a point to which I shall later return. What follows are some examples of the Marvel multiverse in operation, but given the colossal transmedia sprawl, I shall use Spider-Man as a focal point to demonstrate quantum seriality.

In 2000, Marvel inaugurated the Ultimates Universe, which operates as a parallel counterpart to the central spine of Earth-616 and acts as host for reversions and remediations of familiar faces. This strategy allowed creators to begin stories again for the generation of new readers who had not been around to witness the emergence of Spider-Man or the X-Men; at the same time, it invited longtime fans to see how the old materials would be contemporized. The Ultimate imprint was set on Earth-1610, which set it apart from the mainstream continuity, and although it began rather modestly, with a limited number of titles—*Ultimate Spider-Man, Ultimate X-Men,* and *Ultimate Fantastic Four*—it soon sprouted multiple branches and diverted in significant ways from Earth-616. In recent years, for example, Peter Parker was murdered by his archnemesis the Green Goblin and his mantle passed to a new Spider-Man, Miles Morales, who, rather coincidentally, was also bitten by a radioactive spider and endowed with preternatural abilities. Thus, the Ultimate Universe developed its own internal continuity as an appendage to the history of Earth-616.

Yet this isolated pocket universe then breached its own narrative borders. In *Spider-Men*, Peter Parker crossed over from Earth-616 into Earth-1610 to come face to face with his alternate version, learning that his multiversal doppelgänger had perished. Likewise, during the events of the miniseries *Age of Ultron*, Wolverine "repeatedly abused the space-time continuum" (Bendis et al. 25), which led to an ontological instability between the ostensibly disparate realities. As a result of this spatiotemporal disaster, the intergalactic leviathan Galactus broke through time and space and crossed over, both literally and figuratively, from Earth-616 into Earth-1610. This event, and its wholesale destruction of the status quo, shifted the narrative parameters of the Ultimate Universe and led the way for a relaunch of the imprint. The Miles Morales Spider-Man survived: he went on to lead the Ultimates—the Earth-1610 version of the Avengers—in a new series that began in April 2014. Following the events of Jonathan Hickman's Secret Wars, the Ultimate Universe was destroyed (although Miles Morales successfully survived the cull and migrated to Earth-616) (see figs. 12.1 and 12.2).

In place of Spider-Man, then, the Marvel multiverse is home to multiple Spider-Men coexisting in a superposition of quantum states. Alongside Parker and Morales, Miguel O'Hara becomes the Spider-Man of 2099 (Earth-928) following a catastrophic laboratory experiment; he has also appeared in Earth-616, more recently in the pages of *The Superior Spider-Man*. At the end of issue no. 19, O'Hara is stranded in the "master-narrative" continuity of Earth-616 and, like Morales, he has been awarded his own solo series set in that universe (*Spider-Man 2099*). In *Spider-Man 2099 Meets Spider-Man*, both Peter Parker and Miguel O'Hara team up with Max Borne, the Spider-Man of 2211 (Earth-9500), to battle the Hobgoblin of the twenty-third century. On Earth-50101, Peter Parker is ethnically recast as Paviitr Prabhakar to become the Spider-Man of India, alongside principal cast members Mary

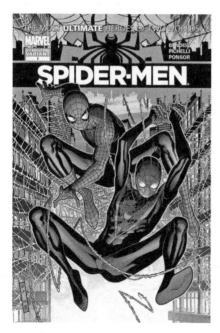

12.1. Tangled webs: Peter Parker and Miles Morales unmasked. *Spider-Men* no. 2 (June 2012).

12.2. Spider-Man goes global: Paviitr Prabhakar as the Spider-Man of India. *Spider-Man: India* (2005).

Jane (Meera Jain), Aunt May (Auntie Maya), Uncle Ben (Uncle Bhim), and Norman Osbourne (Nalin Oberoi). In the alternate past of *Spider-Man: Noir*, (Earth-90214), "old web-head" emerges during the Great Depression of the 1930s rather than in the 1960s. And in another alternate future, in the *Reign* storyline, Spider-Man comes out of retirement to take up his mantle once again. *Reign* borrows its conceit from Frank Miller's *The Dark Knight Returns* (even going so far as calling a character Miller Janson, a portmanteau of creators Frank Miller and Klaus Janson). Moreover, a 2014 crossover series, *Spider-Verse*, includes every iteration of Spider-Man congregating within the same narrative space of quantum seriality (see fig. 12.3).

Marvel's "What If?" stories offer alternate histories of canonical characters by slightly tweaking the events that fans recognize as official continuity. By readjusting a single plot point, "What If?" stories introduce a quantum event that creates an alternate reality, a Borgesian fork in the narrative road. In Spider-Man lore, the death of Peter's Uncle Ben was the catalyst that created Spider-Man's moral code—"with great power comes great responsibility"—and a burden of guilt for his inability to save his surrogate father. Each time Parker dons the Spidey suit, he is paying for the mistake that cost Uncle Ben his life by dedicating his existence to fighting evil and protecting lives.

12.3. Promotional art for *Spider-Verse*, or, "an apocalyptic multiversal spider-orgy."

12.4. *What If?* no. 1 (Feb. 1977).

But consider the question of a 1984 story that reconceptualizes Spider-Man's origin by replacing Uncle Ben's death with that of Aunt May, entitled "What If Spider-Man's Uncle Ben Had Lived?" Although one could consider this storyline to be apocryphal rather than official, Marvel canonized it by giving it a multiverse number, Earth-TRN034, which legitimized its existence as an alternative reality, birthed by a quantum event. Other "What Ifs" have been given similar legitimization, including: "What If Spider-Man Joined the Fantastic Four?" and "What If Someone Else Had Been Bitten by the Radioactive Spider?" These "Schrödinger's Cape" stories are akin to the cat-in-the-box experiment by which Schrödinger posited a superposition of states. As discussed above, Everett's thesis was that the superposition did not collapse into one state or another, but into both states simultaneously. To create the "What If?" thought experiment in a Marvel context is to create a bifurcation in the narrative history and introduce a quantum state into Marvel's multiverse (see fig. 12.4).

Miles Morales, Miguel O'Hara, Max Borne, Paviitr Prabhakar, and the manifold Peter Parkers *are all* Spider-Man, or variations thereof, existing in alternate realities connected by the assemblage of the Marvel multiverse. For many readers, however, the Peter Parker Spider-Man remains the "pure" version, and the others act as illegitimate offspring—although this conclusion depends in large part on the position of the reader. After all, the multiverse is nothing if not relative and nonhierarchical. Within the *Spider-Verse* event-series, however, Peter Parker is tagged as the *central* Spider-Man of the Marvel multiverse, which also positions the mainline Marvel continuity universe, Earth-616, as a central hub, and alternate worlds interconnected with it like spokes on a wheel. From this perspective, the Earth-616 Peter Parker is the "real" Spider-Man, whereas his alternate counterparts are "Spider-Totems," multiversal replicas, or analogues.

Even Peter Parker is not an immutable, stable personality, however, but a character in a state of perpetual flux. As we have seen, there are also multiple variations of Peter Parker coinhabiting the multiverse that problematizes the notion of a congruent, static entity. Even if one decides that the "first" Peter Parker, as created by Stan Lee and Steve Ditko in 1964, is a fixed point in space-time, the Peter Parker that currently exists in Earth-616 is hardly the same character that has gone through multiple ret-cons,[3] relaunches, and character developments. *Amazing Fantasy* no. 15 (Aug. 1962), which first introduced Spider-Man, is not the first and last word on the character, especially when one takes into account the many lives of Spider-Man coexisting within the Marvel multiverse. Like Schrödinger's Cat, Spider-Man (and countless other characters) exist in a superposition of states between different forms. Yet unlike Schrödinger's feline duo, Spider-Man splinters into a multiplicity of alternate superpositions rather than in only the binary context in which Schrödinger's Cat exists.

A recurring feature of these stories is their ability to traverse the multiverse and cross the liminal boundaries between worlds. As discussed above, quantum physics argues that contact between different temporal branches is impossible, and thus Marvel's fictional motif departs from quantum theory. However, as Michio Kaku argues in *Hyperspace*, "physicists, who once thought that this was merely an intellectual exercise, are now seriously studying multiply connected worlds as a practical model for our universe" (19). Normally, parallel universes "never interact with one another," but "wormholes or tubes may open up between them, perhaps making communication and travel possible" between discrete dimensions (ibid.). "As long as you avoid walking into the wormhole, our world seems perfectly normal," continues Kaku, but "if you fall into the wormhole, you are instantly transported to a different region of space and time" (18). Perhaps the future of science will help humanity develop quantum holidays where we, too, can visit our alternative selves and travel the glorious expanse of the multiverse.

Of course, the concept of wormholes and interdimensional portals are par for the course in science fiction and fantasy narratives. *Stargate*'s very existence relies on this factor for its narrative expeditions, for example. Yet for Kaku, the scientific model is analogous to Alice's looking-glass: "When Lewis Carroll's White Rabbit falls down the rabbit hole to enter Wonderland, he actually falls down a wormhole" (18). Once again, the possibility of traveling between different quantum states is prefigured in fiction rather than science.

Bordwell argues that forking-path narratives are typically limited and linear by design. This structure allows for greater understanding by the reader of a potentially complicated text, because it reduces the narrative "to a more cognitively manageable conception" (90). How, then, does one negotiate the many forks in the Marvel multiverse, which splinter into multiple pathways rather than bifurcating into easily manageable quadrants of text? I think Bordwell underestimated the ability of ardent fans to navigate the many worlds of Marvel; they take pleasure in doing so and have no problem cognitively managing the multiple continuities, alternate variations, and counterfactual narratives. (Although Bordwell was discussing cinema texts, he did explicitly state that alternative-world scenarios were limited affairs "in fiction" [89], not only film.)

Readers who attempt to traverse Marvel's sprawling continuity—which is even more complicated than, say, *Doctor Who*, *Star Trek*, and *Star Wars*—must possess substantial intertextual competences in order to navigate one of the "largest and arguably longest-running examples of world-building in any media" (Bainbridge 64). As discussed above, quantum theory suggests that contact between different temporal branches is impossible, and thus Marvel's fictional motif departs from quantum theory. For Douglas Wolk, these are the "super-readers"—that is, "readers familiar enough with enormous numbers of old comics that they'll understand what's really being discussed in the story" (105). There is a practical reason why both Marvel and DC produce large coffee-table concordances that blueprint their respective universes, and why these are reprinted regularly to take shifts in the hyperdiegesis into account.

But Bordwell's point about linearity is important to consider, especially when one takes into account the principle of continuity, which, as discussed above, is a site of pleasure for many fans. Committed readers who follow as many adventures as they can—depending on time constraints and the economic pitfalls that come with staying in tune with the continuum—rearrange the pieces of the nonlinear sprawl into a logical order that obeys the ontology of time and space. "Seeing how the pieces fit is fun," writes Tyler Weaver, for example. "You don't have to find everything to enjoy the story in front of you, but it adds depth and fun to your story experience" (170). Continuity is a linear concept, but this does not mean that the narrative unfolds in causal precision. Rather, the Marvel multiverse is multilinear, and one must read paradigmatically in order to construct a syntagmatic structure.

Some readers may only purchase one or two monthly titles, which reduces the temporal spread considerably. In accordance with quantum physics, everything is relative and depends upon the position of the observer. For some, the adventures of Spider-Man or Captain America may suffice. But following even just one of these superheroes monthly will invariably involve a crossover into other books. Marvel invites readers to follow multiple series in order to understand the range of history that is being told, which is the topic of the next section.

MARVEL/DC

In 1961, four years after Everett advanced his many-worlds thesis,[4] DC Comics pioneered the concept of parallel worlds in the Silver Age story "The Flash of Two Worlds." This story involved the second incarnation of the Flash character, Barry Allen, who crosses the liminal borders between alternate dimensions to meet his Golden Age predecessor, Jay Garrick. Over the years, however, DC's adherence to its own continuity became haphazard—indeed, it was chaotic from its inception—and multiple errors in the story-system destabilized its ontological order. That led to the entire narrative corpus being collapsed in the event series *Crisis on Infinite Earths*, and the multiverse was destroyed (DC reintroduced it in the weekly series 52 in 2006; at the time of writing, the DC multiverse remains limited to fifty-two worlds). Put simply, five decades of narrative history were swept away in one fell swoop, and the DC universe "rebooted" from year one. Since then, DC has put its universe through periodic cataclysms to tidy up its story-system—from *Zero Crisis* (1994) and *Infinite Crisis* (2005) to, more recently, *The New* 52. The goal is to invite new readers into the fray, especially readers who might otherwise by deterred from entering the narrative world on account of its enormous data banks of lore and history. Rather than "super-readers," DC wanted to attract people who could access the material without the necessity of a concordance or encyclopedia.

Of course, Marvel needs to refresh its audience periodically, too. Yet, unlike DC, Marvel has not yet resorted to dramatic tactics that have wiped whole swaths of history from its data banks. Marvel's present-day continuity is still the same continuity that began in 1938 under the Timely Comics banner, despite the events of Jonathan Hickman's *Secret Wars* (2015), which supposedly destroyed continuity (read: it didn't). Instead of rebooting its universe, Marvel has revised and regenerated the story-system to keep it fresh, vital, and contemporary, using ret-con (retroactive continuity), generic updating, and "relaunches" (a strategy of renumbering titles from no. 1 to attract new readers while also remaining "in continuity").

For many readers, the DC Universe has been plagued by the fractures and fissures in its internal continuity. DC has made multiple attempts to wipe the slate clean and begin again, but these attempts invariably birth multivalent paradoxes. Following the introduction of Superman in *Action Comics* no. 1 (1938)—what Michael Chabon describes as "minute zero of the superhero idea" (12)—DC Comics did not obey the principle of continuity, as those who were at its helm saw the comic form as ephemeral and short-lived. Marvel, in contrast, crafted a serialized and sequential system, especially during the 1960s, when the company challenged DC's hegemony with its new wave of comic book heroes and the work of new creators such as Stan Lee, Jack Kirby, and Steve Ditko. During this period, DC began trying, with limited success, to emulate the principle of continuity. As Weaver explains, DC was "managed by multiple editors who rarely spoke to one another" (170). Marvel, on the other hand, was now being stewarded by Stan Lee, who "vigilantly kept a consistent continuity between all the titles, so that, for instance, when the Hulk was captured in *Tales to Astonish*, Reed Richards wondered about his whereabouts in a *Fantastic Four Annual*. If Tony Stark went missing from *Tales of Suspense*, he was also AWOL in the next issue of *The Avengers*. One issue of the World War II–set *Sgt. Fury and the Howling Commandos*, which had previously been isolated from the superhero characters, featured a crossover appearance from Captain America" (Howe 56).

Following Marvel's successful strategy of interlinking books to manifest a congruent story-system, DC set out to replicate this conceit, which meant that "series of islands that had been separated for years" began "suddenly discovering one another and setting up trade routes" (Morrison 117). All those years of self-contained stories and growing arbitrariness, from 1938 onward, meant that editorial stewardship had been nonexistent; continuity had not been policed sufficiently or even been a cause for concern, and this lack of attention had led to fractures and achronological hiccups and errors. DC's editorial control was therefore wanting: it had led to the tangled mess that the 1986 *Crisis* narrative set out to address (with little success).

This is not to imply that the Marvel multiverse is a utopian story-structure without contradiction or continuity fissures and fractures—in fact, Marvel introduced the concept of the "No-Prize" in the 1960s, which invited fans to spot errors in the narrative continuum and write in with their thoughts on how to repair the ontological damage and justify mistakes. (The No-Prize was literally an empty envelope that contained the following words on the front: "CONGRATUALTIONS: THIS ENVELOPE CONTAINS A GENUINE MARVEL NO-PRIZE WHICH YOU HAVE JUST WON!"; see fig. 12.5.) In lieu of financial reward or bestowal of material goods, the No-Prize fostered a connection between fan and producer; it allowed avid readers to display their mastery of continuity as a way to develop cultural capital. Remember, this was well in advance of Internet technologies where fans can communicate at the touch of a button. Marvel, or, more accurately, Stan Lee, understood that generating a two-way dialogue between producers and

12.5. The No-Prize: an empty envelope as an in-joke bonding producers and readers.

———

readers fostered a relationship that could illustrate what worked and what did not. Marvel also recognized the fan commitment necessary to follow a vast narrative continuity; unlike DC, Marvel recognized that creating a cataclysmic event that threw out decades of narrative history (à la *Crisis on Infinite Earths*) could alienate the fan-base, as many of the most avid fans, who had spent an inordinate amount of time and money amassing a collection of comics, would not want to be told that those "did not count" as canon any longer.

It is unknown how DC's latest experiment will turn out, as *The New* 52 has been severely corrupted since its inception in 2011. The decision to reboot some titles while relaunching others only set more fractures in DC's internal ontology into motion. For example, following the events of *Flashpoint* in 2011, and the launch of *The New* 52, the *Superman* titles were rebooted—that is, Superman's past was expunged and wiped clean to make way for a new beginning (Proctor, *Beginning Again*)—whereas Batman's continuity remained intrinsically connected to the pre-*New* 52 universe. Readers criticized the decision to handle the transition in this way (for example, see Greear). The state of continuity in the DC universe remains fraught, and it is arguably only a matter of time before the company decides to reboot its universe once more.

Whereas Marvel has created a multiverse that contains within its ambit the entire contents of its various transmedia adventures, DC has repeatedly stressed that its comic book universe and media extensions, such as film and animation series, are separate entities. DC's burgeoning TV universe, consisting of *Arrow* (2012–), *Gotham* (2014–), *The Flash* (2014–), *Supergirl* (2015–), and *Legends of Tomorrow* (2016–), does not exist within the same continuity as its cinematic counter. As DC Comics creative officer and writer Geoff Johns commented, the TV universe is "a separate universe than film. . . . We will not be integrating the film and television universes" (qtd. in Eisenberg). Characters such as the Flash and Arrow in the DC TV shows are therefore not the same characters set to appear in the DC film universe. They are *separate universes* despite the Season One finale of *The Flash* in which Barry Allen discovers the existence of a multiverse (a concept adapted from 1961's "The Flash of Two Worlds"). Moreover, DC has hired actor Ezra Miller to play the Scarlet Speedster in the forthcoming *Flash* film (2018), which means that there will be two live-action versions operating in parallel.

Obviously, the lack of continuity for DC is a matter of corporate design, and quantum theory would no doubt state that the storyworlds are hyperlinked intertextually despite executive decisions (which would also dovetail with the school of poststructuralism and its dissolution of boundaries as permeable and unstable). But Marvel's stratagem works to canonize its diverse catalog, creating a structure that legitimizes disparate and alternative narrative texts as exemplars of quantum seriality. Privileging the principle of continuity is a case of "quantum entanglement": it is a multiverse by design. But as continuity is often a source of pleasure for "super-readers," such a strategy operates dialogically between the fannish demand for storyworld cohesion and the market-oriented need for a transmedia tactic. The ideal consumer is one who will follow individual episodic threads from, say, a single comic book issue to other titles that may or may not be a part of his or her original "pull list" (fan vernacular for personal orders). *Spider-Verse*, for example, was spread across multiple "Spider-Family" titles, including the *Edge of Spider-Verse* miniseries, *The Amazing Spider-Man*, *Spider-Woman*, and *Spider-Man 2099*. Each issue stands as a micro-narrative episode but also follows a principle of serial continuity; it is bound to a schema of what Wolf describes as "narrative braiding," a process whereby "narrative threads taking place within the same world . . . become grouped together due to the fact that they share the same themes, characters, objects, locations, events, or *chains of cause-and-effect*" (Wolf 378, emphasis added).

And yet narrative braiding is always also "commodity braiding," as theorized by Matthew Freeman, who writes of "the interlocking of . . . media texts, with the production of fictional stories operating . . . like entertainment stepping stones" (46). Freeman's main focus is to historicize the concept of transmedia storytelling, detailing how it emerges not in the contemporary era of digitization and convergence, but at the turn of the twentieth century in the works of, for instance, Frank L. Baum and Edgar Rice Burroughs. Transmedia "bridging" between media texts—those "entertainment stepping stones"—in such work exploited "the popularity of one creation to the boost the readership of its others" (47). For Freeman, commodity braiding, now linked to narrative braiding, is "the commercially designed interlocking of a range of commodities, be it media texts and/or consumer products, through strategies of narrative and authorship as exemplified by the interlocking of . . . storyworlds" (ibid.). From this perspective, continuity principles are bound to market-based commodity logics, an elemental factor that has arguably reached an apotheosis in the twenty-first-century market.

By exploiting the relationship between fans and continuity, Marvel encourages and invites readers to follow comic titles that they may not regularly purchase. In so doing, the company makes multiversal continuity—whether transmedial or intramedial—an element of both narrative and commercial design—that is, there is a dialectical tug-of-war between content and economics. For Marvel, the promotion of continuity between disparate media—even when continuity principles are hardly evident, as in the relationship between Marvel Comics and the Marvel Cinematic Universe—obeys the logics of capitalism through the commodification of narrative forms.

The Marvel Cinematic Universe, in actuality, is a transmedial universe rather than an intramedial one (Proctor, "Avengers Assembled"). The first wave of Marvel films was composed of *The Incredible Hulk* (Louis Leterrier, 2008), *Iron Man* (Jon Favreau, 2008), *Iron Man 2* (Jon Favreau, 2010), *Captain America: The First Avenger* (Joe Johnston, 2011), *Thor* (Kenneth Branagh, 2011), and the ensemble film *The Avengers* (Joss Whedon, 2012). The second wave included *Iron Man 3* (Shane Black, 2013), *Thor: The Dark World* (Alan Taylor, 2013), *Captain America: The Winter Soldier* (Anthony and Joe Russo, 2014), *Guardians of the Galaxy* (James Gunn, 2014), *Ant-Man* (Peyton Reed, 2015), *Avengers: Age of Ultron* (Joss Whedon, 2015), and the TV series *Agents of S.H.I.E.L.D.* (2013–) and *Agent Carter* (2014–). Marvel's plans also include a Netflix deal to produce four TV series, including *Daredevil*, *Luke Cage*, and *Jessica Jones*, with *The Defenders* operating as an ensemble piece, the televisual equivalent of *The Avengers*.

Moreover, Marvel has published several comic book series that operate outside the "master-continuity" of the mainline Marvel Universe—Earth-616—but are welded onto the narrative architecture of the film and TV series as world-building expansions and "mutually locking commercial ventures" (McMahan 145). Titles such as *Black Widow Strikes*, *Avengers Prelude*, and a range of others exploit gaps in Marvel's overarching macro-structure and flesh out narrative events more fully. In 2011, Marvel began to introduce short films into the cinematic continuity with a series of "One-Shots" that were featured as extras on Blu-ray releases of *Thor*, *Captain America*, and *The Avengers* (and are also available on YouTube). The first two shorts feature Phil Coulson, Agent of S.H.I.E.L.D., in *The Consultant* and *Something Funny Happened on the Way to Thor's Hammer*, the latter focusing on the character following his departure from *Iron Man 2* that serves as a prelude to the first *Thor* film.

In many ways, Marvel has adapted the comic book model of continuity to its live-action universe, the largest example of world-building and sequen-tiality in film history.[5] Each film or TV series can be seen as a chapter, or "micro-narrative," in an ongoing saga, or "macrostructure," that adheres to the principles of continuity and sequentiality. The characters repeatedly cross over into each other's diegetic realms, thus forming a hyperdiegesis that continues to grow exponentially into a vast narrative body. More than this, however, rather than having the live-action material function as apoc-rypha or appendages to the comic book universe, Marvel emphatically states that these events take place on Earth-199999, thereby legitimizing the various texts as fully functioning components of the multiverse. Comic book "super-readers" can rationalize film continuity as part of the Marvel multiverse, but non-fans and casual viewers do not need to have extensive knowledge of the Marvel storyworld to visit the cinema and enjoy the latest Marvel film. Marvel's strategy works for comic book fans, film fans, and casual observers alike.

DC's exploits in the live-action marketplace have paled in comparison to Marvel's, both in terms of quantity of output and in terms of economic divi-dends. Although Christopher Nolan's Batman films were successful, *Green Lantern* (Martin Campbell, 2011) was a critical and commercial disaster and *Man of Steel* radically split the fan-base despite its economic dividends. *Sui-cide Squad* (David Ayer, 2016) featured the Joker, Harley Quinn, and Deadshot, among others, and *Batman v Superman: Dawn of Justice* (Zack Snyder, 2016) featured Superman, Batman, Wonder Woman, and Lex Luthor, with brief cameo appearances of Aquaman, Cyborg, and the Flash, perhaps in a rushed attempt by DC to catch up with the Marvel juggernaut (culminating in the ensemble film *Justice League*, slated for release in 2017). DC has announced a forecast for a roster of films based upon other superhero properties, includ-ing *Wonder Woman* (2017), *The Flash* (2018), *Aquaman* (2018), *Shazam* (2019), *Cyborg* (2020), and another attempt at adapting *Green Lantern* (2020).

Marvel's success derives from a patiently constructed storyworld, whereas DC seems to operate in flashes of anxiety. *Batman Begins* is not part of DC's multiverse; neither is *Man of Steel*, *Green Lantern*, or the TV series *Arrow* or the spinoff *Flash* (although *Green Arrow* and *The Flash* occasionally cross over with one another). *Arrow* does not exist in the same universe as Henry Cavill's Superman; and Christopher Nolan has stated that his Bat-man films do not exist in the same diegesis as *Man of Steel*. Even the Marvel films produced by Fox and Sony are given a multiversal designation in the Marvel Cinematic Universe: the X-Men series takes place in Earth-10005;

Sam Raimi's Spider-Man films exist in Earth-96283; and the Marc Webb rebooted timeline is in Earth-120703.

CONCLUSION: THE PANOPTICHRON

In the Marvel multiverse, travel between quantum regions is usually ratio-nalized by way of a cosmological accident or special abilities rather than being pictured as accessible through a simplistic pathway that can be trav-eled by all. In *The Exiles*, we have the Panoptichron, a crystalline structure that exists outside of time and space where the vistas of the multiverse can be viewed and visited. We, as readers, exist in the Panoptichron; hence we can survey the Marvel multiverse as a vast narrative network of complex design. Hypothetically, that is. For Reynolds, there is no single person—on this plain of existence at least—who has digested the entire contents of Marvel's many worlds. However, in cyberspace, individual fans pool their vast encyclopedic knowledge and collaborate to construct enormous data-bases of arcana. Websites such as those in the Marvel/Wikipedia database operate as online reference manuals that are vast pools of collective intel-ligence, and they are painstakingly constructed by fans and "super-readers." Cyberspace is an intricate branch of the Panoptichron whereby the multi-verse and its rich expanse of narrative becomes accessible to all.

As per quantum theory, the multiverse only becomes real once it is observed. For many fans, the regular continuity of Earth-616 is the "real" narrative history; but, equally, Tobey Maguire's performance in Sam Raimi's *Spider-Man* trilogy may be the quintessential version for certain people. As quantum theory would have it, the multiverse is not hierarchical but a relative construct that depends upon the position of the observer. In the multiverse, "all quantum states are equally real" (Gribbin 27).

Despite DC's strategy of containment and separation, all texts exist in what Jim Collins astutely terms "the intertextual array," which means that the entire contents of culture exist in a multiverse of multiple continuities, alternate narrative realities, and quantum locations. This nonhierarchy is, of course, a key feature of poststructuralist discourse. Consider Gilles Deleuze's definition of the rhizome, summarized by Adolphe Haberer as "a network that spreads and sprawls, has no origin, no end, no hierarchical organization" (57).

The dovetailing of literature, philosophy, the quantum and academic paradigms—and comic universes—allows us to view cultural systems from a cosmological position where everything is intrinsically connected and intertwined within a cacophony of text and intertext. From this perspective, all fiction is equally real and exists somewhere across the multiverse. As Scarlett Thomas observes, "if you go along with the Many Worlds interpretation, then every novel we write actually describes some reality out there in the multiverse. Nothing is fiction." In other words, all culture is quantum.

Marvel's commitment to continuity and ontological order cannot be ignored. For fans, canon is important—that which is official and legitimate. For others, that may not always be true—DC need only devise a scheme that canonizes alternate properties through multiversal designation. Yet this is what separates DC from Marvel: it is significant, and it remains a vital component for many readers who enter the multiverse and demand rationality, cohesion, and consistency. Marvel's transmedia firmament is the apotheosis of quantum seriality.

. . . .

NOTES

1. Bordwell focuses on four films: Krzysztof Kieslowski's *Blind Chance* (1981), Tom Tykwer's *Run Lola Run* (1998), Peter Howitt's *Sliding Doors* (1998), and *Too Many Ways to Be No. 1* (1997).

2. Like Crumey, Bordwell excludes comic books from his considerations, which is a significant exclusion given the focus of his argument.

3. "Ret-con" is an abbreviation for "retroactive continuity," which is "the process of revising a fictional serial narrative, altering details that have previously been established in the narrative so that it can be continued in a new direction or so that potential contradictions in previous versions can be reconciled" (Booker 510).

4. Once again, it would be foolhardy to suggest that this was a response to Everett's work, as the many-worlds interpretation was largely ignored at the time and was popularized in the 1970s by physicist Bryce De Witt (Wolf 95).

5. Since Disney purchased Lucasfilm in 2012, the *Star Wars* universe has undergone a series of shifts that have revised the old continuity by casting aside the expanded universe of novels, comics, and so forth; and reconceptualized the hyperdiegesis as Star Wars "fact," and canonical. Henceforth, from 2014, all future Star Wars comics, novels, video games, and other media will be canonical (the old system operated as a tiered continuity with multiple levels of canonicity). In so doing, Disney seems to be following the MCU framework and, by extension, the comic book model of continuity.

———

WORKS CITED

Bainbridge, Jason. "Worlds Within Worlds: The Role of Superheroes in the Marvel and DC Universes." In *The Contemporary Comic Book Superhero*. Ed. Angela Ndalianis. Oxon: Routledge, 2009. 64–85. Print.

Bendis, Brian Michael, and Brian Hitch. *Age of Ultron*. New York: Marvel, 2013. Print.

Booker, Keith M. *The Encyclopaedia of Comic Books and Graphic Novels*. Oxford: Greenwood, 2010. Print.

Bordwell, David. "Film Futures." *SubStance* 31.1 (2002): 88–104. Print.

Borges, Jorge Luis. "The Garden of Forking Paths." In *Labyrinths*. London: Penguin Classics, 2000. Print.

Chabon, Michael. "Secret Skin: An Essay in Unitard Theory." In *Maps and Legends: Reading and Writing Along the Borderlands*. London: Fourth Estate, 2010. 216–224. Print.

Collins, Jim. "Television and Postmodernism." In *Channels of Discourse, Reassembled*. Ed. Robert C. Allen. London: Routledge, 1992. 327–353. Print.

Crumey, Andrew. "Parallel Worlds." *Aeon*, 2013. Web. http://aeon.co/magazine /world-views/can-the-multiverse-explain-the-course-of-history.

———. "Quantum Suicide: Walter Benjamin and the Multiverse." 2010. Web. www.crumey.toucansurf.com /quantum_suicide.html.

Dittmer, Jason. *Captain America and the Nationalist Superhero: Metaphors, Narratives and Geopolitics*. Philadelphia: Temple University Press, 2013. Print.

Duncan, Randy, and Matthew J. Smith. *The Power of Comics: History, Form and Culture*. London: Continuum, 2009. Print.

Eco, Umberto. *The Limits of Interpretation*. Indianapolis: Indiana University Press, 1990. Print.

Eiji, Otsuka. "World and Variation: The Reproduction and Consumption of Narrative." *Mechademia* 5 (2010): 99–116. Print.

Eisenberg, Eric. "Batman v Superman Will Not Be Set in the Same Universe as The Arrow and Flash TV Shows." *Cinema Blend*, 2015. Web. www.cinemablend.com/new /Batman-v-Superman-Set-Same-Universe -Arrow-Flash-TV-Shows-66363.html.

Freeman, Matthew. "The Wonderful Game of Oz and Tarzan Jigsaws: Commodifying Transmedia in Early Twentieth-Century Consumer Culture." *Intensities: The Journal of Cult Media* 7 (2014): 44–54. Print.

Geraghty, Christine. "The Continuous Serial: A Definition." In *Coronation Street*. Ed. Richard Dyer. London: BFI, 1981. 9–27. Print.

Greear, Mike. "Critiquing the Robins of the New 52." Sequart Organization, 10 November 2012. Web. http://sequart.org/magazine/16713/critiquing-the -robins-of-the-new-52.

Gribbin, John. *In Search of the Multiverse*. London: Penguin, 2010. Print.

Haberer, Adolphe. "Intertextuality in Theory and Practice." *Literatura*, 2007. Web. www.literatura.flf.vu.lt/wp-content/uploads/2011/11/Lit_49_5_54-67.pdf.

Harvey, Colin. *Fantastic Transmedia: Narrative, Play and Memory Across Science Fiction and Fantasy Storyworlds*. London: Palgrave, 2015. Print.

Hickman, Jonathan. *Secret Wars*. New York: Marvel, 2015. Print.

Hills, Matt. *Fan Cultures*. London: Routledge, 2002. Print.

Howe, Sean. *Marvel Comics: The Untold Story*. New York: Harper Collins, 2012. Print.

Kaku, Michio. *Hyperspace: A Scientific Odyssey Through the 10th Dimension*. Oxford: Oxford University Press, 1994. Print.

Kaveney, Roz. *Superheroes! Capes and Crusaders in Comics and Films*. London: I. B. Taurus, 2007. Print.

Lloyd, Seth. *Programming the Universe: A Quantum Computer Scientist Takes On the Cosmos*. New York: Random House, 2006. Print.

McMahan, Alison. *The Films of Tim Burton: Animating Live Action in Contemporary Hollywood*. London: Continuum, 2005. Print.

Miettinen, Mervi. "Past as Multiple Choice—Textual Anarchy and the Problems of Continuity in *Batman: Killing Joke*." *Scandinavian Journal of Comic Art* 1:1(Spring 2011). Print.

Moorcock, Michael. "Welcome to My Multiverse." In *Michael Moorcock's Multiverse*, no. 1. Print.

Morrison, Grant. *Supergods: Our World in the Age of the Superhero*. London: Jonathan Cape, 2011. Print.

Parkin, Lance. "Canonicity Matters." In *Time and Relative Dimensions in Space: Critical Perspectives on Doctor Who*. Ed. David Butler. Manchester: Manchester University Press, 2007. 246–263. Print.

———. "Truths Universally Acknowledged: How the 'Rules' of *Doctor Who* Affect the Writing." In *Third Person: Authoring and Exploring Vast Narratives*. Eds. Pat Harrigan and Noah Wardrip Fruin. Cambridge: MIT Press, 2009. 13–25. Print.

Proctor, William. "Avengers Assembled: The Marvel Transmedia Universe." *Scope*, no. 26, February 2014. Web. www.nottingham.ac.uk/scope /documents /2014/February/filmrevf eb2014.pdf.

———. *Beginning Again: The Reboot Phenomenon in Comic Books, Film and Beyond*. London: Palgrave, 2016. Print.

Reynolds, Richard. *Superheroes: A Modern Mythology*. Jackson: University Press of Mississippi, 1992. Print.

Ryan, Marie-Laure. "The Modes of Narrativity and Their Visual Metaphors." *Style* 26.3 (1992): 368–387. Print.

Strehle, Susan. *Fiction in the Quantum Universe*. Chapel Hill: University of North Carolina Press, 1992. Print.

Thomas, Scarlett. "Andrew Crumey: In the Multiverse, Novels Are All True." *The Independent*, 8 April 2006. Web. www.independent.co.uk/arts-entertainment/books/features/andrew-crumey-in-the-multiverse-novels-are-all-true-6104220.html.

Weaver, Tyler. *Comics for Film, Games, and Animation: Using Comics to Construct Your Transmedia Storyworld*. London: Focal Press, 2013. Print.

Wolf, Fred Alan. *Parallel Universes: The Search for Other Worlds*. London: Simon and Schuster, 1988. Print.

Wolf, Mark J. P. *Building Imaginary Worlds: The Theory and History of Subcreation*. London: Routledge, 2012. Print.

Wolk, Douglas. *Reading Comics: How Graphic Novels Work and What They Mean*. Philadelphia: Da Capo Press, 2007. Print.

Notes on Contributors

Felix Brinker is a PhD student at the John F. Kennedy Institute's Graduate School of North American Studies at the Free University of Berlin. He holds a BA in American studies and political science as well as an MA in American studies from Leibniz University Hannover, where he completed his studies in 2012 with a thesis on "The Aesthetics of Conspiracy in Contemporary American Serial Television." His research focuses on film and television, popular seriality, critical theory, and the politics of American popular culture in general. His most recent publications include the chapters "On the Political Economy of the Contemporary (Superhero) Blockbuster Series," in *Post-Cinema: Theorizing 21st Century Film*, edited by Shane Denson and Julia Leyda (Falmer, UK: Reframe Books, 2016), and "NBC's *Hannibal* and the Politics of Audience Engagement," in *Transgressive Television: Politics and Crime in 21st Century American TV Series*, edited by Birgit Dawes, Alexandra Ganser, and Nicole Poppenhagen (Heidelberg: Winter, 2015).

James N. Gilmore is a PhD student in the Department of Communication and Culture at Indiana University. His publications include a co-edited anthology with Matthias Stork entitled *Superhero Synergies: Comic Book Characters Go Digital* (Lanham, MD: Rowman and Littlefield, 2014).

Michael Graves is an assistant professor of communication at the University of Central Missouri. He received his PhD in film and media studies from the University of Kansas in 2011, and his research focuses on the media industry's use of transmedia storytelling, participatory strategies, and new media technologies to engage with audiences.

Dru Jeffries is a postdoctoral fellow at the University of Toronto's Cinema Studies Institute. He received his PhD in film and moving image studies from Concordia University in 2014. His work on comic book cinema has appeared in *Porn Studies, Cinephile, Quarterly Review of Film and Video*, and *World Building: Transmedia, Fans, Industries* (Amsterdam University Press, 2017). He is the author of *Comic Book Film Style: Cinema at 24 Panels per Second* (University of Texas Press, 2017).

Henry Jenkins is the Provost's Professor of Communication, Journalism, and Cinematic Arts at the University of Southern California. His books include *Textual Poachers: Television Fans and Participatory Culture* (London: Routledge, 1992), *Fans, Bloggers and Gamers: Media Consumers in a Digital Age* (New York: New York University Press, 2006), *Convergence Culture: Where Old and New Media Collide* (New York: New York University Press, 2008), and *By Any Media Necessary: The New Youth Activism* (New York: New York University Press, 2016).

Derek Johnson is an associate professor of media and cultural studies at the University of Wisconsin at Madison. He is the author of *Media Franchising: Creative License and Collaboration in the Culture Industries* (New York: New York University Press, 2013) as well as the co-editor of *A Companion to Media Authorship* (London: Wiley-Blackwell, 2013) and *Making Media Work: Cultures of Management in the Entertainment Industries* (New York: New York University Press, 2014).

Mark Minett is an assistant professor in the Department of English Language and Literature and the Film and Media Studies Program at the University of South Carolina. His work has appeared in *The New Review of Film and Television Studies, Film History*, and *A Companion to Robert Altman* (London: Wiley-Blackwell, 2015).

Deron Overpeck is an assistant professor in the Department of Communication and Theatre Arts at Eastern Michigan University. His research has appeared in the journals *Film Quarterly, Film History: An International Journal, Historical Journal of Film, Radio and Television, Horror Studies, Quarterly Review of Film and Video*, and *Moving Image*, and in the collected volumes *American Cinema of the 1980s*, edited by Stephen Prince (New Brunswick,

NJ: Rutgers University Press, 2008) and *Explorations in New Cinema History: Approaches and Case Studies* (London: Wiley, 2011).

Anna F. Peppard is a PhD candidate in English at York University in Toronto, where her research has focused on representations of gender, race, and sexuality in American literature and popular media, including film, television, genre fiction, and comics. Her work has been published in the *Canadian Review of American Studies*, the *International Journal of Comic Art*, and the *Journal of the Fantastic in the Arts*.

William Proctor is a lecturer in media culture and communication at Bournemouth University, UK. He is the author of *The Contemporary Reboot: Comic Books, Film and Television* (London: Palgrave, 2017) and has published articles and book chapters on popular culture characters and ideas such as Batman, James Bond, *The Walking Dead*, One Direction fandom, and *Star Wars*. His research interests include transmedia storytelling, adaptation, rebooting, franchising, and audience/reception studies. He is also the director of "The World Star Wars Project."

Bradley Schauer is an assistant professor at the School of Theatre, Film & Television at the University of Arizona. He is the author of *Escape Velocity: American Science Fiction Film 1950–1982* (Middletown, CT: Wesleyan University Press, 2017). His work has also appeared in several journals and books, including *Film History* and *Behind the Silver Screen: Cinematography*.

Kalervo A. Sinervo is a doctoral candidate at Concordia University, where he researches issues of world-building and intellectual property in media franchises. His research on digital comics piracy has appeared in *Amodern* and IGI Global's *Educational, Psychological, and Behavioral Considerations in Niche Online Communities*, and his work on transmedia geography has recently been published in *First Person Scholar* and *Wide Screen Journal*. Kalervo also works as a researcher for the IMMERSe games research network and serves as vice president for communications for the Canadian Society for the Study of Comics.

Aaron Taylor is an associate professor in the Department of New Media at the University of Lethbridge in Alberta, Canada. He is the editor of *Theorizing*

Film Acting and the author of numerous articles on film performance. His work on superhero comics and film has appeared in *The Journal of Popular Culture* and *The Journal of Adaptation in Film and Performance,* and will also be featured in the forthcoming anthology *Comics, Cinema & Culture,* edited by Barry Keith Grant and Scott Henderson (Austin: University of Texas Press).

Darren Wershler holds the Concordia University Research Chair in Media and Contemporary Literature. His most recent book is *Guy Maddin's My Winnipeg* (Toronto: University of Toronto Press, 2011).

Matt Yockey is an associate professor in the Department of Theatre and Film at the University of Toledo in Ohio. His work on the superhero genre and fandom has appeared in a number of journals and anthologies. He is the author of the monograph *Batman* (TV Milestones Series) (Detroit: Wayne State University Press, 2014).

Index

Page numbers in italics indicate figures.

Aaron, Jason, 177. *See also* Marvel Architects

Adams, Neal, 170

Agent Carter (TV series, 2014), 207, 217, 339

Agents of S.H.I.E.L.D. (TV series, 2013–), 207, 217, 219, 339

All-New X-Men, 138

All-Star Comics, 43–44, 45, 47, 62

Alonso, Axel, 147–148, 173

Amazing Spider-Man, The, 14, 33, 80, 142, 165, 173, 174, 184n13, 236, 273, 274, 282–283, 284, 293, 299, 338

Amazing Spider-Man, The (TV series, 1977–1979), 212, 270

Amazing Spider-Man, The (Webb, 2012), 248, 253, 258, 270, 276, 277, 281, 282, 286–287, 291, 310, 311

Amazing Spider-Man 2, The (Webb, 2014), 248, 253, 270, 277, 281, 282–283, 284, 292, 312

Ant-Man (Reed, 2015), 207, 339

Arad, Avi, 252, 256, 258, 259, 264

Asamiya, Kia, 173

Astonishing X-Men, 174, 180

Avengers, The, 30, 54, 55, 59, 60, 61, 174, 241, 304, 312, 327, 329; film franchise, 138, 144, 216, 250

Avengers, The, 28, 30, 39, 40, 41, 62, 63, 64n1, 165, 168, 299, 317n14, 327, 335; continuity, 56–62, 64n4; industrial context and history, 43, 45, 46; storytelling and characterization, 46, 49, 50–56

Avengers, The (Whedon, 2012), 6, 39, 144, 169, 180, 207, 208, 216, 217, 228n8, 240, 241, 249, 279, 312, 314, 339

Avengers: Age of Ultron (Whedon, 2015), 6, 207, 208, 210, 217, 243, 317n14, 339

Avengers Assemble (animated series, 2013–), 145, 212

Avengers vs. X-Men, 178–179, 182, 199, 327

Azzarello, Brian, 67

bad girls, 119

Bails, Jerry, 25

Batman, 23, 43, 44, 45–46, 49, 58, 59,

81, 110, 113, 337, 340; film franchise, 227n1, 228n9, 340

Batman Begins (Nolan, 2005), 320, 340

Batman v Superman: Dawn of Justice (Snyder, 2016), 131, 226, 287, 340

Bendis, Brian Michael, 63, 67, 69, 90, 92, *98, 99,* 138, 139, 173, 177, 178, 179, 273, 289, 328. *See also* Marvel Architects

body-too-much, 35, 272, 273, 280

Bordwell, David, 30, 40, 41, 42, 50

Borges, Jorge Luis: "Garden of the Forking Paths," 324

bounds of difference, 31, 66, 69–71; Steranko, 87, 100

Bradshaw, Nick: *Guardians of the Galaxy,* 182

Broome, John, 47

Brubaker, Ed, 177. *See also* Marvel Architects

Buckley, Dan, 150, 153, 154, 156

Bullpen Bulletins, 19, 249, 257–258, 299. *See also* Lee, Stan

Bunn, Cullen, 182

Buscema, John, 17

Buscema, Sal, 273

Busiek, Kurt, 172

Caniff, Milton, 78

CAPA-Alpha, 25

Captain America, 3, 5–10, *9,* 20, 21, 22, 27–28, *28,* 45, 52, 54–55, 58, 60–61, 153, 154, 179, 212, 220, 223, 240, 312, 315n2, 327, 334, 335; film franchise, 138, 144, 216, 315n2

Captain America, 20, 159, 222, 298

Captain America (Holcomb, 1979), 5, 212

Captain America (Pyun, 1990), 5–6, 168

Captain America (serial, 1944), 5, 222

Captain America: Civil War (Russo, Anthony and Joe, 2016), 6, 178, 207, 227n1, 270

Captain America: The First Avenger (Johnston, 2011), 3, 5, 6, 8, 207, 216, 217, 219, 222, 228nn7,8, 239, 240, 241, 243, 312, 314, 339

Captain America: The Winter Soldier (Russo, 2014), 6, 169, 207, 217, 218, 229n11, 243, 245, 339

Captain America II: Death Too Soon (Nagy, 1979), 5, 212

Captain Marvel, 31, 114–116; Carol Danvers's relaunch as, 123–124, *125;* costume of, 124, *125;* as source of Ms. Marvel's imagery and superpowers, 115. *See also* Danvers, Carol; Ms. Marvel

Cat, the, 31, 105, *106,* 109, 110–112, 113, 119, 127, 132n4; as a gendered monster, 105; marginalization and incorporation of, 109

chronotope, 4–5

Claremont, Chris, 129, 171, 302, 303, 312

Coipel, Olivier, 173

Colan, Gene, 17, 176

commercial auteurism, 165. *See also* Marvel Architects

convergence culture, 2–5, 209, 249. *See also* Jenkins, Henry

Conway, Gerry: *Ms. Marvel,* 114–116, 132n5

Coover, Coleen: *Girl Comics,* 128

Coppola, Francis Ford, 170

Crain, Clayton, 184n16

Cybercomics, 193–196, 197–198, 203

Danvers, Carol, 113–119, *115,* 117–119, *118,* 123, 124; costume of, 123–124,

125. *See also* Captain Marvel; Ms. Marvel

Daredevil, 66, 71, 74, 81, 82, 83, 83, 84, 85, 86, 86, 88, 90, 93, 127, 327; costume of, 88; and the Marvel Knights, 69

Daredevil (TV series, 2015–), 207, 219, 339

Dark Knight, The (Nolan, 2008), 207

Dark Knight Returns, The, 330

David, Peter, 129

Dazzler, 112–113

DC Comics, 10, 40, 43, 143, 172, 177; fictional cities in, 312; and fissures in internal continuity, 335; and the multiverse concept, 319–320; and *The New* 52, 143, 335, 337; and parallel worlds, 334; readership survey, 108, 131n2–132n2; TV universe of, separate from film universe, 337

decompression, 165–166, 180

DeConnick, Kelly Sue: *Captain Marvel*, 123, 131n1

Defenders, The (TV series), 207, 227, 339

Demeo, Mick, 14

Ditko, Steve, 17, 26, 80, 81, 82, 86, 88, 170, 171, 179, 273, 275, 275, 276, 300, 316n4, 316n13, 332, 335; and authorship, 171, 260; as freelance artist, 316n13; Marvel style of, 81; and Peter Parker, 274, 275, 275, 276, 332; and Spider-Man, 80, 273, 299; and Stan Lee, 268, 299, 332

Donenfeld, Harry, 43

Dyssegaard, Elisabeth, 129

Eisner, Will, 71, 74

Ennis, Garth, 173

Everett, Bill, 45, 81, 83, 86, 88, 93

Everett, Hugh III, 320, 321, 322, 324, 331, 334, 342n4; and many-worlds interpretation, 322–323, 324, 334, 342, 342n4

extractability and immersion, 34, 235, 237–238, 242, 244. *See also* Jenkins, Henry

fan desire, 3, 290

fandom, 4, 14; and collective intelligence, 287, 290, 293; comic book, 25–26; and letters, 1, 11, 14, 18, 25, 28, 45, 116, 117, 122, 124, 132n6, 133n11; and male readers as double-edged sword, 159; and the Merry Marvel Marching Society, 26, 264, 299; and Sam Raimi, 256, 261; transgenerational, 155, 156

Fantastic Four, 10, 12–13, 18, 25, 27, 239, 299, 304, 331

Fantastic Four (animated series, 1967–1970), 263

Fantastic Four (Sassone, 1994), 168

Fantastic Four (Story, 2005), 311, 316n8

Fantastic Four (Trank, 2015), 159

Fantastic Four, The, 1, 10–11, 12, 15, 16, 17, 18, 25, 37n3, 44, 45, 51, 60, 139, 147, 174, 179, 299, 301, 301, 302

Fantastic Four Annual, 302, 308, 309, 335

Fantastic Four: Rise of the Silver Surfer (Story, 2007), 207, 308

Feige, Kevin, 39, 245

Finch, David, 173, 177

Fite, Linda: *The Cat*, 105, 127

Foster, Hal, 78

Fox, Gardner, 44, 46, 47, 48, 49–50, 55, 61, 62

Fraction, Matt, 177. *See also* Marvel Architects

Friedrich, Mike, 63

Fury, Nick, 3–5, 20, 87, 194, 213, 218, 234, 243, 278; and the chronotope, 5; and Cybercomics, 194; in *Iron Man*, 234; Samuel L. Jackson as, 3–4, 278; in S.H.I.E.L.D., 3, 20, 87, 194; in *The Ultimates*, 3, 4; and World War II, 3, 4, 5. *See also* Steranko, Jim

Gaiman, Neil, 173

Gaines, Max, 43

Garfield, Andrew, 35, 270, 271, 273–274, 276, 276, 277, 277, 279, 280–284, 286–287, 288, 290, 291–293, 292, 312

Gerber, Steve, 18

Girl Comics, 126–128, 133n

Goodman, Martin, 10, 44

Goyer, David S., 130–131

Guardians of the Galaxy (Gunn, 2014), 207, 245, 297, 339

Hairsine, Trevor, 176, 177, 184n17

"Hawkeye Initiative, The," 123

Heck, Don, 14, 51

Hickman, Jonathan, 177. *See also* Marvel Architects

historical poetics, 30, 40, 41, 62, 63–64. *See also* Bordwell, David

Hitchcock, Alfred, 97, 297, 298, 303, 304, 305–306, 307, 308, 311

Hogarth, Burne, 78

Holland, Tom, 270, 279, 288

Hulk, The, 13, 18, 39, 45, 51, 52–54, 55, 56, 59, 60, 117, 119, 120, 171, 174, 179, 221, 239, 309, 310, 311, 327, 335; counterculture symbol, 19, 23. *See also Incredible Hulk, The*

Hulk (Lee, 2003), 221, 241, 311

Hulk and the Agents of S.M.A.S.H. (animated series, 2013–2015), 145

Incredible Hulk, The, 173, 174, 175

Incredible Hulk, The (Leterrier, 2008), 207, 216, 219, 221, 223, 234, 239, 241, 310, 311

Incredible Hulk, The (TV series, 1977–1982), 168, 212, 221

Iron Man, 3, 14, 39, 45, 51, 53, 58, 60, 105, 179, 212, 220, 234, 281, 327; Cybercomics, 194; film franchise, 138, 144, 216

Iron Man (Favreau, 2008), 2, 3, 39, 207, 211, 216, 222, 234, 239, 241, 307, 308, 339

Iron Man: Exremis, 198

Iron Man 2 (Favreau, 2010), 3, 207, 216, 219, 232, 239, 241, 308, 339

Iron Man 3 (Black, 2013), 207, 208, 216, 218, 219, 222, 228n8, 240, 241, 308, 339

Jackson, Samuel L., 3, 4, 278

Jemas, Bill, 164–165, 167, 172, 175, 183n6

Jenkins, Henry, 30–31, 34, 140, 196, 209–211, 213–214, 215–216, 225

Jessica Jones (TV series, 2015–), 207, 219, 339

JLA. *See* Justice League of America

Johnston, Joe, 3, 7, 207, 239, 312, 339

JSA. *See* Justice Society of America

Justice League of America (JLA), 30, 44, 46, 48, 49, 50, 51, 54, 61

Justice League of America (JLA), 10, 40, 41, 42, 61, 62, 63, 64n1; continuity, 56–59; industrial context and history, 43, 44, 45 46; storytelling and characterization, 46–47, 48, 49, 50, 51, 52, 53–54, 55, 56

Justice Society of America (JSA), 43, 50, 58. *See also* JSA

King, Stephen, 322, 323

Kirby, Jack, 1, 2, 86, 88, 171, 310, 314, 335; appearance of, in comics, 301–302, *302*, 308, *309*; at Atlas, 11; and authorship, 171; and collage, 18, 179; and the Fantastic Four, 10, 11, 12, 17, 44–45; as freelance artist, 300, 310, 316n13; influences of, 78; and Marvel style, 11–12, 18, 80–81; Nick Fury, 5; and Stan Lee, 10, 15, 24–25, 39, 45, 171, 299, 300, 301, *301*, 302, *302*, 308, *309*, 316n5, 316n6; as a visionary, 15, 18; and World War II, 7

Kirkman, Robert, 170

Lee, Stan, 1, 20, 26, 27, 36, 37, 37–38n4, 43, 50–51, 55, 61, 113, 176, 264, 273, 335; and *The Avengers*, 61–63; and Bullpen Bulletins, 19, 249, 257–258, 299; cameo of, in comics, 25; and collaboration, 17; creative process of, 17; as editor, 17, 45–46, 176, 299, 300, 316n7, 335; editorial voice of, 14, 19, 25, 45; as face and voice of Marvel, 24, 299; and *The Fantastic Four*, 10–13, 25, 44–45; and Jack Kirby, 14–15, 24–25, 39, 45, 171, 299, 300, 301, *301*, 302, *302*, 308, *309*, 316n5, 316n6; and the Marvel brand, 14; as a Marvel pitchman, 10, 17, 19, 25, 28, 300, 306; and the Marvel style, 11, 335; and the Marvel Universe, 46–58, 59; and Stan's

Soapbox, 19, 23, 249, 257–258, 299, 314; as writer, 11, 15, 17, 18, 23, 55, 58

Loeb, Jeph, 92, 149, 154, 174

Luke Cage (TV series, 2015–), 207, 227, 339

Mack, David, 31, 66; and *Daredevil: Echo-Vision Quest*, 31, 66, 75, 79, 88, *91*, 93, 94, 95, 97, 100; and *Daredevil: Wake Up*, 67, 71, 90, 98, 99, 100; as experimental, 67, 70, 101; and *Kabuki*, 68, 69, 87; and multiple modalities, 75; and texture, 93, 94, 101. *See also* bounds of difference

Maguire, Tobey, 35, 256–257, 270, 271, 273, 274–276, *275*, 277, 278, 280, 282–283, 284, 286, 290, 293, 341

Maleev, Alex, 93

male gaze, 107, 118, 122, 128

Manara, Milo, 130

Marvel Architects, 32, 165, 170–171, 176–179, 182

Marvel Comics, 2, 3, 4, 10, 13; and acts of consumption, 14; and affective relationship between characters and audience, 13; popularity of, on college campuses, 17, 19, 23–24; readers of, as collaborators, 26, 28; self-aware editorial approach of, 45; and strategy to attract older readership, 29, 45, 80

Marvel Entertainment, 166, 168, 183n4, 268; and Walt Disney Company, 2, 209, 245

Marvel One-Shots, 34, 126, 207, 210, 211, 218, 219–220, 223, 228n8, 234, 235, 239–243, 244–245, 339

Marvel Studios, 2, 8, 33, 35, 39, 45, 63,

138, 139, 166, 169, 182, 183n4; and
Marvel One-Shots, 239, 241, 242,
244–245, 249, 268; and Stan Lee
cameos, 297, 298, 303, 304, 310,
315n2; and transmedia, 207–209,
213, 220–221, 224, 225, 227n1, 228n7,
229n13, 234–235
Marvel Style, 11, 15, 25, 90, 100; Kirby
and Ditko defined, 81
Marvel Universe, 2, 5, 8, 10, 12–13, 30;
complex storyworld of, 24; fans as
participants in, 37; as genre, 4; and
Kirby, 15; narrative connectivity
in, 58–60
Marx Brothers, 80
McKelvie, Jaime: *Captain Marvel*, 124
McKenzie, Roger, *84, 85, 86*
media convergence, 32, 209
Mighty Thor, 130, 131
Millar, Mark, 69, 173
Miller, Frank: with Bill Sienkiewicz,
88, *89*, 90, *90*; with Klaus Janson,
81, *82*, 83, *83*, 84, 85, 86, *86*, 88, 90.
See also Daredevil
Moench, Doug, 18
Molotiu, Andrei, 80
Moorcock, Michael, 322, 323
Moore, Alan, 173
Morales, Miles, 158–159, 289, *289*, 328,
329, *329*, 332. *See also* Parker, Peter;
Spider-Man
Morrison, Grant, 173
Moscoso, Victor, 80
motion comics, 30, 33, 187–189, 192,
195–196, 197–199, 201, 203–204
Mouse, Stanley, 80
Ms. Marvel, 31, 113–119, *115, 118*;
costume of, 113, 118; and female
hysteria, 117–118; and problematic
invocations of feminism, 116. *See*

also Captain Marvel; Danvers,
Carol
Murase, Sho: *Elektra*, 127

N+1 strategy, 52–53, 62. *See also* split-
up structure
New Mutants, 172
No-Prize, 11, 336, *336*
NuMarvel, 32, 36, 165

O'Neil, Dennis, 63
Origins of Marvel Comics, 10, 26, 37

Pantozzi, Jill, 130, 133n10, 136
Parker, Peter, 34, 132n7, 158, 236, 268,
274, 275, *275*, 276, *276*, 277, *277*, 278,
281, 288, 290, 293, 310, 312, 314, 328,
329, *329*, 330, 332. *See also* Garfield,
Andrew; Maguire, Tobey Maguire;
Spider-Man
Perelman, Ron, 172
Pichelli, Sara: *Guardians of the Galaxy*,
183
postfeminism, 120–122, 128
Pynchon, Thomas, 322

quantum seriality, 36, 320, 326, 328,
338, 342
Quesada, Joe, 198–199, 290; and
Daredevil, 67, 69, 71, *71*, 74–75, *76*,
78, 81, 94, *96*, 100; and Share Your
Universe, 154, 164–165, 171, 172–174,
175–178, 180–182
Quitely, Frank, 173

Raimi, Sam, 165, 195, 197, 207, 248, 251,
252, 255, 256–257, 258, 260, 261–262,
263, 264, 270, 273, 282, 285, 286,
291, 293, 309, 314, 341
Raymond, Alex, 78

Remender, Rick, 182
Rios, Emma: *Captain Marvel*, 131n1
Romita, John, Jr., 177, 273
Romita, John, Sr., 14, 17, 171, 273, 274, 276, 276, 277, 293

Sale, Tim, 92, 93
Savage She-Hulk, The, 119
Schaefer, Jeanine: *Girl Comics*, 126
Schiff, Jack, 46
Schiti, Valerio: *The Avengers*, 182
Schrödinger, Erwin, 320–321, 331, 332
Schrödinger's Cat, 320, 321, 332
Schwartz, Julius, 44, 46, 47, 48–50, 52, 59, 61, 62
second-wave feminism, 110, 112, 120–121
Sekowsky, Mike, 44, 46
Sensational She-Hulk, The, 119–123
Seuling, Carole: Shanna the She-Devil, 110
seven principles of transmedia storytelling, 34, 235
Severin, Marie: The Cat, 105, 127
She-Hulk, 31, 112, 119–123, 121, 126, 127, 127, 128, 129, 131; institutionalized sexism of, 122–123; postfeminism of, 120–122; self-aware sense of humor of, 119, 120; and sexualization, 120–121; and *The She-Hulk Diaries*, 129–130; and Weezie, 119, 121. See also Walters, Jennifer
Sienkiewicz, Bill, 31; and *Daredevil: Love and War*, 87, 88, 89; and *Elektra: Assassin*, 87, 88, 90; painterly aesthetic of, 87
Simon, Joe, 7
Simone, Gail: "Women in Refrigerators," 123
Sinnott, Joe, 17

Smith, Kevin, 69, 173
Spider-Girl, 132n7
Spider-Man, 2, 13, 18, 26, 35, 45, 59, 81, 105, 132n7, 150, 158, 167, 171, 175, 194, 228n9, 236, 239, 248, 251, 255–256, 257, 261, 268, 273, 290–291, 304, 309, 314, 327, 334; authorship, 260; body-too-much, 273; counterculture symbol, 19, 23–24; Cybercomic, 194; film franchise, 34–35, 144, 168, 227n1, 249–250, 251–253, 254, 258, 259, 261, 262, 264, 281, 285; as range brand, 269, 270
Spider-Man (animated series, 1967–1970), 197, 263
Spider-Man (Raimi, 2002), 165, 248, 251, 253, 255, 256, 262–263, 270, 280, 309, 313
Spider-Man: India, 236, 329
Spider-Man 2 (Raimi, 2004), 195, 248, 251, 253, 255, 256, 259, 261, 262–263, 270, 282–283, 284, 284, 293, 309, 314
Spider-Man 3 (Raimi, 2007), 207, 248, 255, 260, 261, 285, 285, 291, 314
Spider-Man 2099, 236, 329
Spider-Man and His Amazing Friends (animated series, 1981–1983), 168
Spider-Man Unlimited, 196
Spider-Verse, 330, 330, 332, 338
Spider-Woman, 112
Spider-Woman, 130, 336
split-up structure, 47, 50, 52, 53–54, 62. See also N+1 strategy
Stan's Soapbox, 19, 23, 249, 257–258, 299, 314. See also Lee, Stan
Starlin, Jim, 18, 170
Steinberg, Flo, 26
Steinem, Gloria, 114
Steranko, Jim, 5, 17, 87; graphic design of, 87; surrealistic style of, 20, 21, 22

Strange Tales, 27–28, 28
Superman, 13, 20, 23, 43, 44, 45–46, 49, 57, 58, 113, 335, 337, 340
Superman, 57, 59, 336

Tales of Suspense, 58, 59–60, 335
Takeda, Sana: *She-Hulk*, 127, 127
Thomas, Jean: *Night Nurse*, 110
Thomas, Roy, 18, 25, 37–38n4, 176
Thor, 13, 14, 39, 45, 51, 53–54, 56, 58, 59, 178, 220, 327; as a woman, 131, 159
Thor, 180
Thor (Branagh, 2011), 138, 144, 174, 175, 179, 207, 219, 228n8, 239, 241, 279, 313, 339
Thor: The Dark World (Taylor, 2013), 216, 219, 228n8, 241, 313–314, 339
Trial of the Incredible Hulk, The (TV movie, 1989), 307, 309

Ultimate Fantastic Four, 328
Ultimate X-Men, 328
Uncanny X-Men, 126, 138, 172, 299

Wacker, Stephen: *Captain Marvel*, 124
Walters, Jennifer, 119, 120, 129. *See also* She-Hulk
Webb, Marc, 248, 258–259, 260, 261, 270, 276, 282, 286, 287, 291–292, 310, 312, 341

Weisinger, Mort, 46, 57, 58, 59
Whedon, Joss, 174, 175, 180
Wilson, Wes, 80
Witterstaetter, Renée, 122
"Women of Marvel," 126
Wonder Woman, 43, 44, 114, 131, 132n3, 340
Wonder Woman (Jenkins, 2017), 226, 340
Wood, Brian: *X-Men*, 126, 132–133n10

X-Force, 172
X-Men, 33, 139, 147, 165, 172, 302–303, 302, 312
X-Men (animated series 1992–1997), 168
X-Men (comics franchise), 126, 138, 172, 173, 174, 179
X-Men (Cybercomic), 194
X-Men (Singer, 2000), 2, 165, 166, 175, 241, 311
X-Men (2013 relaunch), 126, 128, 133n11
X-Men, The, 59, 129, 171, 299, 303, 304, 309, 327, 328
X-Men: Days of Future Past (Singer, 2014), 138, 316n10
X-Men: The Last Stand (Ratner, 2006) 309
X-Men No. 1 (1991), 142